A Guide to the Lands of the Bible

A Guide to the Lands of the Bible

Leslie J. Hoppe, O.F.M.

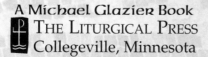

A Michael Glazier Book
THE LITURGICAL PRESS
Collegeville, Minnesota

A Michael Glazier Book published by The Liturgical Press.

Cover: The Old City of Jerusalem as seen from the Mount of Olives (front); Jewish worshipers at the Western Wall, Jerusalem (back). Photos and design by Robin Pierzina O.S.B.

1   2   3   4   5   6   7   8

Library of Congress Cataloging-in-Publication Data

Hoppe, Leslie J.
    A guide to the lands of the Bible / Leslie J. Hoppe.
        p.   cm.
    "A Michael Glazier book."
    Includes bibliographical references and index.
    ISBN 0-8146-5886-5 (alk. paper)
    1. Israel—Guidebooks.   2. Middle East—Guidebooks.   3. Bible-
-Geography.   I. Title.
DS103.H63   1999
915.604'53—dc21   98-33864
                                                                        CIP

For Carroll Stuhlmueller, C.P.,
Professor of Old Testament at Catholic Theological Union
who loved the Lands of the Bible

Contents

Foreword

"Of the making of many books there is no end . . ." (Eccl 12:12) is particularly true of guidebooks for the lands of the Bible. Besides those geared for the general leisure-time traveler, there are specialized guidebooks for particular religious groups, for those interested in history and archaeology, for those on a pilgrimage, and for those interested in nature study and hiking. Each guidebook has something to offer to those planning a trip to the Middle East. Besides the guidebooks available in print, the countries of the Middle East, which try to foster tourism, all have web-sites on the Internet to attract visitors.

Why add another guidebook to the list of those already available? First, this book tries to help enhance the reader's appreciation for the Bible as a collection of books produced by real people, who lived in a real place and at a specific time. The best way to accomplish this is to visit those lands whose people lived the experiences described in the Bible. Visiting the lands of the Bible allows the believer to read the Bible in its geographical, historical, and cultural context. This guidebook makes a special effort to direct readers to the biblical texts related to the sites that they may visit. Most people who visit the lands of the Bible say that they read the biblical text with new understanding, appreciation, and enthusiasm because of the experiences they had as visitors to these lands.

Second, while the primary reason people visit the lands of the Bible has to do with their religious past, it is very important for visitors to recognize that these lands are home to people today. It is far too common for tourists to the Middle East to return from their visit without having paid much attention to the problems and concerns of the people who live in the lands of the Bible. No visitor should walk about this region as if it were a large outdoor museum or shrine. That is why the guidebook devotes significant space to some of the political and social issues the people of the Middle East have to face. This is particularly true of the relations between the Israeli and Palestinian peoples. After decades of conflict, the Israelis and Palestinians have begun to speak together about their common concerns. Visitors should not allow themselves to spend time in the Holy Land without coming away with a greater understanding of the problems that still face the people who live there. In particular, Christians should speak with and learn from their sisters and brothers in faith that are trying to live the gospel in the land Jesus called home. An informed visit to the region will help outsiders realize that the people of the Middle East face difficult issues that do not admit of simple solutions. As guests, tourists should be interested in the concerns of their hosts.

While the relations between the Israeli government and the Palestinian National Authority are developing, there is no clear idea of the final settlement. Important matters are still subject to negotiation. Nothing in this book should be taken as an endorsement of any one side's position. One day soon peace will finally come to the Israelis and Palestinians. It will come because these two peoples will have learned what they must do to live together in the land they both consider a gift from God. People of good will throughout the world ought to wish them well in their search for peace.

Third, a practical consequence of the normalization of diplomatic relations between the State of Israel and its neighbors in the Middle East is that tourists are able to visit other countries in the region more easily. Some itineraries include not only Israel but will add stops in Jordan or Egypt as well. Similarly, visitors whose interest was piqued by a tour to Israel may come back to the region to visit Greece and Turkey to see where the early Church developed because of the ministry of St. Paul and other early missionaries. What this guidebook offers is one handy guide for all the lands of the Bible. One does not have to haul around two or three guidebooks. This book should help you prepare for and enjoy your visit to the lands of the Bible.

Finally, I want to thank Carolyn Osiek, R.S.C.J., a colleague at Catholic Theological Union for writing Chapter Eleven: Jordan, and Robin Pierzina, O.S.B., who illustrated this volume. I also want to thank my colleagues in the Biblical Literature and Languages Department of CTU and the hundreds of participants in CTU's Israel Study Programs, who have inspired and encouraged the writing of this book.

Abbreviations

A	Arabic
A.D.	*Anno Domini* "In the Year of the Lord" = C.E. [Common Era], which is used primarily by Jews who consider the use of A.D. as an implicit acceptance of the claims of Christianity about Jesus.
ANET	*Ancient Near Eastern Texts Relating to the Old Testament.* James B. Pritchard, ed.
B.C.	Before Christ = B.C.E. [Before the Common Era], which is used primarily by Jews who consider the use of B.C. an implicit acceptance of the claims of Christianity about Jesus.
c.	*circa.* L: around, about
EBA	Early Bronze Age
G	Greek
H	Hebrew
L	Latin
LBA	Late Bronze Age
MBA	Middle Bronze Age
NT	New Testament
OT	Old Testament

CHAPTER ONE

Preparing for Your Trip

Set Your Goals. Enjoying your trip to the lands of the Bible and deriving the most benefit from it will involve some preparation beyond simply joining a tour group, getting a passport, and packing. The preparation you will need to make depends on the goals you have. Is your trip to the lands of the Bible a pilgrimage? Is it an opportunity for you to study the Bible in context? Are you primarily interested in archaeology, history, architecture, or spiritual renewal? Is your trip an occasion to visit an exotic place with a culture different from your own? Perhaps you want to visit the lands of the Bible for more than one purpose. The goals you have should determine the choice you make of the type of group you should join, the time you should set aside for your trip, the sites you will visit, and the people you should meet. The first step in preparing for your visit is to decide what goals you have for your trip. This will help you make a good choice about the tour or program you will select to help you meet those goals.

The Types of Tours. Many Christian pilgrimages to the Holy Land last ten days. Three days are necessary for air travel to and from Israel, leaving seven days for touring. A priest or minister usually accompanies participants and acts as chaplain. Local licensed guides lead the groups on visits to Christian holy places. These pilgrimages are attractive because the cost is reasonable and their thrust is devotional. Many believers view a pilgrimage to the Holy Land "a trip of a lifetime." The disadvantage of these short tours is that there is not enough time to visit all the holy places. The pace is sometimes too fast with little time or energy to reflect on the experience, which can be overwhelming. Finally, little or no attention is paid to the complex political, religious, and social issues that the people who live in Israel have to face. Still, many people do not have the flexibility to do anything more than a ten-day pilgrimage. That is why it is important to choose your group carefully. It is best to go with a chaplain who has had some experience in Israel and whom you know personally. Once you have set your goals for your trip, ask the chaplain questions to be sure that his or her tour will help you achieve most of your goals. Examine the itinerary. Be sure you will visit most of the sites you want to see.

Some tours to Israel include optional side trips to one or another of the lands of the Bible: Jordan, Egypt, Greece, or Turkey. Such add-ons are an economical way to visit these other lands though the stay will be short and the sites visited the absolute minimum. If it is possible for you, Egypt deserves more time. It can be the destination of another trip. Those who have already visited Israel sometimes return to the eastern Mediterranean region to visit sites in Greece and Turkey associated with the journeys of St. Paul and the churches mentioned in the Book of Revelation.

Other possibilities for visiting the lands of the Bible are study-tours that last from three weeks to three months or more, depending on the particular program. Educational institutions here and abroad have developed these tours and make them available to interested and qualified participants. Besides Christian shrines, participants in these programs visit historical, archaeological, and nature sites. The tour leaders are teachers and usually take some role in guiding the group, though local guides may still be necessary.

The advantage of study-tours is that more time is available. This makes for an easier pace when visiting sites. Also, it allows for visiting more than does a typical ten-day pilgrimage. Study-tours typically visit more than just Israel. Visits to other lands of the Bible are made. Depending on the length of the study-tour, it is possible to become more acquainted with the local scene by meeting people other than guides, bus drivers, and shopkeepers. The disadvantage of study-tours is that they require more time and involve a greater expense. Still, the more time you allow yourself in the lands of the Bible, the more rewarding your experience will be.

Touring the lands of the Bible by yourself or with a small group without professional guides is usually not advisable unless you have had previous experience in these countries. Israel is the one country where private touring is both possible and practical for the experienced traveler. With careful planning, a good road map, and a guidebook, the adventurous are free to follow their interests at their pace. Help is available from Israeli tourist offices in Israel and abroad. If necessary, you can hire a guide for particular trips. Once in Israel, it is possible to join tours for trips in the specific itineraries. It is always advisable to have an experienced guide for trips into wilderness areas or sites near closed military areas. While it is possible to travel in Greece without a professional guide, it is not advisable to travel alone in Jordan, Egypt, or Turkey.

Whichever way you choose to go, it is important to plan your trip. National tourist offices located in major American cities, travel agents, and good guidebooks can help you explore options and make your plans. If you are committed to visiting the lands of the Bible, you will find that your planning sessions will not be work but enjoyment—a harbinger of what is yet to come. You can contact these tourist offices by mail or telephone for practical advice. Each country's tourism ministry maintains a web page. If you have access to the Internet, you will find these sites very helpful in preparing for your trip, even if you are going on a guided, package tour.

Government Tourist Offices. The modern states of the eastern Mediterranean region depend on tourism and make special efforts to be helpful to people who wish to visit their countries. They provide maps, brochures, travel tips, hotel lists, and other useful information at no charge. Below are addresses of the tourist offices maintained in New York, Chicago, and Los Angeles by the countries in the Middle East. You can go to the offices in person, write, telephone, or fax your questions and the staff at these offices will do all they can to be of help. If you have access to the Internet, you will find that these offices have pages on the Net with hyperlinks to other sites where you can get information and also make hotel or car rental reservations. Some hotels even offer discounts to guests who reserve by the Internet. The value of these sites is that the information is kept current.

Israel Government Tourist Office

800 2nd Ave. 16th Floor	5 S. Wabash Ave.	6380 Wilshire Blvd.
New York, NY 10117	Chicago, IL 60603-3073	Los Angeles, CA 90048
Tel: 800-596-1199	Tel: 800-782-4306	Tel: 213-658-7462-3
FAX: 212-499-5645	FAX: 312-782-1243	FAX: 213-658-6543

Internet: http://www.travelnet.co.il/tnet/mintourism/index.htm

The Palestinian National Authority

Internet: http://www.arab.net/palestine/palestine_contents.html

The **Franciscan Custody of the Holy Land** also has a web page that visitors to Israel and Jordan will find helpful, especially in preparing for visits to the Holy Places:

http://www.Christusrex.org/www1/ofm/TSmain.html

The Kingdom of Jordan

Consulate of Jordan
5423 W. 95th Street
Oak Lawn, IL 60453
Tel: 708-422-9733

Internet:http://www.arabia.com/Jordan/

Egyptian Tourist Authority

630 5th Ave.	645 N. Michigan Ave.	8283 Wilshire Blvd.
Suite 1706	Suite 829	Beverly Hills, CA 90211
New York, NY 10111	Chicago, IL 60611	Tel: 213-653-8815
Tel: 212-336-3570	Tel: 312-280-4666	

Internet: http://its~idsc.gov.eg/tourism/

Greek National Tourist Organization

Olympic Tower	168 N. Michigan Ave.	611 W. 6th St.
645 5th Ave.	Suite 600	Suite 2198
New York, NY 10022	Chicago, IL 60601	Los Angeles, CA 92668
Tel: 212-421-5777	Tel: 312-782-1084	Tel: 213-626-6696-9

Internet: http://agn.hol.gr./info/data.htm

Turkish Government Tourist Office

821 United Nations Plaza
New York, NY 10017
Tel: 212-687-2194
FAX: 212-599-7561

Internet: http://www.turkey.org/tourism.htm

Reading. After deciding on the goals of your trip and choosing a group that meets those goals, you can start reading. You can begin with this book though your interests may take you beyond it. Read something about the history of the lands you will visit. Having a general grasp of a particular country's history will help you place the sites you will visit in a context. It will also make your guide's comments more meaningful. Your reading should be as detailed as your interest requires. Second, read something about the contemporary society, its culture, religion, politics, and economics. You need to know something about the people who will be your hosts during your trip.

The Local Church. For Christians, it is important to learn something about the local church in the places they will visit. The lands of the Bible are the cradle of the Church. It is especially important to learn about the Christian community in Israel. This community is small and divided. There are several ecclesial communities in Israel though ecumenical relationships between these communities is improving. The Christians in Israel are proud of their history but fearful about their future. Egypt's Christians, the Copts, are ready to welcome you to their churches and monasteries. Most Christians in Greece belong to the Orthodox Church. Roman Catholic visitors should know something about the relationship between the Eastern (Orthodox) and Western (Roman) Churches. Jordan and Turkey, though Muslim countries, are home to small Christian communities. When visiting the lands of the Bible, Christian visitors must recognize that these countries are more than the setting for shrines and historical sites. These lands are home to Christian communities that are trying to live the gospel today in circumstances that sometimes require great personal sacrifice to remain faithful to the ideals of Jesus.

Getting in Shape. Another important part of your preparation requires you to get in shape. This is especially important if you have a sedentary life-style. When you decide to make a trip to the lands of the Bible, start walking. This is the easiest and most practical way to get in shape for your trip. Also, get into the habit of drinking water. You should always be careful about dehydration. This is a serious medical problem that can ruin your trip, but it is something you can avoid by simply drinking water. Start before your trip and while on tour always have a water bottle nearby and drink regularly.

Your physician can suggest a diet that can help you lessen the effects of jet lag and prepare you for the change in environment—a change that can affect your digestion. Some people's systems tolerate the change of environment very well. Other people may experience a minor case of dysentery. To lessen the chances of this problem, eat food prepared in your hotel or in restaurants. Avoid buying food from street vendors. Eat fresh fruits and vegetables that you know have been washed thoroughly. Peel any uncooked fruit or vegetable you eat. If you experience any distress, a day of rest will often be enough to deal with the problem. Check with your physician about anti-diarrheal medicines. Usually it is wiser to take a day off from the tour and let the mild dysentery run its course and avoid the anti-diarrheal prescriptions. No vaccinations are required for visiting the lands of the Bible though it is prudent to get a tetanus booster.

What to Take. Packing for your trip is your next task. First, make certain to limit your baggage to one suitcase and one carry-on piece of luggage. Concentrate on casual clothes that are hand-washable and lightweight. Since the climate in the lands of the Bible ranges from temperate to subtropical, it is wise to take clothes that can be layered. As the temperature rises, you can take off layers. Even in the summer a lightweight jacket or sweater will be necessary in the mornings and evenings. You may want to take items of clothing that you are willing to leave behind since this will give you some space for things you purchase during your trip.

There are particular items that you should attend to when preparing your wardrobe for Israel. You will find loose-fitting clothes to be most comfortable for the transatlantic flight. Many people fly in a running or warmup suit. Women should take a skirt that covers their knees and blouses that cover their shoulders since they will not be admitted to Holy Places in shorts or with bare arms. Men, too, will need to have long pants for entrance into Holy Places. Shorts are not usually worn by local people. You may offend some people's sense of modesty if you wear shorts. It is important to have comfortable walking shoes. These should have rubber soles—especially if one is visiting Israel during the rainy season, from November to February, when the rain makes stone pavements very slippery. Also, take a hat and wear it whenever you are outdoors. Walking about without a hat invites sunstroke. Sunglasses, too, are indispensable. Without them the glare will be difficult to tolerate. If you wear prescription eyeglasses, take an extra pair or at least an old pair. If you wear contact lenses, take also a pair of glasses. Sometimes the dust makes wearing contacts uncomfortable.

Make certain you pack your over-the-counter medications such as aspirin. These are available in the region, but are very expensive. You may find a small first-aid kit will come in handy (Band-Aids, an antiseptic, aspirin, insect repellant, an anti-itch ointment). Take sun block and use it liberally once you begin your tour. It is very important to carry a sufficient supply of any prescription medicines you take. Pack them in carry-on luggage.

Other useful items include needle and thread, a water bottle, camera and film, several cheap pens, your address book, and a notebook or journal. Take all the film you will need since buying it in the region is expensive. If you visit Israel during the months of November to February you should take an umbrella or plastic poncho since it will rain often during those months.

The electrical current in the countries of the Middle East is 220 volts with European-style plugs. While you can find adapters for the plugs in most travel stores, this is not enough. One must also have a transformer so that the American-made appliances will not burn out because of the higher voltage. It is possible to get a portable transformer for appliances such as hair dryers that you use for short periods. For equipment like computers and typewriters that are in use for longer periods, it is necessary to have a heavy-duty transformer. It is best to consult with technicians familiar with your appliances and the 220 system before you take your electrical appliances to the Middle East.

Money. It is not wise to carry a lot of cash. Travelers' checks in American dollars are much safer. Bank cards and American Express and other charge cards are accepted in most places though it may not always be possible to pay with a personal check. The amount of money you should take depends upon how much of your trip was prepaid and how much you plan to spend on gifts and souvenirs. You will need some cash for personal expenses, tips, postcards and stamps, and any meals not covered by your tour. It is better to exchange American currency or traveler's checks once you arrive in each country rather than to buy foreign currency in the United States. Exchange only the amount you expect to spend. It is helpful to have one-dollar bills since these are often accepted for small items.

The Bible and a Journal. One item that you should not forget is a Bible. Pick up a cheap paperback edition since the Bible should be your constant companion during your visit. Find and read the biblical citations related to the sites you are visiting. You should do this as a way to prepare for your visit and as a way to reflect on the places you have seen. The Christian Information Office in Jerusalem has a booklet with biblical references to all the sites that tourists usually visit in Israel.

Besides reading and reflecting on the biblical texts related to your visit, you may want to keep a journal. You can take notes while you are visiting sites and, more importantly, jot down your thoughts and prayers at the end of the day. Unless you take the time to do something like this, you will soon notice the days and sites blending into one another. Your visit can become a blur rather than a sharply focused experience. After your trip, you will consider your journal the most valuable remembrance of your visit.

CHAPTER TWO

Israel: The Setting

"For the LORD, your God, is bringing you into a good country,
a land with streams of water, with springs and fountains welling
up in the hills and valleys, a land of wheat and barley, of vines and
fig trees and pomegranates, of olive trees and of honey, a land where
you can eat bread without stint and where you will lack nothing,
a land whose stones contain iron and in whose hills you can mine
copper" (Deut 8:7-9).

GEOGRAPHY

Israel is a small country—about the size of New Jersey. The distance from Dan to Beersheva (see 1 Sam 3:20; 2 Sam 3:10; 17:11; 24:2; 1 Kgs 4:25) is just 125 miles. From the Mediterranean Sea to the Jordan River (running through Jerusalem) is just 50 miles. Still, it has been a crossroads for millennia—even before the rise of the Israelite national states. Why? The answer is simple—geography.

East-West Communications. A look at a good map of the Eastern Hemisphere shows that there are three main barriers to east-west communications there: mountains, deserts, and seas. There are mountains from the Pyrenees in Western Europe to the Tsingling Shan in Western Asia. Deserts stretch from the Sahara in North Africa to the Gobi in Mongolia. The difference is that in the west the mountain ranges are in the north and the deserts in the south. It is the opposite in Asia. Then, of course, there are the five seas: the Mediterranean, Black, Caspian, and Red Seas, and the Persian Gulf. Look back at the map, and these three great obstacles to land movement converge in the territory of the former Israelite kingdoms. Armies and caravans from all over the ancient world met on a 125-mile corridor between the eastern Mediterranean and the Arabian desert. Until modern times, it was the only land passage between Egypt, Africa, Arabia to the south, and the empires of Asia to the north and east. When

Alexander came to Palestine in the fourth century B.C., he added the West to this volatile mix. This accident of geography made it impossible for the ancient Israelites to live in isolation. The only time in its history during which ancient Israel could conduct an independent foreign policy was possibly during David's time (1000–960 B.C.).

The Fertile Crescent. The Fertile Crescent is where the east-west lines of communication met in the ancient world. This is a sickle-shaped piece of land north of the Arabian desert, which has water supplies sufficient to support agriculture and which, in turn, makes possible settlement in towns and villages. The Fertile Crescent is divided into two subsections. The eastern section we know by its Greek name *Mesopotamia*, "[the land] between the rivers." In the northern part of this region, the two rivers supplied water necessary for agriculture, plus rainfall was sufficient to allow for villages and towns away from the river. The south was subject to spring flooding because the melting winter snows in the mountains ran off into its low-lying areas. Drought was not a problem in Mesopotamia. Here the empires of Sumer, Babylon, and Assyria held hegemony until the Greeks came in the fourth century B.C. The Romans ruled here for seven hundred years until the Arabs defeated them in A.D. 636.

Politically and economically the western part of the Fertile Crescent was not as stable as Mesopotamia. This area is also known as the *Levant,* comprising the territories now controlled by the modern states of Syria, Lebanon, Israel, and Jordan. The area of the Levant extends from the mountains of the north to the Red Sea (five hundred miles) and is a complex area geographically. There are four geographic zones that run north-south: the Coastal Plain, the Western Highlands, the Central Rift Valley, and the Eastern Plateau. Besides these zones, there are depressions that run northeast-southwest. None of these is of any consequence to the modern traveler, but they formed serious obstacles to people in antiquity. Each subregion of the Levant, formed by these depressions, developed its own distinct character that set it apart from the others.

The Biblical Heartland. At the foot of Mount Hermon, there is a major transverse fault that causes the Central Rift to drop suddenly as it begins its descent to the Red Sea. For most of that descent, the Rift Valley will be below sea level. This rift effectively cuts off the east and west banks of the Jordan River, i.e., the Transjordan from Cisjordan. The Coastal Plain widens beginning just south of Mount Carmel until Gaza where the Philistines found a home. The Western Highlands descend in two steps (Upper and Lower Galilee) to the low-lying Valley of Jezreel that connects the Jordan Valley with the Mediterranean coast at Acco. To the south of the Jezreel Valley are the highlands of Manasseh, Ephraim, and Judah. The mountains of Manasseh are like an uplifted basin. Instead of providing an obstacle to invasion, they provided an easy route for armies striking at the center of the Israelite and Judahite kingdoms.

Other important geographical subdivisions of the Levant include the **northern regions**. Here were located Ugarit and the Kingdom of Hamath. These were famous for their grain production and pastures. Next is the **Syro-**

Phoenician region along the northeastern coast. People here were wealthy traders. The **southwestern region** did not have much agricultural potential, but caravan routes crisscrossed through the region and people lived off trade. The **southeastern region** received barely enough rain to support village agriculture. This was the territory of Edomites and the Nabateans.

People living in these regions of the Levant did not cooperate with one another very easily—perhaps due to the geographical barriers separating them. People here had a strong regional consciousness that regarded outsiders with suspicion. This does not mean that integration was impossible. Both Rome and Arabia imposed it near the beginning of the Christian era.

Geology. The foundation stone in the Levant is Arabian granite. This stone is not exposed in Israel though it emerges in the Sinai. Above this is red Nubian sandstone. (It can also be yellow or purple.) While this is the major rock of Transjordan, it is not visible in Israel except near the Gulf of Eilat. What you will see much of is Cenomanian limestone, a hard, white sedimentary rock that is the major rock of the highlands. It sometimes is yellow or red. This rock provides excellent building material. Above it is Senonian chalk and above this is Eocene limestone or chalk.

The soil with high chalk content is easier to plow because the soft chalk erodes easier than limestone. The downside is that the soil is not as fertile as that made from the much harder limestone, which decomposes into a rich, soft, red, porous soil. It sops up the winter rains and releases the moisture during the long summer drought. In antiquity, the areas of Cenomanian limestone were thickly forested. Now they are devoted to the cultivation of olive trees that thrive in the red soil.

Alluvial soil covered the valleys of Palestine (along the Coastal Plain, the Jezreel, and the Rift Valley). With a good water supply, these regions can be very productive agriculturally. The one exception was the Plain of Sharon that has a red, sandy soil that was not good for the grain, grapes, and olives that were staples in antiquity. The region was only marginally exploited for agriculture in antiquity and remained a sandy marsh. Today, citrus fruits flourish there.

Climate. The western part of the Fertile Crescent does not have anything like the two great rivers [the Tigris and Euphrates] that are in the east. Most rivers flow only part of the year and the Jordan is at the bottom of the Rift Valley. This rendered it almost useless for irrigation in antiquity. The area is blessed with some springs, but not enough to meet the needs of agriculture. The water for the soil and its crops has to come as rain. The agriculture of Palestine is dry agriculture, i.e., without irrigation. That is why weather and climate were critical concerns for people in antiquity. They meant survival.

It is difficult to speculate about the general weather patterns of antiquity. We simply do not have the data. Still, it is likely that the climate fluctuated here over the centuries as it did in places where we do have sufficient data to chart these fluctuations. It is probably a mistake to think that the climate in the Levant has not changed appreciably since the Old Testament Period. What follows is a description of the climate today. We need to remember that there may have been some variations during the biblical period.

There are several phenomena that influence the climate of the Levant. First, the Mediterranean Sea and the Arabian desert are just over one hundred miles apart. The proximity of these two geographical features affects the climate of the region very much. Second, the weather patterns run west to east while the mountains in the center of the Levant run north and south. The effect of this is to stall weather west of the mountains. Third, the Levant is close enough to the Sahara and Arabian deserts to feel their intense summer heat, and close enough to the Russian and Siberian Plains to be influenced by their cold in the winter. Finally, during the summer the sun is over the Tropic of Cancer while during the winter it is over the Tropic of Capricorn.

These four phenomena combine with the following results. First, in Israel there are two seasons. One is a dry season that begins on June 15 and runs to September 15. The beginning and end of this season are regular. It almost never rains during this time. Before and after this dry season, there are transition periods of between four and six weeks. The other principal season is the wet season. Its beginning unfortunately is not as predictable as that of the dry season. This is what caused farmers in antiquity so much anxiety.

Second, the rains that do come do not fall evenly throughout the land. It rains more in the north than in the south and more in the west than in the east. Antioch in the far north of the Levant receives forty inches of rain a year and has no dry season. Beersheva receives about eight inches and is totally dry for five months (May–September). Rainfall is always greater on the west side of a mountain than on the east side since the former is closer to the sea. Finally, moisture will evaporate quickly on the south side of a mountain because of greater exposure to the sun. The best place to plant, then, is on the north and west sides of hills.

Life-styles. What life-styles did this geography of the Levant encourage among ordinary folk? There were shepherds, farmers, and merchants. The shepherds led their flocks from one pasture to another, taking advantage of every hill and valley that had grass to feed their sheep. They could not stay in one place for long because the sheep would soon deplete the available resources. For shepherds, **mobility** was the key to survival. For farmers, the key was **stability** and rain. Farmers cared for their land generation after generation. The land was the means of survival. On the other hand, sometimes oppressive taxation led farmers to convert their wealth in land to herds and flocks so that they could evade the tax collectors. The merchants required both mobility and stability. Without safe roads commerce would be impossible. These three groups interacted and even cooperated. For example, the merchants depended on animals bred by the shepherds and farmers. They also needed guides in unfamiliar areas. The shepherds provided animals to help with both the plowing and the threshing. While society in antiquity was much more complex than this schema proposes, still it does give an idea of how society ordered itself as it adapted to the resources available and the potential of the land.

HISTORY

The first datable event in Israel's history is the surrender of Jerusalem to Nebuchadnezzar (2 Kgs 24:12). From information found in the *Babylonian Chronicles,* this event took place on March 15–16, 597 B.C. This is not to imply that it is impossible to reconstruct earlier Israelite history; however, clearly any reconstruction is tentative and therefore subject to revision.

There are two types of sources that historians use in writing the history of ancient Israel: literary (the Bible and ancient Near Eastern texts) and material (the results of excavations). There are problems with both sources. First, the Bible is not concerned about providing a history in the contemporary sense of the term. Also, most biblical stories were written by people who were not witnesses to the events the stories describe. In fact, the writers may have been separated from the events they tell of by hundreds of years. The stories of origins of Israel in Canaan inform us what people of a much later age in Israelite history thought those origins to be. Second, references to ancient Israel in ancient Near Eastern texts are occasional. At most these can provide us with the broad outlines of Israelite history rather than the details that could fill in that outline.

Finally, the archaeological data suffer on two accounts. First, the are fragmentary. There might be something yet to be discovered that may require current hypotheses to be revised. Second, archaeology in Palestine is silent. Usually no texts are found with the material remains that can help in their interpretation. For example, excavators of Hazor came upon a stratum from the Late Bronze Age that shows a violent destruction. Still, there is no material evidence that can identify those responsible for the destruction. It is tempting to use Josh 11:10 to interpret those data. Unfortunately, the Late Bronze Age in Canaan was a time of severe disruptions. There is no way to be certain that the Israelites were responsible for the destruction that took place in thirteenth century Hazor.

With these cautions in mind, you can use what follows as a guide in placing the archaeological sites and artifacts that we see in Israel into a chronological framework.

An Outline of the History of the Holy Land

Chalcolithic Period   4500–3150 B.C.
    advanced crafts and the beginnings of a metal industry

Bronze Age   **3150–1200**
    Early   3150–2200
        walled towns and international trade
    Middle   2200–1550
        the alphabet; advanced urban cultures
    Late   1550–1200
        Egyptian hegemony over Canaanite
          town-states

The Iron Age	**1200–586**
The breakdown of Egyptian control leads to conflicts between the Israelites and Philistines for control.	1150–1000
Saul	1020
David	1000–960
Solomon; First Temple	960–922
The Two Israelite Kingdoms	
Israel (North)	922–721
Judah (South)	922–587
Early Prophets	800–700
Amos and Hosea in Israel	
Micah and Isaiah in Judah	
Assyrian Conquest of Israel	721
Jeremiah	625–587
The Babylonian Conquest; the destruction of the Temple and end of the Davidic dynasty	587
The Persian Period	**539–333**
The return from Exile	539
The Jerusalem Temple rebuilt	515
The Hellenistic Period	**333–63**
Alexander conquers Palestine	333
Ptolemaic Rule	323–200
Seleucid Period	200–164
The Maccabean Revolt	167–164
The Hasmonean Period	164–63
The Roman Period	**63 B.C.–A.D. 324**
Pompey enters Jerusalem.	63 B.C.
Herod the Great	37–4 B.C.
Birth of Jesus	c. 7 B.C.
Pontius Pilate	A.D. 26–36
Ministry of Jesus	c. A.D. 30
First Revolt	A.D. 66–70
Destruction of the Temple	A.D. 70
Second Revolt	132–135
Aelia Capitolina	135
The Byzantine Period	**324–640**
Holy Sepulchre built	326–335
Persian Invasion	614
The Arab Period	**640–1099**
Conquest of Jerusalem by Omar	638
Omayyid (Umayyad) Rule (Damascus)	640–750
Dome of the Rock completed	691

Abissid Rule (Baghdad)	750–973
Fatimid (Cairo)	973–1071

Seljuk Turks **1071–1099**

Crusader Period **1099–1291**
Jerusalem captured and sacked	1099
Crusader Church of the Holy Sepulchre	1149
Saladin's victory at the Horns of Hattin	1187
Acco (Acre) falls.	1291

Mamluke Period **1250–1517**
| Franciscan custody of the Holy Land | 1342 |

The Ottoman (Turkish) Period **1517–1918**
Suleiman builds Old City walls.	1537
Latin Patriarchate	1847
Herzl comes to Palestine.	1898
Tel Aviv founded	1909
Turks surrender Jerusalem to Lord Allenby.	1917
Balfour Declaration	1917

The Mandate Period **1918–1948**
The UN partitions Palestine
   into Jewish and Arab states. 1947

The Modern State of Israel **1948–**
| Israel proclaims itself a state. | May 14, 1948 |
| Invasion of Jewish state by Arab states | May 15, 1948 |

The Six-Day War;
   annexation of East Jerusalem and occupation
   of Sinai, Gaza, Golan Heights, and West Bank 1967
| Yom Kippur War | 1973 |

Peace Treaty with Egypt;
   return of the Sinai 1979
Oslo Accords with PLO	1993
Peace Treaty with Jordan	1994
Assassination of Rabin	1995

ARCHAEOLOGY

Many of the sites that visitors to Israel see have been excavated in order to reconstruct the history of pre-Israelite Palestine, of ancient Israel, early Judaism, and early Christianity. Archaeologists working with the National Parks Authority, the Society for the Protections of Nature, the Israeli Department of Antiquities and other official bodies have prepared these sites to receive visitors. In order to appreciate the achievement of the archaeologists and to have a good idea of what their work can contribute to biblical studies it is helpful to understand the discipline of biblical archaeology.

What Is Archaeology? The definitions of archaeology vary. Most helpful is the one that designates archaeology as the study of the material remains of antiquity as opposed to its literary remains. Sometimes during excavations literary remains are found. This is the case more often outside Israel than in excavations within Israel. In Israel, archaeology is silent, with rare exceptions such as the Dead Sea Scrolls. In any case, whenever written materials are found they are handed over to epigraphers, philologists, textual critics, paleographers who may not be archaeologists themselves.

This is not to undervalue the study of literary texts uncovered during archaeological work. Little more than a century ago the Bible was an isolated artifact of ancient Near Eastern civilization, a monument without known context or ancestry. Today, thanks to archaeological exploration throughout the Middle East, the history of Israel has become part of the history of the ancient world. Ancient Israel's literature can be viewed as evolving out of the forms of related literature. The religion of ancient Israel stands both in continuity and discontinuity with contemporary Near Eastern mythology and cult. The student of biblical literature is forced by the impact of archaeological research to place Israelite literature in the context of Canaanite literature. Israel was heir to a rich literary heritage. To be sure, Israel changed, developed, and transformed this heritage. The results of these efforts have not only helped translate and understand difficult passages of the Bible, but they have caused the reevaluation of early theories about the development of ancient Israel's literary and religious traditions.

Still, archaeology proper is a field of study that deals with nonliterary remains from an ancient culture. These range from monumental structures to seeds and even pollens. Any object that gives evidence of human activity is fair game for the archaeologist. Archaeology uncovers these objects, identifies them, reconstructs them when possible and necessary, and then classifies them. Once these preliminary tasks have been completed, the more difficult ones begin: the artifacts are compared with examples from other regions, they are arranged in a chronological sequence, and they are related to previously known information about antiquity.

All this is done to reconstruct life in the ancient world, to trace the development of the people who left these remains behind, and to help define the various types of human responses to different situations. Archaeology fills a void where literary sources are insufficient or nonexistent. The Bible is, after all, literature that comes from an elite group in ancient Israel. While the people who composed the books of the Bible may not have been part of the social and economic upper class, they came from those people who had a keen sense of the values and beliefs of their ancestral religious tradition. But is this the way most Israelites believed? Archaeology then puts the Bible into a living context. To say this in a more theological key: archaeology makes us sensitive to the incarnational aspect of revelation.

Students of the OT have been more receptive to the archaeological task than those of the NT. There has been a tendency to relegate the books of the NT to the domain of theology exclusively. Still, NT scholars do not deny that the NT presupposes an historical situation, but they ask what can be learned about NT background from archaeology that we cannot learn from ancient literary sources like Josephus, other Jewish texts, and the large body of Greco-Roman literature from the period? Slowly this attitude is changing, in part because of the influence of social studies on NT interpretation.

The goal of archaeology is to recreate the world of the Bible using the material remains left by the people of that world. This assumes that the Bible is the product of real people, who lived at a real time, had certain values, political, economic, and social structures. It also assumes that the more we know about these people, the more we can know about the literature that they produced.

The Methods of Archaeology. Archaeological research comprises three aspects: the discovery and surface survey of the site, excavation and recording of data, and interpretation and publication of the data.

Discovery and Survey. One may select a site for one of several reasons: (1) its historical importance, (2) chance finds of great consequence, (3) the impressiveness and accessibility of the site, (4) to check finds from previous excavations, and (5) as a salvage operation before the site is lost to modern development. This first phase is marked by a study of surface remains, a survey of the immediate area. Aerial photographs and surface sherding are two techniques among others that help determine the value of excavating at the certain site.

Excavation and Recording. Archaeology is one science that systematically destroys its evidence as it progresses. Beginning at the surface and proceeding through the layers of occupation, excavators must remove what is above to uncover what is below until the excavators reach bedrock or virgin soil. This is why special techniques of excavation and recording have been developed. These make it possible to reconstruct the excavation in the library months and even years after it has taken place.

The method used in excavating biblical sites is usually some variation of the Wheeler-Kenyon method. Mortimer Wheeler developed this method of stratigraphic excavation for use with sites from the classical period; Kathleen Kenyon adapted his method for use on biblical sites. The basic approach is to peel off occupational layer by occupational layer, recover artifacts and other evidence of human presence at the site, and then to use the recovered data to reconstruct the site's history, economy, politics, religions, and society.

While the excavation needs to be done carefully, the recording of data requires special attention. Those who study biblical texts have the same data before them. Those who study the material remains of an ancient society have only one opportunity to see these remains in their context unless the progress of the excavation has been recorded with such detail that the entire process can be reconstructed from the final reports.

A vital element in any project is reporting finds through prompt publication. Here is where many archaeologists fail. What good is careful excavation and recording if results are not published? About one half of all excavation projects begun in Israel since 1948 have not been published. Not publishing the record of one's excavations is like withholding a text from one's colleagues.

Interpretation. Archaeology is both a science and an art. What has been described so far is the scientific part. What follows is the art. Interpretation is the most important element in the whole enterprise. Without it excavation has no value for the advancement of knowledge. What we will have is a mass of unrelated data that are not even accessible to the scholarly community. Pottery, coins, bones, seeds, metal, stone and wood objects, structures uncovered must all be related in a coherent fashion. The interpretation of data is so crucial in Palestinian archaeology because of its "silence." The results of this interpretation appear in a published report that includes a history of earlier excavation projects, a summary of the goals of the current project, and the description and interpretation of the remains found.

Visiting Archaeological Sites. There are two types of archaeological sites in Israel: the *tel* ("mound" A: *tell*) and the *khirbeh* ("ruin" H: *horvah*). The latter are sites from the Roman-Byzantine Periods. Tels are the remains of earlier occupations.

A *tel* is an artificial mound formed by successive occupations at the same site. These occupations may cover more than one thousand years as at Megiddo and Hazor. People returned to the same sites to build on the ruins of previous occupations since there are only a few places where a town or city settlement was possible. To be successful a city must have three features. The site must be defensible. Usually this means that people will settle on a site elevated above the surrounding territory. This allows defenders to catch sight of potential threats and forces attackers to fight their way uphill. Second, the site must be near a water source sufficient to supply the needs of its inhabitants. The water supply also must be available in time of siege. Third, a city must be near an important trade route to make possible commercial relations with other cities.

A tel is easy to spot. It is a hill with a flat top. Though there is usually some pottery visible on the surface, excavation is necessary to reveal major structures. When visiting a tel, look first for the **probe trench**. Archaeologists usually begin excavation by digging a trench from the top of the tel to bedrock or virgin soil. Tel es-Sultan (OT Jericho) and Megiddo offer good examples of such trenches. A record on the site's occupational history is visible on the walls of the trench called the balks. Unfortunately, after being exposed to sun and rain for so long, these balks do not tell their story to visitors. But, one can sometimes still see the telltale signs that guide the excavation on a tel. Look for walls in the balk. These are easy to spot. You may see dressed stones [stones worked by masons] or field stones. You will sometimes see mud brick above the stones or small field stones that served as the foundational makeup for the wall. Look for evidence of surfaces: a layer of beaten earth, cobbles, or plaster. Sometimes you will see a layer of ash that suggests destruction by fire. Black ash shows that there were attempts to extinguish the fire. White ash shows that the fire burnt itself out. When looking at a balk, try to see how many occupational layers you can detect.

As you walk about the tel, you will see various structures uncovered and reconstructed by the archaeologists. Remember that not all the structures you will see are contemporaneous. Most sites will have signs that identify the structures and the dates of their use. For tels, gates and walls are important. Notice the patterns used for gates. Especially important is the defensive value of city gates. When looking at walls, notice if they are solid or casemate. Look for a glacis attached to the outer wall. Look also at the makeup of the wall. Is it made of dressed or field stones or mud brick?

Another important installation on a tel is the cult center. Look for the outline of the temple and its interior architecture. Can you recognize the entrance, the "holy of holies," and other rooms? Can you spot the altar? It is outside the temple and is a structure usually made of field stones. Sometimes the royal residence is near the temple. Other structures found on a tel will be storage facilities, silos, a water system, private homes. Sometimes one can also see industrial areas where pottery and other items were manufactured.

When you visit a tel, you want to have some sense of its occupational history, its wealth, its religious life, its vulnerability to attack, its political system, and its industries. You can discover all this by walking about the site and keeping track of what archaeology has uncovered. Of course, to get a complete and accurate profile of the tel, it is necessary to look at the small finds uncovered during excavation. Many sites have small museums nearby to help you do this.

Sites from the Greco-Roman and Byzantine Periods usually have remnants of monumental buildings visible above ground. The names of such sites often have the Arabic word **khirbet** or the Hebrew word **horvat** prefixed to them as in *Khirbet Qumran*. Because the license to excavate in Israel carries with it the requirement that archaeologists reconstruct whenever possible, most sites from the Roman-Byzantine Period that we visit show extensive reconstruction. At all sites, whether tels or khirbehs, look for a solid black line on structures. What is below the line is original; what is above the line is the result of reconstruction by the archaeologists. Reconstruction is necessary because Israel is in an earthquake region because of the Aravah fault line. Monumental buildings from antiquity usually show some evidence of earthquake destruction.

When visiting a khirbeh, look for the monumental buildings. Whether churches or synagogues, these will usually be **basilicas**, a Greco-Roman architectural form common in Roman and Byzantine Palestine. A basilica is a rectangular building whose interior space is divided into a central nave and two side aisles by two rows of columns. Sometimes there will also be a row of columns at the front, the rear, or both. Variations on this form include the **broadhouse** in which the orienting interior wall will be a long wall instead of the short wall. Another variation is the **apsidal** basilica. Here the wall of orientation will have an apse. Variations more common in church buildings include a **transept** and a **triple apse**.

The residential and industrial areas in the khirbeh will not differ radically from those from earlier periods. People built their homes from stone if it was readily available. Limestone is the most common building material because it is widely available and it is easy to work with. In some sites near the Sea of Galilee and in the Golan, basalt is the building stone used. Basalt is a very difficult stone to work because of its density, but this region contains an abundance of this volcanic rock.

When visiting Crusader sites—especially fortresses, look for evidence that the Crusaders reused stones from earlier structures when they built. Good examples are the Crusader castles at Caesarea and Belvoir. The former used stones from the hippodrome and other Byzantine Period structures. The latter used stones from a nearby Jewish village and its synagogue.

The Israeli National Parks Authority has reconstructed and identified many sites from the Roman-Byzantine Period to help visitors appreciate the skill and achievements of the people of that period. Usually there is no problem except that the identifications are sometimes disputed. For example, at Masada you will see a room in the casemate wall along the western side identified as a "synagogue." Most often a structure will be identified as a synagogue only if it has an inscription or an architectural fragment with a Jewish religious symbol that makes such an identification reasonable. The structure on Masada had neither, but since scrolls containing biblical texts were found nearby, the excavators were confident that they had found the synagogue of the Zealots.

Ancient Synagogues

Excavations in the area called *Palestina Prima* by the Romans have uncovered thirty-six structures that are clearly identified as synagogues. The location of forty-eight structures from which architectural fragments have survived is unknown and the identification of sixty other structures as synagogues is a matter of dispute. Clearly there is a problem identifying a particular building as a synagogue.

The most indisputable means of identification is through an inscription that confirms the building's use as a place for liturgical assembly. Unfortunately, buildings with such inscriptional evidence are few. Another criterion is that the building must show decoration that reflects Jewish religious practice. For example, a typical decorative feature of many synagogues is a menorah. Sometimes a building's architectural style and decorative motifs are used to identify it as a synagogue. Unless these decorations involve religious symbols, such an identification has little to commend it because the Jews of Roman and Byzantine Periods adopted the Greco-Roman style of decorating monumental buildings common in the region. Similarly, the Jews adopted the Greco-Roman basilica as the standard for synagogue architecture in the Roman and Byzantine eras.

Though both Josephus and the NT speak of the synagogue as a place of Jewish liturgical assembly, no building dating from the first century A.D. or earlier in Palestine has been indisputably identified as a synagogue. There are at least five first century structures that some archaeologists identify as synagogues: a building in the casemate wall at Masada, a triclinium at the Herodium supposedly converted by the Zealots to a synagogue during the First Revolt, the basilica at Gamla, a structure at Migdal, and a building at Chorazin that can no longer be found. Some archaeologists identify these five buildings as synagogues because of architectural characteristics they share with later buildings that are definitely synagogues. Still, there is no indication that the buildings served any religious purpose or that their architecture conformed to any set of specifications that marked them for liturgical use.

Probably buildings used for non-Temple worship in the first century were not distinguishable from domestic architecture. Though the first-century buildings identified as synagogues were used for worship, there is no way to decide that merely from their architecture. It is more likely that before the third century, buildings used only for worship and having a unique architectural form did not exist. Jews in early Roman Palestine met for communal prayer and the reading of Scripture in private homes modified for liturgical assembly or in public buildings built to accommodate a variety of communal functions. At present, archaeology and available literary sources can establish no firm date for the origin of the synagogue. Though written sources from the first century such as the gospels (e.g., Matt 6:5; Mark 1:39; Luke 4:44), say that Jews worshiped in synagogues, it is not clear that these buildings were, in fact, monumental buildings constructed and used primarily for worship.

The synagogue became the central institution of Jewish life and religion during the Roman and Byzantine Periods. It effected genuine changes in the way Jewish religious rituals were carried on. Most obviously, sacrifice was replaced by prayer and the reading of the Scriptures once the synagogue replaced the Temple as the central Jewish liturgical institution. Second, the priesthood had no essential role in the ritual of the synagogue. Any adult male could lead the service. Still, the liturgy was not the synagogue's only function. It was the religious, social, and cultural center of every Jewish community in Palestine. It served as a place for religious instruction, a place of assembly for communal meetings. It housed the courts that decided legal cases. It sometimes served as the place to keep community funds, and was a hostel for travelers. It is little wonder, then, that the centerpiece of Justinian's anti-Jewish laws was his edict forbidding the building of synagogues.

The ancient synagogues that you will see in Israel will all reflect architectural adaptations of the Greco-Roman basilica. One practical problem with that form is that the entrance faced Jerusalem. Since worshipers offered their prayers while facing the same direction, this required an awkward about-face maneuver upon entering the synagogue. There were two ways synagogue architects dealt with this problem. One was to make the wall of orientation not the narrow wall at the entrance of the building, but one of the broad walls of the prayer hall. A second adaptation was the addition of an apse to the short wall opposite the entrance. The apse oriented the worshiper to Jerusalem. In both adaptations, the entrance of the building no longer faced Jerusalem.

Another interesting feature of Israel's ancient synagogues is the variety of style in their decoration. This variety reflects the diversity there was in interpreting the commandment regarding images. Some communities were obviously very conservative. The only ornamentation is geometric as in the Meiron synagogue. Others will use floral patterns along with geometric ones as does the Baram synagogue. Still others will depict animal forms as found in the Capernaum synagogue. The most unexpected type of decoration involved depicting foreign deities. When you visit the synagogue at Chorazin, look for the image of Medusa (or Helios) incised on a frieze from the synagogue. The most dramatic examples of the latitude that some Jewish communities allowed themselves in this area are found at the synagogues of Hamat Tiberias and Beth Alpha. While mosaic floors of both synagogues depict some traditional Jewish religious symbols and scenes, the centerpiece of both is a zodiac with the Greek god Helios riding his chariot in the sky. The precise function of the zodiac as a decorative element in a synagogue is not clear. Still, the zodiac mosaics make it clear that Judaism in the Roman and Byzantine Periods was a diverse religious phenomenon. This flexibility was one key to Judaism's survival through the centuries.

Ancient Churches

Many structures that you will see during your stay in Israel will be churches or synagogues. While the origins of the synagogue are still a debated issue, the beginnings of Christian architecture are not so mysterious. We know where and when the first church buildings appeared. Unfortunately, there is very little left of those first churches. Most of the churches you will see date from the Crusader Period or later. The only church from the Byzantine Period that has survived intact is the Church of the Nativity in Bethlehem. The Church of the Multiplication of Loaves is a reconstructed version of a Byzantine Period church. Excavators have reconstructed the Byzantine church at Kursi. But little else beyond foundations and some architectural fragments remains of the 276 churches from the Byzantine Period in Palestine. That number is five times the number of ancient synagogues discovered from the Roman and Byzantine Periods—including those whose identification is a matter of dispute. The Fatimid caliph, Hakim the Mad (eleventh century) destroyed most of Palestine's ancient churches. It was this orgy of destruction that led to the Crusades.

The first Christians continued to worship in the Temple (Acts 3:1) and in synagogues as long as they were welcome to do so. Eventually the Jews who believed that Jesus was the Messiah had to find their own places of worship. But these early Christians did not have the economic resources, the organizational structure, nor even the need to develop a distinctive form of Christian architecture. They met where convenient. But from the beginning, a distinctive liturgy developed that required regular gatherings the nature of which led to holding these in the homes of believers. The core of the service was a meal (Acts 2:46).

Christians then met in each other's homes. In time, some of these homes were modified to serve exclusively as places of worship, e.g., Peter's house in Capernaum. These were the *domus ecclesiae*—the house churches. In terms of their exterior architecture, they were indistinguishable from other houses. The first Christians did not want to call attention to themselves since attention might bring with it hostility.

According to the fourth-century church historian Eusebius, there was a large church in Jerusalem before the Second Revolt against Rome (132–135). He also asserts that churches went up throughout Palestine during the reign of Gallienus (260–268) and at the beginning of Diocletian's rule (284–305). Unfortunately, archaeology has not been able to locate these Roman Period churches. Results of excavations show that there were three periods of church building in Palestine. The first followed Constantine's Edict of Milan in 313. The emperor built the Church of the Nativity in Bethlehem, the Church of the Resurrection (now known as the Holy Sepulchre) in Jerusalem, and the Eleona Church on the Mount of Olives. He also encouraged the building of churches in Galilee to achieve Christian inroads into the heavily Jewish population of that region.

A second spate of church building activity took place in the fifth century at the initiative of Eudocia, the estranged wife of Theodosius II (401–460). She built several churches in Jerusalem and its environs. Among these was the Church of St. Stephen. The Church of St. Stephen that serves the Dominican Community of the École biblique is a nineteenth-century structure built on the foundations of Eudocia's fifth-century church.

The last great period of church building before the Crusaders Period was during the reign of Justinian I (527–563). Sixty-nine churches have been dated to this period. Only one of these has survived to the present and that is the Church of the Nativity, which Justinian built to replace the Constantinian structure.

Byzantine Period churches fall into three main categories in terms of the use to which they were put. Most of the churches served the liturgical needs of local congregations of Christians. Archaeologists have identified the remains of forty-five such churches. These were the *dedicated churches* since they often honored the memory of a particular person—usually a saint. A second type of church was the *memorial church* built to commemorate some event in the life of Jesus. The Church of the Nativity is one example. Archaeologists have identified twenty-six memorial churches. Finally, over one hundred churches were part of a larger complex, including monastic settlements, cemeteries, fortresses, or guest houses.

Like the synagogue, the church building was an adaptation of the Greco-Roman basilica. One hundred fifty-five churches of Palestine exemplify this architectural form. One reason for the predominance of this form was the simplicity and ease of construction. Both architects and laborers were familiar with the basilica. Christians, however, introduced some innovations in this form. One was the addition of a transept, which appears in neither the secular nor synagogal basilicas. This made the church cruciform in appearance and had the practical effect of allowing more worshipers to stand close to the altar.

An apse appears in some non-church basilicas, but some churches appear with a triple apse, an innovation of ecclesiastical architecture. The central apse was the setting for the altar and the place of the clergy. The apse on the right, known as the *diaconicon,* was a robing room for the clergy, and the one on the left, known as the *prothesis,* was the place for the preparation of the gifts. The churches at Avdat have a triple apse.

Byzantine architects used two forms other than the basilica in building churches. One is the chapel. This is a single hall with an apse. The Church of the Multiplication of Loaves is an example. The other form is the centralized church. This form shows the influence of the circular Roman mausoleums.

Seven have been identified. There are two forms of the centralized church: the octagonal and the circular. The Church of St. Peter in Capernaum is an example of the former and the Church of the Ascension on the Mount of Olives is an example of the latter.

Archaeology has not found examples of ecclesiastical architecture before the time of Constantine (fourth century). Before that time Christians worshiped in the Temple, in synagogues, and in private homes. There is some evidence that the first Christians also worshiped in caves like those in Bethlehem. The Byzantine era witnessed the building of stately basilicas to serve as the setting for Christian worship. It is unfortunate so little has survived from this period.

THE POLITICAL SCENE

Israel and the Arabs

The State of Israel was proclaimed on May 14, 1948. This proclamation was possible because of a United Nations vote to divide the territory of the former League of Nations Mandate in Palestine into two states: one Jewish, the other Arab. While the Jews accepted the U.N. decision, the Arabs did not. The armies of several Arab states attacked the Jewish population of Palestine on May 15, 1948. The Arab armies were unable to defeat the Israelis and eventually Ralph Bunche, an African-American diplomat, arranged a cease-fire. Mr. Bunche received the Nobel Peace Prize for his efforts. The borders of the State of Israel after the 1948 war enclosed more territory than the U.N. resolution allowed the Jewish state. Jordan annexed the territory of the former Mandate not controlled by the Israelis except for the Gaza Strip, which Egypt annexed. Thus, no Arab Palestinian state was ever established. Also, Jerusalem was divided: the western portion of the city was controlled by the Israelis; East Jerusalem and the Old City were annexed by Jordan.

Though the Arab states agreed to a cease-fire, they did not recognize the existence of the State of Israel and made no peace treaty with it. The Israelis did not allow the Arabs who fled its territory during the war to return following the cessation of hostilities. The Israeli government expropriated their land and homes and the refugees settled in camps on the West Bank and in Gaza. The Arabs who remained in the territory claimed by the State of Israel became Israeli citizens with civil rights and obligations except that of compulsory military service. The unwillingness of the Arab states to recognize Israel and the Arab refugees made the continuing Arab-Israeli conflict inevitable.

Though the cease-fire ended most military activity, there began a war of attrition between Israel and its Arab neighbors and terror attacks from Palestinian groups like the Palestine Liberation Organization [PLO]. Several times these conflicts resulted in war between Israel and Arab states. In 1956, Israel, with England and France, invaded the Sinai peninsula to regain control of the Suez Canal, which Egypt nationalized. The United States and the U.N. insisted that Israel, France, and England withdraw. In 1967, Israel made a preemptive strike against Egypt and Syria when it became clear that they were about to invade Israel. Jordan then joined the conflict. In just six days, the armies and air forces of the three Arab states were all but destroyed, and Israel accepted a U.N.–imposed cease-fire. It occupied the Sinai peninsula and Gaza Strip (Egypt), the Golan Heights (Syria), and East Jerusalem, the Old City, and the West Bank (Jordan), with the hope that these territories, except Jerusalem, could be exchanged for peace treaties. The Arab states refused. The state of war continued and Israeli occupation of Arab territory began.

The occupation of Arab territories after 1967 compounded Israel's security problems and the army established military settlements in the territories. Soon afterward came civilian settlements supported by a conservative government that called the West Bank "Judea and Samaria" and regarded it as integral to Israel. These settlements will be a serious obstacle in any settlement with the Palestinian Authority. The settlers will be unwilling to leave and they have many supporters.

In 1973, Egypt and Syria coordinated attacks on Israel that took place on Yom Kippur. After some serious initial setbacks, the Israelis were able to push the Syrians and Egyptians back to their borders. The United States airlifted military equipment to Israel to replace that which was destroyed in the first days of fighting. This enabled Israel to turn the tide. Once the tide turned against Egypt and Syria, the Soviet Union demanded a cease-fire. The U.S. and Israel acceded.

The Egyptians remembered their victories in the first days of the Yom Kippur War, which they call the October War, and chose to forget how the war ended. With the memories of these initial victories, Anwar Sadat was convinced that he was in a position to seek peace with the Israelis. Egypt was in need of massive economic aid that he knew would be forthcoming from the U.S. if he were to sign a peace treaty with the Israelis. After difficult, personal negotiations between Sadat and Menachem Begin, the Israeli Prime Minister, facilitated by President Jimmy Carter, the Camp David Accords were signed in 1979. These became the basis of peace between Egypt and Israel. Israel returned the Sinai to Egypt and Egypt granted diplomatic recognition to Israel.

After being driven out of Jordan in 1975 (the Black September), the PLO settled in Lebanon. The government of Lebanon was unable to control the PLO, which used that country as a base for terror attacks on Israel—especially settlements in the north of the country. In 1981, Menachem Begin, the Prime Minister, and Ariel Sharon, the Defense Minister, decided to end these attacks by invading Lebanon. After some initial success, they decided to widen the scope of the incursion to destroy the PLO. The Israelis besieged Beirut and forced the PLO leadership to flee to Tunis. The war bogged down as the Israeli army had to face not only the PLO but also Lebanese Muslim forces in what became a guerrilla-type conflict. There was also the threat that the conflict might widen to include Syria. Israeli problems were compounded when Lebanese Christian forces massacred Palestinians in two refugee camps (Sabra and Shintilla) while the Israeli forces were supposedly in charge of security. Eventually the Israeli forces withdrew to a seven-mile, self-proclaimed security zone that abuts the Israeli-Lebanese border.

The Israeli incursion led to civil war in Lebanon between the Christian minority, who controlled the government, and the Muslim majority. Syria entered

Lebanon as a peace-keeping force though they tipped the balance of power to the Muslims. Currently Lebanon is little more than a Syrian protectorate. Christian Lebanese forces (South Lebanese Army or SLA) are concentrated in the Israeli security zone and cooperate with the Israelis in controlling Palestinian guerrilla forces that still harass the Israeli forces in Lebanon and occasionally the extreme north of Israel.

In 1987, the Arabs of the occupied territories began what has been called the Intifada, an Arabic word for separation. It was the result of a spontaneous uprising led by young Arabs who grew up under Israeli occupation. The Intifada expressed itself through the harassment of Israeli military forces and settlers and through general strikes by the Arab population. Although the Intifada never seriously threatened Israel's security, it became a public relations nightmare. The media carried pictures of battle-equipped Israeli soldiers firing their M16s at children who were pelting them with stones. It sparked a debate within Israel itself about the wisdom of holding on to the territories.

To remove the stalemate in Arab-Israeli relations, the United States and the Soviet Union jointly sponsored a multilateral peace conference in Madrid in the fall 1991. The U.S. hoped to capitalize on the goodwill that resulted from the recently concluded victory of the allied forces over Sadam Hussein. One goal was to get Arab nations to negotiate directly with Israel. Israel had to be willing to accept the PLO as a party to these negotiations. Though the conference had no immediate success, the peace process began.

After the Israeli national elections of 1992, Yitzhak Rabin of the Labor Party was able to put together a coalition that was willing to seek some way to move the peace process along. In the fall of 1993, Rabin's government recognized the PLO and granted limited autonomy to the Palestinian National Authority to administer Gaza and Jericho. After five years, the future of the rest of the territories was to be the subject of negotiation. In the fall 1994, Jordan signed a peace treaty with Israel. In the fall 1995, a religious Jew, who opposed the "land for peace" policy of the Labor government, assassinated Rabin. The following spring, elections brought Benjamin Netanyahu of the Likud Party to power as prime minister. Though he is willing to continue the peace process, it will go on at a more deliberate pace. Still, negotiations continue and Israel has turned over major population centers of the West Bank to the administration of the Palestinian National Authority.

There are both Arabs and Israelis who want to undermine the peace process. It is not a simple matter to reverse almost fifty years of distrust, conflict, and hatred. The next step in the process will be a peace treaty with Syria, which is demanding the return of the Golan Heights. The Israeli settlers in the Golan and their supporters are adamant in their refusal to return the Golan. What Israel wants is secure borders and peaceful, normal relations with all Arab states. What the Palestinians want is a state of their own. Negotiations to realize the latter ambition will be perhaps the most difficult of all.

It is important for you as a visitor to the region to become familiar with the political struggles that have shaped the lives of the people who will welcome you to their homeland. These issues are complex. It is important to listen and learn before making judgments. Still, it is important to remember that there are *two* sides to every question. All Christians should pray that the peace process continue so that the land Jesus called home could experience a just and durable peace.

The Israeli Political System

Israel is a parliamentary democracy. In this system, governmental power is concentrated in the legislature [H: *Knesset,* assembly]. This is unlike the U.S. system in which the executive, legislature, and judiciary are coequal branches of the government. The Knesset is the chief policy-making body of the State. Elections to Knesset must take place at least every four years. The party that has the majority in the Knesset can form a government. The prime minister must be a member of the Knesset; members of his cabinet do not. Their appointment is subject to approval by the Knesset. At any time, the Knesset can vote "no confidence" in the government, which must then resign and new elections are held. All governmental policies, then, must enjoy the approval of the majority in the Knesset.

The Israeli election system has made the reality more complicated. Members of the Knesset do not represent districts or constituencies. In elections, voters select a party. Every party that garners at least one percent of the vote receives a seat in the Knesset. The one hundred twenty seats of the Knesset are divided among the parties contesting the election according to the percentage of the votes they have received. Individual members are certified by parties from a list developed through party meetings.

Since the founding of the State, no party has ever won a majority. This requires the formation of a coalition government, i.e., representatives from more than one party will be members of the cabinet. The prime minister is elected separately. Parties forming the coalition make an agreement that will insure that the program of those parties will be supported by the government. If a coalition party is dissatisfied with the performance of the government, it can withdraw from the coalition. If it takes away enough votes from the government, it can bring the government down.

This system gives more power to small parties than their numbers demand. In recent elections, two parties, Labor and Likud, split most of the votes. The Labor Party is more liberal in orientation while the Likud is more conservative. Each of these parties usually commands about forty to forty-five seats in the Knesset, but sixty-one are necessary to form a government. The party receiving the most votes must look for help in forming a coalition from smaller parties that usually control between one and five votes each. Several of these smaller parties are religious and they require the government to support their religious institutions and policies. This causes tensions within Israel because most of the population is secular.

Attempts at reforming the electoral system have not succeeded. The smaller parties that know their power in the government will end or at least be curtailed severely if the members of the Knesset are elected by districts. The only change in election laws that passed allows the electorate to choose the prime minister directly. Thus, voters make two choices: one for the prime minister and another for the party they wish to control the government.

The Head of State is the president [H: *Nasi*]. This post is ceremonial. The president is not a member of the government. The prime minister offers a name to the Knesset which elects the president, who can have two five-year terms.

The judicial system originally followed the British system, but is now based on the Israeli experience and legislation. The most striking difference in the criminal system from that of the United States is that there is no right of *habeas corpus*. In the U.S. almost every defendant has the right to bail because of this law, but here the court has more discretion in releasing defendants before trial. Judges can "remand" the accused for specified periods before trial. There are magistrate and district courts with a Supreme Court as the final court of appeal. In matters of personal status, such as marriage and divorce, courts of recognized religious communities enjoy jurisdiction. The judicial system is independent of the Knesset and the government. Special committees nominate judges and the president makes appointments from the list of recommended candidates. Judges have no term of office, but must retire at age seventy.

Israel's Political Parties

Labor. This party is a coalition of several parties that have had a more socialist orientation. The base of support comes from the secular kibbutzim and the Histradrut [the Israeli labor union]. Its policy regarding peace has been a willingness to trade some occupied territory for secure borders, peace treaties, and normal relations with Israel's Arab neighbors. After elections in 1996, the Labor Party no longer controlled the government but is the chief opposition party.

Likud. This is a conservative, nationalist party, supporting a market-oriented economy and the continuation of settlements in the occupied West Bank, which it calls "Judea and Samaria." It opposes the return of the Golan to Syria and does not support the agreement with the PLO in Gaza and Samaria. Still, it is willing to come to agreement with Arab governments. A Likud prime minister, Menachem Begin, negotiated the treaty with Egypt and the Likud has supported the treaty with Jordan. Besides its conservative, nationalist constituency, it has wide support from the Sephardic community. In the 1996 elections, this party won the most seats in the Knesset and is the major party in the current governing coalition.

The National Religious Party. This party's influence is diminishing. In recent years it has had fewer than five members in the Knesset. It has been part of coalitions formed by both Labor and Likud. Its orientation is religious Zionism. Most of its support comes from the Orthodox Ashkenazi community. Other religious parties have been more successful in attracting the religious vote.

Shas (an acronym for the Sephardic Torah Guardians). This is an ultraorthodox religious and nationalist party of the Sephardic community. It has been a part of governing coalitions to win economic support for its religious institutions and to maintain the *status quo* in terms of religious and secular relationships. Some of its leaders have been implicated in financial irregularities.

Agudat Israel (H: "the association of Israel"). Originally this ultraorthodox religious party opposed Zionism. It has now entered the political system to make its influence felt especially in terms of issues that affect its constituency: the ultraorthodox religious community.

Arab Democratic Party. This party's orientation is communist and it represents Arabs who are Israeli citizens. All Arabs within the pre-1967 borders of Israel are Israeli citizens and entitled to vote in national and municipal elections. Many do not participate, but those who do have elected several representatives to the Knesset. The Arabs of the Old City and East Jerusalem are considered citizens since Israel has annexed these areas; most do not vote in Israeli elections. The Palestinian Authority wants East Jerusalem for the capital of the state it wishes to establish. Most Israelis do not want to divide Jerusalem again and oppose this.

Meretz. This is a secular, left-wing party whose members include Jews and Arabs. It calls for the exchange of land for peace, civil rights for Arab citizens, and the rights of secular Jews to be free of restrictions brought on by the religious.

Naturei Karta (Aramaic: "The Guardians of the Wall"). This is an "anti-party" of ultraorthodox religious Jews who reject the State of Israel, believing that only the Messiah can reestablish Jewish rule. They do not participate in the political process in Israel, but have had extensive contacts with the PLO whom they recognize as the region's rightful rulers until replaced by the Messiah. One member of this group sits in Arafat's cabinet of advisers for the Palestinian Authority.

There are several more small parties whose existence and influence are perpetuated by the Israeli electoral system. Some parties do not last long or are absorbed by larger ones. Because of the variety of parties, vigorous debate about all issues characterizes Israel's political system. It is a very democratic system whose principal flaw is the extraordinary power of small parties. The majority sees this as an imposition of the will of the minority. The minority sees this as a way to protect its rights.

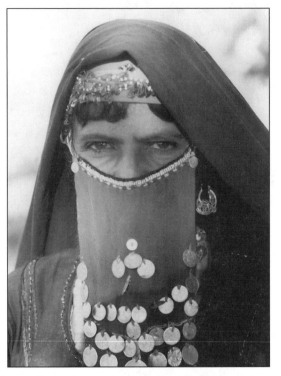

CHAPTER THREE

Israel: The Religious Scene

THE JEWS

*"For you are a people sacred to the LORD, your God; God has chosen
you from all the nations on the face of the earth to be a people peculiarly
God's own"* (Deut 7:6).

Who Is a Jew? Most of Israel's population, excluding the Occupied Territories,
is Jewish. Immigrants make up about one half the population. Jews born in
Israel are called *sabras*. The name comes from the Arabic word for the fruit of
the cactus plant. You will see Bedouin women selling this fruit in early September. They will peel the tough, prickly skin so you can taste the soft and
sweet fruit. Native-born Israelis like to think of themselves as having a tough
exterior but with a kind heart. The name *sabra* seemed to fit this self-image.

The ingathering of Jews from around the world is the reason for the existence of the State of Israel. This is embodied in the Law of Return. This law
establishes the right of all Jews—no matter where they come from—to live in
Israel as citizens. It is ironic that both the ultraorthodox Jews and the Arabs oppose this law. The latter see the Law of Return as discriminatory. The ultraorthodox oppose the law's failure to define a Jew according to rabbinic tradition.

According to rabbinic law, a Jew is a person born of a Jewish mother or
converted to Judaism (by an orthodox rabbi). In practice, people who do not
fit this definition are accepted as citizens of the Jewish state, e.g., a person
whose father but not mother is Jewish or the spouse of any immigrant Jew. But
since the religious establishment in Israel does not recognize Reform or Conservative rabbis, their converts are not accepted as Jews unless they submit to
a "reconversion" by an orthodox rabbi. This, of course, causes problems for
American Jews many of whom belong to the Reform or Conservative movements.

Jewishness, as understood by the Law of Return, is not dependent on
religious or philosophical convictions. A Jew then may be an ultraorthodox
Talmudic scholar or a secularist. The latter's motivation for living in Israel may
vary from devotion to the land to a concern to establish an equitable social

order. In fact, about eighty percent of the Jewish population of Israel is secular. Because of the Israeli political system, the religious establishment has an inordinate amount of power over the life-style of secular people. For example, there is no such thing as a civil marriage in Israel. Jews must be married by a rabbi. Rabbinic law also governs divorce; consequently, a man can divorce his wife but a woman cannot divorce her husband. This prevents a woman whose husband has not granted her a divorce from remarrying.

Sometimes the strategies to which the secularist will go to be free of religious control are ingenious. The religious parties in the Knesset managed to pass a law that forbade the raising of pigs on "the land of Israel." Several secular kibbutzim produce pork for consumption by Christians and nonobservant Jews and for export. After the Knesset enacted this law, the pork producers built small platforms for their pigs so that they would no longer be standing "on" the land of Israel—they were slightly "above" it. Still, many secular Jews in Israel live according to the rhythms of Judaism. For example, while they may not spend Shabbat in a synagogue, they carefully guard their day of rest. Though they may not fast on Yom Kippur, they observe it as a solemn, reflective day. They will have their infant boys circumcised. The day of the latters' *bar mitzvah* is a day of joy and pride for the family. Every Jew in Israel wants to be home for the Passover *Seder*.

What Is Judaism? Though defining who is a Jew is difficult, defining the Jewish faith is another matter. Judaism, as a religious faith, is based on the Torah and the Talmud. The latter is a great collection of religious and ethical teachings, legal decisions, and folklore. It dates from A.D. 600 and fills about thirty substantial volumes. In addition, Jewish faith and the life, which is its expression, are nourished by other ancient rabbinic writings such as the Midrash, an early form of biblical interpretation containing both edifying stories and norms for behavior. The Torah, Talmud, and Midrash can be objects of lifelong study. Indeed some religious Jews do exactly that—they spend their lives in the study of Judaism's religious literature. The word Talmud means "learning."

But this is a deceptively simple explanation of Judaism as a religion. This becomes clear when one learns that Israel has two Chief Rabbis and that many religious Jews pay attention to neither. How can one people have two supreme religious authorities? One chief rabbi comes from the **Ashkenazi** community. This is made up of Jews whose ancestors came from Central and Eastern Europe. "Ashkenaz" appears in the Table of Nations in Gen 10:3. Jewish tradition identifies Ashkenaz as Germany. The other chief rabbi comes from the **Sephardic** community. These are Jews whose ancestors came from Spain, Portugal, or North Africa. Ferdinand and Isabella expelled the Jews from Spain in 1492. Many settled in North Africa, Italy, the Balkans, and Turkey. The word "Sepharad" that appears in Obadiah 20 was understood by early rabbis to refer to Spain.

These two communities have different liturgical traditions and legal traditions though both are based on Torah and Talmud. The differences between the two communities go beyond religious issues. Political leadership of the State has come primarily from the Ashkenazi community. For example, there has never been a prime minister from the Sephardic community though the Sephardim are a majority in Israel. A Sephardi, Yitzhak Navon, has served as president. But this is primarily a ceremonial position without much political power. Business and industry, too, are largely in Ashkenazi hands. The Ashkenazim came with greater educational background than the Sephardim, who came primarily from Arab countries where they did not have access to the opportunities afforded to some Jews in Europe.

Oriental Jews. Besides the two largest groups of Jews, the Ashkenazi and the Sephardi, there are other important groups, each with traditions that made them different from other Jews. There are the **Yemenites** who came to Israel from the Arabian Peninsula. **Iraqi Jews**, the remnants of the Babylonian Jewish community began settling in Israel in the nineteenth century and came in great numbers just after the founding of the State. Finally, the **Bukharian Jews** trace their origins to Uzbekistan. There is a sizeable Bukharian community in Jerusalem.

Distinguishing between the Ashkenazi, Sephardic, and Oriental communities still does not explain the diversity of Judaism as a religion. When you visit the Western Wall, you will note that most of the men who pray there have beards and side curls. They wear black overcoats and broad-brimmed hats. On Shabbat, many wear fur-trimmed hats. The black overcoats and fur hats seem out of place in Israel. That is because they originated in Eastern Europe. This was the attire of the merchant and landlord class there. On Shabbat and holidays, some Jews took to wearing the clothes of the upper class to mark these special days. Gradually wearing this attire became "traditional." When these Jews came from Central and Eastern Europe, they brought their black overcoats and fur hats with them. They wear them on even those hottest days of summer.

The men wearing the black coats are the **ultraorthodox**. Other names for the ultraorthodox are the *hasidim* (H: the pious) and the *haredim* (H: those who tremble, see Isa 66:2, 5). The ultraorthodox movement began as an attempt to bring more joy and exuberance to not only the liturgy but to Jewish life. It is a form of Jewish enthusiasm. The movement's inspiration was a rabbi known as *Baal Shem Tov* [the Master of the Good Name]. The movement quickly spread throughout Eastern Europe.

Though all the men wearing the black coats look alike to the uninitiated, there are subtle differences in their attire. Each of the *haredi* groups follows a particular rabbi—a revered, authoritative, and charismatic religious leader. One example of such a person is the late Rabbi Menachem Schneerson who was the leader of the Lubavitcher Hasidim. Lubavitch is the name of the town in Russia where this movement began in the nineteenth century. His followers were so devoted to him that some hoped he would announce that he was the Messiah. He lived in the Crown Heights neighborhood of Brooklyn and though he never visited Israel, he had many Israeli disciples who followed his advice implicitly. For example, the Lubavitchers of Israel voted as Rabbi Schneerson instructed them and this irritated secular Jews because a non-citizen was influencing the outcome of Israeli elections.

Nonorthodox Jews. Contemporary Judaism is a diverse religious phenomenon. Nowhere is this more obvious than in Israel itself. Still, there are limits to this diversity—at least from the perspective of the religious establishment, which is firmly in **Orthodox** hands. For example, **Conservative** and **Reform** rabbis are not considered legitimate and do not sit on state supported religious councils. Their synagogues and other institutions do not share in the financial aid given to religious institutions of the Orthodox. The marriages they witness and the conversions they oversee are not considered valid. This situation is changing slowly and with great effort. One obvious problem for the Orthodox religious establishment is the role and status of women in the Conservative and Reform traditions. When you visit the Western Wall, you will notice that men and women worship separately. The women cannot worship in a group, but only individually and in silence so that the sound of their voices does not distract the men at prayer. Even some Orthodox women are challenging this. Occasionally, the "Women of the Wall" will pray together at the Western Wall. The rabbi of the Wall, who is appointed by the Orthodox religious establishment, usually sees that such demonstrations are stopped.

The Karaites. What binds these diverse groups of religious Jews is their common acceptance of the Torah and Talmud. There is one small Jewish community that does not accept the Talmud. These are the Karaites. This community was founded in Persia by Anan Ben-David in the eighth century A.D., who advised his followers, "Search well in the Torah, and do not rely on my opinion." The Karaites hold that the laws of the Torah should be interpreted literally and not according to rabbinic usage. For example, they will not leave lights burning on Shabbat as other religious Jews do. For a long time, most Karaites lived in Egypt, but many moved to Israel after the founding of the State. Most live in the area around Ramla. They number about twelve thousand. You can visit the **Karaite Museum and Synagogue** in the Jewish Quarter of Jerusalem's Old City at 3 HaKaraim St. near Hurva Square. Call 6280657 for an appointment to visit. Sometimes it will be open and you can walk in. There is no fee, but there is a box near the synagogue's entrance for offerings.

Jewish Festivals

Sabbath (H: *Shabbat*). The rhythms of your time in Israel will reflect Jewish religious observance. This will take some adjustment for most people coming from countries that follow the Christian calendar. Perhaps the most obvious difference will be the observance of *Shabbat*. The importance that religious Jews place on the Sabbath observance is, in part, a recognition that it is the only religious observance that is mentioned in the Ten Commandments (Exod 20:8-11; Deut 5:12-15). One ancient rabbi believed that observance of the Sabbath was so fundamental to Israel's relationship with God that if all Israel observed just one Sabbath faithfully, the Messiah would come.

Though only about twenty percent of Israelis are religiously observant, the Sabbath brings a real change in the way Israeli society as a whole operates. The pace moves quickly from Sunday through Thursday. It even picks up Friday morning as people make final preparations for the Sabbath. They bid farewell to each other with the words *Shabbat shalom,* "a peaceful Sabbath." About noon or so in the winter—a little later in the summer—things start slowing down. Shops close down, the buses stop running, and streets begin to clear. There may be a few flower sellers left on corners in the city center since it is customary to bring flowers home for the Sabbath. Still, as dusk approaches, the business district becomes deserted. If you are near the Jaffa Gate late on Friday afternoon, you will witness a procession of taxis ferrying people to the Western Wall. You will also see some hasidic families dressed in their Sabbath finery making the trip on foot.

The Fall Holidays (See Leviticus 23). This cycle of feasts begins on the first day of Tishri (Sept.–Oct.). Since the Jewish calendar follows a lunar cycle, the festivals do not fall on the same date in the Gregorian calendar each year.

Rosh HaShanah (New Year's Day). This is a two-day festival that not only inaugurates a New Jewish year, but also begins the Days of Awe or the Days of Repentance, the ten days between Rosh HaShanah and Yom Kippur. Tradition holds that on New Year's Day God writes the destinies of all human beings into the Book of Life or the Book of Death. The Days of Repentance give an opportunity to mend one's ways. The New Year begins with service in the synagogue. It is followed by a family feast. The traditional foods include apple slices dipped in honey as a way of wishing a sweet year ahead. The greeting people give each other in the weeks ahead of New Year's day is *shanah tovah* (lit., "Good Year"). The *shofar* (ram's horn trumpet) is sounded at the morning service. On the first day, there is the ceremony of *tashlich* (lit., "sending") in which men cast their sins away by throwing bread crumbs on a moving body of water. The ultraorthodox of Jerusalem do this at the Pool of Siloam. Other religious people will go to the Mediterranean.

Yom Kippur (The Day of Atonement). This is the most solemn day in Jewish religion. It begins forty minutes before sundown on the eve and continues until three stars have appeared on the following night. For these twenty-five hours, religious Jews observe a total fast of food and drink. They spend most of the day in the synagogue. It is a day of quiet reflection when people ask God's forgiveness after having asked forgiveness of their neighbor. Secular Jews do not disturb the holiness of this day. There is no radio or television. All commercial activities cease. The only vehicles that move are for medical or military emergencies. Among the traditions of this day is that wearing leather shoes is forbidden. You will see the *haredim* walking about with athletic shoes. The day ends with a light meal after sundown. After they break their fast, many religious Jerusalemites will go to the Western Wall for singing and dancing.

Sukkot (Booths or Tabernacles). This is one of the three pilgrimage feasts, the others being *Pesach* (Passover) and *Shavuot* (Weeks or Pentecost). See Deut 16:1-17 and John 7. It begins four days after *Yom Kippur* and lasts eight days.

Like other ancient Israelite religious observances, *Sukkot* was a feast borrowed from the Canaanites. It celebrated the fall harvest. The *sukkot* represent the temporary dwellings that farmers used during the fall harvest. The ancient Israelites reinterpreted the feast to remember the guidance in the wilderness when the Israelites lived in tents. It is the only one of the three pilgrimage festivals that Christianity did not reinterpret. Religious and some secular families (and some restaurants) will build *sukkot* outside. These are decorated with palm branches, fruit, streamers, and children's drawings. People will take their meals in the *sukkot*. Some religious people will sleep in them.

Among the special customs of this festival is that of the four species. Before the feast, stands are set up all over the city to sell palm, myrtle, and willow branches and the *ethrog* (or citron—a citrus fruit that looks like an overgrown lime). These are held during part of the synagogue service while a special blessing is said over them. The first and last days of *Sukkot* are observed like *Shabbat*. During the intervening days, many businesses have reduced hours or close entirely. Many secular Jews take a vacation during this time. The President of the State and the Mayor of Jerusalem host receptions for any who wish to attend. On the third day of the feast, the *kohanim* (priests) gather at the Western Wall at 9:00 a.m. for the priestly blessing. On the fifth day, there is the walk around Jerusalem beginning at 6:00 a.m. Walkers choose a 12, 22, or 25 kilometer route. It ends with a parade down Jaffa Road in the early afternoon.

Evangelical Christians from throughout the world come to Jerusalem for *Sukkot*, which they call "The Feast of Tabernacles." This annual pilgrimage of Evangelicals is organized by the *International Christian Embassy* in Jerusalem and it has attracted more than five thousand participants. It is a combination religious and political rally that the Israeli government welcomes, but most Israeli Jews ignore or disdain.

Simhat Torah (The Joy of the Torah), the last day of *Sukkot*. In the synagogues, the last chapters of Deuteronomy are read, closing out the cycle of readings for the year, and then immediately the first portion of Genesis is read to begin the new cycle. To mark the completion of the annual cycle of Torah reading, the scrolls are carried about the synagogue with dancing and rejoicing that sometimes spills onto the streets. Men from synagogues all over Jerusalem converge at the Western Wall to continue the dancing. Secular Jews have their own celebration at Jerusalem's Liberty Bell Park after sundown. It is a combination rock concert and folk-dancing festival that attract thousands of young people.

THE SAMARITANS

The Samaritan woman said to (Jesus), "How can you, a Jew, ask me, a Samaritan woman, for a drink?" (John 4:9).

There are only about five hundred individuals left of the ancient Samaritan people. They live in Nablus (Shechem) and Holon, a suburb of Tel Aviv. These are the people who consider themselves descendants of those who lived in the former Northern Kingdom and therefore legitimate heirs of the ancient Israelite religion. A unique feature of contemporary Samaritan religious practice is the Passover sacrifice that they offer on Mount Gerizim near Shechem.

The origin of the Samaritans is still a matter of discussion among historians. Most probably the Samaritans as a religious group with their own distinct ideology developed about the fourth-third century B.C. The Jews who returned from the Babylonian Exile regarded themselves as a religious elite—the purified remnant. They did not want or accept help in rebuilding the Jerusalem Temple from people living in the territory of the former Northern Kingdom although these people offered their help (Ezra 4:1-5). Nehemiah says that the Samaritans opposed his rebuilding of Jerusalem's walls (Neh 3:33–4:5). It is probable that the Persian subprovince of *Yehud* (Judah) was politically and economically dependent on Samaria and the Jews wanted to assert their religious autonomy at the very least. In any case, the Jews rebuilt the Temple of Jerusalem in 515 B.C. and in 400 B.C. the worshipers of Yahweh in Samaria built a temple for their use on Mount Gerizim.

The Jews believed that Jerusalem was the only place where sacrificial worship was legitimate. They tried to undercut Samaritan claims by asserting that the Samaritans were not true Israelites but the products of intermarriage with exiles from Mesopotamia introduced into the region by the Assyrians (see 2 Kgs 17:24-33; Ezra 4:2). The Jews characterized the worship of the Samaritans as crudely syncretistic and idolatrous (2 Kgs 17:34-41). The act that cemented feelings of animosity between the Jews and Samaritans was the destruction of the Gerizim temple by the Hasmonean, John Hyrcanus in 107 B.C.

The New Testament reflects separation of the two religious communities that were the descendants of the ancient Israelites. In John 8:48, Jesus' enemies try to damage his reputation by calling him a demon-possessed Samaritan. In Matthew, Jesus seems to share the Jewish prejudice against the Samaritans since he instructs the Twelve whom he is sending on mission to avoid Samaritan towns and take their message to "the lost sheep of the house of Israel" (10:5-6). Similarly in Luke, Jesus characterizes as a "foreigner" the Samaritan leper whom he healed (17:18). Also in Luke, some Samaritans refused to welcome Jesus to their towns (9:51-56). Still, Luke maintains that the risen Jesus ordered the gospel to be taken to Samaria (Acts 1:8) and he reports the success of Philip's preaching in Samaria—success that prompted a visit by Peter and John (Acts 8:4-17). Luke's parable of the good Samaritan (10:25-37) turns on the irony of the Samaritan acting as a neighbor to a Jew in distress. Jesus speaks to the Samaritan woman at the well of Shechem that one day true worship will transcend the differences between Jew and Samaritan (John 4:20). The Samaritans then welcome Jesus and beg him to extend his visit with them (John 4:39-40).

The Samaritans consider only the Torah of Moses as authoritative. It is not surprising that they reject the Prophets and the Writings because several books in the latter two collections have a clear bias in favor of Judah. They also do not look forward to a Davidic Messiah; rather, they are waiting for a *Taheb* ("restorer") who is "the prophet like Moses" (Deut 18:15). Samaritan religious literature lays particular blame on Ezra as one who perverted the revelation of Moses. The Samaritans consider Ezra responsible for the split with the Jews.

THE CHRISTIANS

"Do not think that I have come to abolish the law or the prophets.
I have come not to abolish but to fulfill" (Matt 5:17).

Jewish Christianity

Excavations at several sites in Israel, e.g., Capernaum and Nazareth, have raised the issue of Jewish Christianity. That there was a type of Christianity within a Jewish context in Palestine whose adherents remained strongly influenced by Jewish beliefs and practices is clear enough from the literary evidence. The NT assumes the existence of Christian communities of Jews who accepted the message of Jesus. The Acts of the Apostles often refers to the Church in Jerusalem. The same work describes the missions of Peter, John, and the deacon Philip in Samaritan villages (Acts 8:5-25). Summarizing the growth of the Church in Palestine, Luke wrote: "The church throughout all Judea, Galilee and Samaria was at peace. It was being built up and walked in the fear of the Lord, and with the consolation of the holy Spirit it grew in numbers" (Acts 9:31).

Paul mentions the "churches of Judea that are in Christ" (Gal 1:22). The Letter of James also supports the existence of Jewish Christianity. Deploring a type of caste system that was invading the Church, James wrote: "If people with gold rings and in fine clothing come into your *synagogue,* you are not to show them any deferential treatment" (Jas 2:2 [*NJB*]). In the same letter, the author uses the usual Greek word for the Christian community, *ekklesia* (5:14). That some Christians used the word *synagogue* for their assemblies is significant. These literary sources that speak about Jewish Christianity have been supplemented by material remains from Palestine. Archaeologists have been attempting to interpret the graffiti, amulets, lamps, pottery, tomb decorations, and inscriptions that seem to point to the existence of Christian Jews in Roman-Period Palestine. At present, archaeological remains are few and their significance is unclear. No consensus has emerged. The problem is that the Jewish Christians during the first two hundred years of the Church's existence used no distinctively Christian symbols, built no churches, and left no other material remains that distinguished them from other Jews in Roman Palestine. The development of a distinctive Christian symbol system in Palestine began in the Byzantine Period.

From a rabbinic perspective, one could consider Jewish Christians as Jews who had gone astray as long as they fulfilled the basic requirements of Jewish identity such as circumcision. The early rabbis may have regarded Jewish Christians as outside the Jewish community without, however, denying the Jewishness of those who became Christians. This situation changed during the Second Revolt. Rabbi Akiba acclaimed the leader of that revolt as the Messiah.

Jewish Christians who, of course, confessed Jesus as the Messiah refused to fight on the side of another "messiah." Bar Kochba executed many Jewish Christians as traitors to his revolution. This decimated the ranks of the Jewish Christian community. In turn, the rabbis came to regard Jewish Christians as members of a different and hostile religious community rather than just Jews who had been led astray by the messianic claims made for Jesus of Nazareth.

The excavations of the Franciscan archaeologist, Bellarmino Bagatti, called into question the so-called "Pella hypothesis" according to which the first Christian community left Jerusalem and Palestine during the First Revolt (66–70). Pella was a Hellenistic city on the plateau across the Jordan about twenty-eight miles south of the Sea of Galilee. Supposedly the Christian community went there to flee the violence of the Jewish revolt against Rome. More than this, Bagatti believed that as a social-religious phenomenon, Jewish Christianity survived the problems of the Bar Kochba revolt. He offered archaeological proof to support this conclusion. Bagatti pointed, for example, to what he regarded as a Jewish Christian synagogue in Nazareth. Some view the evidence he offered as ambiguous to the extent that Bagatti's argument becomes circular. One needs to accept the hypothesis of Jewish Christianity to interpret the very evidence that Bagatti cited to prove his hypothesis. According to Bagatti's hypothesis, the Jewish Christian community of Palestine was absorbed by the Gentile church that had the support of the imperial government after the fourth century. Others suggest that Jewish Christianity's end was inevitable because it limited its mission to Jews. It was this self-imposed limitation rather than Byzantine pressure that relegated Jewish-Christianity to the fringe.

While the literary evidence from both Christian and Jewish sources provides evidence for the existence of a community of Christians in Palestine who were still strongly influenced by Judaism and who were still recognized as Jews by some rabbis, the archaeological evidence that can be used to fill out the picture of that community needs more careful study and interpretation. The pre-Constantinian chapter of church history in Palestine is an obscure one. Perhaps new excavations and interpretive approaches will provide more insight into Jewish and Christian relationships and the development of both Jewish and Christian identity in Palestine. Many Arab Christians in Palestine today consider themselves descendants of the first Christian communities.

The Crusades

It is particularly important for Christians visiting the Holy Land to be familiar with the Crusades. Many structures that visitors to Israel see are Crusader in origin. What is more important, however, is that the memory of the Crusades has greatly affected interfaith relations in Israel. The Crusades were several European Christian military expeditions into Palestine beginning with the sack of Jerusalem in 1099 and ending with the fall of Acco in 1291. The original goal of these expeditions was to take control of the Christian holy places from the Muslims to make these safe for Christian pilgrims. What the Crusaders did was to set up European-style kingdoms in the region.

The lasting effects of the Crusades in Israel can be seen in architecture and attitudes. Among the more important examples of Crusader period architecture in Israel are the Church of the Holy Sepulchre and the Church of St. Ann in Jerusalem, and castles at Caesarea, Acco, and Belvoir. There were some three hundred ecclesiastical buildings credited to the Crusaders who built in the Romanesque style. The hardened and negative Muslim attitude toward Christianity is the result of memories of the Crusader massacre of Jerusalem's inhabitants in 1099. Before the Crusades, the Muslims generally tolerated Christians though the Muslims sometimes required Christians to pay a special tax.

Origins. The last of the early Muslim period dynasties to rule Palestine was the Fatimid (969–1171). They were Shiʾites who ruled from Cairo. At first they were tolerant of Christians and Jews. The exception was Hakim the Mad (996–1021) who destroyed many churches and the tomb of Christ in 1009. This, of course, led to severe tensions with Christians in Europe. After Hakim's death, his successors resumed the more characteristic Muslim tolerance toward the Church. But in 1078, the Seljuk Turks wrested control from the Fatimids. They severely restricted the accessibility to the Christian holy places. In reaction, Pope Urban II called for a crusade in 1095. Though the Fatimids expelled the Turks in 1098 and signaled their desire to resume friendly relationships with Christians, the First Crusade was on its way and its momentum was unstoppable.

The First Crusade (1099). Godfrey of Bouillon led the First Crusade. He captured Jerusalem on July 15, 1099. His soldiers killed most of the city's Muslim and Jewish inhabitants. They expelled the few survivors. The taking of Jerusalem led to the establishment of the Latin Kingdom under Baldwin I (1100–1118). The territory of the kingdom included not only Jerusalem but the coast up to and including Lebanon, the Transjordan up to Aqaba, and most of the Cisjordan. The Crusaders turned the Muslim shrines on the Haram in Jerusalem into Christian churches. The Crusaders set up three other states north of the Kingdom of Jerusalem along the Mediterranean coast. They were (from south to north) the county of Tripoli, the principality of Antioch, and the county of Edessa. The Crusaders were good administrators and energetic builders.

The Second Crusade (1147). The Crusaders enjoyed initial success because their Muslim opponents did not present a united front. When the Emir of Aleppo overcame the division among the Muslims, Crusader realms came under serious attack. The first to fall was the county of Edessa in 1144. This prompted the second Crusade. At first the Crusaders were successful. The situation changed with the rise of Saladin, who ended Fatimid rule in Egypt and established the Ayyubid dynasty there in 1171. He turned his attention to Palestine and crushed the Crusader army at Galilee's Horns of Hattin on July 3, 1187. The defeat at Hattin meant the loss of virtually the whole Latin Kingdom. Saladin took Jerusalem three months later. Saladin did not massacre the

Christians of Jerusalem. He either sold them into slavery or held them for ransom. He converted several Christian churches to Muslim institutions. For example, the Church of St. Ann became a Muslim religious school. He also reconverted the Crusader churches on the Haram to mosques.

The Third Crusade (1189). Saladin's victory and the fall of Jerusalem prompted the Third Crusade. This was the one led by Frederick Barbarossa and Richard the Lionheart. Frederick's Teutonic Knights were the power behind the Third Crusade. They used not only brute force but also diplomacy to establish another Latin Kingdom that included much of the coast and Galilee, though they failed to take Jerusalem.

Other Crusades. Later Crusades had little effect on Palestine since the Crusaders realized that Egypt was the key to holding Palestine so they redirected their energies there. The **Fourth Crusade** (1203–1204) never made it to the Middle East, but ended with the sack of Constantinople in 1204. This finished Byzantium as a great state. The **Fifth Crusade** (1217–1221) was fought primarily in Egypt. It was during this Crusade that St. Francis went to speak to the Sultan (probably Kamil I) at Damietta. The **Sixth Crusade** (1228–1229) involved little fighting but led to negotiations that gave the Crusaders Jerusalem, Bethlehem, and Nazareth for ten years. They held on to Jerusalem for another five years before losing it in 1244 to Turks. Louis IX of France led the **Seventh Crusade** (1248–1254). He built the castle at Caesarea though most of his activity was in Egypt. Although successful at first, Louis and his entire army surrendered to the Egyptians, who held the king for a great ransom. Two more crusades were launched, but the fall of the Crusader forces at Acco in 1291 marked the end of European rule in Palestine until the twentieth century. Almost two hundred years after the last military adventures of the Europeans in Palestine, the Ottoman Turks were still wary about the intentions of the Europeans. Suleiman built the present walls of Jerusalem in the sixteenth century to protect the city from a supposed Crusader attack. By this time, of course, western Christians were fighting among themselves and the setting for their religious wars was Europe itself.

The Effects. Though there may have been some reason to be concerned about the protection of Christians visiting the holy places, the almost six hundred years of Muslim tolerance should have given the Europeans cause to negotiate rather than resort to war. War and its spoils were too much for the Crusaders to resist. Unfortunately, the hatred and distrust engendered by these wars still affect Christian-Muslim relations. The Crusades are a grim and shameful period of Christian history. The Jewish population also suffered because of the devastation caused by these wars. Some fled to Egypt; others moved to towns like Ashkelon that withstood Crusader attacks. Jews in rural Galilee suffered minimally. The Crusaders denied Jews access to Jerusalem, but Saladin invited Jews to return to Jerusalem and Palestine. The fall of Jerusalem to the Turks in 1244 ended Jewish life in the city. When Nachmanides came to the city from Spain in 1267, he found only a few Jewish families living there.

The Local Church Today

The local Christian community of the Holy Land is Arab. These Arab Christians regard themselves as the descendants of the original Christian community. That is why some will become upset when visitors, assuming Arab Christians must be converts, ask "When do you become a Christian?" Conversions from Islam are rare. Islam is so fundamental to Arab culture that conversion—even by a nonobservant Muslim—is exceptional. In some ways, Arab Christians feel alienated from their own culture. This has led to great pressure being placed on the Christian Arabs to give public expression for the struggle for a Palestinian State. The conflict with the Israelis has had some theological and pastoral consequences since it has led to the tendency to distance Christianity from any links with Judaism.

These pressures have been, in part, a stimulus for Arab Christians to emigrate to the West. If left unchecked, this trend will result in the end of the local Christian community. Already in 1964, Pope Paul VI was alarmed by this possibility. At his initiative, Bethlehem University was founded to train Palestinians for professions that would tie them to their homeland. While the Christian population of Israel has grown, it has not kept up with the birthrate of Arab Christians. Emigration then is continuing. Another attempt at building up the Church here is the appointment of a Palestinian as the Latin Patriarch. Msgr. Michel Sabbah is the first Arab to hold this pastoral responsibility.

There are about 110,000 Christian Arabs in the Holy Land. The largest Christian Church is the Greek Orthodox. The church is the heir of Byzantine Christianity that has been an important Christian presence in Palestine since the 300s. Also, the Armenian Orthodox, who claim to be the descendants of the first nation to embrace Christianity, are an ancient and significant Christian community in Palestine.

The Christians of Palestine are divided into thirty denominations that fall into four main groups. Orthodox Churches comprise the largest group. These include the Greek, Rumanian, and Russian. The next highest in number are the Catholic Churches. Beside the Latin Catholics, there are also Maronite, Greek, Syrian, Armenian, and Chaldean Catholics. The Monophysite Churches form a third group. These are ecclesial communities that do not accept the Council of Chalcedon, which taught that Christ had two natures: human and divine. The Monophysites held that Jesus' human nature was absorbed by the divine. For the most part, the controversy is historical. Roman Catholic and the non-Chalcedonian theologians have come to an understanding about the person and nature of Christ. The question of the Petrine Office is more sticky. Included in these groups are the Armenian, Coptic, Syrian, and Ethiopian. The smallest group of Christians belongs to the Protestant tradition. Among these are the Anglican, Presbyterian, Lutheran, Baptist, and several others.

The Franciscan Custody of the Holy Land

Almost all holy places controlled by Catholics are administered by the Franciscan *Custody of the Holy Land*. The origin of the Franciscan presence here goes back to Francis himself. The poor man of Assisi thought that he could end the brutality and organized murder that were the Crusades by proclaiming the gospel to the sultan. With the holy naiveté that inspired many of his actions, Francis went to Egypt to visit al-Kamil, the Ayyubid sultan in 1219. What happened during their conversations is unknown, but the sultan was sufficiently impressed with Francis' sincerity and holiness that he allowed Francis safe passage to return to Assisi. The sultan, however, was not sufficiently impressed to accept the gospel.

Whether Francis used this opportunity to visit the Holy Land itself is not certain. But he did show a special interest in the Arabs. The last chapter of the Rule of St. Francis concerns "those who go among the Saracens and other infidels." A Franciscan province of the Holy Land was established in 1263 to facilitate evangelization in the Middle East. Because of this Franciscan interest and presence in the region, Pope Clement VI entrusted the guardianship of the holy places to the Franciscans on November 21, 1342. The Custody received the financial support for the work of the friars from the House of Savoy and other Catholic ruling houses of Europe. This enabled them to purchase many holy places, insuring that pilgrims would have access to them.

The Franciscans administer fifty-eight shrines in Israel, Syria, and Jordan. They share the administration of sixteen more with representatives of other Christian churches. The Custody's work goes beyond administering shrines. It has established sixteen schools, two orphanages, several housing projects, credit unions, and other educational and charitable works not only in Israel but also in Jordan, Syria, Lebanon, Egypt, and Cyprus. It also helps support the *Jerusalem Theological Studium,* a seminary for Franciscans preparing for the ordained ministry, the *Studium Biblicum Franciscanum,* a graduate school of biblical studies in Jerusalem, and the Franciscan Center for the Study of Eastern Christianity in Cairo. The SBF publishes scholarly journals and monographs and sponsors excavations in the region. The Custody derives support for this work, in part, from the Good Friday collection. The current Latin Patriarch of Jerusalem, Michel Sabbah, has suggested that the local church be entrusted with more responsibility regarding the shrines. This has caused some tension with the Franciscan Custody, which does not want to see its six-hundred-and-fifty-year-old guardianship of the Holy Places curtailed.

The Status Quo

Of course, the Franciscans were not the only Christians who believed it was their responsibility to look after the holy places. There were the Greeks, Syrians, Copts, Ethiopians, and Armenians. Protestants came in some numbers only in the 1700s, but they did not seek to control any shrines. To say that relationships between these Christian Churches were not cordial is an understatement. The rivalry was passionate and extreme especially at the Church of the Holy Sepulchre and the Church of the Nativity. Conflicts over "rights" led to assaults and even murders. Being a sacristan at the Holy Sepulchre was a dangerous occupation.

The situation got so bad that in 1757 the Ottoman government decided to control these conflicts by issuing a ruling called *The Status Quo in the Holy Places*. This document lists with minute specificity the rights of possession and worship that each Christian group has at the shrines. It is concerned with minutiae—like what group can sweep the floor at what time, how many candles each group can light, which pictures may be hung where—because the rival custodians were killing each other over just such insignificant matters. Ironically, the Turks could not trust any one Christian group with the keys to the Holy Sepulchre so they gave these to a Muslim family, the Nusseibeh, who open and close the church to this day. To compound the problems between the Christians in the Holy Land, the European powers were interested in the Holy Land. France supported the Catholics and Russia supported the Greek Orthodox. One of the sparks that set off the Crimean War in the nineteenth century was the removal of the star that marked the birthplace of Christ from the cave beneath the Church of the Nativity.

Some Catholics felt that the *Status Quo* favored the Greeks since they were subjects of the sultan at the time it was issued. Still, the British maintained the *Status Quo* during the Mandate Period, so did the Jordanians when they ruled the Old City and Bethlehem. The Israelis have continued this policy. This eighteenth-century law still determines how some Holy Places are administered. Note that this law does not apply to shrines the Custody alone owns such as the Church of All Nations. It applies only to those shrines where several Christian groups have "rights."

One can distinguish the shrines administered by the Franciscans by the coat of arms of the Custody: a Crusader Cross (one large Maltese cross with four smaller crosses in each quadrant) above the crossed arms of Christ and Francis. The shrines administered by the Greeks will show the Greek letter Tau (T) superimposed upon the Greek letter Phi (Φ). This is an abbreviation of the Greek word ταφος, "sepulchre."

The relationship among Christian groups in the Holy Land is far better than it was when the Ottoman Turks had to intervene to bring order to the chaos engendered by piety run amok. After Vatican II and the visit of Pope Paul VI to the Holy Land in 1964, relationships have improved—particularly between the Catholics and the Greeks. Still, a lot depends on the personalities of the leadership of these churches on the local level and the conduct of those who serve at the shrines.

In 1990, the Israeli government had to intervene when the Greek Orthodox unilaterally decided to repair the roof at the Church of the Nativity. While the roof did need repair, the Armenians and Franciscans interpreted the failure of the Greeks to consult them and secure their agreement to the repairs as an act of proprietorship that is contrary to the *Status Quo*. The Christians have agreed on the extensive repairs necessary at the Church of the Holy Sepulchre. The work in progress for more than twenty years is still going on. Currently, the Franciscans are trying to raise funds to help finance the replacement of the aedicula over the tomb of Christ. The one-hundred-and-fifty-year-old dispute between the Ethiopians and the Copts regarding the monastery on the roof of the Holy Sepulchre keeps simmering and occasionally boils over, forcing the Israelis to restore order.

Christian Pilgrims

The Franciscans, the Orthodox, the Armenians, and others vie for control of the shrines for the express purpose of making them available to Christian pilgrims. It is ironic that of the three major faiths in the Holy Land, Christianity is the only one that does not mandate pilgrimage as a religious duty yet so many Christians come to visit the holy places.

It is clear that early Christians venerated the site of Calvary and the tomb of Jesus, the cave of his birth, and a house in Capernaum that was believed to be that of Peter (see Mark 1:29-31). After Constantine made Christianity the religion of the Empire, his mother Helena came to Palestine and built several churches: the Church of the Nativity in Bethlehem, the Church of the Holy Sepulchre in Jerusalem, and the Eleona Church on the Mount of Olives. Pilgrimage to the holy places then took off. Several of these pilgrims left behind the diaries that give us information about the appearance of these buildings and the liturgies carried on in them. The most famous of these is the diary of a nun named Egeria, who came on pilgrimage in 385.

The Crusades were launched because of the action of the Fatimid caliph Hakim (996–1035). He claimed to be an incarnation of Allah for which some of his subjects gave him the sobriquet "The Mad." In addition, he was determined to convert all his Jewish and Christian subjects to Islam. In 1009, he ended all pilgrimages to the Holy Land and ordered the destruction of all synagogues and churches in his domain —except the Church of the Nativity because Moslems used its southern transept for prayers.

Although Hakim's successors (Zahir [1021–1035] and Mustansir [1035–1094]) allowed the Church of the Holy Sepulchre to be rebuilt and pilgrimages to resume, the Crusaders were on their way. Meanwhile, the Seljuk Turks invaded Palestine, intent on depriving the Fatimids of their holdings in Palestine. They took Jerusalem in 1071 and renewed the prohibition of Christian pilgrimages. The Fatimids retook Jerusalem in 1098. The conflict wore out the Fatimids who were unable to repulse the Crusaders when they came to Jerusalem a year later.

The early victories of the Crusaders allowed pilgrimages to resume, but Saladin's victory at the Horns of Hattin in 1187 returned Jerusalem to the Muslims, who carefully controlled the activities of Christians in the Holy Land. When the Mamlukes determined to bring an end to Crusader presence, they embarked on a campaign marked by the destruction of churches and the murder of worshipers. Despite this, Christian pilgrims continued to come. Pilgrims like Jacques of Verona, Ludolph of Suchem, Felix Fabri, and Martin Kabtanik left diaries that describe the way the Muslims allowed but controlled pilgrim activity. In the sixteenth century, pilgrims began making the Via Dolorosa and this time rivalry among Christian Churches for control of the holy places became intense with the greatest conflict between the Greeks and Latins.

The 1800s witnessed efforts by European powers to protect their citizens visiting the Holy Land and the shrines they came to see. For example, the Russians built a huge compound on the top of the Mount of Olives. One can still see the tall tower of the Russian church built to commemorate the Ascension.

They also built St. Mary Magdalene Church on the Mount of Olives, and a hospice near the Church of the Holy Sepulchre. They built substantial facilities in West Jerusalem that the Israelis lease as government offices, the so-called *Russian Compound.* Wilhelm II of Germany had the Lutheran Church of the Redeemer built close to the Holy Sepulchre. He donated land to German Catholics for the Dormition Abbey on Mount Zion, and he built the Augusta Victoria Hospital between the Mount of Olives and Mount Scopus. The Austrian government established its own postal system to serve its citizens on pilgrimage because the Turkish system was unreliable. The Christian Information Office now occupies the building that housed that Austrian post office.

The State of Israel encourages Christian pilgrimages to Israel and there is never a lull in this activity. Of course, Christmas, Easter, and the summer are the high seasons. Today pilgrimage is nothing like it was for pilgrims of the Byzantine and medieval times. Such pilgrimages took a year or more to complete, and were costly and dangerous. Even pilgrims in the nineteenth century had to worry about Bedouin raids. Today pilgrims jet in, move around the land in air-conditioned buses, and spend the night in comfortable hotels. Jet lag, the guide's pace, and mild dysentery are their biggest concerns.

For many people, the opportunity to visit the Holy Land is a dream of a lifetime. If not properly prepared and led, the trip can be a disappointment. The best way to experience the Holy Land is to spend the amount of time that most of today's pilgrims do not have, despite the conveniences of modern travel. A pilgrimage to the Holy Land can be a spiritually uplifting experience as long as the pilgrim goes with an open mind, patience, and a readiness to listen to all the voices of this land—both past and present.

The Jerusalem Syndrome

An unusual development that appears to have coincided with the rise of pilgrimages by evangelicals to the Holy Land is a psychological condition that Israeli physicians have called the "Jerusalem syndrome." Some people become overwhelmed with the experience of being in the Holy Land, "the place where Jesus walked." For so many it is a lifelong dream come true. After months of eager anticipation and excited preparation, they are finally there and sometimes it becomes too much. Some people react by identifying with the biblical figures they hear about as they travel the land, and the identification can become pathological. That is when the "Jerusalem syndrome" can be observed.

The afflicted person can be observed preaching repentance to the crowds like John the Baptist or Elijah. They take on the persona of these biblical figures and imagine themselves preparing the way for the Messiah. They are largely ignored by the local people who usually have more urgent business that precludes their listening to a prophet. If the behavior of the twentieth-century John the Baptist becomes too disruptive or if they are observed wandering about the city aimlessly, the police will become involved. First, the police try to locate the group the "prophet" belongs to so they can get him or her back among familiar faces. That is sometimes enough to restore them to their senses. Sometimes the police will contact someone from the person's home.

Hearing the familiar voice of a relative or friend can bring the "prophet" back to reality. In more severe cases, a short hospital stay may be necessary, followed by a flight home.

The number of incidents in which a tourist identifies with some biblical figure and begins acting out has been high enough for the local medical community to be aware of the problem. They have developed treatments that help restore the patient to reality with relative ease, and they have given the affliction its own name—"the Jerusalem syndrome."

Jewish-Christian Relations

If the State of Israel imposed the type of restrictions on Christians that the latter placed on Jews when Christianity dominated this region, the Church would experience great problems. Constantine kept in place the decree of Hadrian that forbade Jews to live in Jerusalem, though he did alter the law to the extent that he allowed them to stand on the Mount of Olives on the ninth of Ab to lament the destruction of the Temple. Under Constantius, Constantine's son and successor, the Jews were pushed to revolt because of the anti-Jewish policies of Gallus whom Constantius placed in charge of the eastern part of the Empire. The Romans suppressed revolt with great ferocity.

Under Theodosius II, new laws were passed to restrict Judaism. In 429, the emperor ended the Jewish office of "patriarch" that gave the Jewish community a sense of solidarity. Another attempt to divide the community was the appointment of a Sanhedrin in Caesarea to rival that of Tiberias. The Jews largely ignored the Sanhedrin of Caesarea. Other anti-Jewish laws from Theodosius' reign prevented Jews from holding public office, building new synagogues, or converting Christians.

It was Eudocia, Theodosius' wife, who improved conditions for the Jews. After she and her husband became estranged, she moved to Jerusalem. She saw to it that Jews could visit Jerusalem more often and even live there. Excavations have revealed synagogues that date from the middle of the fifth century, so perhaps she helped insure that the imperial ban against such building projects was not enforced strictly. Still, the anti-Jewish legislation had its effect. By the sixth century, Jews made up only about ten to fifteen percent of the population of Palestine.

Matters took a turn for the worse during the reign of Justinian the Great (527–565). He believed that it was his responsibility as a Christian emperor to suppress all religious groups that did not accept the decrees of the Council of Chalcedon (451). This meant, first of all, the Monophysites, but the emperor redefined heresy to include Judaism and the Samaritan religion. The old anti-Jewish laws were reaffirmed and new laws were promulgated. The one that had the most damaging effect was that which revoked Judaism's status as a lawful religion. This led to a series of revolts that the Byzantine armies had no difficulty quashing. The worst was yet to come. Emperor Phocas (601–610) decreed that all Jews of the Empire had to submit to baptism and become "good Christians." Before this program of forced conversions could be carried out, the Persians threatened the continued existence of the Byzantine Empire.

When the Persians came to Palestine, the Jews welcomed them as liberators. Several thousand Jews joined the Persian army to rid the land of the hated Byzantines. As a reward, the Persians briefly placed the Jews in control of Jerusalem (614–617) before giving control back to the Christians. In 629, the Byzantine Emperor Heraclius retook Palestine from the Persians. Of course, the Jews had to pay a price for the help they gave the Persians. The Byzantines expelled the Jews from Jerusalem.

By the middle of the seventh century, the Byzantine and Persian Empires exhausted themselves fighting each other. This gave an opening to a new force from the desert of Arabia. The Arabs defeated the Byzantine army in 636 at the Yarmuk River. This defeat ended Byzantine rule in Palestine. Jerusalem surrendered in 638. Even while Sephronius, the Patriarch of Jerusalem, was surrendering the city to the Muslim caliph Omar, he could not forget the Jews. He asked that the Muslims forbid the Jews from settling in Jerusalem. Because some Jews helped in the Muslim conquest, Omar did not honor the Patriarch's request, but allowed two hundred Jewish families to move into the city.

Christians had no power in Palestine until the Crusader Period (1099–1291). The Jews who considered themselves fortunate to live in Jerusalem were not so fortunate when the city fell to the Crusaders on July 15, 1099. The Crusaders indiscriminately massacred anyone they found in the city: Muslim, Jew, or Christian—probably because they were angry over the stiff resistance shown by the Jerusalemites during the siege.

Despite these problems, there were a few Jews who settled in Palestine during the Crusader Period. They came from both Europe and North Africa. At first, the Crusaders did not allow these Jews to settle in Jerusalem, but eventually they reversed themselves and did allow some Jews to take up residence there. The twelfth-century Jewish pilgrim Benjamin of Tuleda left his diary describing how the Jews of Palestine fared under the Crusaders. He notes that the Jewish population of the city was just two hundred people, who lived near David's Tower. He also remarked that these Jews went to the Western Wall for prayers. Finally, he observed the Christians using stones from the Jewish cemetery on the Mount of Olives to build their houses. The Crusaders allowed Jewish pilgrims to visit Palestine. The most famous was the Ramban (Rabbi Moshe ben Nachman) who came from Spain in 1267. In a letter describing his travels, he referred to a massacre of Jerusalem's Jews in 1260 and a synagogue he established in the city to restore Jewish life there. The Mamlukes ended the Crusader rule in Palestine when they took the fortress in Acco (1291). Though the economic conditions of the Jews were bad, they fared better under the Mamlukes than they ever did under the Crusaders.

Jewish-Christian relations in Israel are complicated not only by this history but by the even more tragic history of Jewish-Christian relations in Europe. Many of the State's founders and early leaders experienced this tragic history first hand. For example, as a child in Kiev, Golda Meir had to cower in fear because of the Ukrainian peasants who came to her neighborhood looking for Jews to harass. Menachem Begin came from Poland to Israel in 1941; members of his family who remained in Poland died in the Holocaust.

Other complications in Jewish-Christian relations flow from the Arab and Israeli conflict. The people for whom the Church has pastoral responsibility in Israel are Arabs. The Latin Patriarch is an Arab. Most of the local clergy are Arab. It is difficult for the local Christian community to remain above the political debates and the struggle for justice. Until the peace process began, the Vatican had no diplomatic relations with Israel because of the question of Jerusalem's status. Because the Oslo Accords between Israel and the PLO calls for a determination to be made on Jerusalem at the conclusion to negotiations, the Vatican has begun normalizing its relationships with the State of Israel. Currently the Vatican's representative in Israel is Archbishop Pietro Sambi. He lives on Shemuel Ben Adaya Street at the north end of the Mount of Olives. He holds the rank of Apostolic Delegate but as relations between the Vatican and Israel progress, his status will be upgraded to that of Papal Nuncio.

The State of Israel is a Jewish State, but it guarantees freedom of worship for all. It has made it a policy that the shrines of all faiths are accessible to all. Sometimes security concerns require a modification of this policy, but under normal conditions the government encourages the shrines and holy places to be open to all who come to visit and pray. The Church is also free to pursue its educational and charitable ministries. This does not mean that there are no practical problems such as securing building permits, but with tact and persistence these can be solved. The area that requires special discretion is proselytizing. Both Jews and Muslims are very sensitive about Christian missionary activity. There is a law that prohibits giving monetary inducements to foster conversions and this can be interpreted quite broadly.

The most serious problem regarding the Church's relationship with the State of Israel is less overt than legal prohibitions and restrictions. It is the matter of economic opportunities for the Palestinians. Christian Arabs are emigrating largely for economic reasons. Creating economic opportunities for Arabs is not a priority for Israel. It is dealing with problems absorbing immigrants from the former Soviet Union. Unless the emigration trends among Palestinian Christians change, the local Church will desiccate. The Christian presence in Israel will be limited to foreigners who watch over shrines.

The International Christian Embassy

In the last twenty years, there has been a new development in Christian-Jewish relationships here. Following the Arab oil embargo in the mid-1970s, countries that maintained an embassy in Jerusalem moved their legations to Tel Aviv under pressure from the Arab oil states. (The embassy of the United States has always been in Tel Aviv.) This prompted some Christian Evangelicals from Europe to establish what they call the *International Christian Embassy* (10 Brenner St., Jerusalem). These people believe that it is the divine will for Israel to possess all the land promised to Abraham and his descendants. The "embassy" exists to encourage support for the State of Israel among Christians and to express that support to the Israeli government. To that end, each year during Sukkot the International Christian Embassy sponsors its "Feast of Tabernacles" celebration. It attracts evangelicals from around the world, who are warmly greeted by the Prime Minister and other governmental leaders. Similarly, some prominent evangelical preachers from the United States, like Jerry Falwell, sponsor "pilgrimages" that are as much political as religious. Falwell's groups spend as much time getting briefings from military officers at army bases as they do attending worship services.

All this attention from the evangelicals does not mean that they value the State of Israel in itself. Israel's continued existence is necessary for the playing out of the evangelical eschatological scenario. According to a simplified version of their beliefs, sometime after the building of the Third Temple, Jesus will "rapture" Christians from this world (see 1 Thess 4:16-17). (Falwell boasts that he has not purchased a cemetery plot since he believes that the rapture will take place during his lifetime.) After this, Jews will have another opportunity to accept the gospel. Many will, but then seven years of tribulation will begin when the anti-Christ will enter the Temple. Many will believe in him (See Matt 24:1-14). During these seven years, the unfulfilled prophecies of Ezekiel, Daniel, and Revelation will be fulfilled. There will be a great conflict between a coalition of nations led by Russia against Israel. This will conclude with the Battle of Armageddon. Following the victory of Christ in that battle in which millions of non-Christians will die, the thousand-year reign of Christ (Revelation 20) will begin. But for any of this to happen, the State of Israel needs to exist and the Third Temple built. That is why evangelicals are so staunch in their support for Israel.

The Mormons

Another religious body that claims to be Christian is the Mormon Church, though they are unrelated to either the Catholic, Orthodox, or Protestant branches of Christianity and their fundamental beliefs are at odds with traditional Christian doctrines. During the 1980s the Mormons sought permission to build a permanent study center in Jerusalem. There was a storm of protest— especially by the Jewish religious establishment. Israel has very strict laws limiting proselytizing and the Mormons are active, enthusiastic proselytizers. Most Mormon men spend two years as unpaid missionaries. Eventually the Mormons received permission to build their study center though they could not buy but only lease the land on which it is built. In addition, Mormon officials had to sign an agreement not to proselytize in Israel. The Mormon center in Jerusalem is on the Mount of Olives. You can see their beautifully designed and landscaped building as you go to the Old City by bus. It is the building with the arches just below the Hebrew University.

THE MUSLIMS

"There is no God but Allah, and Mohammed is his prophet" (Muslim profession of faith).

The overwhelming majority of Arabs in Israel are Muslims. The word *Muslim* means "one who submits (to God)." The religion of the Muslims is called *Islam,* which means "submission (to God)." Muslims believe Islam to be the only true religion professed by prophets from Adam to Abraham to Mohammed, who was the last of the prophets.

Islam is based on the teachings of the prophet Mohammed (570–632), who began to set these forth around the year 610. He saw himself in a line of prophets that began with Abraham and included both Moses and Jesus. Mohammed believed that his teaching completed the message of Judaism and Christianity. His first great success occurred when the city of Medina requested Mohammed's help to mediate a dispute among rival tribes. His move from Mecca to Medina in 622 marks the beginning of the Moslem calendar. Islam spread quickly among the tribes of Arabia. The Byzantine Empire, exhausted by internal conflicts, e.g., the doctrinal controversies between the Orthodox and the Monophysites and external threats from Persia succumbed to the Islamic advance. In 636, Arabs defeated Byzantine forces at the Yarmuk River. Jerusalem fell two years later and Caesarea capitulated in 640, bringing to an end Byzantine rule in Palestine.

The teachings of Mohammed are found in the *Koran,* a book of one hundred fourteen chapters called *surahs.* Mohammed taught orally and his sayings were compiled after his death. The Koran contains not only teachings unique to Islam but it also contains stories that are familiar to readers of the Bible. Muslims honor Abraham, Moses, David, and Jesus as prophets. Mohammed regarded the revelation he received as bringing to completion earlier revelation given through the prophets of the Bible and so saw himself as the final prophet of God. He fully expected Jews and Christians to accept Islam and was bitterly disappointed when they did not.

The Pillars of Faith. Muslims have five principal religious duties, which are called "the pillars of faith." First is the recitation of the profession of faith: "There is no God but Allah, and Mohammed is his prophet." The Muslims are monotheists who regard the Trinitarianism of Christianity a departure from true belief. One inscription inside the Dome of the Rock calls Christians to recognize that God does not have a son. Similarly, the profession of faith distinguishes Islam from the other monotheistic faith—Judaism. It believes that true faith requires the recognition of Mohammed's unique role in proclaiming God's final revelation.

A second requirement is the offering of prayers toward Mecca five times a day. Mohammed detested bells so he had his followers called to prayer by a muezzin, who sings out the invitation to prayer at the appropriate times. Though Moslems usually assemble at a mosque for prayer, it is not necessary to do so. Islam does not have a "Sabbath" in the same sense Judaism does, but Muslims consider coming to the mosque for noonday prayers on Friday an important practice of piety. You will notice that crowds of Muslims will assemble for Friday noon prayers at the Haram es-Sharif. Men and women worship separately and non-Muslims are not admitted to the Haram at the time of prayer. At first, the orientation for prayer was toward Jerusalem, but this was changed to Mecca when it became clear that Jews were not accepting Islam nor recognizing Mohammed as a prophet.

The third pillar is almsgiving. In Jerusalem, Muslim charity is administered by the Waqf. It is also responsible for maintaining the Islamic shrines of Jerusalem. The members of the Waqf receive a salary from the Kingdom of Jordan that has exercised responsibility for the Muslim holy places in Jerusalem since 1948. The Palestinian Authority has challenged Jordan on this score. When the Mufti of Jerusalem (the principal Islamic clergyman) died in 1994, both Jordan and the Palestinian Authority appointed separate replacements. King Hussein of Jordan and Yassir Arafat of the Palestinian Authority have agreed that Jordan will continue its religious responsibilities in Jerusalem until the city's final status is decided in negotiations with Israel. In its peace treaty with Jordan, Israel recognized Jordan's role as guardian of the Islamic shrines of Jerusalem. Muslim clergymen within the pre-1967 borders are paid by the State of Israel.

Fasting is the fourth pillar of the faith. The great fast of Islam takes place during Ramadan, the ninth month of the lunar year. Islam follows a lunar calendar like Judaism, but it does not have "leap years" that correct the disparity between the lunar and solar years. As a result, Ramadan has no fixed date in the solar calendar. During this month total abstinence from food and drink is required during daylight hours. Food is taken after sunset. This is a difficult discipline when Ramadan occurs during the winter, but it requires great devotion when Ramadan occurs during the summer with its long and hot days. The fast is not done for ascetical or penitential reasons but to mark the giving of the Koran.

The pilgrimage to Mecca is the last of the five duties of Muslims. If possible, all Muslims are to make the pilgrimage to Mecca at least once in the lifetime. Muslims who have made this pilgrimage sometimes place a sign on the front of their homes depicting the Kaʾba, a square building covered by a black cloth. Muslims believe that the Kaʾba was built by Abraham and his son Ishmael, whom the Arabs regard as their father. It was a magnet for pilgrims in pre-Islamic Arabia. Mohammed emptied the building of its images and kept it as an object of pilgrimage.

Diversity in Islam. There are several branches of Islam, the two principal ones being Sunni and Shiʾite. The two split over the question of the succession to Mohammed, who died without a male heir. Sunnis are the majority in the Islamic world and in Israel. The Shiʾites view themselves as an oppressed minority and this sometimes manifests itself in fanaticism like that of Iran where the Muslims are Shiʾites. Most of the Muslims in Israel are Sunni though Shiʾite groups have significant popular appeal among those frustrated by the political problems of the region.

All forms of Islam are experiencing a wave of fundamentalism—not over doctrine but over traditional values and mores. Muslim fundamentalism is a rejection of Western ideas and customs and Western economic and political domination. One manifestation of this new wave of Muslim fundamentalism is the more conservative style of dress worn by women. Fewer Muslim women will wear Western clothes in public. Those who oppose the State of Israel have exploited this more conservative and traditional direction of Islam by presenting acts of terrorism against Israelis as acts of piety.

THE DRUZE

The Druze comprise an important religious minority in Israel. Their religion is an eleventh-century offshoot from Islam. It began when the Fatimid caliph al-Hakim (996–1021) allowed himself to be considered an incarnation of God. This is the same person who destroyed Christian shrines, including the Holy Sepulchre, in the territories under his control. One night Hakim went riding and never returned. He was probably assassinated because many of his subjects considered him a tyrant, but his unexplained disappearance fueled the speculation among his supporters that he was divine.

Like the Muslims, the Druze believe in a series of prophets including Abraham, Moses, Jesus, and Mohammed. But unlike the Muslims, they believe that the one God has been made known by successive incarnations, the last and most perfect of which was Hakim. Orthodox Muslims see this belief as a compromise of monotheism. The Druze do not; they call themselves *Muwahhidin* ("Unitarians").

Having a good grasp of Druze doctrine is difficult because their society is closed and secretive when it comes to religious matters. Only a select few Druze are fully initiated into their religion. They must show themselves worthy before they learn the secrets of their people's faith. The Druze believe in predestination and the transmigration of souls. They do not seek converts because they believe the number of Druze is divinely determined and constant. When one dies, his soul enters the body of a newborn Druze.

Most Druze live in Syria, Lebanon, and northern Israel. Several Druze villages are in the area around Mount Hermon. They bear political allegiance to the country in which they live. Those who live in Israel serve in the army and accept all other obligations of citizenship. Druze men can be recognized by the walrus-like mustaches, their white veils, and black robes.

The Druze consider questions about their religious beliefs to be improper. Those who are initiated into the secrets of their religion are not allowed to reveal these. Women are allowed to be among the initiated. There are seven fundamental duties that the initiated are to observe: (1) the recognition of Hakim and belief in his teachings, (2) rejection of all non-Druze religious beliefs, (3) rejection of the devil, (4) acceptance of God's acts, (5) submission to God, (6) truthfulness, and (7) solidarity with all other Druze.

THE HOLY PLACES

"When Jacob awoke from his sleep, he exclaimed, 'Truly, the LORD is in this spot, although I did not know it" (Gen 28:16).

Judaism. The notion of a "holy place" is almost nonexistent in the primary sources of Judaism: the Bible and the Talmud. The term "Holy Land" occurs only once in the Bible—in Zech 2:16. Holiness in rabbinic Judaism is determined by the laws applying to the place in question, e.g., the Temple—and not according to what may have occurred at the site. For example, Mount Sinai is not a Jewish holy place. At its summit, there are a mosque and a church but no synagogue. When Anwar Sadat suggested building one there, he did not receive a positive reply from the Israelis. Also notice that sites connected with the history of Israel have no shrines and are not the objects of pilgrimage—except Jerusalem and the Western Wall.

In time—and perhaps under non-Jewish influence—Jews came to regard some places as being holy and prayers offered there as more efficacious than those offered at other places. Among these holy places are the Western Wall, the tombs of biblical figures (the tombs of the patriarchs and their wives in Hebron, the tomb of Joseph in Nablus, Rachel's tomb near Bethlehem, and David's tomb on Mount Zion are all special places of prayer for religious Jews), and the tombs of early rabbis such as those in Upper Galilee near Meiron. Visiting the tombs of revered rabbis and pious men is considered particularly desirable by the ultraorthodox and other Jews of a mystical bent. The purpose of those visits is to commune with the departed saint and absorb some of his qualities.

Christianity. At first, Christians showed little interest in "holy sites" for two reasons. First, the apocalyptic orientation of early Christianity made shrine-building and pilgrimage irrelevant. Second, the first Christians were persecuted and needed to avoid public displays like pilgrimages to holy sites to avoid calling attention to themselves. There is evidence that some early Christians did regard the caves at Bethlehem, the tomb of Jesus in Jerusalem, the caves in Nazareth, and the house of Peter in Capernaum as holy places. Most Christian holy places were identified during the Byzantine Period (fourth through seventh centuries) when Christianity became the official religion of the Roman Empire. Imperial policy led to the building of shrines for the service of pilgrims. Christian holy places were sites associated with the life of Jesus. Pilgrimage to the Holy Land became a very popular pious practice among Christians though Christianity does not require pilgrimage as a religious duty.

Islam. Jerusalem holds a special status in Islam. *Sura* 17 of the Koran, the holy book of Islam, speaks of a night journey that Mohammed took to the "farthest mosque." After spending time in prayer there, he was taken to the very presence of God in heaven. He then returned to earth and traveled back to Mecca. Traditionally, the site of this "farthest mosque" has been identified as Jerusalem though the Koran does not specifically name the site. When the Arabs wrested control of Palestine from the Byzantines in the seventh century, among their first projects was to build shrines to commemorate Mohammed's night journey and ascension. These shrines were built on the platform that was the site of the Temple. During the Byzantine Period, this area became a refuse dump for the city. The Muslims had the area cleaned and began the construction of their shrines.

One shrine is the **Dome of the Rock**. This octagonal building covered with blue tiles and a golden dome was built over the rock from which Muslims believe Mohammed ascended into heaven. The second shrine on the Temple platform is the **al-Aksa** ("the farthest") **Mosque**, which commemorates the site of Mohammed's prayer in Jerusalem. The Muslims refer to the Temple platform as the **Haram es-Sharif**, "the noble sanctuary." The Muslim authorities are very wary of any archaeological work or pilgrim activity that threatens their presence on the **Haram** or imperils the physical integrity of the buildings there. Because of the Arab-Israeli conflict, there is no pilgrimage to this sanctuary from outside Israel and the Occupied Territories, though the State of Israel offers the assurance that it will maintain access to the shrines of all religions to anyone coming to Israel. The successful conclusion of the peace process may lead to Islamic pilgrims from around the world coming to Jerusalem, which they call *al-Quds*, "the Holy."

The Samaritans. There is only one holy place sacred to the few Samaritans of Israel. It is **Mount Gerizim**, the site of the Samaritan Temple. This is located just outside the city of Nablus. Samaritans gather there for their Passover celebration each year.

The Druze. This eleventh-century off-shoot of Islam has a special devotion to Jethro, the father-in-law of Moses (see Exod 3:1), whom they call Nabi Shuʾeib. They gather each year at his tomb that they locate near the Horns of Hattin, that overlook the Sea of Galilee.

The Bahai. The Bahai faith that originated in Persia (Iran) could not maintain its headquarters there because the Muslims regard adherents of the Bahai faith as heretics. The principal shrines of the Bahai are two tombs. One is just north of Acco and is the burial place of BahaʾAllah. The second is the tomb of Mizrah Ali Muhammed, the founder of the faith, in the Persian Gardens of Haifa.

CHAPTER FOUR

Israel: The Preliminaries

Psalm 122

With joy I heard them say,
"Let us go to the Lord's house!"
And now, Jerusalem,
we stand inside your gates.

Jerusalem, the city so built,
that city and temple are one.
To you the tribes go up,
every tribe of the Lord.

It is the law of Israel
to honor God's name.
The seats of law are here
the throne of David's line.

Pray peace for Jerusalem:
happiness for your homes,
safety inside your walls,
peace in your great houses.

For love and family and friends
I say, "Peace be with you!"
For love of the Lord's own house
I pray for your good.

The Psalter (Chicago: Liturgical Training Publications)

ARRIVAL

Travel to Israel. Christian pilgrims have been going to the Holy Land since the fourth century. Until the middle of this century making a pilgrimage was a costly, lengthy, and dangerous undertaking. The trip from the port of Jaffa to Jerusalem alone took almost three days. The jet age has made travel to Israel affordable and quick. Just a few hours of flight time separates Israel from the rest of the world. The cost of package tours is not beyond the means of most people.

Travel from North America to Israel usually involves a stopover and change of planes in a European city. When boarding a plane for Israel, be ready for the security measures that will be in force. These measures may require you to identify your checked baggage and may include an examination of the contents of your luggage. Patient cooperation with these procedures will insure a safe flight. It is important that you take all security procedures seriously.

Though your ticket will say that your destination is Tel Aviv, the airport where you will be landing is near the town of Lod. The airport's name honors David Ben Gurion, the first prime minister of the State of Israel. Ben Gurion Airport is the principal international airport in Israel. Eighteen international airlines land there. There is an airport in a suburb north of Jerusalem, but it is small and handles mostly domestic flights.

Formalities. A bus will take you from the airplane to the arrival section of the terminal building. There you will present your passport and receive your tourist visa if you are from Western Europe or North America. Visitors from other regions need to have a visa issued by the Israeli government before arriving in Israel. If you plan to travel to any country that does not recognize Israel, *before* you hand your passport to the agent, ask that the agent not stamp it. Be sure to keep the white entry card the agent will give you, along with your passport. You will need to have this card when you leave Israel.

After going through passport control, get a luggage cart and pick up your luggage at the proper carousel. After claiming your luggage, wait for the other members of your group. If you have nothing but items for personal use during your visit, you can pass through the green "nothing to declare" line at customs. Your guide will escort you to a bus that will take you to your first destination in Israel.

Distance to Jerusalem. Jerusalem is about thirty-six miles southeast of the airport. The airport is on the eastern edge of the plain that runs along the Mediterranean coast. You will pass through the foothills (H: *Shephelah*) before reaching the central highlands. Jerusalem is in the central heights—about 2,600 feet above sea level. The last five miles of the trip from the airport to Jerusalem requires a steep ascent. It is at this point that you will leave the foothills and enter the central highlands. The trip from the airport to Jerusalem will take about an hour.

Entering Jerusalem. You will approach Jerusalem from the west so you will enter that part of the city that is almost exclusively Jewish in population. This western part of the city is not yet one hundred fifty years old. Until the middle of the nineteenth century, all Jerusalem's citizens lived inside the walled city that today is known as "the Old City." An Anglo-Jewish philanthropist named Moses Montefiore tried to encourage the Jews of the Old City, who lived on charity, to become self-reliant. Montefiore made his fortune in banking and the stock market. He retired at the age of forty and devoted himself to Jewish charities and principally the settlement and welfare of Jews in Palestine. He urged them to move outside the walled city to farm the surrounding fields and hills. Montefiore built a windmill to process the grain harvest. His windmill is still a familiar part of the Jerusalem scene. He also built homes near the windmill, but the people were afraid of bandits so they went back to their hovels in the Old City each night after working in the fields. Gradually, however, people began to settle outside the walls. Neighborhoods, each with its own character, developed so that the western part of Jerusalem is a large city made up of small neighborhoods, each with its own appeal.

GENERAL INFORMATION

Dress. The Israelis tend to favor informal dress for the most part. Even the best restaurants do not require a suit and tie of their male patrons. In neighborhoods where religious people reside, it is important to wear modest clothing. For women, this means that shoulders should be covered and skirts should reach below the knee. Shorts for both women and men are inappropriate. Arabs, too, expect women to dress modestly. You will not be admitted to synagogues, churches, or mosques in shorts or with bare shoulders. When visiting historical and archaeological sites, there is no dress code. On days when you visit both holy sites and historical sites, women should carry a wrap-around skirt with them. Men should have a head covering for visits to synagogues and mosques. Muslims take off their shoes inside mosques. You will be expected to do the same when you visit these Muslim places of prayer.

Israeli Currency. The currency in Israel is the *New Israeli Shekel* (NIS). The name comes from a measure for weight in the Bible (e.g., Gen 24:22; Exod 30:13, 24; Neh 10:33). The NIS is divided into one hundred *agorot* (sing: *agorah*). You may change your currency for NIS at your hotel, a bank, or with a money changer. Changing at a bank is an unnecessarily long and complicated process, and the bank charges a commission for this service. Hotels usually give a very bad exchange rate. It is more convenient to use the services of an authorized money changer. Do not change money with anyone on the street. If you are not extremely careful, you can be short-changed. There are money changers in the western (Jewish) and eastern (Arab) parts of the city though they are far more common in East Jerusalem. You will need Israeli shekels for bus and taxi fares, postage, snacks, and other incidental expenses. Some restaurants will accept payment in dollars though the exchange rate may not always be favorable. Most shops that cater to tourists will accept payment in American dollars. All major **credit cards** are accepted in Israel. You will be charged in dollars according to the exchange rate prevailing at the time your purchase is posted.

Postal Services and Telephones. Post offices are conveniently located throughout the country. They are open daily except Saturday. They close at 1:00 p.m. on Friday afternoon. Some offices are closed in the early afternoon. Tourists in Jerusalem will find two post offices in the Old City. One is in the Jewish Quarter. The other is inside the Jaffa Gate across from the Citadel. There is a post office on Saladin Street across from Herod's Gate. The city's main post office is on Jaffa Road across from the City Hall. People pay various bills, cash some checks, and buy telephone cards at post offices so sometimes there can be a wait for services. If you want to send packages by mail, you can buy boxes at the post office. Do not seal them until they have been inspected by postal authorities.

Telephone calls made through hotel switchboards can be expensive because of surcharges. One can make international calls from the main post office in Jerusalem, Haifa, and other cities. Most American long distance carriers (AT&T, MCI, Sprint) have numbers in Israel that will connect you directly to an operator in the United States who will connect you. Check with your long distance carrier for this number before you leave. This is the easiest way to make a call to the U.S. from Israel. Local calls can be made from public phones that are available throughout the country. Public telephones accept prepaid telephone cards that are available at the post office. These cards can be used for international calls made through the Israeli system.

Entertainment. Israel offers an array of entertainment possibilities: plays, concerts, movies, clubs. The Friday edition of the *Jerusalem Post* includes a magazine called "Time Out," which lists many of these. Also, tourist publications will have a listing of those that may be of special interest to visitors. These publications are available at the Municipal Tourist Office at 17 Jaffa Road and at major hotels. Tickets for most events can be purchased at ticket agencies. During the summer, there are usually many cultural events that tourists will enjoy for free or for a modest charge.

News in English. The *Jerusalem Post* is an Israeli daily (except Saturday) newspaper published in English. Its editorial bent is toward the right-wing of the Israeli political spectrum. Both the *International Herald-Tribune* and *USA Today* are available in bookstores and newsstands. *Time* and *Newsweek* are also available. There are English-language newscasts on radio throughout the day: Israel Radio (576AM and 1458AM) (Israeli news with some international news). BBC (1323AM) has a newscast every hour on the hour devoted to international news.

Personal Safety. Despite image problems Jerusalem and Israel are safe places. For example, in 1993 there were one hundred murders in Seattle, Washington. In Jerusalem that same year there were ten. Also, the incidence of street crime is low. One reason for Jerusalem's relative safety is the presence and visibility of the police. Still, there are common sense safety precautions that prudent people take no matter where they are living. Keep your wallet or purse in a place where pickpockets would have a hard time reaching. Putting them in a backpack is *not* a good idea. Know where you are going and how to get there. Traveling with others is more enjoyable and safer. The best way to insure your personal safety is to follow the same sort of prudent procedures that you would at home. Also, Israel is a country where everyone carries a government-issued identity card. For foreigners, the passport serves this purpose. It is a good idea to carry your passport with you, but be certain that you keep it where it will be safe.

EATING OUT

Most tours include some if not all meals. You may want to strike out on your own to sample some of Israel's restaurants. Israel has everything from French to Chinese restaurants. Lately, American fast food has made its presence felt with McDonald's, Burger King, and Pizza Hut. The distinctive Israeli cuisine is an adaptation of Middle Eastern cooking that is found throughout the region. The following list represents some typical Middle Eastern foods:

pita: a round and flat bread. It can be slit open and used as a pocket to hold different types of food such as *falafel* and *shwarma*.

houmus: a sauce made from ground chickpeas (garbanzo beans) and olive oil. Used as a dip with *pita*.

tehina: a sauce made from sesame seeds; also used as a dip with *pita*.

falafel: round balls made of fried ground chickpeas; also the name of a sandwich. A *pita* is stuffed with various salads, garnished with a few *falafel* balls, and topped by various sauces to taste. This is the Middle Eastern version of fast food.

shwarma: meat (usually lamb) cooked on an upright spit and thinly sliced. It can be served as an entree or stuffed into a *pita*.

kebab: ground, spicy meat cooked on a skewer.

shishlik: cubes of meat (lamb, beef, chicken, or turkey) cooked on a skewer.

Kosher. Most restaurants in Israel are *kosher*. This means more than limiting their menu to "clean" foods (see Lev 11) and avoiding unclean foods such as pork. The rules of *kashrut* are based on the text that commands the Israelites: "You shall not boil a kid in its mother's milk" (Exod 23:19; 34:26; Deut 14:21). The early rabbis extrapolated this text by forbidding dairy and meat products to be eaten at the same meal. Kosher restaurants will be either meat or dairy (vegetarian and fish). For example, at a restaurant that serves meat, you will not be able to have butter on your bread, milk in your coffee, or ice cream for dessert. At a kosher pizzeria, you will not find any meat toppings.

The requirements of *kashrut* also call for separate dishes and cutlery for dairy and meat meals. That is why even in malls that have food courts, the dairy and meat sections are separate and customers are asked to observe this separation by sitting in the appropriate part of the food court. If you are having a shwarma sandwich and your companion is having a slice of pizza, you should sit in separate sections. Different religious organizations supervise the kosher character of restaurants and provide certificates attesting to their observance.

Keeping kosher is important for restaurants in Jerusalem since much of the city's Jewish population keeps kosher kitchens at home and will avoid restaurants that are not certified as kosher. Still, there are restaurants in the city that do not keep kosher. Of course, Arab restaurants do not, but they do not serve pork since Islam forbids this food. In other cities where the percentage of the population that is religious may be smaller, there will be fewer kosher restaurants.

Recommendations. Two fine non-kosher restaurants outside the western part of Jerusalem are those in the American Colony Hotel on Saladin St. and in the Notre Dame Center (across from the New Gate). A booklet listing restaurants in various price ranges is available from the municipal tourist office at 17 Jaffa Road. Many restaurants and cafés are located in the city center (Ben Yehuda Mall area and the Nahalat Shiva area). You will also find fast food places in the Ben Yehuda Mall area. Israel Government tourist offices will provide you with recommendations for restaurants throughout the country.

SHOPPING

The Old City. Shopping in the Old City of Jerusalem can be economical and fun for people who like to "bargain" or haggle over prices. Most tourist shops in the Old City have no fixed prices. The seller and the buyer engage in a process that leads to a price agreeable to both. You have to assess the quality of the merchandise so that your bargaining will be realistic. Shops in the Old City's Jewish Quarter have fixed prices and no bargaining. Remember that there is no word in Arabic or Hebrew that translates the English word "shopping." In the U.S., shopping is a leisure-time activity that may or may not end with an actual purchase. In Jerusalem one does not shop; one "buys" and this is serious business. (The Hebrew word for "shopping mall" means "place for buying.") Despite the invitations to visit an Arab's shop with words like "No need to buy; only look," shopkeepers expect to make a sale. This is especially true after investing time in answering questions, bargaining, showing different selections, and perhaps serving tea, coffee, or a cold drink. Once you express interest in an item, the shopkeepers are relentless. The only way to resist is to be firm. That is not insensitive, but the way things work there. Never buy anything unless *you* are satisfied with the quality and price. If you enjoy bargaining, you will have many opportunities to engage in this special form of "interaction."

Moslem girls at the Damascus Gate market.

West Jerusalem. Stores here have fixed prices and no bargaining. Prices for most items are much higher than in the U.S. There is no tax added to the price. The Value Added Tax (VAT) is already included. If you purchase items in tourist shops and pay for them in foreign currency, you may be entitled to a VAT refund. Usually items must cost $50 or more to qualify for a refund. To receive this refund you need to have the proper receipt. You will receive your refund at the airport. Consult the merchant for other requirements and procedures. The two main shopping areas in West Jerusalem are the **City Center** (the triangle formed by Jaffa Road, King George Street, and the Ben Yehuda pedestrian mall) and the **Mall** (*Canion Jerushalayim, Mahla* ["The Jerusalem Mall"] Bus 6 from Jaffa Road or 31 from King George Street). These contain the usual mix of department stores, shops, restaurants, fast-food outlets, and movie theaters.

There are shops that cater to tourists throughout the country. You will find them in hotels and at places that tourists frequent. You will find some variation in prices and quality for items that you may wish to purchase as souvenirs or gifts. It is best to do some comparison shopping if you have the time. Do not be rushed into a decision. Make certain that you are happy with the item and satisfied that you are paying a fair price.

TRANSPORTATION

Jerusalem has a good public transport system that makes getting around the city easy. During peak hours travel on buses can be time-consuming because Jerusalem's streets were not designed for mass transit.

The Israeli System. The *Egged* (H: cooperative) Bus Company serves the western part of the city. These buses run from about 5:30 a.m. to midnight. They do not run on Friday from two hours before sundown until about an hour after sundown on Saturday when service on most lines resumes. To use the system one has to be familiar with the particular route that services your destination. (Call the Municipal Tourist Office for information.) You pay a fare each time you board a bus; there are no transfers. You may buy a card (H: *cartesia*) that gives eleven rides for the price of ten. (People over sixty are entitled to a card that gives fifteen rides for the price of ten.) You can also pay cash for each ride; exact change is not necessary.

Travel by taxi around the western part of the city is also an option (H: *monit*). If you choose to travel by taxi, make certain the driver uses the meter. This will prevent problems. The rate after dark is higher than during the day. Still, rates are cheaper than in the U.S. and drivers do not expect tips.

The Arab System. Jerusalem has two public transportation systems—one Arab and one Israeli. The Arab bus system has a terminal across from the Damascus Gate. Buses take riders to points in East Jerusalem and to the city's Arab suburbs. For example, Arab bus nos. 22 or 47 will take you to Bethlehem and no. 75 will take you to the top of the Mount of Olives. Arab buses run seven days a week, but do not run after dark. There are Arab taxi companies that will take you to any destination in Jerusalem. Such a ride is called a "special." Make certain that you know the fare before you get in.

Information. The Christian Information Office puts out a sheet with information about bus routes to many tourist sites in Jerusalem and some interurban routes as well. You can also get help from the Municipal Tourist Office on Jaffa Road or from an information booth at the Central Bus Station. You can call Egged at 6304555 for information, but you may not always get a person who speaks English well. A call to the Municipal Tourist Office is the best bet.

Interurban Transportation. The Egged Bus Company has interurban lines that connect Jerusalem with the rest of Israel. The terminal for these lines is the Central Bus Station on Jaffa Road. Information and tickets are available there. Israel also has a few passenger trains. You can take a train from Jerusalem to Tel Aviv and Haifa. The depot is at Remez Square near Hebron Road.

Taxis. You can use taxis within a city or to travel between cities. When traveling within a city make certain the driver uses the meter. When using a taxi for interurban transportation, have the driver use the meter or have the driver consult the price list from the Ministry of Transport. The fare will be about the same. Taxi drivers do not expect a tip. If you have complaints about taxi service, you can lodge them at the Ministry of Transport, Clal Bldg., 97 Jaffa Road, 94342 Jerusalem.

Israelis use public transport more frequently than Americans do. Other Israeli cities have bus systems similar to that of Jerusalem. If you want to use the system, ask for help at the Israeli Government Tourist Office or at the Central Bus Station in any city.

YOUR ITINERARY

If this is your first visit to Israel, you will probably be going on a guided tour with a set itinerary. You will see many religious and historical sites in a short time, and you will certainly feel that your trip has just whetted your appetite. With a little bit of planning you will be able to do your next trip on your own but it will be necessary for you to set an itinerary for yourself. For information, use this book, consult other books referred to here, and check the Internet if it is available to you. Setting an itinerary involves the art of selection. Have a goal for your trip and choose sites that contribute to meeting that goal. Eliminate those that will make a lesser impact. Give yourself the time to visit places at a leisurely pace so that you can enjoy your visit.

National Parks Authority. Most historical and archaeological sites in Israel are administered by the National Parks Authority (NPA). There is an entrance fee at each of the parks. Get a brochure from the Israel National Tourist Office or visit the NPA web site (http://www.webscape. com/inpa). You can choose the sites that fit your goals before you leave for Israel. You can then decide if you should purchase the NPA "Green Card." This card is valid for two weeks and allows you to visit more than twenty sites for one price. You can purchase it at the first site you visit.

Israel's Nature Reserves. Some historical sites are located in nature reserves administered by the Society for the Protection of Nature in Israel (SPNI). These reserves are areas of unique flora, fauna, and landscape that the SPNI protects from destruction. Among the most beautiful is the Tel Dan Reserve in Galilee. There is an entrance fee to these reserves. Visiting these reserves can be a welcome break from the usual tourist sites, and many will show you an Israel that you did not expect to find.

CHAPTER FIVE

Israel: Jerusalem

"Ten measures of beauty were bestowed upon the world; nine were taken by Jerusalem and one by the rest of the world" (Babylonian Talmud, Tractate *Kiddushin* 49:2).

HISTORY

The Pre-Israelite City. The presence of flint tools suggests that there was a settlement in the area already in the Stone Age. People were drawn here by the waters of the Gihon Spring. Sherds from the Early Bronze Age testify to the beginning of permanent habitation from 3000 B.C. The first time the city is mentioned in a literary text is in the Egyptian *Execration Texts* of the nineteenth century B.C. This text calls the city *Rushalimum* while the Amarna letters of five hundred years later call this city *Urusalim*. At the end of the Late Bronze Age, Jerusalem was a small Canaanite city-state that controlled East-West communications at the southern end of the central highlands. Since the major trade routes ran north-south, Jerusalem was not an important trade center.

The Judahite Monarchy. Jerusalem became part of the Israelite national state when David conquered the city in 1005 B.C. (2 Sam 5:6-13). During the Israelite Period (or Iron Age 1005–586), the city served first as the capital of the Davidic-Solomonic Empire. Solomon built the Temple on a threshing floor just north of David's City in 969 B.C. With the empire's breakup after the death of Solomon (922), Jerusalem remained the capital of Judah (the southern of the two Israelite kingdoms). In the eighth century, Judah became a vassal state of the Assyrian Empire. In 701 B.C., the Assyrians attacked Jerusalem because of its participation in a revolt against their hegemony. The Assyrians lifted the siege before the city fell (see 2 Kings 18–19). When the Assyrian Empire collapsed in the seventh century, Judah became a vassal of the Babylonian Empire. At the end of an ill-advised revolt against Babylon, Nebuchadnezzar took

Jerusalem in 587 B.C. The city and its Temple were destroyed and its leading citizens were taken into Exile (2 Kings 25). The Davidic dynasty came to an end, the priesthood was scattered, and the institutions that gave the city its cultural and religious identity were no more.

Restoration. Following the fall of Babylon to the Persian Empire in 539, the Jews in Babylon were allowed to return to Jerusalem. The Persians encouraged them to rebuild the Temple and reinstate worship there (2 Chr 36:22-23). The Temple was rebuilt in 515 (Ezra 4:14–5:17). Nehemiah oversaw the rebuilding of the city's walls c. 440 (Neh 12:27-28). Jerusalem, however, did not regain its political independence. It was one city in the Persian satrapy called "Beyond the River."

The Hellenistic Period. In 333 B.C., Alexander's victory at the Battle of Issus ended Persian domination in the ancient Near East and brought the territory of the former Israelite kingdoms into his domain. Alexander respected the achievements of ancient cultures. He hoped that the infusion of Greek perspectives into these ancient cultures would bring new vigor to what he considered an old world. After Alexander's death in 323 B.C., his generals divided his empire among themselves. Judah and Jerusalem came under the control of Ptolemy who ruled from Egypt. Seleucus, who ruled from Babylon, thought that Judah and Jerusalem properly belonged to him. Eventually, Antiochus III brought Judah and Jerusalem under Seleucid rule in 198 B.C.

Antiochus IV encouraged Jews to abandon their ancestral traditions. He renamed Jerusalem "Antioch-in-Jerusalem." Though some Jews voluntarily cooperated with Antiochus (1 Maccabees 1), many did not. His rule became despotic when his plans to hellenize Jerusalem were not completely successful. His anti-Jewish legislation and desecration of the Temple led to the Maccabean revolt in 167 B.C. The Maccabees succeeded in defeating the Seleucid armies and established an independent Jewish State in Palestine in 164 B.C. They retook Jerusalem and rededicated the Temple. At first, the Maccabees served as high priests of the Jerusalem Temple (1 Maccabees 14), but eventually the Hasmoneans (as this dynasty was called) took the title of king. Alexander Yannai (103–72 B.C.) extended the rule of the Hasmoneans to practically the entire area once ruled by David.

The Roman Period. The Roman rule of Palestine began with Pompey's entrance into Jerusalem in 63 B.C. The Romans effectively ended Hasmonean rule although the dynasty continued to reign until Herod the Great eliminated the last Hasmonean. Augustus confirmed Herod as king in 30 B.C. Herod made Jerusalem his capital and beautified the city and its Temple. Jesus was born in Bethlehem during Herod's reign. At his death in 4 B.C., the Romans divided Herod's kingdom among his sons. Jerusalem was in the territory ruled by Archelaus who proved to be incompetent. The Romans decided to rule his territory directly through a procurator whose seat of government was not in Jerusalem but in Caesarea Maritima. The procurator Pontius Pilate condemned Jesus to death about A.D. 30.

A revolt against the Romans began in Caesarea in A.D. 66. It spread to Jerusalem, which the Romans besieged. The city fell in A.D. 70 and the victorious Roman legions burnt the Temple and part of the city. In A.D. 132, the Emperor Hadrian decided to rebuild Jerusalem as a Roman-Hellenistic city and to rename it Aelia Capitolina. When word of his plans leaked out, the Jews under Bar Kochba began a second revolt. The Romans suppressed this revolt in 135 and Hadrian went ahead with his plans. The present street plan of the Old City is that of Hadrian.

The Byzantines. When Christianity became the official religion of the Empire in A.D. 324, Jerusalem was transformed into a Christian city. The emperor's mother Helena visited Jerusalem in 326. Constantine built the Church of the Resurrection over the Tomb of Christ and the Church of the Ascension on the Mount of Olives. These churches attracted many Christian pilgrims. The Byzantines expelled the few Jews who lived in Jerusalem, but Julian the Apostate (361–363) allowed them to return to the city. Later Byzantine emperors renewed the anti-Jewish legislation that effectively eliminated Jewish presence in Jerusalem. Byzantine rule began to unravel when the Persians took Jerusalem in 614, though the Byzantines retook the city in 629.

The Arabs. Byzantine rule over Jerusalem ended when the city passed peacefully into Arab hands in 638. Jews were again allowed to live in Jerusalem. The Muslims built a mosque on the platform that supported the Temple. They also built a shrine to commemorate Mohammed's ascension to heaven (The Dome of the Rock in 691). South of the platform, they built a palace. Because of internal conflicts among the Arabs, Jerusalem passed under the control of three Arab dynasties: the Omayyid of Damascus, the Abissid of Baghdad, and the Fatimid of Cairo. The Seljuk Turks ended Arab rule in Palestine just before the First Crusade.

The Crusaders and the Turks. Relationships between Jews, Christians, and Muslims were good during the succession of Arab dynasties. But in 1009, the Caliph Hakim the Mad began to destroy Christian shrines and this was the spark that led to the Crusades. In 1071, the new masters of Jerusalem, the Seljuk Turks, forbade pilgrimages to the Holy Land. This led Pope Urban II to call for a crusade to retake the holy places. The Fatimids retook Jerusalem from the Seljuk Turks and welcomed Christian pilgrims but it was too late to stop the Crusaders.

The Crusaders arrived in Jerusalem in 1099 and massacred its Jewish and Muslim inhabitants. The city passed back and forth between the Crusaders and the Muslims until 1244 when the Turks expelled the last of the Crusaders. Jerusalem was in ruins until the Ottoman Turks became the rulers of Palestine. Suleiman the Magnificent, their Sultan, had the city's walls rebuilt in 1538. These walls still stand today.

In 1700, Rabbi Yehuda HeHassid began the construction of the Hurva Synagogue. The British philanthropist Moses Montefiore visited the city in 1836 and determined to better the living conditions of its Jewish population. The British government was the first to open a consulate in Jerusalem, in 1838.

The first settlement outside the walls started in 1860. In 1898 Theodor Herzl, the founder of the World Zionist Organization, arrived in Jerusalem.

The British Mandate. Turkish rule over Jerusalem ended in 1918 when the League of Nations gave Britain a mandate to govern Palestine. Jewish emigration began to enlarge the newer western part of the city. Chaim Weizmann laid the foundation stone of Hebrew University on Mount Scopus the same year the mandate began. The British Mandate ended in 1948 when the United Nations decided to partition Palestine into a Jewish state and an Arab state. Jerusalem was to be an international city.

The Jewish State. The partition plan never had a chance to work because several Arab states invaded the region of the Jewish State, which proclaimed its independence on May 14, 1948. When the armistice ended the 1948 war, Jordan controlled the Old City and East Jerusalem. Israel, the Jewish State, controlled West Jerusalem. During the Six-Day War the Old City and East Jerusalem were captured by the Israelis and Jerusalem became one city on June 7, 1967. The United States government has never officially recognized Jerusalem as the capital of Israel and maintains its embassy in Tel Aviv though the State of Israel declared Jerusalem its capital city on December 12, 1949. The Vatican also did not recognize the status of Jerusalem and had no diplomatic relations with Israel until the Oslo Agreement of 1993 in which Israel granted limited autonomy to Gaza and Jericho. The Palestinian Authority was to administer these areas while further negotiations were to continue. The last step in the negotiations will involve deciding the status of Jerusalem.

THE OLD CITY

"Jerusalem, built as a city with compact unity" (Ps 122:3).

The Old City is not very old when one considers the history of Jerusalem. Its walls date from the sixteenth century A.D. Its street pattern follows that of Hadrian's second-century rebuild of the city. The Crusaders added ceilings that cover some streets. The original Canaanite was located to the south of the Old City on the Ophel Hill above the Gihon Spring. David took that city and made it his capital (2 Sam 5:6-12). Since there were steep ravines on all but the north side of this city, northwards was the only direction that it could expand. When Solomon built the Temple, he built it north of David's city. Sometime later the city expanded to the west of the Temple area. In the first century, the city began expanding to the north again. Two unsuccessful wars with Rome ended the expansion. When the Byzantines built their wall around Jerusalem in the fourth century, they did not include David's city and it was forgotten. When Suleiman the Magnificent rebuilt the walls of Jerusalem four hundred years ago, his intention was to include within the walls all the places that Muslims, Christians, and Jews considered holy. The area enclosed by Suleiman's wall has come to be known as the Old City.

The Old City of Jerusalem as viewed from the east.

Some Cautions. Until you become familiar with the Old City, walking about in it can sometimes be a problem. A map does not always help since street signs in the Muslim Quarter are sometimes defaced or missing. There are plenty of men and boys who will offer "help" or will volunteer to serve as your guide. They expect a "tip" for their "services" and will disappear immediately after receiving your money. It is best to politely but firmly decline their service. You can always get accurate directions from the Christian Information Office. There are, of course, people who will help you if *you* ask. They will not demand a tip.

Because of the tension between the Israelis and the Arabs over the status of Jerusalem, one needs to be careful about walking in the Muslim Quarter. It is best not to go alone—this is especially true of women. Also it is important for both women and men to respect the standards of modest dress expected of guests here. Avoid behavior that calls attention to your presence. There are many children about the streets of the Muslim Quarter and most are as curious as are all children; that is part of their charm. Also, some school-age children will practice their English skills with you.

Be aware of your wallet or purse because pickpockets work congested areas in the Old City. Do not place anything of value in a backpack because thieves can go through it without your realizing it. Be alert to your surroundings and always look as if you know where you are going. Petty crime used to be almost unknown in Israel, but the situation has changed. Use the same type of vigilance that you would use anywhere and you will have a safe and enjoyable time in the Old City.

Some Help. The Christian Information Office and the Franciscan Pilgrims Office (Mon.–Sat. 8–12; 2–4) are across from the Citadel just inside the Jaffa Gate. Besides providing the usual maps and help to tourists, the staffs are specially skilled in answering questions that Christian visitors to Jerusalem may have. For example, they list the time and place of all Christian worship services in Jerusalem that are open to the public. They also sell pamphlets and booklets that provide help to pilgrims during their stay here. A Franciscan from the Custody of the Holy Land will take reservations for the celebration of Mass at the shrines in Jerusalem. These reservations are necessary and are free of any charge. The city of Jerusalem maintains a tourist office at 17 Jaffa Road (across from City Hall). Sun.–Thurs. 8:30–4:30; Fri. 8:30–12:00.

Photo Opportunities. There are plenty opportunities to take photographs in the Old City. It all looks charming and "oriental." You need to remember that some devout Muslims object to having their picture taken. You need to ask someone's permission before you take their picture—unless you are far enough away. There is no photography allowed at the Western Wall Friday evening to Saturday evening and on Jewish holidays.

Walls and Gates

"And now we have set foot within your gates, O Jerusalem . . . May peace be within your walls . . ." (Ps 122:2, 7).

The walls of the Old City date from the sixteenth century. The Turkish sultan, Suleiman the Magnificent, built them because he feared another crusade. As much as possible the architects used the foundations of earlier walls. That is probably why Suleiman's walls did not include Mount Zion—contrary to the Sultan's instructions. The builders simply followed the outline of Hadrian's wall, which did not include Mount Zion. It is possible to walk the ramparts of Suleiman's wall. The distance is about two and one-half miles. One can begin the walk at the following gates: Jaffa, Zion, St. Stephen's, and Damascus. One can exit at the other gates. Fee. 9–5 daily. The ticket is good for two days.

The Eastern Section. The eastern section of the wall is 2,540 feet in length with two gates: The Golden Gate and St. Stephen's Gate.
   The Golden Gate was closed by Muslims in the seventh century when they denied access to Haram to all non-Muslims. The gate's name is the result of confusing the Greek *horaia* (beautiful; see Acts 3:2, 10) with the Latin *aurea* (golden). Before the Crusades, the Muslims opened the gate on Palm Sunday and the Feast of the Exaltation of the Cross. The Muslims call one part of the gate the Gate of Mercy and the other the Gate of Penance. According to Jewish tradition, it is the gate through which the Messiah will enter the city from the Mount of Olives (see Zech 14:4). A medieval Jewish tradition holds that the Muslims blocked the gate to prevent the Messiah's entrance.

St. Stephen's Gate (H: Shaᶜar Ariyot "Lions' Gate"; A: Bab Sittna Mariam "Mary's Gate"). The gate's Hebrew name comes from the lions carved on each side of it. The Arabic name honors Mary since one pious belief holds that the house of Joachim and Anna was just inside the gate (St. Ann's Church). Another pious belief locates their home in Sepphoris, a town near Nazareth. It is called St. Stephen's Gate because pilgrims from the Crusader period honored St. Stephen's martyrdom just outside this gate. The Byzantines located the place of the Protomartyr's death outside the Damascus Gate. They built a church in his honor nearby. After Saladin defeated the Crusaders at the Horns of Hattin in 1187, he forbade Christians from gathering to the north of the city, the only vulnerable approach. Christian pilgrims moved their devotions on the eastern side of the city and with this move went the "tradition" about the site of St. Stephen's martyrdom. A short walk from this gate down al-Mujahadeen Road is the beginning of the Via Dolorosa. During the 1967 war, Israeli Defense Forces made their first entrance to the Old City through this gate that opens to the Muslim Quarter.

The Northern Section. The northern section of the wall is 4,270 feet in length and has three gates: Herod's Gate, the Damascus Gate, and the New Gate.

Herod's Gate: (A: Bab al-Zahir; H: Shaᶜar HaPrachim, "Flowers Gate"). Medieval pilgrims were told by their guides that a house inside this gate was the house of Herod Antipas; hence, the name of the gate. In both Hebrew and Arabic, this gate is known as the Flowers Gate because of the floral decoration on the outer walls of the gate. This gate leads into the Muslim Quarter.

Damascus Gate: (H: Shaᶜar Shkem "The Gate of Shechem"; A: Bab el-Amud, "the Gate of the Column"). This is the largest and most impressive of the gates. It was the northern terminus of the Cardo, the main north-south street of Hadrian's city. The Romans also built two arched gates that have been excavated and can be seen below the present gate. In Hebrew this gate is named after the town of Shechem (Nablus) because the gate opens on the road that leads to this city. The Arabic name for the gate probably recalls the column that stood just inside this gate during the Byzantine period (see the Madeba map). This gate leads to the Khan es-Zeit, "the Inn of the Olives," the main commercial street of the Muslim Quarter and el-Wad Road (H: HaGai; the Valley Road) that crosses the Via Dolorosa at the Third Station and leads to the Western Wall esplanade. Excavations: Daily 9–4, Friday 9–1. Fee.

New Gate: (H: Shaᶜar Hadash; A: Bab el Jadid). This gate was cut into the wall in 1887 to ease movement to what was then the northern suburbs. It leads to the Christian quarter of the city. Nearby are the cathedral of the Latin Patriarch and the St. Savior's Monastery, the headquarters of the Franciscan Custody of the Holy Land, and other Christian institutions. Unlike Herod's and the Damascus Gates, entering the Old City by the New Gate does not require a left and then right turn. This gate opens directly into the Old City. The more complicated entrances of the other gates were defensive measures taken by the Turkish builders of the walls. The L-shaped entrance of these gates was intended to prevent a cavalry charge into the city and to slow down soldiers entering on foot.

The Western Section. The western section of the wall is 2,900 feet long and has only one gate: **Jaffa Gate** (H: Sha'ar Yafo; A: Bab el-Khalil "The Gate of the Friend"). In Hebrew this gate is named for the road leading from it to the west going to Jaffa. It was also the western end of the *Decumanus,* the main east-west street of Hadrian's city. Part of the wall at the Jaffa Gate was dismantled to allow Wilhelm II and his entourage to enter the city on horseback in 1898. In Arabic this gate is named for Abraham ("the friend of God" in Islamic tradition) because the road going to the south from this gate leads to Hebron where Abraham is buried. The Jaffa Gate opens to David Street, where are found many tourist shops and some restaurants. From David Street one can walk to both the Christian and Jewish Quarters. Turning right from the Jaffa Gate leads to the Armenian Quarter.

The Southern Section. The southern portion of the wall is 1,100 feet long and has two gates: the Zion Gate and the Dung Gate.

Zion Gate: (A: Bab en Nabi Daoud "Gate of the Prophet David"). Mount Zion, with its Jewish and Christian shrines, is located just outside this gate and was a part of Jerusalem until Hadrian failed to include it in the walls he built. Suleiman's architects, building on Hadrian's foundations, also failed to include the shrines on Mount Zion. After walking through the gate, taking the road straight ahead will take you to the Jewish Quarter. Turning around on that road will take you to the Armenian Quarter. The gate's façade is heavily pockmarked due to the heavy fighting that took place here in 1948.

Dung Gate: (A: "Gate of the Moors"; see Neh 3:13). The area outside the gate served as the city's refuse dump in the second century. This is the gate closest to the Western Wall. It tends to be very congested with tour buses. It is best to avoid this area if you are getting around Jerusalem by car. On Mondays and Thursdays, families whose sons have just celebrated their bar mitzvah at the Western Wall have picnics in the area outside the gate.

The Four Quarters

"So Hilkiah the priest . . . and Asaiah betook themselves to the Second Quarter in Jerusalem, where the prophetess Huldah resided" (2 Kgs 22:14).

The residents of the Old City live in separate sections, depending on the religious affiliation. Each section's residents live near the shrine of their respective communities. The Moslems live north of the Haram, the Jews live west of the Western Wall, the Armenians live south of the Cathedral of St. James, and the Greek and Latin Christians live north and west of the Holy Sepulchre. The division of the Old City into separate quarters dates from the Mandate Period. Before that time, the population in the Old City was more mixed than it is today.

The Muslim Quarter is the northeast quadrant of the Old City. One enters this quarter through the Damascus Gate, Herod's Gate, or St. Stephen's Gate. It is the largest of the quarters in area and density of population. Since 1967, Israeli Jews have been moving into the quarter. For example, Ariel Sharon, an important Likud politician, purchased a home on el-Wad Street. He does not live there, but has allowed some religious nationalists to use it. There are always soldiers there for security. Jewish presence in the Muslim Quarter is a matter of some tension though Jews lived there before 1948.

Most of the shops in the Muslim Quarter service the local population. The commercial area storms the senses with a mass of sights, smells, and sounds. For example, the sheep and beef quarters hanging from hooks take some getting used to by people accustomed to buying their meat in small cellophane-wrapped packages. The spice and coffee shops combine to give the area a distinctive aroma. There are restaurants where you can have a falafel or a full meal. The Arab pastries are particularly tempting to the eye. There are shops that sell everything from gold jewelry to power tools, from Levis to Nikes. Before the Intifada, Israelis frequented the shops of the Arab *suq* (bazaar) looking for bargains.

From the Damascus Gate the road to the left is **el-Wad** (H: HaGai; the Valley) Road. It leads to several entrances to the Temple Mount and its Islamic shrines. These entrances are for Moslems only. Other visitors enter the Temple Mount area by walking up the incline from the plaza in front of the Western Wall. While walking along el-Wad Road, you may find a home with a picture of the Dome of the Rock and Mecca's shrine in Ka'aba painted on the wall. This shows that the residents of that home have made the pilgrimage to Mecca required of Muslims.

Also look for the fountains that are remnants of the Turkish Period. Though they no longer are in use, they still give an idea of Muslim art with its emphasis on geometric, floral, and scribal patterns rather than human or animal forms. This emphasis is necessary since Islam prohibits the depiction of the latter. Among the sites of the Muslim Quarter are:

St. Ann's Church (see also Bethesda, Pool of). There are two legends about the birthplace of Mary. One from the Byzantine Period locates the home of Joachim and Anna in Sepphoris where there is a small church to commemorate Mary's birth. A Crusader-period legend locates Mary's birthplace in Jerusalem in a cave near the Pool of Bethesda. They built a church on the site. Entrance to the cave is in the nave of the church. When the Muslims ended Crusader control of Jerusalem, the built-up animosity led them to use the church as a stable and later as a garbage dump. Ironically, this preserved the pristine character of the church's architecture from modification, motivated by piety rather than aesthetics. When the Muslims returned the structure to the control of French authorities, the building was cleaned and is now the best example of a Crusader church in Israel. Pilgrims are fascinated by its fine acoustics. Priests of the Missionaries of Africa administer the church. It is closed on Sundays. There is a fee charged for entrance to the church and the adjacent Bethesda excavations.

You can reach St. Ann's church from St. Stephen's Gate (Lions' Gate). Entrance to the church is a few feet from the gate on the right. You can also reach the church by entering Herod's Gate and following El Qadisieh Road until it dead-ends at Mujahadeen Road. Turn left and the entrance of the church is a short walk.

Via Dolorosa, near the Ecce Homo Arch.

The **Pool of Bethesda** (John 5:1-15). Near St. Ann's Church excavations have uncovered two adjacent reservoirs. These reservoirs originally served the Temple whose sacrificial cult required large amounts of readily available water to preserve the cleanliness of the site. By the first century, the pool was associated with healing. The Romans built a shrine to Asclepios, the Greek patron of the healing arts, at this site. In the fifth century, the Byzantines built a church on a dam between the two pools to commemorate the healing of the lame man narrated in John 5. The Persians destroyed the church in the seventh century. The Crusaders built a small chapel in what was the left side aisle of the Byzantine church. Little remains of this structure. South of the reservoir, the Crusaders built a church over a cave they believed to be the home of Joachim and Anna where Mary was born. Daily except Sunday: 8–12; 2:30–5. Fee.

The **Via Dolorosa** begins a short distance west of St. Ann's Church. It was in the middle of the sixteenth century that the name *Via Dolorosa* was given to the route along which pilgrims walked in remembrance of Jesus' final journey to Calvary. The current route of the Way of the Cross was determined finally in the nineteenth century when stations 1, 4, 5, and 8 were set in place. Before that time the number of "stations" varied. The current route is based on the premise that the trial of Jesus took place in the Antonia Fortress that was north of the Temple area. The Via Dolorosa passes through a heavily used commercial area. There are tourist shops and a local market. Sometimes pilgrims are disconcerted by the din and crowds on the street, but on the way to Calvary Jesus likely passed through a similar area. In this case, the Via Dolorosa helps recreate the original Way of the Cross. The easiest way to get to the Via Dolorosa is to enter the Old City at Herod's Gate and follow the street until it dead-ends on Mujahadeen Street. Turn right and stop when you reach the Franciscan Monastery of the Flagellation.

The **first station** is in the courtyard of the El-Omariyah school across from the Flagellation Monastery. It is open for visit and prayer only on Fridays at 3:00 p.m. when the Franciscans lead the Way of the Cross.

The **second station** is opposite the entrance of the school. Its location is marked on the wall that abuts the street. The Flagellation Chapel is open 8–12; 2–5. Free.

The **third station** is near the intersection of the Via Dolorosa and El-Wad Road. Next to the station is the Armenian Catholic Patriarchate. Near the station on el-Wad Road, there are large pavers from the early Roman period that were found nine feet below street level when the Israelis installed a sewer system. They raised the pavers to today's street level.

The **fourth station** is in the grounds of the Byzantine Period St. Sophia Church. During the Turkish Period it was converted to baths, which were in use until the eighteenth century.

The **fifth station** is at the intersection of el-Wad Road and where the Via Dolorosa Street resumes and turns west.

The **sixth station** is marked by a fragment of a pillar embedded into the south wall of the street. Part of the building is owned by the Little Sisters of Jesus and houses a school. The sisters also run a small shop that sells pictures

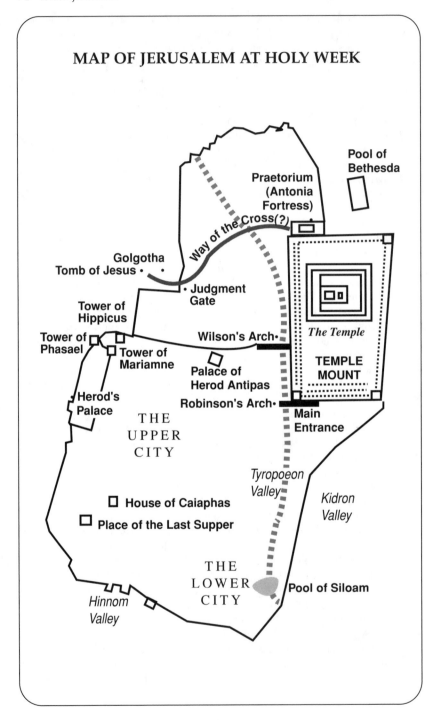

MAP OF JERUSALEM AT HOLY WEEK

of icons laminated on wood. They are not genuine icons, but they are inexpensive and attractive. The proceeds support the charities of the sisters.

The **seventh station** is at the intersection of the Via Dolorosa and Khan es-Zeit (the Byzantine Cardo Maximus). It is a small Coptic Chapel acquired by the Franciscans in 1875. While the area was being cleaned, several large columns and pilasters were found here. Preliminary reports identify them as Crusader. It is at this point that the Via Dolorosa meets an important market in the Muslim Quarter.

To reach the **eighth station** cross the Khan es-Zeit Street and walk up the slight incline of Aqabat el-Khan Street. A building on the south side of the street bears a Latin Cross and the Greek inscription *IC XC NIKA* (Jesus Christ has conquered).

Retrace your steps to Khan es-Zeit Street and turn right. Follow the street until you see a flight of stairs. Walk up the stairs to the Coptic Orthodox Patriarchate to find the **ninth station**.

Return to Khan es-Zeit Street and turn right. At the next intersection turn right again onto the Suq ed-Deabbagha and follow the street to the Church of the Redeemer. It is a Lutheran Church built in 1909 by Kaiser Wilhelm II. You can walk up to its bell tower, which affords a grand view of the Old City. It is a great "photo-op." There is a fee for the tower. Mon.–Sat. 9–1, 2–5:30.

Continue on the same street to the Church of the Holy Sepulchre. As you enter, climb the stairs to the right to Calvary. The **tenth station** is the right nave of the Chapel of the Sorrows. The **eleventh station** is nearby. The **twelfth station** is the Greek Orthodox Chapel. The **thirteenth station** is marked by the small seventeenth-century wooden statue of the Sorrowful Mother.

Take the stairs down from Calvary to the Tomb of Christ, the **fourteenth station**. (Note: A description of the Church of the Holy Sepulchre can be found in the section devoted to the Christian Quarter below.)

At the second station is the **Franciscan Monastery of the Flagellation.** Inside the grounds of the Flagellation Monastery are two chapels. The one on the left is the Chapel of Judgment and the one on the right is the Chapel of Flagellation. At one time, the floor of the Chapel of Judgment was thought to be part of the Lithostrotos (the Stone Pavement, see John 19:13) where the trial before Pilate took place, but excavations under the Ecce Homo Convent next door where the pavement continues have shown that it comes from Hadrian's second-century city. Free. Daily 6–12; 2–5.

Near the Chapel of Flagellation is the **Franciscan Biblical Museum**. The focus here is on the archaeological sites excavated by members of the faculty of the Studium Biblicum Franciscanum located next to the monastery. Among the sites represented are Capernaum, Nazareth, the Herodium, Mount of Olives, Mount Nebo (Jordan), and Bethlehem. Also, on display is one of the best collections of ancient coins in Israel. Mon.–Sat. 9–11:30; Sun. by appointment. Limited to groups of 20. Free.

East of the Museum is the **Studium Biblicum Franciscanum**, a graduate school of biblical studies and archaeology. Originally the Studium served students from the Franciscan Order, but now its facilities are open to anyone interested in studying the Bible on a graduate level.

Detail of the Dome of the Rock.

The **Ecce Homo Convent** of the Sisters of Zion is west of the Flagellation Monastery. It is possible to visit the excavations below the convent. These show that the pavement and the Ecce Homo Arch were not from the Antonia Fortress as once thought but from Hadrian's second-century city. Daily except Sunday 8:30–4.

The Temple Mount (A: Haram es-Sharif "The Noble Sanctuary" H: Har HaMiqdosh "the Temple Mount"). Though there are entrances to the Temple Mount along the Via Dolorosa, these are for Muslims only. All others are to enter by way of the incline that leads from the plaza in front of the Western Wall to the Temple Mount. At the top of the incline is the Gate of the Moors. You will pass through security here. Police will inspect all bags. Entrance to the area is free, but there is a fee to enter the Dome of the Rock, the Aksa Mosque, and the Islamic Museum.

The Haram is the rectangular esplanade in the southeast corner of the Old City. It is atop Mount Moriah (2427 feet above sea level) and is surrounded by walls on all sides. The southern and eastern walls serve as the city's walls as well. The area measures 35.5 acres. This is seventeen percent of the Old City. The platform at the center sanctuary is fourteen feet higher than the rest of the esplanade. It covers 9.2 acres. At the center of the platform is the Dome of the Rock. There are eight staircases that lead up to it. The other major structure in the area is the el-Aksa mosque. There are also about one hundred other structures in the esplanade from different periods beginning with the seventh century. Of course the Arabs consider the Haram to be the most important site in Jerusalem. Though it was the site of the Temple, the platform now supports two Muslim shrines. The Israeli government has allowed the Muslims to retain control of the Haram although the Israeli border police are responsible for security. Muslim authorities, however, control access to the Temple Mount.

Biblical Background. The Second Book of Samuel tells the story of David's purchase of the site that had been a threshing floor belonging to the Jebusite Arauna (24:18-25). David wanted to build a shrine for the Ark there (See 2 Samuel 7). According to the Chronicler, David built an altar here (1 Chr 21:26-30), but it was Solomon who built the First Temple in 950 B.C. (1 Kings 5–8; 2 Chr 3:1). Isaiah experienced his call as a prophet there (Isa 6:1-8). Queen Athaliah who ruled Judah was assassinated outside the Temple (2 Kgs 11:1-20). The building was restored by Joash (2 Kgs 12:5-9) and Josiah (2 Kgs 22:3-7). Jeremiah criticized those who believed that the Temple protected them from God's judgment (Jer 7:1-15; 26:1-6). The Babylonians destroyed the Temple in retaliation for the revolt under Zedekiah in 587 B.C. (2 Kings 25). In a vision, Ezekiel witnessed the worship of Tammuz in the Temple itself (Ezek 8:1-14) and the glory of God leaving the Temple (Ezek 10:18-22). He also saw God's return following the Exile (Ezek 10:1-22; 43:1-12). This inaugurated the Temple's glorious restoration (Ezekiel 40; 44). Post-biblical Jewish tradition identified the Temple Mount with the Mount Moriah that is the site of Abraham's aborted sacrifice of Isaac (Genesis 22).

Cyrus, the king of Persia, defeated the Babylonians in 539 B.C. and urged the Jews in exile to return to Jerusalem and rebuild their Temple (2 Chr 36:23; Ezra 1:2). The prophet Haggai (1:2-11) called the people of Judah to build a temple though most people were indifferent to completing the project. The Second Temple was built after some delays and was dedicated in 515 B.C.— almost twenty-five years after the return (Ezra 4:24; 6:1-18). Eventually the Deuteronomic perspective on the Temple as the only legitimate place for sacrificial worship came to dominate Judaism (see Deuteronomy 12; 2 Kings 22) and the building came to have immense religious significance.

In 167 B.C. Antiochus IV desecrated this Temple by erecting a statue to Zeus upon its altar (1 Macc 1:20-42). This led to the Maccabean revolt. Judas Maccabee defeated Antiochus' armies and rededicated the Temple after removing the offensive statue (1 Macc 4:36-59). This is the origin of the Feast of Hanukkah (H: "dedication"). Internal strife within the Hasmonean family that served as the ruling house of the Jews following the defeat of Antiochus made it easy for the Romans to add Palestine to their empire. Pompey conquered Jerusalem in 63 B.C. and entered the Temple's Holy of Holies. He was surprised to find the room empty.

Herod the Great doubled the size of the Temple esplanade. He had to build large retaining walls to hold the fill brought in to accomplish this. The Western Wall is one of these retaining walls. He rebuilt and beautified the Temple and erected the Antonia fortress in the northwest corner of the Temple Mount. It was Herod's Temple that Jesus visited and where the first Christians worshiped. The Romans destroyed this Temple in A.D. 70.

The Temple figures prominently in the NT. It is the setting for the annunciation to Zachary regarding the birth of John the Baptist (Luke 1:5-25). Mary and Joseph presented Jesus in the Temple according to the requirements of the Law (Luke 2:40-52). During a pilgrimage to the Temple, Jesus remained there unbeknownst to his parents. When they returned to Jerusalem, they found him discussing the Law with scholars (Luke 2:41-52). At the beginning of his ministry, Jesus was taken to the pinnacle of the Temple during his temptations (Luke 4:9-13).

According to John 2:13, the cleansing of the Temple took place at the beginning of Jesus' ministry, while the Synoptics, who have Jesus go to Jerusalem only once during his ministry, must place it at the end (Matt 21:12-17; Mark 11:15-19; Luke 19:45-46). Because John has Jesus make more than one trip to Jerusalem, the Temple provided the setting for several incidents: Jesus met the man he cured at Bethesda (5:14); apparently it was where he explained the reason for his "work" on the Sabbath (5:16-47); and during Sukkot, Jesus spoke about his relationship with God (7:1-53; 8:12-59). The Pharisees brought the woman taken in adultery to Jesus while he was teaching in the Temple (8:1-11). During Hanukkah, which the Fourth Gospel calls the Feast of the Dedication, Jesus went to the Temple and the people asked him if he were the Messiah (10:22-39).

In the Synoptic Gospels, the Temple is the place where the religious authorities challenged Jesus' authority (Matt 21:23). It is where he called attention to the gift of the widow (Mark 12:41-44) and foretold the destruction of

Jerusalem and its Temple (Matt 24:1-25). In the Passion Story, Judas went to the Temple to return the fee given him for betraying Jesus (Matt 27:3-10). As Jesus died, the veil in the Temple was torn in two (Matt 27:52). Acts notes that the first Christians continued to go to the Temple for prayer and while there Peter healed a lame man (Acts 3). Paul too went to the Temple (Acts 21:26) and his presence there caused a riot (Acts 21:27–22:29). The Book of Revelation, however, envisions a new Jerusalem that will not need a temple since God is its temple (Rev 21:22).

History of the Site. After the Romans destroyed the Temple, the site was abandoned until Hadrian built a temple to Jupiter there. Once Christianity became the Empire's religion, the site became a refuse dump. Eusebius informs us that this was done to fulfill the words of Christ in Matt 23:38 (*Theophany* IV). For most of the Byzantine Period, Jews were forbidden to live in Jerusalem. Still, on the Ninth of Ab, when Jews commemorate the two destructions of the Temple, the Christians allowed them to stand on the Mount of Olives and look down at the Temple Mount while praying their lamentations. Jerome notes that the Jews had to buy permits to pray on the Mount of Olives on that day.

When Omar, the Arab caliph who defeated the Byzantines, entered Jerusalem in 638, he was horrified at the sad state of the Temple Mount. After all, the site was sacred to Muslims who regarded it as the place from where Mohammed ascended into heaven. Omar had Monomachus, the Patriarch of Jerusalem, lead the effort to remove all the refuse that littered the site. The Muslims built the Dome of the Rock (691) and the Aksa Mosque (705–715), transforming the Temple Mount into a Muslim shrine. When the Crusaders conquered Jerusalem (1099), they turned both buildings into Christian churches. After their departure (1187), they reverted to Muslim places of prayer. When the Israelis annexed Jerusalem in 1967, they made no changes to the religious status quo on the Haram. The shrines are administered by the Waqf, a Muslim charitable trust. The principal administrator of Muslim affairs in Jerusalem, the Grand Mufti, is an appointee of the King of Jordan, who considers himself to be the guardian of these shrines. Since the establishment of the Palestinian Authority, Yasir Arafat has claimed this authority and appointed his own Grand Mufti.

Rabbinic authorities forbade any Jew from going to the Temple Mount to prevent any possibility of profaning the site of the Holy of Holies. Still, there are some religious Zionists who claim that there are places on the Temple Mount where a Jew can pray without endangering the holiness of the site. They have tried to pray on the Temple Mount. The Muslims forbid anyone but a Muslim from praying on the Haram. A still more problematic phenomenon is the intention of some Jews to begin work on the "Third Temple." For the last few years there have been attempts to lay the cornerstone for this building during Sukkot. Understandably, this has created tensions among the Muslims for they recognize that building a Third Temple would involve the destruction of their shrines.

There is a curious alliance between the Jews who want to build a Third Temple and some fundamentalist Christians. The latter want this building to go forward because it is necessary for the fulfillment of their eschatological vision. They believe the Temple must be rebuilt before the return of Christ. Every year, evangelicals and fundamentalists from around the world gather in Jerusalem for Sukkot and one purpose is to encourage Jews to build the Third Temple. The Israeli government opposes this project, in part, because of the havoc it would cause throughout the Muslim world.

Unfortunately, this area has been the sight of several tragedies in modern times. In 1951, King Abdullah of Jordan was assassinated outside the Aksa Mosque for his efforts to seek some accommodation with the Israelis. In 1969, a deranged Australian tourist set fire to the Aksa Mosque with the hopes of starting a conflict that would hasten the return of Christ. In 1990, twenty-four Arabs were killed when Israeli police, fearing their lives were in danger, opened fire during a severe disturbance. Though non-Muslims are not to pray on the Temple Mount, surely every visitor's thoughts should turn to the efforts to bring a just peace to the region.

The **Dome of the Rock** is the octagonal building with the Golden Dome. It is sometimes called the Mosque of Omar. It is not a mosque and it was not built by Omar but by Abd el-Malik, the Omayyid Caliph in 691. Its dome covers the rock from which Mohammed ascended to heaven before returning to Mecca. The Koran does not specially mention Jerusalem as the site of Mohammed's ascension though traditional interpretation of Sura 17 understands the site to be Jerusalem. Also there is no historical evidence that Mohammed ever visited Jerusalem. Still, the shrine represents the triumph of the Arab Muslims over the Byzantine Christians. The inscription beneath the cupola calls upon Christians to accept Islam's notion of the Divine Unity, which makes it impossible for God to have a son.

This eight-sided building is one of Jerusalem's most striking sites. Most of its forty-five thousand exterior blue tiles were set in place during the 1950s but some go back to the days of Suleiman. The dome has just been gilded with gold leaf, personally paid for by King Hussein of Jordan. The mosaics on the interior are original and magnificent. The Rock is surrounded by a wooden fence and nearby there is a container holding three hairs from Mohammed's beard. These were gifts to the shrine by a Turkish sultan in 1609. There is a declivity at the base of the rock where people gather for prayer. They believe that the souls of the dead are present there for worship. In this room, you can see the oldest *mirhab* (eighth century) in Jerusalem. A *mirhab* is that feature of a mosque that orients worshipers toward Mecca.

The **al-Aksa Mosque** ("The Farthest Mosque"—the name given to the mosque where Mohammed prayed before his ascension). The original building dates to 670. There is little that remains of this building which was larger than the present one. This building can hold five thousand worshipers, but that is usually not big enough for Friday noon prayers that are held outdoors. Mussolini donated the white Carrara pillars in the building. The back wall of the mosque has undergone extensive repairs over the last twenty years because the fire of 1969 severely damaged it. Recently the silver-colored dome was replaced by a lead dome that is much darker in color.

Interior of the Dome of the Rock.

The **Islamic Museum**. This houses a display of items from the Haram and its buildings. It should not be confused with the Museum of Islamic Art, which is in the new city at 2 Palmach Street and focuses on the arts and crafts of the Islamic world. Entrance to site and mosques: Daily 8–11:30; 12:30–2. Summer 12:30–4. Friday closed. Islamic Museum: Daily except Friday 12–3. Entrance to the site is free. There is a fee to visit the mosques and the museum.

The Jewish Quarter is the southeast quadrant of the Old City. The buildings in this quarter were almost entirely rebuilt. Most of the area was destroyed after the Jews left the area during the 1948 war. While some buildings have been restored, most are new though they have been designed to mesh with the architectural character of the Old City. While builders were laying the foundations for many of the Jewish Quarter's new buildings, several archaeological discoveries were made. These have been integrated into the layout of the quarter and several exist as part of new structures. Among the archaeological discoveries that visitors can examine are:

The **German Hospice**. At the top of the stairs leading to the Western Wall at Rabbi Judah Halevi St. These are the ruins of a Crusader Period church destroyed by Saladin in the twelfth century.

The **Burnt House**. West of the stairs on Tiferet Yisrael St. (H: "Blossoming of Israel"), this house was destroyed during the First Revolt against Rome. An excellent multimedia show recreates the dramatic events and highlights the archaeological finds. The house belonged to an aristocratic family and was located in the Upper City that remained in Jewish hands for a month after the fall of the Temple. An Aramaic inscription on a stone weight has led to the conclusion that the house was owned by a certain Bar Kathros. Fee. Buy the combination ticket that will also admit you to the Wohl Museum. Sun.–Thurs. 9–5; Fri. 9–1; closed Saturday. The slide show is shown in English every two hours from 9:30. Fee.

Wohl Archaeological Museum. Located on HaKaraim St. (H: "Karaites") just off Hurvah Square. This museum, located ten feet below the present street level, houses the reconstructed remains of six mansions from the early Roman period. The area is sometimes called "The Herodian Quarter." These six mansions were the homes of the wealthy who lived in the Upper City across the Tyropaean Valley from the Temple. The largest house of the six covers an area of two thousand square feet. The houses are similar in design to the villas of Pompeii. One of the houses has been restored to show the Roman destruction in A.D. 70. Fee. A combination ticket will also admit you to Burnt House. Sun.–Thurs. 9–5; Fri. 9–1. Closed Saturday. Fee.

The **Nea Church** (G: "the New Church"). Down a staircase on the south side of the Bate Mahse square you will find the remnants of one apse from this Byzantine church. The size of the apse will give you an idea of the immense proportions of this church. Along the wall are diagrams with the archaeologist's reconstruction of this church that extend from here to the Cardo. This is an archaeological site—not a shrine or active church. The way to it is not posted very well, but entrance is free. Sun.–Thurs. 9–5; Fri. 9–1.

The **Four Sephardi Synagogues**. Located near the northeast corner of the parking lot in the Jewish Quarter. These are four interconnected synagogues that date from the sixteenth century. They were founded by Jews from Spain. They were built below street level because the Muslim rulers of Jerusalem required that synagogues be built below the level of mosques. They were restored after 1967. From 1948 to 1967, the Jordanians used them as warehouses. Pictures in a small museum show the condition of the synagogues during this period.

The first synagogue is named in honor of Rabbi Yohanan ben Zakkai, a first-century rabbi who is said to have taught on this spot. The unusual feature of this synagogue is its double ark. The Eliyahu HaNavi (Elijah the prophet) synagogue is the oldest of the four. A chair near the door is reserved for Elijah because of the story that he once came as the tenth man (to make the required number [minyan] for prayer) on one Yom Kippur. The smallest of the four is the Emtza'i (middle) synagogue. The art work on the ceiling is original. The Istanbuli Synagogue was founded by Turkish Jews in 1764. The ark, which houses the Torah scrolls, and the bema, the platform from which one reads the Torah, were imported from Italy. Sun.–Thurs. 9–4; Fri. 9–1. Fee.

Hurva Square. This is a public square east of the reconstructed Cardo. It derives its name from the **Hurva Synagogue** whose arch dominates the area. It was built in 1700 and destroyed twice. Its original name was the Judah Ha-Hasid Synagogue, but it received the nickname *Hurva* (H: "ruin") because of its sad history. The arch and four broken walls are all that remain after its destruction during the 1948 war.

Below the Hurva Synagogue is another Jewish place of prayer named in honor of **Ramban** (Rabbi Moshe ben Nachman, also known as Nachmanides) who visited Jerusalem from Spain in 1267. He founded a synagogue in what is now the Jewish Quarter seven years after a massacre of Jews in Jerusalem. In 1473, the synagogue was taken from the Jewish community, but later restored to it by the Mamluke sultan. In 1599 the synagogue was again taken from the Jews and became a cheesemaker's shop. After the 1967 war, the synagogue was restored and is again a place for prayer. It is likely that this synagogue is Jerusalem's oldest. Above the Ramban synagogue is the only minaret in the Jewish Quarter. It was part of the Sidna Omar mosque located south of the synagogue. Today the Ramban synagogue serves the residents of the Jewish Quarter and is a popular place for worship. Daily 10–1. Fee.

The **Broad Wall** is on Plugat HaKotel St. (H: "Division of the Wall") to the north of Hurva Square. Here is a section of a wall probably built by Hezekiah when the population of Jerusalem swelled with refugees following the fall of Samaria in 721, and there was need to protect the city from the Assyrians. The Bible does not mention the building of this wall, but it may enclose what the Bible calls the *Mishneh* or Second (Quarter) (2 Kgs 22:14). There may be an allusion to the building of this wall in Isa 22:10: "you counted the houses of Jerusalem, and you broke down the houses to fortify the wall." The section that can be seen is 23 feet by 131 feet. What we see are the foundations of the wall. The visible part of the wall would have been of dressed stones.

The **Cardo** (L: "the hinge"). This is the principal north-south street in a Roman and Byzantine city. The part of the Cardo that has been reconstructed is the Byzantine Period extension of Hadrian's Cardo that was a commercial center housing shops. There is also evidence of the reuse of the area in the Crusader Period. Part of the Cardo has been converted to a shopping area for tourists. Portions of Israelite and Hasmonean Period walls are visible in this area. The shops are closed on Saturday.

The **Western Wall** (formerly known as the Wailing Wall; H: HaKotel "The Wall"). This is what remains from the Temple area built by Herod the Great. It served as a retaining wall that kept the platform on which the Temple was built from eroding into the Tyropean Valley below. When the Romans destroyed the Temple in A.D. 70, they did not dismantle this wall—probably because debris from the top of the Temple Mount filled the space below and protected it. It serves then as the tangible connection with the Temple of Jerusalem. One can see Herodian stones (the bottom seven courses of the wall). The courses above these were added during the Ottoman Period and differ in style from the massive and exquisitely bossed Herodian stones. There are another seventeen courses of Herodian stone below the present street level. The name "Wailing Wall" was given to this area by the British who witnessed religious Jews lamenting the destruction of the Temple. Between 1948 and 1967, when Jordan ruled Jerusalem, Jews were not allowed to pray at the wall. The plaza in front of the wall dates from 1967. The Israelis bulldozed a housing area to create it.

The Western Wall serves as an outdoor synagogue so men and women have separate sections for prayer. It is a favorite site for the celebration of "bar mitzvah," when a boy reaches the age of responsibility (13). This ceremony can be held only on days when the Torah is read in the synagogue service. Those days are Monday, Thursday, and Saturday. To avoid profaning the site, no bar mitzvah ceremonies are held on Saturday, but Monday and Thursday mornings are alive with family celebrations at the wall. On Shabbat, all visitors are to refrain from taking pictures or smoking in the area because of Sabbath observance.

The most direct way to the wall is to walk through the Damascus Gate. At the fork, take the street to the left (el-Wad Street). A ten-minute walk on el-Wad Street will take you directly to the square in front of the wall. A more dramatic entrance is through the Jewish Quarter. From the stairs that lead to the wall from Rabbi Judah haLevi Street, one has a beautiful vista of the area. Before entering the area around the wall, all visitors must pass through security. Anything you are carrying is subject to search. There is also a tunnel that connects the Western Wall area with the Via Dolorosa. The opening of the tunnel in the fall of 1996 caused violent reactions from the Muslims who feared that the tunnel could somehow threaten their shrines that are located on the Haram.

Access to the wall is available at all times. Modest dress is required. Men must wear a head covering. Free.

The **Southern Wall**. The entrance to the archaeological site is just inside the Dung Gate on the right. You will see the kiosk where tickets to the site are purchased. Just before the 1967 war, the Jordanians wanted to build a girls'

Jewish worshipers at the Western Wall.

high school on the area of the archaeological park. This, of course, was before any excavations took place. Before work on the high school began, Jordanian authorities asked Roland de Vaux, O.P., the excavator of Qumran, and Kathleen Kenyon, the excavator of Jericho, to examine the site. They put in some probes and assured the Jordanians that there was nothing of archaeological significance in the area. (Their excavations were never published since de Vaux died before he could prepare his field notes for publication.) When the Israelis annexed Jerusalem in 1967, this was the end of the high school building project. The Israelis decided to excavate in the area despite the assessment of de Vaux and Kenyon. Excavations there have yielded one surprise after another.

The visit begins along the western wall of the Temple platform. This is an extension of the Western Wall, which is just north of the incline leading up to the Haram. In the area facing the wall, one can see evidence of the several uses to which this area was put. In evidence are warehouses and baths. Also visible are large ashlars toppled into this area—no doubt by the Romans who were dismantling the top courses of the wall surrounding the Temple Mount during the destruction of A.D. 70.

If one looks at the wall of the platform carefully, one will see an inscription in Hebrew. It is a citation of Isa 66:14a: "When you see this, your heart shall rejoice, and your bodies flourish like the grass." Excavators suggest that this was inscribed on the wall during the reign of Julian the Apostate, who ruled the Empire from A.D. 361–363. He followed the old Greco-Roman religion. He wanted to reduce the influence of Christians who made up about forty percent of his subjects. His plan was to revive the older religions by re-opening temples and encouraging worship of the old gods. His plans included the reconstruction of Jerusalem's Temple. Julian's sudden death brought an end to these plans and Jewish hopes based on them.

In the same area, one can see Robinson's arch spring from the wall. It is named for the British archaeologist who first uncovered it in the nineteenth century. Before the excavations here, archaeologists assumed that this arch supported a walkway that led from the Temple Mount to the hill across the Tyropean Valley to make access to the Temple easier for those people who lived in what is now the Jewish Quarter. This is how the Holyland Hotel Model of first-century Jerusalem depicted Robinson's arch. Excavations below the arch make it clear that it supported the top of a stairway that led from the Temple Mount to the valley below. The model had to be modified accordingly.

Beyond the wall are the bottom courses of a monumental building that was part of an Arab Period palace complex. Before excavations no one knew of its existence. One can also see evidence in the southern wall of the Haram that there was a walkway from this palace to the Aksa Mosque. Beyond the palace complex to the east, there are Byzantine Period houses, one of which was reconstructed, displaying a fine mosaic floor and several rooms. Turning the corner to the east, one can see remnants of a Crusader tower. In the area below, there are more than sixty *mikveot* (ritual baths) used by pilgrims who had to purify themselves before entering the Temple. Looking back toward the wall, one sees a great stairway leading to double and triple gates to the Temple area. It is clear then that during the Second Temple Period, pilgrims entered the Temple area from the south. Daily 9–4; Fri. 9–2. Closed Saturdays. Fee.

The Armenian Quarter takes up the southwest quadrant of the Old City. It can be reached by entering the Jaffa Gate and walking south along the Armenian Orthodox Patriarchate Road or by entering the Zion Gate and walking west along the wall. After entering the Jaffa Gate and turning right to the Armenian Quarter, you will come on the site of **David's Tower**, also known as the **Citadel**. Fee. Sun.–Thurs. 8:30–4:30; Fri. 8:30–2. Herod the Great built a palace here in 24 B.C. Its entrance had three towers. You can see the one remaining. The Romans who leveled most of Jerusalem in A.D. 70 used the lone remaining part of Herod's palace as a watchtower for their camp. David had nothing to do with this structure though it is also known as David's Tower. This name comes from the assumption of Byzantine Christian pilgrims who believed that only David could have built such an impressive building. When the Muslims came in the seventh century, they were influenced by the Byzantine identification, but they called this site *Mirhab Daud* (A: "David's Place of Prayer"). The Crusaders gave the site the name "Tower of David." This is one example of how a "traditional" identification of a site develops.

The archaeology of the site revealed its complex history. You will see remnants of Hasmonean, Herodian, Roman, Arab, Crusader, Mamluke, and Turkish construction. There is an important biblical connection with this site. Although the details given in the Gospels do not make it possible to pinpoint the site of Jesus' trial, it is likely that when Pilate came to Jerusalem from his residence in Caesarea, he stayed at the Herodian palace, located here. The trial before Pilate probably took place here rather than in the Fortress Antonia, which was a military barracks.

The Citadel offers not only a self-guided tour that points out the elements of the structure from different periods, it also has a modern museum that traces Jerusalem's growth. With well-done relief maps of the city and other visual aids, you will be thoroughly introduced to Jerusalem and its citizens throughout the ages. You can see catapult stones with the inscription LXF of the Tenth Roman Legion (Fratensis) that carried out the destruction of Jerusalem in A.D. 70. Jerusalem's diverse ethnic and religious groups are depicted through handmade dolls whose costumes and poses show careful attention to detail. There is a "Sound and Light Show" at the Citadel. The English version begins at 9:15. Since it cools off considerably at night in Jerusalem, take a jacket or sweater. Fee.

The **Armenians** believe themselves to be the first entire nation to convert to Christianity. They date their conversion to A.D. 303. The first Armenians to come to Jerusalem arrived in the first century as part of the Roman army. More Armenians came to Jerusalem as part of the great influx of pilgrims in the Byzantine Period. Some stayed on and settled, becoming the progenitors of the contemporary community. They established the city's first printery in 1833.

Most Armenian Christians here are not in communion with Rome though there is a small Armenian Catholic community in Jerusalem. The quarter centers on the Armenian Orthodox **Cathedral of St. James,** built on the spot where Armenian tradition holds that Herod Agrippa I had James, the brother of John, beheaded in A.D. 44 (see Acts 12:2). A chapel to the left side of the cathedral holds the relics. The Armenians also honor a tomb under the main altar as that of James the Less, apostle and the first bishop of Jerusalem. The cathedral was built in the twelfth century over two earlier churches. A wooden clapper still calls the worshipers. Bells were forbidden by the Moslem rulers of Jerusalem until 1840 since Mohammed hated their sound. A distinctive Armenian art form is the *kachkar*—an elaborately carved cross. These are inlaid in the walls around the cathedral courtyard. The cathedral is open to visitors only during the service of vespers. Mon.–Fri. 3–3:30; Sat.–Sun. 2:30–3:15.

South of the cathedral on the right is the **Armenian Seminary** that is not open to the public. The entrance to the area of private homes of the quarter is on the left. About two thousand Armenians live here though the area looks deserted except for the few shops on the Armenian Patriarchate Road. There are several pottery shops in this area. The Armenians have become renowned for their distinctive techniques of decorating pottery. Still, the most well known of the Armenian potters has a shop in the Muslim Quarter on Via Dolorosa near the Sixth Station.

Further south on the left is the **Armenian Museum,** which introduces visitors to the world of the Armenian people. It is housed in the old seminary building. The most important part of its collection is related to the liturgy. Also interesting is its collection of the first photographs of Jerusalem taken by an Armenian, Yessayi Gaberdian in the 1850s. There are also artifacts from excavations on Mount Zion. Daily except Sunday and Tuesday, 10–4. Fee.

The Christian Quarter. This is principally a residential area for the Old City's Latin and Orthodox Christians. It is located to the north and west of the Holy Sepulchre. Other than the Holy Sepulchre there are no tourist sites here. Among the Christian institutions located in this part of the Old City are St. Savior's Monastery, the headquarters of the Franciscan Custody of the Holy Land, St. Savior's Church, the Latin Patriarchate, the Greek Orthodox Patriarchate, the Greek Catholic Patriarchate. Also, there are several Catholic schools in the quarter besides Jerusalem's Casa Nova, a hospice for pilgrims.

The Holy Sepulchre is a Crusader Church in the Old City built over the site of the Constantinian Basilica of the *Anastasis* (Resurrection). The best time to visit the church is in the late afternoon. Most tour groups visit earlier in the day. With the great number of people who come here every day, it is important to find a time when the church is less crowded.

   History and Archaeology. Excavations have shown that the area covered by the church was outside the city before the time of Hadrian and his Aelia Capitolina. It is located about 660 feet north of the first wall (the Hasmonean wall) and 390 feet north of the second wall (the Herodian wall). The area was brought inside the city with the Third Wall (c. 41–44 A.D.) built by Agrippa. There is evidence of tombs being quarried in the area from the eighth–sixth centuries B.C. and more in the first century A.D. In 135 Hadrian built a temple to Venus on the site, perhaps to discourage Christian veneration here. Eusebius says that Constantine built his church on this site though this involved the added expense of dismantling the temple to Venus and though the nearby forum had open space available. Constantine's fourth-century basilica was intended to unite the tomb of Jesus and the site of the crucifixion in a single architectural complex. It was dedicated in 335. The Persians destroyed Constantine's basilica in 614. The Patriarch Modestus rebuilt the church with little change to its basic architecture, following the victory of the Emperor Heraclius over the Persians in 628. In 1009, the Caliph Hakim the Mad tore down the church and demolished the tomb. In 1042, the Patriarch Monomachus rebuilt the church after an agreement with the Muslim rulers. He restored the rotunda over the tomb. In front of the tomb was an open court yard called the Holy Garden. The Crusaders incorporated Monomachus's construction in the present structure dedicated in 1149.

   Architecturally, the church represents a transitional form between Romanesque and Gothic. Unfortunately, it is impossible to appreciate the external architecture because of the buildings that abut the church. The room divisions made by the various Christian groups that have rights in the church under the *status quo* make it difficult to see the lines of its internal architecture, though recent renovations have improved the situation.

   The **Authenticity of the Site.** Archaeology has shown that the site was a quarry abandoned about 100 B.C. In one corner of the quarry was a big block of stone left by the quarriers because it was cracked and made of inferior, soft stone. You can see a part of this stone in Adam's Chapel below Calvary. It is not certain when people began to exploit the abandoned quarry for tombs, but such places are ideal for tombs because the quarry eliminated the need to dig down before digging in to make the catacombs for tombs.

The Romans did not have a specific site in Jerusalem designated for executions. When Pilate condemned Jesus, a Roman centurion was appointed to execute the judgment. For some reason, he chose the block of stone abandoned by the quarriers. Jesus died close to the time for the beginning of the Sabbath. His disciples took his body off the cross and looked for the first tomb to place his body temporarily until they could make more permanent arrangements after the Sabbath. When the women returned to the tomb, Jesus' body was gone. The entire area was outside the walls of Jerusalem until A.D. 41 when Herod Agrippa began building a third wall in the north. It was then almost ten years after the death of Jesus that Calvary was included within the city walls.

According to Eusebius, Christians of the first century venerated this spot. With the failure of the First Revolt against Rome and the destruction of the city, this veneration came to a halt. Still, the Christians of Jerusalem remembered the location of Jesus' tomb. Matters got more complicated after the Second Revolt in 135. Hadrian flattened the ruins of Jerusalem. He filled in the area of the quarry to support a platform on which he constructed two buildings that abutted his Cardo and Forum: one building was a Temple to Venus (Aphrodite) and the other was a commercial building. Still, the Christians of Jerusalem kept alive the memory that Jesus' tomb was beneath these new structures.

The Christians of Jerusalem were finally able to do something to mark the site of Jesus' tomb at the beginning of the fourth century when Christianity became a legitimate religion. The bishop of Jerusalem, Makarios, wanted to build a church on the site of Jesus' tomb, but he did not have the money to tear down two buildings and put up a third. The situation changed when Constantine decided to build churches on sites associated with the life of Christ. He sent his mother Helena to locate the appropriate places. The bishop was able to convince her to spend the money necessary to tear down the two Hadrianic buildings and put up the church to honor Christ's resurrection in their place. Helen was convinced by his argumentation though some empty space was just fifty yards away. Building the church in Hadrian's forum would have been much cheaper, but the memory of the local church would not allow it.

The **Visit**. There are many small structures in the area of the church—each with its own traditions. What follows are comments on a few more significant elements in the church. Below the courtyard is a cistern built to exploit the declivity made by the quarry. The pavers are from the Crusader Period. The chapels to the left of the courtyard are Greek Orthodox and were built in the eleventh century. The building to the right is the **Monastery of St. Abraham** where the Greeks believe the sacrifice of Isaac took place. The **stone of unction** just inside the atrium first made an appearance in the twelfth century. The present one dates from the nineteenth century. To the right of the stone is the **Chapel of Adam** where Greek tradition maintains that Adam was buried. One can see the stone of Golgotha and its crack.

Coming back into the atrium, turn right and climb the stairs to the top of **Calvary**. The mosaics on the Latin side are modern except the one depicting the Ascension that is twelfth century. Coming down from Calvary, we go to the **rotunda**. The columns have been restored during repairs made in the 1970s. Several cracked because of the nineteenth-century fire that burnt the aediculum

The stone of unction at the entry to the Church of the Holy Sepulchre.

over the remnants of the tomb. The rotunda looks smaller than it should because portions of it have been converted into stock rooms.

The original **tomb** was cut away from the other tombs in the area by Constantine. John Wilkinson of the British School of Archaeology in Palestine has offered a suggestion of how the tomb looked based on a pre-tenth-century model found at Narbonne, and on pictures of the Holy Sepulchre found on sixth-century pilgrim flasks. It resembled Roman mausoleums. Over the years various aedicules were built over what little remained of the tomb after its destruction by Hakim the Mad. Excavation needs to be done on the tomb to see what is left of the original and what is from the various aedicules built since the 1100s.

Just behind the **Chapel of St. Mary Magdalene,** to the right of the tomb are two rows of pillars. The larger load-bearing ones (inside) are Crusader, the smaller outside ones with their Byzantine basket capitals are from Monomachus' eleventh-century courtyard in front of the Rotunda.

The area just in front of the rotunda is the **Greek Orthodox church.** This is the nave and apse of the Crusader church. Note that the apse orients the church to the east. However, Constantine's church was oriented to the west to face the tomb. Note the stone chalice at the west end of the nave. It marks the "navel of the earth," which Jewish and Christian tradition place in Jerusalem (see Ezek 38:12).

Stairs lead down to lower chapels. As one goes down to the chapels, one can see crosses etched into the wall by pilgrims over the years. The first chapel is Armenian. The mosaic on the floor depicts important shrines in Armenia. Beyond this chapel is one dedicated to St. Helena, who is credited with finding the cross of Jesus in this area. Daily 4:30–8:00; Summer 5–9. Free.

THE CITY OF DAVID

"But David did take the stronghold of Zion, which is the City of David" (2 Sam 5:7).

This area is south of the Old City on the Ophel Hill. To reach the northern entrance to the City of David, descend the slope to the east of the Dung Gate. Continue past the parking lot until you see a building with a blue UN sign. It is at the point where the road begins to curve to the north. The east side of the building faces the Observation Point to the City of David. It is a short descent to the entrance.

The Ophel Hill was the location of the pre-Israelite city. Recent excavations have revealed twenty-five occupational strata, going back to the Chalcolithic Period. Unfortunately, archaeologists had to stop these excavations prematurely because of the disruptions caused by the ultraorthodox Jews who believed that the excavations were disturbing ancient Jewish graves.

Jerusalem came into the Israelite coalition at the time of David, who made it his capital. The Bible refers to the pre-Israelite city as Jebus and its inhabitants Jebusites (1 Chr 11:4). The Book of Joshua mentions Jerusalem as standing on the northern border of Judah (15:8) and states that the Israelites were not able to drive the Jebusites out of the city. It implies that even after Jerusalem came into the Israelite coalition it had a mixed population of Jebusites and Israelites (15:63; see also Judg 1:21). Excavations have brought to light a one-room house from the pre-Israelite period.

The excavations on the Ophel Hill have been prepared for tourists by the National Parks Authority. We will see what might be a retaining wall that made it possible for large structures to be built on the steep slopes of the hill. This may be the Millo (2 Sam 5:9) that the biblical text mentions. We will also see some Iron Age houses that showed evidence of violent destruction during the sixth century B.C.—probably Nebuchadnezzar's destruction of the city that took place in 587 B.C. The archaeologists have also kept on display two stone toilet seats from the eighth century B.C. Excavators cleared out **Warren's Shaft**, another element in ancient Jerusalem's water system. This shaft is named for the British archaeologist who located it in 1867. Second Samuel 5:6-8 asserts that David took the city by having his soldiers climb the shaft—a feat that Alpine mountain climbers had difficulty recreating (See also 1 Chr 11:4-9). Daily 9–4, Friday 9–1. Fee.

MOUNT ZION

"Mount Zion . . . is the city of the great King" (Ps 43:3).

Mount Zion has always been an integral part of Jerusalem. The Bible often uses the name "Zion" to refer to Jerusalem as a whole. Originally Zion referred to a small fortified area on the southeast ridge, south of what would become the Temple Mount (1 Kgs 8:1). This led to the Temple being called Zion, Mount Zion, or the holy hill of Zion (Pss 9:11; 50:2; 76:2; Isa 8:7, 18; Joel 3:17). In the fourth century, Christians called the southwest hill of Jerusalem "Zion." This part of the city was the least damaged during the First Revolt and was close to the Holy Sepulchre. Also, Christians venerated Mount Zion as the location of the Upper Room. It became the site of a large basilica named Holy Mount Zion, the Mother of All Churches. The sixth century Madaba map depicts this church.

In Jesus' day this area was within the walls of the city; however, from the time of Hadrian (135) the area has been left outside the walls. When Suleiman ordered the construction of the present walls of the Old City in the 1500s, he wanted to include within the walls all shrines of the city. He was angry when he discovered that Mount Zion and its shrines were left outside the walls. Just inside the Jaffa Gate, one can see two Muslim tombs. Legend has it that the architects of the city walls were buried there after their execution for failing to include Mount Zion within the city. Zionism, the nineteenth-century political movement that had as its goal the establishment of a Jewish state in Palestine takes its name from Mount Zion. There are three principal tourist sites here: the Cenacle, the Tomb of David, and the Dormition Abbey.

The Cenacle. Walking directly south from the Zion Gate, one comes to a grey metal doorway. This leads to the oratory that looks into the Cenacle. The *Status Quo* allows Catholics to celebrate Mass in the Cenacle itself on Holy Thursday and Pentecost Sunday. At all other times, Mass and any other prayers are said in this oratory that looks into the Cenacle. To gain entrance into the oratory it is necessary to ring the bell and you will be buzzed in. Daily 9–12; 3–6. Free.

Leaving the oratory and turning to the left, one comes to a building complex whose elements are holy to Jew, Christian, and Muslim. Until the Israelis gained control of Mount Zion during the 1948 war, Jews and Christians were unable to enter this area. Upon entering the building, turn left and take the stairs to the second floor. The room at the top of the stairs is the **Cenacle** where most Christians commemorate the Last Supper and the coming of the Holy Spirit on Pentecost. The Syrian Orthodox commemorate these two events at St. Mark's Church on Ararat St. in the Armenian Quarter. They believe this church to be built over St. Mark's house where the Last Supper was held.

To reach the Cenacle, follow the signs that read *Coenaculum* until you come to a building on the left with a round stone column, a remnant of a Byzantine church. Above the entrance is an arch with an inscription in Arabic from the 1400s. The upper floor of the building is the Cenacle. Go up the stairs on the left. The Cenacle is part of the twelfth-century Crusader Church of Our Lady of Mount Zion though there are elements from the earlier Byzantine structure as well. Note the Crusader arches and the coats of arms in the room. Because of disputes between Christians and Jews over this building, the Muslims expelled both in the 1400s and converted it to a mosque. Note the *mirhab* in the southern wall. Daily 8:30–4:30, Friday 8:30–12. Free.

The Tomb of David. Outside the Cenacle and downstairs is a darkened room that contains a cenotaph dating from the Crusader Period. A velvet cloth covers it. The crowns atop the tomb once decorated the Torah scrolls from communities destroyed during the Holocaust. Since it is a Jewish place of prayer, men entering the room need to have their head covered. The first time this site was mentioned as the burial place of David was in 985 in the work of Muqadassi, a Muslim historian. Since then, Jews, Christians, and Muslims have honored the memory of David here. Excavations have revealed a niche behind the cenotaph facing the Temple, and a mosaic from the Roman or Byzantine Period. This led some to conclude that a synagogue stood here. The Pilgrim of Bordeaux maintained that the synagogues of Mount Zion were the meeting places of the first Christian community. Daily 8–5; Friday 8–1. Free.

Dormition Abbey. In the same area is a monastery and church of German Benedictines built in 1910 on land given by the Turkish Sultan to Kaiser Wilhelm II in 1898 when the latter visited Jerusalem. The Kaiser laid the cornerstone of the church and gave it to the Catholics of Germany to complete. It is built over earlier churches that commemorated the place of Mary's Tomb. The interior of the church is decorated with impressive mosaics of scenes from biblical, ecclesiastical, and Benedictine history. There is a mosaic floor with a zodiac whose signs are arranged in a circle of three interlocking rings to represent the Trinity.

The outer circle of the mosaic depicts the prophets and apostles. Downstairs, in the center of the crypt, is a life-size statue of a sleeping Mary. It is made of cherry wood and ivory. In the dome is a mosaic of Jesus surrounded by some women of the Bible. The Greek Orthodox commemorate Mary's Tomb at the base of the Mount of Olives next to Gethsemane. Daily 7–12:30; 2–7. Free.

THE KIDRON VALLEY

". . . Jesus went out with his disciples across the Kidron valley to where there was a garden into which he and his disciples entered" (John 18:1).

The Kidron Valley separates the Mount of Olives from the Old City. The diary of the Jewish pilgrim Benjamin of Tudela tells us in the twelfth century A.D. the Kidron was identified with the Valley of Jehoshaphat (See Joel 3:2, 12). Both Jeremiah (31–40) and Joel speak of this valley in connection with the beginning of God's final intervention in Israel's life. The New Testament probably alludes to the monumental tombs here where Jesus criticizes the honoring of the prophets with such impressive tombs but the failure to observe the prophets' teachings (Matt 23:29).

The Kidron Valley was a favorite place for burials from the time of the Exile until the fall of Jerusalem. It was outside the city and therefore in accord with Jewish practice but near enough to allow the bereaved access to it. The usual pattern for burials at this time involved using natural or quarried caves in the side of bedrock formations that formed the eastern side of this valley. Inside these caves, ledges were cut into the walls and the dead were laid on these ledges so their bodies could desiccate. Once this occurred, the bones were placed in an ossuary that was set further back in the cave. The ledge was free for the next burial. One can still see the openings of these caves along the eastern wall of the valley. The tombs have long since been emptied by robbers or archaeologists.

The Tombs. The Kidron Valley also has four monumental tombs. The northernmost is called **Absalom's Pillar**. The first mention of this monument's relationship with Absalom came during the Crusader Period. Benjamin of Tudela spoke about the pillar standing on the site of Absalom's palace in the Valley of Jehoshaphat (See 2 Sam 18:18.). The monument dates from the later years of the Hellenistic Period (second-first centuries B.C.)—some nine hundred years after Absalom. The next tomb is that of **Jehoshaphat**. It was uncovered in 1924. Inside were found many old Jewish prayer books and other ritual texts. Since these contain the name of God, they are reverently buried rather than destroyed. Evidently the Jews of Jerusalem believed that this tomb provided a fitting burial place. This supposedly was the tomb of King Jehoshaphat who ruled Judah in the ninth century B.C. He was one of the few Judahite kings who received a favorable evaluation by the Deuteronomistic Historian (see 1 Kgs 22:43) though the Chronicler is less positive in his estimate (2 Chr 20:35-37). The Bible, however, states that he was buried in the "City of David" (1 Kgs

Kidron Valley tombs (the tomb of Zechariah is on the right).

22:51; 2 Chr 21:1). The third tomb is that of the **Sons of Hezir**. An inscription on the tomb makes this identification possible. The males of the Hezir family were priests (see Neh 10:20). The tomb has several rooms and dates to the Hasmonean Period. The southernmost of the four monumental tombs is that of **Zechariah**. Another local tradition also places the prophet's tomb on the Mount of Olives. The rabbis dealt with one person and two tombs by stating that the people prepared two tombs for the prophet as a way of making amends for stoning him.

No one has yet thought to protect these great tombs and charge visitors for entering them. They are always open to exploration, but one needs a flashlight, a nimble body to get in and out of tight spots, and great care.

Gihon Spring. The site of ancient Jerusalem's source of water is a short distance south of the tombs. Having a dependable and nearby supply of water was essential for the development of any city. The spring originally percolated water unpredictably. Engineers, however, have controlled the spring so that it releases water evenly. Solomon was proclaimed king here (1 Kgs 1:28-55, esp.

v. 38). Pious Christian tradition calls this "The Fountain of the Virgin" because some Christians located the home of Joachim and Anna at Jerusalem. Here then is where Mary would have drawn water for use in her parents' home.

Hezekiah's Tunnel. This connects the Gihon Spring with the Pool of Siloam. It was prepared during the reign of Hezekiah (2 Kgs 20; 2 Chr 32:30; Sir 48:17) to enable Jerusalem to survive the inevitable siege that the Assyrians would lay once they arrived at the city. The object was to prevent the Assyrians from controlling the city's water supply. This would have forced Jerusalem to surrender in short order. Hezekiah's engineers plugged the spring and had a tunnel dug from the spring that was outside the city walls to the Pool of Siloam that was inside. When this was complete, the entrance to the tunnel from outside the walls was blocked.

Hezekiah's workers split into two groups: one began at the Gihon Spring; the other at the Pool of Siloam. They started cutting into the bedrock, hoping to meet each other. They did meet and inscribed the wall at their place of meeting. This inscription was removed during the Turkish period and is on display in a museum in Istanbul. Though it is remarkable that the two work parties managed to meet, it is probable that they followed a fault in the bed rock to guide their digging. The tunnel is 570 yards long. In the end, the Assyrians lifted their siege and Jerusalem did not fall. The Bible says that an angel came to destroy the Assyrian army while it was in its camp (2 Kgs 19:35-36; 2 Chr 32:21-23). Some interpreters suggest that the text refers to a plague. Still, historians have not been able to find a satisfactory explanation for the lifting of the siege. One possibility is that there were some disturbances in another part of the Assyrian Empire that required the presence of King Sennacherib and his army.

The seemingly miraculous lifting of the Assyrian siege of 701 left some people believing that Jerusalem was inviolable—that despite Judah's infidelity God would never allow the city to fall since it was the place of God's dwelling on earth. It was a matter of divine honor. During the Babylonian crisis about one hundred years later, Jeremiah had a difficult time trying to convince people that Jerusalem was going to fall to Babylon by divine decree. This led some people to call for his death (Jer 26:1-19).

It is possible to wade through the tunnel. The water will be cool. Its height varies, but a person of average height should expect the water to reach thigh level. You will need to wear clothes that you are willing to get wet. A flashlight is essential. Also helpful are nonslip sneakers. It takes twenty to thirty minutes to walk through the tunnel. Daily except Saturday 10–4. Friday 10–2. Fee.

Pool of Siloam (H: Shiloah). This pool figures prominently in the Book of Isaiah. It is the place where Isaiah speaks to Ahaz about Immanuel (Isa 7:3). The prophet also mentions the pool in two oracles against Jerusalem (8:6; 22:9-11). It is the setting for Jesus' cure of a blind man in John 9:7. In Luke 13:4-5, Jesus refers to an accident that occurred here, which is otherwise unknown.

Silwan (H: Kefar HaShiloah). By looking across the Kidron Valley at the village of Silwan, one can see how homes were built along the slopes of the Ophel

Hill during the biblical period. The roof of one house is the porch of the house above it. Also it is possible to see caves in the bedrock below the village that served as tombs in the first century. One of these has acquired the identification "the tomb of Pharaoh's daughter." One of Solomon's wives was "the daughter of pharaoh" (1 Kgs 11:1), but there are no archaeological grounds for this identification.

THE MOUNT OF OLIVES

"That day his feet shall rest upon the Mount of Olives, which is oppo-site Jerusalem to the East" (Zech 14:3).

Both Testaments mention the Mount of Olives several times. When Absalom began his revolt, David fled Jerusalem by crossing here (2 Sam 15:30-32). Solomon built palaces here to house his foreign wives (1 Kgs 11:7-8). Josiah destroyed the altars here during his attempt to centralize all sacrificial worship in the Temple (2 Kgs 23:12-13). According to Ezekiel, before the glory of the Lord left Jerusalem, it paused here (Ezek 11:23). It is the place where the Messiah will make his appearance (Zech 14:3-4). According to John 18:2, Jesus often met his disciples here. It is the place from which Jesus made his triumphal entrance to Jerusalem (Matt 21:1-6) and from where Jesus predicted the destruction of the Temple (Mark 13:3). It is the place where Jesus spent his final night in prayer (Matt 20:30-56; Mark 14; Luke 22). According to Luke, Jesus ascended to heaven from the Mount of Olives (Luke 24:50; Acts 1:4-12).

A good place to get an overview of the Old City, close-by the Judean Wilderness, and part of the modern city is the Panorama on top of the Mount of Olives. The best way to visit most of the other sites on the mount is to start at the Panorama and follow the paths down to the Church of All Nations.

The Panorama. This is located just below the Seven Arches Hotel that sits atop the summit of the Mount of Olives. At the Panorama, we look west toward Jerusalem. Immediately below is a Jewish cemetery. The Mount of Olives is a favorite place for Jews to be buried because of the rabbinic interpretation of Zechariah 14 that expects the Messiah to descend from the Mount of Olives. The dead buried here will be awakened first and join the Messiah in Jerusalem while others will have to make their way here by rolling underground. Immediately in front of the Old City walls is a Muslim cemetery. The Muslims believe the final judgment will take place on Haram es-Sharif. Open at all times. Free.

Directly opposite the Panorama is the **Haram es-Sharif**, the site of the **Dome of the Rock** and the **Aksa Mosque**. One can also see the domes of the **Church of the Holy Sepulchre**: the smaller one over Calvary, the larger one over the Tomb of Jesus. The white steeple nearby is that of **Church of the Redeemer** (Lutheran).

South of the Old City is the **Ophel Hill**, on which David's City stood. Southwest of the Old City is Mount Zion. The Church on its summit is **Dormition**

Abbey. Below it is **St. Peter in Gallicantu.** This church commemorates Peter's denial and the imprisonment of Christ. Daily 8:30–12; 2–5. Fee.

Beyond the Old City to the West, one can see the modern city with its high-rise buildings. The cluster of buildings to the north on the summit of Mount Scopus is the **Hebrew University.** Another campus is in the Givat Ram neighborhood near the Israeli Government Center.

Looking to the south, one can see a hill with a flat top. That is the **Herodium,** one of the several palace-fortress complexes Herod the Great built. The tree-topped hill to the southwest with the barely visible UN flag flying above one of the buildings is the headquarters of the United Nations. It is also known as the **Mount of Evil Counsel.** It received this dubious honor because local legend holds that the meeting of the Sanhedrin during which Caiaphas urged it to take action against Jesus was held there. (See John 11:45-53. The text gives no information about the location of the meeting.)

There are several churches near the top of the Mount of Olives. One that has been renovated recently is the **Eleona Church.** It is across from the Panorama. The word *Eleona* is an Aramaicized version of the Greek word for olive. The enclosure houses a cave associated with the teaching of Jesus—especially the Lord's Prayer (see Luke 11:1-4 that places Jesus' teaching on prayer immediately following his stay in Bethany). In the cloisters are plaques with the Lord's Prayer in many languages. Several churches have been built and destroyed on this spot from the Byzantine Period. The present church dates from 1874. In the courtyard, there is a partial reconstruction of the Byzantine Period church. Daily except Sunday 8:30–12; 3–4:30. Free.

North of the Panorama is the **Church of the Ascension.** It can be recognized by the dome and minaret. What you see are remnants of a Crusader church commemorating the ascension of Jesus (Luke 24:30-32). The Byzantine church built by Constantine was destroyed in the eleventh century. The building now serves as a mosque. The Muslims also believe that Jesus ascended into heaven though this is not mentioned in the Koran. The Arab caretakers will point you to an imprint in the bedrock made by Jesus' foot.

Return to the area of the Panorama and begin moving down the Mount of Olives along the edge of the Jewish cemetery. You will see signs directing you to the **Tombs of the prophets Haggai, Zechariah, and Malachi.** The identification of these tombs as belonging to the prophets rests on local legend. You will need a flashlight to see the inside of the tombs. Entrance is free, but there are always Arab boys around who want to "give" you a candle to illuminate the tombs or to serve as your guide. They expect a tip. Be firm in your refusals if you do not want their help.

Continuing down the mount, one comes to the chapel of **Dominus Flevit** built in 1955 to commemorate Jesus' lamentation over Jerusalem (Matt 21:1-6). The new building incorporates elements from the Byzantine and Crusader churches that stood here. The cupola of the church is intended to look like a teardrop. The view toward the Temple Mount from the altar is magnificent. Daily 8–12; 3–6. Free.

The **Church of Mary Magdalene.** Further down the hill is the church whose golden onion domes make it the most distinctive building on the

Mount of Olives. Tsar Alexander III built it in 1888, but the interior was never completed and is disappointing compared with the exterior. The church does not commemorate any event in the Bible, but was built in honor of Alexander's mother. Tuesday and Thursday 10–11:30. Fee.

At the foot of the Mount of Olives is the Garden of Gethsemane with its ancient olive trees. Olive trees are hardy. They require a minimum of care and have been known to grow continuously for hundreds of years. It is not out of the realm of possibility that these trees were growing in Jesus' day though some consider this unlikely because they assume the Romans cut down the trees on the Mount of Olives during their siege of Jerusalem in A.D. 67–70. It is more likely that the trees in Gethsemane today could have grown from the roots of those trees. Passing through the garden one comes to the **Church of All Nations**. Its name comes from the twelve nations that contributed the funds for its building in 1924. Symbols of these nations can be found on the mosaic that covers the ceiling. It was built over earlier Crusader and Byzantine buildings, remnants of which are still visible. Daily 8–12; 2:30–5; Summer 2:30–6. Free.

After leaving the Garden of Gethsemane and going down to the Jericho road, turn to the left to go down to the Greek Orthodox **Tomb of Mary**. Before going to the tomb, walk along the eastern wall of the enclosure and follow the sign marked "Grotto." That will take you to the Roman Catholic **Grotto of Gethsemane** that commemorates where Jesus left his disciples when he went off to pray (Matt 26:36). After the visit to the grotto, walk down the steps to the tomb of Mary. Upon entering the church, it is necessary to walk down a long flight of steps to the tomb itself. Gethsemane Grotto: Daily 8:30–12; 2:30–5. Free; Tomb of Mary: Daily 6–11:45; 2:30–5:30. Free.

On the eastern slope of the Mount of Olives one can find Bethphage and Bethany. The small church that marks the site of **Bethphage** (Matt 21:1; Mark 11:1; Luke 19:29) commemorates the beginning of Jesus' triumphal entrance to Jerusalem. The Palm Sunday procession begins at this chapel.

Bethany. Neh 11:32 mentions a town called Ananiah, a place of resettlement after the Exile near Jerusalem. W. F. Albright suggested that in the first century this town would have been known as Beth Ananiah (H: the house of Ananiah) that the NT renders as the Greek *Betania*. Today it is an Arab village of about 3600 people, both Muslim and Christian. *Azariyeh*, the Arabic name for the town, derives from the Greek *Lazarion*. *Azariah*, the Hebrew name is based on the Arabic.

The Byzantines believed that this town was the Bethany of the New Testament. John names Bethany as the home of Lazarus and his sisters Mary and Martha (11:1; 12:1-2). Mark identifies it as the home of Simon the Leper (14:3). While Jesus is dining at Simon's home, a woman whom Mark does not identify anoints Jesus' head with perfume (Mark 14:3-9; see also Matt 26:6-13). John 12:1-8 reports a similar episode but identifies Mary, the sister of Martha and Lazarus, as the woman and says that she poured the perfume on Jesus' feet. Luke 7:36-50 has a similar episode taking place in Galilee at the home of a Pharisee named Simon. There, it is an unnamed woman, regarded by Simon as

Bethany. The Latin Roman Catholic Church (left) and Greek Orthodox Church (right) honor Jesus' friends, Martha, Mary, and Lazarus.

a sinner, who pours perfumed oil on Jesus' feet. Luke also has Jesus stop in a village that is home to Martha and Mary, but Luke does not name the village (Luke 10:38-42). John names Bethany as the site of Lazarus' tomb and of his raising by Jesus (11:1-44). John also mentions a place called Bethany that is described as "across the Jordan" (1:28). This place is otherwise unknown. There may be a textual error here. The Syriac reads "the place of crossing over" (Bethabara).

Eusebius (330) and the Bordeaux Pilgrim (333) do not mention a church, but only a crypt containing a tomb at Bethany. St. Jerome, writing in 390, says that a church was built on the site of Lazarus' tomb. The first church then was built sometime between 333 and 390. Egeria (410) describes an Easter Vigil Service at the church. Franciscan Church 7:30–11:30; 2–5:15. Free.

Antiquities. Excavations on an unoccupied hill west of the tomb of Lazarus revealed caves with rooms and a bakery with a small silo. Ceramic finds (oil lamps, storage jars, and pitchers) and coins show that the site was occupied from the sixth century B.C. to the fourteenth century A.D. Excavations at the Church of Lazarus reveal three major occupational levels: (1) twelfth-century (Crusader) convent for Benedictine sisters with some accommodations for pilgrims, (2) a fifth-century (Middle Byzantine) basilica, and (3) a fourth-century (Early Byzantine) basilica. The present church was designed by Barluzzi, the architect for Dominus Flevit and the Church of All Nations, and built in 1954.

The Tomb of Lazarus. The entrance to the tomb is up the hill from the church. Its Muslim guardians will give you a dramatic account of the raising of Lazarus. Near the tomb is a mosque where the Moslems honor el-Uzeir whom they regard as the brother of Lazarus. Above the tomb is a Greek Orthodox church that honors Lazarus. The tomb has a vestibule and a burial chamber. It is quarried out of soft limestone. A flight of twenty-four stairs leads to a small vestibule. Three more steps lead to the burial chamber that contains three niches. Daily 8–12; 2–5. Fee.

EAST JERUSALEM

This area was part of Jordan until 1967. It is opposite the northern gates of the Old City. The population is Arab. Although the Israelis annexed it to their city, most Arabs here do not participate in local or national elections. Their loyalty is to the Palestinian Authority. Most of the sites of interest can be found on three streets: Suleiman St., the street that runs along the northern wall of the Old City; Saladin St., the main commercial street of East Jerusalem, which intersects Suleiman St. at Herod's Gate; and Nablus Road which begins opposite the Damascus Gate.

Suleiman Street. Rockefeller Museum is near the northeast corner of Jericho Road and Suleiman Street. This archaeological museum was built with a $2 million gift from John D. Rockefeller in 1927 while Palestine was under the British Mandate. The museum opened its doors in 1938. It boasts one of the most important collections of antiquities in the region. Its distinctive architecture makes it a Jerusalem landmark. Its courtyard has a fountain and a tiled pool covered with water lilies. It is a thing of beauty in its own right.

The exhibition galleries do not display the artifacts as more modern museums do; still the importance of most of the finds on display demands close study. Every period from the Stone Age to the Crusader Period is covered with some of the most famous discoveries in the history of Syro-Palestinian archaeology on display. The museum has a library and a study collection of ceramics that are open to students and scholars by appointment. The unpublished Dead Sea Scroll fragments are kept in the museum where scholars working on these have facilities for their work. This area is not open to the public. Sun.–Thurs. 10–5; Fri.–Sat. 10–2.

Solomon's Quarries (also known as Zedekiah's Cave or Suleiman's Cave). This limestone quarry is located across from the Central Bus Station on Suleiman St. Such quarries abound in and about Jerusalem. Jewish legend says that Zedekiah fled from the Babylonians in 587 B.C. through a tunnel that connected his palace with this quarry. The Bible describes his escape route and capture in 2 Kings 25:4-5. It is possible to explore the five acres without a flashlight since it is all illuminated. The limestone provides a natural air-conditioning so it can get cool. A light jacket or sweater may be necessary. Daily 9–5. Fee.

The **Central Bus Station of East Jerusalem**. This is the terminus for the nos. 36 and 63 that will take you to Bethany, the no. 75 that goes to the top of the Mount of Olives, and the nos. 22 and 47 bus that goes to Bethlehem. In the front of the station you can find shared taxis that shuttle riders to various Arab suburbs of Jerusalem.

The **Notre Dame Center**. Across from the New Gate. Before 1948, this was a monastery of the Assumptionist Order. Between 1948 and 1967, it was in no man's land between the Israeli and Jordanian sides of Jerusalem. The building was abandoned. After 1967, when Israel annexed East Jerusalem and the Old City, the Assumptionist Order agreed to sell the building to the Israeli Government, but the Vatican voided the sale and purchased the property. The Vatican rehabilitated the building to serve as a hospice for Catholic pilgrims. It also has a snack shop and two fine restaurants.

Saladin Street. This is the main commercial street of East Jerusalem. Whatever goods or services you need can be found somewhere along Saladin Street, from a hairdresser to a money changer, from groceries to stationery and stamps.

W.F. Albright Institute of Archaeology. This is the headquarters of the American Schools of Oriental Research (ASOR—a scholarly association of schools and individuals interested in archaeology). It serves as a kind of accrediting agency for American archaeologists working in Israel. There are other branches of ASOR in Jordan and Cyprus. The Jerusalem center is named for William Foxwell Albright, a giant in the field of biblical archaeology. The Institute offers members a place for research and study and offers grants each year that provide scholars with support for their research. It also provides field archaeologists a place to prepare their reports.

The **Third Wall.** The entrance of the Albright Institute faces Amr be Ela²as Street. If you walk west on that street, almost to Nablus Road, you can see what some suggest are courses of the Third Wall, built by Agrippa to provide additional protection for the city's vulnerable north end. The wall is along the north side of the street.

The **Tombs of the Kings**. This tomb is that of Queen Helene of Adiabene who ruled an ancient kingdom in what is now northern Iraq. The tomb is an example of a family tomb in the Greco-Roman Period. Rabbinic tradition identifies the tomb as that of the father-in-law of Rabbi Akiva who was also active during a first-century famine. He was nicknamed *Kalba Savua* (Aramaic: the sated dog) from the saying that anyone who came to his house as hungry as a dog left it sated. Jews used to come here to pray during drought. The value of a visit to these tombs is that they illustrate what the tomb of Jesus looked like before Constantine built the *Anastasis* (Resurrection) basilica.

Jewish merchants led Queen Helene and two of her sons to convert to Judaism. The queen moved to Jerusalem following her husband's death and the accession of her son Izates to the throne in A.D. 41. During the famine in Jerusalem mentioned in Acts 11:27-30, she imported food from Cyprus and Egypt. She built a palace southeast of the Temple. She returned to Adiabene when her son Izates died in 65 and she died shortly after him. Another son, Monobazes, returned both bodies to Jerusalem for burial in this tomb. Because the First Revolt was on the horizon, the queen's body was not buried in the central room of the tomb, but in a side room behind a secret entrance. The corners of her sarcophagus had to be chipped off to fit into the area. Josephus described this tomb (*Antiquities* 20.17-96, 191; *Jewish Wars* 5.147) and three pyramids on top of the tomb. These no longer exist.

The French archaeologist de Saulcy excavated the tomb in 1863. He was struck by the magnificence of the tombs and pronounced them "The Tombs of the Kings of Judah." This incorrect identification has stuck. The Turks removed several sarcophagi and used them in constructing fountains in the city. De Saulcy discovered Helene's sarcophagus and took it to the Louvre in Paris. The tomb was purchased by a wealthy French family, the Pereyeres, who gave it to the French government.

From the entrance, one walks down twenty-four steps that were probably cut into the ramp that served the area when it was a quarry. Channels were also cut into the center and sides of the stairs to direct rain water into two cisterns. This water was used in preparing bodies for burial. To the left there is an arch cut out of the stone that leads to an eighty-five-square-foot court that was dug out when the area was a quarry. To the left of the vestibule are steps that lead to the burial chambers. There is a round stone that covered the entrance, and grooves in front of the round stone for slabs that would completely seal the tomb. Daily 8:30–5. Fee.

The **American Colony** (H: *Moshava Ameriqanit*) in East Jerusalem was founded by Christians from the U.S. in 1881. Its centerpiece is the American Colony Hotel, which was a residence of the Pasha during the Turkish period. The hotel has fine restaurants and is well known for its Saturday lunch buffet. It is at the north end of Saladin Street past St. George's Cathedral.

Nablus Road. The **Garden Tomb** is north on Nablus Road from the Damascus Gate on the east side of the street. A sign will tell you when to turn into the side-street entrance. The British General Charles Gordon held that the Holy Sepulchre could not be the tomb of Jesus since it was inside the walls of the city. He noticed a hill above what is now the Central Bus Station looked like a skull (the Skull Place of John 19:17). Nearby he found a tomb that he identified as that of Christ. Those who administer this place do not make the kind of claims about it that Gordon did, but it is still a favorite spot for evangelical Christians to remember the death and resurrection of Jesus. It is a well-groomed garden and quiet place for prayer—unlike the Holy Sepulchre. The tomb itself is probably connected with Iron Age tombs found on the property of the adjacent École biblique. Daily 8–12:30; 2:30–5. Free.

The **École biblique** was founded by Marie-Joseph Lagrange, O.P. (1855–1938) in 1890. Lagrange and the École played an important role in the Catholic Church as modern biblical criticism was developing. Lagrange showed that it was possible for Catholics to engage in the scientific study of the Bible without having to compromise their faith. For many years the École offered an excellent program of postdoctoral studies in biblical studies. Recently they have been authorized to grant the doctorate in biblical studies. Professors from the École have been leaders in biblical archaeology. Most notable was the contribution of Roland DeVaux, O.P., who excavated Qumran.

The **Church of St. Stephen**, which serves the Dominican community at the École, dates from the late 1800s. It was constructed over the foundations of a fifth-century basilica built by the Empress Eudocia to house the relics of St. Stephen whose martyrdom the Byzantines located outside the Damascus Gate. Lagrange is buried in this church.

The **Damascus Gate Bus Station**. Here are buses that go to the Arab towns near Jerusalem. It is also the terminus for Egged bus 27. You can take the bus here to the Center of the City, the Central Bus Station on Jaffa Road, to Yad VaShem, and the Hadassah Hospital.

The **American Consulate**. This serves the residents of East Jerusalem. There is another consulate on the western side of the city at 16 Agron St.

St. George's Cathedral. This is the seat of the Anglican Bishop in Jerusalem. At the end of the 1800s, the Anglicans and German Lutherans agreed to have a Protestant bishop in Jerusalem. The idea was to alternate an Anglican and a Lutheran. The First World War found England and Germany on opposite sides so the agreement fell through, but the Anglicans built this cathedral and school and have maintained a bishop here.

WEST JERUSALEM

A Divided City or One City. The Israelis do not care to speak of East Jerusalem and West Jerusalem. For them, it is one city—the undivided capital of the State of Israel. Still, between 1948 and 1967 Jerusalem was a divided city. East Jerusalem and the Old City were part of the Kingdom of Jordan. West Jerusalem was the capital of the State of Israel. The populations of the two are also different. West Jerusalem is almost exclusively Jewish while East Jerusalem has more of a mixed population, but the vast majority are Arabs. Jews used to visit East Jerusalem and especially the Old City to shop for bargains. Since the Intifada began, Jews stay away although there are a few religious and nationalistic Jews who have settled in the Muslim Quarter of the Old City. Some Arabs visit West Jerusalem for shopping, work, and recreation. They are subject to identification checks by the border police as a security measure.

The two parts of Jerusalem obviously have different characters. The western part of the city is a place where eastern and western cultures meet—except for the ultraorthodox neighborhoods where residents live as their ancestors did in Eastern Europe since the sixteenth century. Ironically, these ultraorthodox Jews are like their Muslim Arab cousins who are uncomfortable with the inroads of western culture into their society. Today more Muslim women eschew western dress than was the case twenty years ago. They will wear a loose-fitting robe and a veil. The contrast between the two parts of the city is most obvious after dark. East Jerusalem shuts down at night; the western part of the city comes alive with its clubs, theaters, and concert halls. Though the Israelis speak of one Jerusalem, the Arabs complain that East Jerusalem and the Old City, except for the Jewish Quarter, do not enjoy the same level of city services as does the rest of the city. The final status of Jerusalem is still to be negotiated between Israel and the Palestinian Authority.

The western part of the city dates from only 1860 when Moses Montefiore founded *Mishkenot Shaʿananim*, the first residential quarter outside the Old City. Montefiore encouraged some Jews to set up an agricultural settlement just west of the walled city. This was the beginning of west Jerusalem. He was convinced that the only way the Jews could ever control their fate in Palestine was for them to begin working the land. In 1855, he received permission from the Turkish sultan to acquire land outside the walls of Jerusalem. He built homes and a mill for grinding grain to encourage the Jews to move out of the Old City. From this beginning, west Jerusalem has grown into a city of neighborhoods, each with its distinct character and history. *Mea Sheʿarim* in the center of the city is an ultraorthodox neighborhood where signs warn visitors to act and dress with regard to the religious sensibilities of the residents. *Rehavia,* where the president and prime minister have their official residences, was once *the* address in Jerusalem. *Yemin Moshe* is an artists' quarters with studios and shops selling original works. *Nahalat Shivʿa* is an old residential quarter founded in 1869 but which has now become the city's night club and restaurant center. There are many more neighborhoods in this beautiful city.

What to See. What follows is a partial list, in alphabetical order, of sites that are worth a visit. A comprehensive list with helpful information is available at the Municipal Tourist Office, 17 Jaffa Rd.

The **Bible Lands Museum.** Across the street from the Israel Museum is one of the city's newest museums. It helps the visitor see ancient Israel as part of a wider ancient Near Eastern culture. It contains almost three thousand artifacts illustrating the material culture of the ancient Near East. Sun.–Tues., Thurs. 9:30–5:00; Wed. 1:30–8:30; Fri. 9:30–2:00; Sat. 11:00–3:00. Tours Sun.–Tues., Thurs. at 10. Fee.

The **Biblical Zoo** (The Tisch Family Zoological Gardens in Jerusalem). This is among the most modern and innovative zoos in the world. It was opened in 1994 and replaced an outdated facility. Like many modern zoos, the animals live in open spaces. There are few cages and bars. There are only natural barriers and low fences between the animals and visitors. Though the collection is small, the zoo is growing. Its beautiful setting in the southwestern hills makes it worth a visit. A unique feature of this zoo is that it provides the relevant citation if a particular animal in its collection is mentioned in the Bible. Sun.–Thurs. 9–7; Fri. 9–3; Sat. 10–3. Fee.

Canion Jerushalayim ("The Jerusalem Mall" also known as the Canion Mahla). Restaurants open to midnight. Egged bus no. 6 from the City Hall or no. 31 from King George and Ben Yehuda. This is a modern indoor shopping mall with eight movie screens and several restaurants and fast-food outlets.

City Center (H: Merkaz Ha'ir). The area bounded by Jaffa Road, King George St., and the Ben Yehuda Pedestrian Mall. This is Jerusalem's main shopping, dining, and entertainment district, and is the place "to see and be seen" Saturday night after Shabbat ends.

The **City Hall** (Safra Square). At the corner of Jaffa Road and Paratroopers Street. There is a large menorah at the top of the building. Below the menorah you can see the pockmarks made by Jordanian bullets. These are reminders of the pre-1967 days when the building was just outside "no man's land." Recently, the city expanded its city hall to a civic center. A tour in English is given every Monday at 9:30. Fee.

The **Great Synagogue**. On King George St. near Agron St. This synagogue is next to the Hechal Shlomo, which is the seat of the two chief rabbis of Israel. Its liturgy is "high church," which some consider "stuffy." To an American, it will not appear that formal. If you want to experience the synagogue liturgy, here is one place to visit. The best time to visit is the Saturday morning liturgy that begins about 8:30 and ends about 11:00. You do not have to be present for the whole service. They have an excellent cantor and choir. Men must have a head covering. Women observe the liturgy from an upstairs gallery.

Hadassah Medical Center. Egged bus 27 from the Damascus Road Bus Station. Marc Chagall made twelve stained glass windows for the synagogue of this hospital in 1962. Each window represents one of the Twelve Tribes. Since he was unable to depict the human form (because of Jewish religious sensibilities about images), Chagall's work is an ingenious effort at depicting the characteristics of the tribes in symbolic form. During the 1967 war, the Jordanians shelled the hospital and severely damaged four of the windows, which Chagall replaced. One slightly damaged window was kept as a reminder of the war. The windows are exquisite and well worth the trip to Ein Kerem. Besides, the final leg of the trip gives you a picturesque view of the village and the surrounding Judean hills. English Tours every half hour from 8:30–2:30, Sunday to Thursday. Last tour on Friday is at 11:30. Closed on Saturday.

The **Hebrew University** was founded in 1921. Its campus was on Mount Scopus. After 1948, the campus was surrounded by Jordanian-controlled territory. This made it impossible to use this campus so another campus was built near the Knesset in Givat Ram. After 1967, the main campus was moved back to Mount Scopus and beautiful, modern buildings were constructed. The Givat Ram campus is still used for some courses and also houses the National Library. Free tours of the Mount Scopus Campus in English Thursday at 11 a.m.

The **Holyland Hotel Model.** This is a model of Jerusalem at the beginning of the First Revolt (A.D. 67). Its scale is 1:50. A person of average height would be about 1.25 inches high in this scale. As far as possible the model was built from the types of material used in the construction of first century A.D. Jerusalem and its buildings: marble, limestone, wood, copper, and iron. Professor Michael Avi-Yonah of the Hebrew University served as the first archaeological consultant for the project. Since Avi-Yonah's death, Professor Yoram Tsafrir has guided the continuing work on the model, which is regularly reworked in accord with the results of archaeological work.

Since excavations in Jerusalem are incomplete for practical and religious reasons (people live here and orthodox Jews and Muslims object to excavations) reliance on literary sources in planning this model was necessary. Avi-Yonah used the NT, Josephus, and rabbinic literature (the Mishnah and Talmud) as guides in his reconstruction. These written sources provide geographic details that are incidental and imprecise. The Mishnah (A.D. 200) and

The Holyland Hotel model of first-century A.D. Jerusalem.

Talmud (A.D. 600) are not contemporaneous with the city they attempt to describe. A significant part of the model is speculative, but it still gives a fair idea of Jerusalem at the beginning of the Christian era. Note especially the Herodian structures: the three towers and the Herodian palace in the northwest, the fortress Antonia north of the Temple, the Temple structures (the royal stoa, the enlargement of the platform, and the beautification of the building), the theater, and stadium. Herod engaged in these large-scale building projects to immortalize his name, to secure the loyalty of a hostile population by giving them jobs, and to impress his Roman patrons. Herod Agrippa I (A.D. 41–44) began work on the northernmost wall, which was completed just before the First Revolt in A.D. 67. It did not exist at the time of Jesus' death so Calvary and the site of Jesus' tomb were located outside the "Second Wall" and the "Water Gate." Jerusalem was defended by three walls on its vulnerable northern side. The western, southern, and eastern sides of the cities were bounded by deep valleys and needed only a single wall. At the north end, those who were outside the city were on a higher elevation than the city's defenders. The north side of the city was most susceptible to attack and therefore, the most fortified area.

The model is not definitive but gives the visitor a sense of what first-century Jerusalem looked like. Revising the model is a complicated matter and is not always possible. For example, notice where the theater is placed. This location is in the present-day Jewish Quarter. Following the 1967 war, excavations were possible before rebuilding the quarter devastated between 1948 and 1967. Excavations in the area in which Professor Avi-Yonah placed the theater

provided no evidence at all of the presence of a theater there. But it is imprac-
tical to remove the theater. Where will it be placed? What will take its place on
the model?

Sometimes updating the model is possible. For example, the original
model had Robinson's arch supporting a bridge connecting the Temple area
with the upper city (the present Jewish Quarter). Excavations along the southern wall led by Professor Avi-Yonah himself showed that the stairway led to
the southwest corner of the Temple area. The model was modified to look as it
does now. Excavations have also proved that the main access to the Temple
was from the south through the Huldah gates and not from the west as shown
on the original model. Again, the necessary changes were possible and so were
made.

This model, besides giving visitors an idea of how first-century Jerusalem
looked, helps to illustrate the relationship between literary and material sources
for historical reconstruction. Though there are many literary sources that give
information about the topography and architecture of Jerusalem, archaeology
has shown that the only way to be certain is to excavate. None of the literary
sources—even those from the first century—had as their purpose to provide
topographical and architectural information. Daily 8–9; Friday and Saturday
8–5. Fee.

Israel Museum. This is a collection of museums that emphasize the history
and art of Israel and the Jewish people. There are museums dedicated to the
archaeology of Israel, Judaica, and art. There is a beautiful sculpture garden
and children's museum. There are always some special exhibits and a theater
that shows classic and educational films. The highlight of the museum is the
Shrine of the Book. It is where the Dead Sea Scrolls and other documents
found in the Judean desert are kept. The exterior of Shrine of the Book is
shaped like the lid of the jars in which the scrolls were found. The dome is
white and the walls are black basalt, symbolizing the conflict between light
and darkness—an important motif in the writings of the Qumran community.

The museum is large—too large for a single visit. If you have time for only
one visit concentrate on what is unique to this museum: the archaeological collection and the Dead Sea Scrolls collection. There are guided tours in English
of the various parts of the museum. Check the advertisements in the *Jerusalem
Post* and the tourist information booklets for the times of these tours. They are
very well done and a good way to see the museum. Fee (an additional fee for
the Shrine of the Book). Sun., Mon., Wed., Thurs. 10–5; Tues. 4–10 p.m. Fri.–Sat.
10–4. There is a cafeteria serving dairy and vegetarian meals. Guided Tours: at
4:30 Sun.–Fri. 11 a.m., except Tuesday (highlights of the museum); Shrine of
the Book Sun., Mon., Wed., Thurs. 1:30; Tues. 3:00; Fri. 12:45; Archaeology Galleries Mon.–Thurs. 3:00.

The **Jerusalem Center for the Performing Arts** (the Jerusalem Theater). 20
Marcus Street. Bus 15 from Jaffa Road going east. This is the home of the Jeru-
salem Symphony Orchestra. There is a movie theater here and also the
Sherover Theater for live performances. Check the *Jerusalem Post* or *Events in
Jerusalem* (distributed by the Municipal Tourist Office) for cultural events here.
Tickets may be purchased at the Box Office or at ticket agencies.

Knesset (H: "Assembly"). Bus 9 from the Jaffa Road Central Bus Station. The Knesset is Israel's parliament. When the Knesset is not in session, it is possible to take a tour of the building where the Knesset meets. Your guide will be able to answer all your questions about how the Israeli political system works. The building is worth seeing just for the beauty of its interior architecture. Most striking are tapestries by Marc Chagall that adorn the formal reception area. Tours are on Sunday and Thursday from 8:30–2:30 (The tours are given in English.). You need to show your passport for admittance. When the Knesset is in session (Monday and Tuesday, 4–9 p.m.), you can be admitted to the visitor's gallery to witness the debates that can sometimes be raucous. Of course, the debates are conducted in Hebrew.

Mahaneh Yehuda (H: "The camp of Judah"; popularly known as the Jewish market). On Jaffa Road west of the City Center. Buses 27, 6, 13, 20. This is an outdoor market that sells fresh produce at prices below those of the newer supermarkets. There are also merchants selling bakery goods, sweets, housewares, clothing, nuts, tapes and CDs —and just about anything else. The prices here account for its popularity. It is always crowded, especially on Friday morning.

L.A. Mayer Museum of Islamic Art. 2 HaPalmach St. Tel: 661291. Bus 15. Founded to promote an appreciation of the artistic achievement of Israel's Muslim neighbors, especially Egypt, Syria, Iraq, Iran, and Turkey. Daily 10–5. Tuesday, 4 p.m.–8 p.m.; Friday and Saturday, 10–4. Fee.

Mea She'arim ("One hundred gates" see Gen 26:12). Bus 1. The city's oldest ultraorthodox quarter. The men wear side curls *(pe'ot)* and distinctive clothes. All visitors must dress modestly.

Nahalat Shiva ("the settlement of the seven") is named for the seven founders of the neighborhood established in 1869 in the area now bounded by Jaffa Road, Hillel, Rivlin, and Yoel Salomon Streets. It was renovated in 1990 and is now a pedestrian mall with restaurants, shops, and bars. It is very popular with younger Israelis and visitors.

Yad VaShem (H: "A Monument and a Name"; see Isa 56:5) on Har HaZikaron (H: "the mountain of remembrance"). This is the monument to the victims of the Holocaust. A visit to this place is necessary to have a fundamental understanding of the State of Israel, for the founding of the State is in large part an outcome of the Holocaust. Although it is not always easy to understand someone else's pain, this memorial comes as close as possible to help us understand what it means to be a Jew after 1945. It also shows the horror of antisemitism for which Christians must take responsibility. Egged bus 27 from the Nablus Road bus station and buses 17, 18 from the Central Bus Station on Jaffa Road. Free. Sun.–Thurs. 9–5; Fri. 9–2. Cafeteria.

Upon entering the site, you will walk up a slight tree-lined incline. It is the Avenue of the Righteous Gentiles. Each of the five hundred trees is dedicated to a Gentile who risked his or her life to save Jews during the Nazi Period. This avenue leads to the museum that describes the diversity and vitality of Jewish life in Europe before Nazism. It chronicles the rise of Hitler and the Final Solution. The museum also houses the Hall of Names, which has gathered biographical information on about one half of Hitler's victims.

"Korczak & the Children of the Ghetto," sculpture by Henryk Goldschmidt at Yad VaShem. Janusz Korczak was the head of an orphange in the Warsaw Ghetto. In August 1942, when the Nazis deported the children to Treblinka, he volunteered to join them—and died with them.

Garden memorial to the children of the Holocaust, Yad VaShem.

Across from the museum is the Hall of Remembrance. Inside this dark and silent structure is an eternal flame burning in memory of the six million victims. The ashes of some are buried below the floor that is emblazoned with the names of the death camps. Open areas outside contain sculptures that memorialize the one million children who died in the Holocaust, the Warsaw uprising, and the five thousand Jewish communities that the Nazis destroyed. There is also a facility for scholarly research on the Holocaust.

There are no words to describe the experience of walking through this place. It is impossible to comprehend the evil that this place depicts. The sadness that it evokes is overwhelming. Most moving is the exhibit at the exit of the museum. It is a torn shoe—a child's shoe. This brings the enormity of the Holocaust to a scale that anyone can grasp. It must be a place of pilgrimage for every Christian visitor to Israel. Daily 9–5:30, Friday 9–1. Closed Saturday. Free.

Y.M.C.A. 26 King David Street. Most evenings the Y has a folklore show that is entertaining and enriching. There are two restaurants, a pool, and other athletic facilities available. One can have a marvelous view of Jerusalem from the building's tower. The Madaba map is reproduced on the floor of the entrance.

CHAPTER SIX

Israel: The Jerusalem Area

THE JUDEAN HILLS

"Mountains and hills, bless the Lord" (Dan 3:75).

The Judean hills are part of the central highlands that run north to south through Israel. Historically this was the core of the Kingdom of Judah that emerged following the breakup of the Davidic-Solomonic Empire (921 B.C.) and lasted until the destruction of Jerusalem (587 B.C.). The Judean hills begin at Mount Baal Hazor in the north (about seven miles north of Ramallah) and end at Beersheva. Their western boundary is the Shephelah (see below) and their eastern boundary is the Judean desert. Most of this region is part of the West Bank. Its future political status will be negotiated with the Palestinian Authority.

The agricultural potential of these hills was not easily exploited in antiquity. The building and maintenance of **terraces** were necessary. This is very labor-intensive agriculture. Natural stepped-limestone formations provided the foundation for the terraces. At the front of the horizontal surface, the farmer built a retaining wall of field stones. It is this retaining wall that is the telltale sign of terracing. The farmer filled the space created by the retaining wall with gravel and fill. Atop the fill, he placed silt and organic matter that formed a rich soil. Terraces prevented large-scale erosion. Rain was absorbed by the fill beneath the soil. When the soil could absorb no more, the excess flowed slowly to the terrace below.

At first these terraces were used to grow grain, which was the dietary staple. Later, with the development of large estates in place of family farming (See Isa 5:8), these terraces were given over to the production of olives—also a dietary staple (the oil was used to eat with bread and for cooking). The oil was also needed for lamps. The large estates, however, produced olive oil for export. This made less land available for the production of grain, which, in turn, led to higher prices and great misery for the poor. One can still see the terraces on these hills.

Abu Gosh

". . . The inhabitants of Kiriath-jearim came for the ark of the LORD *and brought it into the house of Abinadab on the hill . . ."* (1 Sam 7:1).

Location. This is a Muslim Arab village about eight miles from Jerusalem. Its name recalls a sixteenth-century Arab sheik who imposed tolls on travelers to Jerusalem. He always held Franciscans for ransom if he could because he knew that the Custody of the Holy Land would redeem them. The museum of the Custody has a few of the ransom notes. The coming of the railroad link between Jaffa and Jerusalem ruined what became a profitable family business. Descendants of Abu Gosh still live in the village, but they have found other means of support. You can reach Abu Gosh by taking an intercity bus from the Central Bus Station on Jaffa Road, where you can find information about schedules and fares.

History. This is the Kiriath-jearim of the Bible. It was one of the four Gibeonite cities that made treaties with Joshua and escaped destruction (Josh 9:17). After the Philistines returned the Ark to the Israelites, following their capture of this Israelite battle palladium (1 Sam 4:4-11; 5:1–6:21), it remained here in the home of Abinadab under the guardianship of Eleazar. Arabs call the site of the Byzantine church built to commemorate this *Deir el ʿAzar* ("the monastery of Azar" apparently after Eleazar). After David took Jerusalem (2 Sam 5:6-12), he personally went to Kiriath-jearim to escort the Ark to his city (1 Chr 13:5-8). The Byzantines believed the site to be the place of Abinadab's house since the Bible says that it was located on a hill (1 Sam 7:1).

The Churches. In 1924, a church was built on the foundations of the Byzantine Period basilica. The site is visible from a distance not only because of its location on a hill but also because of the huge statue of Mary holding the infant Jesus on the roof of the building. The French sisters who live in the convent next to the church call it *Notre Dame de l'Arche d'Alliance.* Daily 8:30–12:00; 3–5. Free.

The other church in the town, which serves a Benedictine community of women and men, was built in 1899 over the foundations of a Crusader church built in 1142 and destroyed in 1187. The building is a good example of Crusader architectural style. Below the church is a Roman Period pool built over a spring. Evidently the Crusaders built their church over a Roman Period structure—perhaps a fortress since there is an inscription placed there by the famous Tenth Legion (Fretensis) stationed in Jerusalem during the first century A.D. The Benedictines welcome visitors to their Sunday morning Mass whose liturgy is enhanced with Gregorian chant. Daily 8:30–12:00, 3–5. Free.

Ein Kerem

". . . among those born of women there has been none greater than John the Baptist" (Matt 11:11).

Location. This Jewish village lies in a small valley between Mount Herzl and the Hadassah Hospital at the southwestern end of Jerusalem. Before 1948, Ein

Kerem was an Arab village. During the war, the Arabs left and have not been allowed to return. Its name means "the well of the vineyard." It is not difficult to imagine grapes being cultivated on the terraces in the surrounding hills. You can reach Ein Kerem by taking bus no. 17 from the Central Bus Station on Jaffa Road. The line ends at St. John's Church.

History. Christians honor the village as the birthplace of John the Baptist though the NT does not name the place of the Baptist's birth. Several early Christian writers, i.e., Jerome and Augustine, maintained that John was born in Jerusalem though other sites including Hebron have been suggested. The first text that associates Ein Kerem with John the Baptist is a Jerusalem lectionary from the late Byzantine Period.

St. John's Church. The Franciscans came to the village and bought the Crusader Church of St. John in 1621 from the Ottoman Turks. The latter had a change of heart, confiscated the church and used it as a stable. In 1674 the Ottoman authorities again gave permission to the Franciscans to take possession of the church. Its restoration was in progress until the end of the 1800s. Excavations in front of the church revealed the existence of two Byzantine Period churches next to one another. The one below the entrance of the modern church has a mosaic floor with an inscription that reads: "Hail, martyrs of God." You can view this mosaic through a grill just before the entrance of the modern church. South of this church is another with a single apse. Also discovered near the churches were Herodian and Byzantine Period tombs, terraces and wine presses, and a statue of Aphrodite that suggest that this area was used for worship before the Christian era. The Byzantines simply replaced Ein Kerem's Greco-Roman cult with a Christian one.

In the church now in use, there is a grotto at the end of the left aisle that is venerated as the spot of John's birth (Luke 1:5-25). The blue and white tiles of the interior date from the 1865 renovation of the building. These tiles reflect the aesthetics of the Spanish benefactors who underwrote the renovation. Although extensively refurbished, this church is essentially a Crusader structure. The text of Zechariah's Canticle (the *Benedictus*; Luke 1:68-79) in several languages adorns the walls of the courtyard in front of the church. Daily 8:30– 12:00; 3–5. Free.

The Church of the Visitation (see Luke 1:39-56). Walking to the south past the spring from which the town derives its name, you can walk up a hill to the Church of the Visitation. Again, the location is not determined by the NT but by Byzantine Period texts. The church has two stories. The lower story is a converted Byzantine Period cistern. In an alcove is a rock behind which, according to legend, Elizabeth hid John from Herod's soldiers at the time of the slaughter of the innocents that Matthew describes in 2:16-18. The upper story is a church completed in 1938 reusing the apse of a twelfth-century Crusader church. The walls of the upper church are decorated with pictures relating to the church's veneration of Mary. One pictures the Council of Ephesus, which proclaimed Mary the Mother of God. Next is a portrait of Mary as the Mother of Mercy. There is also a portrait of the wedding at Cana (John 2:1-11). Another painting depicts a papal legate blessing the sword of the admiral who led the Christian

Church of Saint John the Baptist in the hills of Ein Kerem.

fleet at the Battle of Lepanto (1571) against the Turks. The last picture shows the Franciscan Duns Scotus defending the Immaculate Conception at the University of Paris in 1307. Above these paintings are portraits of prominent women in the biblical tradition. In the courtyard, there are panels with Mary's Canticle (The *Magnificat*, see Luke 1:46-55) in more than twenty languages.

After your visit, look out at the Judean hills and notice the terraces. Some of these date to the Iron Age (1100–700 B.C.). Cutting out terraces in the hills and carefully maintaining them was the only way that Israelite farmers were able to exploit the hills for agriculture. Daily 8:30–12:00; 3–5.

Lachish

"The LORD delivered Lachish into the power of Israel . . ." (Josh 10:32).

Lachish was a large fortified city that commanded an important trade route that led from the Philistine region and southern plains to the hill country of Judah. Excavations have found evidence of human occupation as early as the fourth millennium B.C. Following the breakup of the Davidic-Solomonic Empire, Rehoboam fortified Lachish and other cities on his southern flank because of problems with Egypt. It fell to Sennacherib in the eighth century. The Lachish Letters, which are correspondence between the military commander of Lachish and his superiors in Jerusalem, showed how desperate the military situation was during the Babylonian invasion of Judah in the early part of the sixth century. Excavations have revealed palaces and a temple from the second century. Lachish was virtually abandoned during the Roman Period. The site has recently been prepared to receive visitors although excavations continue. Daily 8–4; Friday 8–2. Fee.

Motza

"Now that very day two of (the disciples) were going to a village seven miles from Jerusalem called Emmaus . . ." (Luke 24:13).

This settlement just four miles from Jerusalem was named after a city in Benjamin's tribal allotment (Josh 18:26). According to Josephus, this was the site of a town called *Colonia* established for retired Roman soldiers (*Jewish Wars* 7, 6, 6). Jerome Murphy-O'Connor maintains that this is the most likely location for the Emmaus of Luke 24. The sixty stadia (v. 13) reflects the length of a journey from Jerusalem to this site and back.

Nebi Samuil (A: the prophet Samuel)

"Samuel died, and all Israel gathered to mourn him; they buried him at his home in Ramah" (1 Sam 25:1).

Looking to the right (north) from the Tel Aviv-Jerusalem highway, one can see a deep gorge (the Brook of Sorek). Beyond it on a high ridge, there is a mosque with its minaret. This is the site of a Muslim shrine to Samuel. Muslims regard it as his tomb. Jews also came to this place during the Middle Ages, identifying it with Ramah where the Bible says the prophet was buried (1 Sam 25:1). But it was the Byzantines who identified this site as Mizpeh (See 1 Sam 7:6; 10:24-25) and the burial place of the prophet. Justinian built a church here over the prophet's tomb. The Crusaders called the place "Mount Joy" because from this summit (2900 feet above sea level), they caught their first sight of Jerusalem. They identified the site as Shiloh. You can visit the prophet's tomb. Daily 8–4; Friday 8–1; Summer 8–5.

THE FOOTHILLS
(H: Shephelah)

"So Joshua captured all this land: the mountains . . . the foothills . . ." (Josh 11:16).

This hilly region is in the center of the country between the Judean hills on the east and the Coastal Plain on the west. The hills of Samaria are the northern boundary of the Shephelah and the Negev its southern boundary. The Shephelah region is eighty-three miles long and between sixteen and thirty miles wide. In antiquity the area was important economically because its agricultural potential was much easier to exploit than that of the Judean hills where terracing was necessary. Also, the region was important strategically since it allowed for travel north and south as well as east and west. There were few north-south routes in ancient Israel because of the highlands that extended the length of the country. The Egyptians controlled the area until the middle of the thirteenth century B.C. When their control waned, it became a battleground for the conflicts between the Philistines and the Israelites. The Kingdom of Judah controlled the foothills until the Babylonian Period (sixth century B.C.) during which settlements here were devastated. It was resettled during the Persian Period (late sixth century to fourth century B.C.), but became a scene of conflict during the Hellenistic Period when Antiochus IV proscribed the practice of Judaism (67 B.C.). The Maccabees came from Modein (1 Macc 2:1), a town in the foothills, to lead a successful revolution against Antiochus. It was in these foothills that Judas Maccabee led the Jews to their first victories over the Greeks (1 Macc 3:38–4:25). The foothills remained under Jewish control until the Roman Period. After the fall of Jerusalem in A.D. 70, Jewish population here diminished.

Aijalon (Ayyalon) Valley

"Stand still, O sun, at Gibeon, O moon, in the valley of Aijalon!"
(Josh 10:12).

This valley in the Judean Foothills (Shephelah) lies between the Coastal Plain to the west and the Judean Hills to the east. The southwestern tip of this valley meets the Latrun junction on the Tel-Aviv Jerusalem highway. It guards two important approaches to these hills. One is through the Shaᶜar HaGai and the other is through the Maᶜale Beth Horon (H: the heights of Beth Horon). The Amarna Letters (fourteenth century B.C.) mention that caravans from Egypt passed through this valley. Its commercial importance almost guaranteed that contending armies were to fight over it.

According to the Bible, this is the route Joshua took from the Judean hills in his pursuit of the Amorite kings who were allied against the Israelites (Josh 9:1–10:14, esp. vv. 11-12). It was here that Joshua prayed for the sun and moon to stand still so that his victory over the Amorites would be complete. Saul repulsed a Philistine invasion of the Israelite highlands here (1 Sam 14:31). A millennium after Saul, the Romans assembled their forces here before marching on Jerusalem during the First Revolt. The Crusaders did the same after another thousand years. Anyone who wanted to approach Jerusalem from the west usually had to pass through the Aijalon Valley.

Aphek-Antipatris

"Now the Philistines had mustered all their forces in Aphek . . ."
(1 Sam 29:1).

"So the soldiers, according to their orders, took Paul and escorted him by night to Antipatris" (Acts 23:31).

Name. (H: Tell Afeq; G: Pegae [springs]; A: Fajja [corruption of the Greek] and Qalat Ras el-Ein "the castle of the source of the spring" [of the Yarkon River];

NT: Antipatris). Before the time of Herod, this town was known as Aphek, a name that occurs eight times in the OT (Josh 12:18; 13:4; 19:30; 1 Sam 4:1; 29:1; 1 Kgs 20:26, 30; 2 Kgs 13:17). Study of these references makes it clear that they do not all refer to the same town. Current consensus is that there were eight towns in ancient Israel with the name Aphek. This site is the Aphek in the Plain of Sharon. OT references to it are Josh 12:18; 1 Sam 4:1; 29:1. In the Hellenistic Period, when the Plain of Sharon was thoroughly Hellenized, the city received a new name *Pegae*. When Herod the Great added this city to his domains, he renamed it *Antipatris* in honor of his father, Antipater.

Location. The site, twenty-six miles south of Caesarea, is at the source of the Yarkon River that flows westward into the Mediterranean after a twenty-five-mile tortuous course. The Arabic name for the river is *el-Awja*, "the twisted one." Most of the water from the springs in the area is diverted to irrigate the Negev. It was a stop along the Via Maris. Its water and the shade of its trees made it attractive. The park near the antiquities gives some idea of how the site must have appeared to travelers of the past.

History. The area was already inhabited in the Chalcolithic Period. It became a walled city at the end of the fourth millennium B.C., making it one of the earliest walled cities in the region. Aphek was important because of its proximity to the source of the Yarkon River. It became an important stop along the coastal highway because it dominated the narrow strip between the Yarkon and the foothills to the west. It is mentioned in both the Egyptian Execration Texts (nineteenth century B.C.) and the Amarna Letters (fourteenth century B.C.). Joshua (12:18) speaks of the taking of the city, but it may have fallen during the internecine conflicts that marked the end of Egyptian hegemony in Canaan.

Aphek was at the northern end of territory controlled by the Philistines who used it as a marshaling point in campaigns against the Israelites. It was connected by an east-west road to Shiloh from where the Israelites came to meet the Philistine threat (1 Samuel 4). The Philistines defeated them and captured the Ark of the Covenant. In the second battle (1 Sam 29–31), they defeated Saul at Mount Gilboa in Lower Galilee. The OT does not mention Aphek again though Assyrian and Babylonian texts attest its importance as a fortress in the seventh century B.C.

Herod rebuilt the city in 20 B.C. and renamed it for his father. It was an important link between Caesarea and Jerusalem. Paul spent a night here on his way from Jerusalem to Caesarea for transport to Rome for his appeal to the emperor (Acts 23:31). Vespasian destroyed the town during the First Revolt, but it was rebuilt. An earthquake in A.D. 363 leveled the town and it was not restored.

The Crusaders built a fortress called *Le Toron aux Fountains Sourdes* (The Tower at the Quiet Fountains). In the 1600s, the Turks built a fortified caravanserai on the foundations of the Crusader ruins. The walls you see are the remnants of the Turkish construction.

Antiquities. Below the north wall of the fort, one can see the foundation courses of an EBA **city wall**. This is a very important structure since Aphek was among the first towns in Canaan to build a wall (c. 3200 B.C.). Entering the gate in the west wall of the fort, one can see the LB monumental building. It was a **palace** from the period of Egyptian presence here. In the palace were found cuneiform documents—something of a rarity in Palestinian archaeology. This simply testifies to the city's importance during Egyptian rule. There was evidence of a great battle here. Excavators found arrows stuck in the masonry. The attack took place during the thirteenth century as Egyptian hegemony in Canaan was breaking down. Walking outside the fort to the southern wall, one can notice **pavers** from the first-century Herodian street that lies under the eastern wall. Continuing south of the Turkish fort there is a Roman Period **mansion**, a **Cardo** at the end of which is an **odeion**. Daily 8–4; Summers 8–5. Fee.

Hazan Caves

Discovered only in 1980, the man-made caves cut in the region's soft limestone bedrock were inhabited in the first century A.D. The caves housed a facility for the production and storage of olive oil. Perhaps these facilities were located below ground to avoid taxation. During the Second Revolt, the caves were modified to serve as a place of refuge for the Jewish rebels. The site is on the Moshav Amatzya whose members lead visitors through the caves. There is an orientation film that is shown before the tours. Take sturdy shoes and clothing. Going through the caves requires some tight squeezes so this is not for the claustrophobic. Daily 9–4; Friday, 9–2:30. Fee.

Latrun

"Setting out with all their forces, they came and pitched their tent near Emmaus in the plain" (1 Macc 3:40).

Both Eusebius and Jerome identify this site as the Emmaus mentioned in Luke 24, but a plague devastated the area in the 600s A.D. and the site was abandoned. When the Crusaders arrived here at the end of the eleventh century, they were unaware of the Byzantine identification. They saw a church here, but they located Emmaus elsewhere (see **Abu Gosh**). The Crusaders built their church within the ruins of the Byzantine church. Here they honored "the good thief" (see Luke 24:39-43). *Latrun* is an Arabic corruption for the Latin word for thief, *latro*. Others derive the name "Latrun" from a Crusader fortress whose ruins are to the southeast of the junction. Its name was *Le Toron des Chevaliers* ("the knight's fortress"). An Arab village was built near the ancient site and was named *Imwas,* which is the Arabic equivalent of the name *Emmaus.*

Location. Latrun is at the southwestern edge of the **Aijalon (Ayyalon) Valley**. It is at the junction of the Jerusalem-Tel Aviv highway with Ashkelon-Ramallah Road. It is twenty-eight miles west of Jerusalem. It can be reached by intercity bus from the Central Bus Station on Jaffa Road.

History. The First Book of Maccabees notes that Judas Maccabee led the Jewish forces to important victories over the Syrians at "Emmaus in the plain" (1 Macc 3:40, 57; 4:3). A note in the NAB to 1 Macc 3:40 suggests that this is "probably not the village mentioned in Luke 24:13." The citizens of this Emmaus were not docile subjects of Rome and in 43 B.C. they refused to pay their taxes. Many were sold into slavery. Three years later, Emmaus revolted against Herod, who ruled as king by the Emperor's favor. The Romans set fire to the town, which was then abandoned until the third century A.D.

The town was reconstructed in A.D. 221 under a charter granted by the Emperor Elagabalus to Julius Africanus and renamed *Nicopolis*, "the city of victory." Both Eusebius and Jerome assert that Nicopolis was the Emmaus of Luke 24. Obviously, they were unaware that the site had not been occupied in the first century. In the 400s, the Byzantines built an imposing triapsidal basilica here though there are no inscriptions or mosaics to suggest that they intended to memorialize the events of Luke 24 with the basilica. The identification of the site as Emmaus by Eusebius and Jerome, however, makes it probable that the builders of the basilica believed that their church was standing on the site of that post-resurrection appearance.

Antiquities. Two Dominicans for the École biblique, L.H. Vincent and F.M. Abel, excavated the site from 1924 to 1927. Since they worked before the development of stratigraphic archaeology, some of their dating needs to be checked by new excavations. Currently the site is being reexcavated and the results may provide more reliable conclusions. Vincent and Abel identified five separate structures on the site. The earliest were foundations of walls from the second-first century B.C. The second was a Roman villa from the second century. Its floors were adorned with mosaics with geometric, floral, and faunal themes. These mosaics were reused in the triapsidal basilica built as a church in the third century. Today no one accepts a third-century date for the church. At that time, Christianity was still a prohibited and persecuted religion. No Christians in their right mind would call attention to their presence by building a huge (150 feet by 80 feet) church. Also, the triapsidal form is a popular fifth-century form. Both these observations are based on *historical* grounds. Firm conclusions about dating await stratigraphic excavation below the foundations of the Byzantine church. A fourth structure that was north of the church is a separate baptistery. Water came from a well to the north of the building. There was a small basilica (65 feet by 32 feet) in front of the baptistery. It had a single central apse and a narthex. The Crusaders built the fifth structure in the 1100s. It was a Romanesque church that reused the central apse of the south church.

The Environs. The modern building above the archaeological site is the headquarters of a French archaeological institute, which is reexcavating the site. Just off the southeast corner of the Latrun junction is a Trappist monastery nestled in a small forest. The current monastery building dates from 1927. The monks support themselves from their vineyards. Their wine is sold in Israel under the "Latrun" label. The monks welcome visitors from 8–11:30 and 2:30–4:30, except on Sunday.

Across from the monastery, you will see a tank sitting atop a large beam. This is the museum of the tank battalions of the Israel Defense Forces. The museum is open daily 9–4; Friday 9–12. The juxtaposition of a Trappist monastery and a military museum makes for an interesting contrast in this land of contrasts.

Lod

"The sons of Elpaal were Eber, Misham, Shemed, who built Ono and Lod with its nearby towns" (1 Chr 8:12).

This town is on the border between the Shephelah and the Coastal Plain and is the town closest to Ben Gurion Airport. Lod appears in the fifteenth century B.C. city list of Pharaoh Tutmoses III. According to 1 Chr 8:12, Elpaal, the son of Benjamin, built the city. Lod did not play a role in the history of Israel though it became an important rabbinic center after the First Revolt. There was an early Christian community there. Acts 9:32 has Peter visit the city, which it calls *Lydda*. The Romans burnt the city during the First Revolt. Hadrian rebuilt it and colonized it with non-Jews though Jews were allowed to live there as well. Its name was changed to *Diospolis* (G: "the city of god"). During the Byzantine Period, the city's name changed again—this time to Georgiopolis. The Byzantine Christians believed that St. George was buried in the city. After the Arab conquest, Lod served as the capital of the Arabian province of *el-Filastin* (Palestine) until the Arabs built the city of Ramla two miles south and transferred their capital there in 717. The Crusaders restored the name of St. George to the city and built a church over his tomb but Jews could no longer live in the city. When Saladin captured the city in 1191, he allowed Jews to return, but Mongols destroyed St. George in 1271. During the Ottoman Period, it was a small Muslim town and remained so until taken by the Jews in the 1948 war.

Neot Kedumim (H: Ancient Places of Beauty)

"For the LORD, your God, is bringing you into a good country, a land with streams of water, with springs and fountains welling up in the hills and valleys, a land of wheat and barley, of vines and fig trees and pomegranates, of olive trees and of honey" (Deut 8:7-8).

Location. This recreation of the landscapes of Biblical Period Israel is located on the Ramot Road (Rt. 443), about nine miles southeast of Ben Gurion Airport in the Modein region that was the home of Mattathias Maccabee and his sons.

Visit. This is a privately financed nature reserve that attempts to recreate the landscapes of Biblical Period Israel. It features the flora of the Sharon Plain, the Carmel Range, the Jordan Valley, the Negev, and the eastern Mediterranean forest. Some animals mentioned in the Bible roam a special area of the park. There are four trails through the park and three of these are paved. It is recommended that visitors walk the trails, which vary in length from two to three and one-half miles. Electric carts are available for those who have difficulty walking. Depending on one's pace, a visit here should take at least two hours. This offers those whose time in Israel is limited, to see the variety of the country's flora in one stop. Sun.–Thurs. 8:30 to sunset. Fridays and eves of holidays: 8:30–1:00. Last entrance two hours before sunset. Closed on Saturdays and holidays. Fee.

Sha'ar HaGai (A: Bab el Wad; "The Gate of the Valley")

This is the point of transition from the Judean Hills to the Shephelah. On the southeast corner of the junction, one can see the remains of a Turkish Period inn. Pilgrims who landed at Jaffa and traveled by donkey caravan to Jerusalem spent the night here before arriving in Jerusalem. The inn was abandoned when Jerusalem was connected to Jaffa by rail in the 1800s. During the 1948 war, this area was the scene of the most intense fighting. The Jews wanted to keep the Jerusalem-Tel Aviv highway open so that Jerusalem could receive supplies, while the Arabs wanted to close the road to force the Jews of Jerusalem to surrender. The control of this junction was vital. It remained in Arab hands, but the Jews built the "Burma Road" in the adjacent hills to bypass Sha'ar HaGai in supplying Jerusalem.

THE JERUSALEM TO JERICHO ROAD

"A man fell victim to robbers as he went down from Jerusalem to Jericho"
(Luke 10:30).

Judean Desert

This hilly region on Israel's eastern boundary is bordered on the west by the Judean hills, on the east by the Dead Sea and the Jordan Valley, on the north by the hills of Samaria, and on the south by the hills of the Negev. It is eighty-three miles long and seventeen miles wide. The desert is made up of hills that descend from west to east from a height of 3250 feet above sea level to 1300 feet below sea level. Its climate is harsh and the soil is poor. Still, the desert has been occupied from the Chalcolithic Period to the present. Today it is home to a few Bedouin whose encampments can be seen near the Jericho Road. In the Biblical Period, there were few permanent settlements here, the most famous of which was at the oasis of Ein Gedi (see below). The Mishnah says the scapegoat that was to be sent into the desert bearing the people's sins on the Day of Atonement (Lev 16:20-28) was sent into the Judean Wilderness (M. Yoma 4:1).

Herod the Great built several fortresses in this area to protect his southern flank. The most famous of these are Cypros (near Jericho), the Herodium (near Bethlehem), and Masada (see below). Because of the region's harsh conditions and sparse population, the Judean desert served as an ideal redoubt for revolutionaries like Bar Kochba, fugitives like the Zealots of Masada, and the religious refugees like the Qumran community. During the Byzantine Period, this desert was home to an estimated five thousand monks, some of whom lived as hermits and others in monastic settlements called *lauras*. Many of their monasteries have been excavated, but the Israelis have not developed them for tourism. Founded in the fifth century, the Mar Saba monastery seven miles east of Bethlehem is still active. Once the largest monastery in the region, it is now home to fewer than ten Greek Orthodox monks.

Maale Adummim (H: "the red heights")

The name derives from the color of the limestone in the area. The Arabic name for the area is *Tal'at ed Damm* ("the ascent of blood"). Popular legend says that the soil in the area became red from the blood of all the travelers killed by the robbers who plied the Jerusalem-Jericho road. The traveler in Jesus' parable of the Good Samaritan was attacked on this road (Luke 10:30). This is also the name of an Israeli settlement town in Occupied Territory east of Bethany on the Jericho-Jerusalem road. The Bible mentions an Adummim as part of the tribal allotment of Benjamin (Josh 18:17). The settlement is on Occupied Territory, but there is a move on by the settlers to have the area annexed to Jerusalem. Within the settlements are remains of the Byzantine monastery and a Crusader Fortress, which was built on the ruins of a Roman Fort near the Khan el Hatruri.

The Martyrious Monastery. The Judean wilderness was home to an estimated five thousand monks during the Byzantine Period. This monastic complex is among the best preserved and most accessible in Israel. Several beautiful mosaics have survived. Also in evidence are several churches, a water system, and a hostel for guests. Daily 8–4; Friday, 8–1. Closed Saturday. Fee.

The Inn of the Good Samaritan (A: Khan el Hatruri)

This caravanserai from the Mamluke Period is at the summit of "the Red Heights." It was in use until the beginning of the 1900s. The Turks used it as a fortress. Byzantine pilgrims believed the ruins of the Roman Period fort near the caravanserai to be the inn mentioned in the parable of the Good Samaritan (Luke 10:30-37). Pilgrims today use it as a rest stop. Free.

Nebi Musa

A short distance from the Inn of the Good Samaritan is a turnoff from the main road to the south. After about one mile, the side road leads to where Muslims contend that Moses is buried. The Bible maintains that Moses was buried in Moab, which is east of the Jordan, though the exact spot is unknown (Deut 34:5-6). The shrine is known as Nebi Musa (A: The Prophet Moses). The Mamluke sultan Baybars built it in 1269. Each spring there was a procession from Jerusalem to Nebi Musa. The Israelis have stopped this practice because of the nationalistic overtones that the procession had taken on. Until 1990 the shrine was in a closed military area. Now there is free access to the tomb and the mosque that surrounds it. Daily except Friday 8–4. Free.

THE DEAD SEA REGION

The Dead Sea (H: Yam HaMelach "The Salt Sea")

". . . the boundary shall continue along the Jordan and terminate with the Salt Sea" (Num 34:12).

The salt content of the Dead Sea is nine times higher than that of the Mediterranean. The salts are chlorides of sodium (table salt), calcium, magnesium, and potassium. There are also high concentrations of bromides and iodine. The Dead Sea is fed by the Jordan River and runoff rain water from the hills of Judah and Moab. On their way to the Dead Sea, these waters carry traces of these chemicals. If the Dead Sea had an outlet to the ocean, its waters would be fresh since these chemicals would flow into the sea. Without an outlet, the chemicals remain. They reach such high proportions (about thirty percent of the Dead Sea is solids in solution) because of the enormous evaporation of the water. At 106 feet below sea level, the surface of the Dead Sea is the lowest point on earth. The heat there leads to the evaporation by the hundreds of thousands of gallons each day. Because of the high level of solids in the water and the low level of oxygen, no plant or animal life can sustain itself; hence, the name "The Dead Sea."

Because Israel diverts the water from the Jordan for its water system and because the rainfall in the past ten years has been low, the level of the Dead Sea is diminishing rapidly. The southern and shallow part would have dried up years ago were not a canal dug to bring water from the deeper northern part. It is important that the southern part of the Dead Sea not dry up because both Israel and Jordan have industrial installations there that extract the chemicals from the waters. This is an important, profit-making industry for both countries. To prevent the Dead Sea from drying up, a proposal was made to run a canal from the Mediterranean to the Dead Sea. Besides bringing water to the Dead Sea, the canal could generate electricity as the waters drop from the Judean highlands to the Dead Sea. Preliminary work started on this canal, but work had to stop because of the lack of financing. Another proposal is to run a canal from the Red Sea to the Dead Sea through the Aravah Valley. This would be a joint project for Jordan and Israel. Now that these two countries have made peace, this project may proceed.

Part of a trip to Israel usually includes some time in the Dead Sea. The density of the waters makes for great buoyancy. It is not only almost impossible to drown in the Dead Sea; it is difficult to swim. The best one can do is float. It is important to insure that you enter and leave the water carefully. Do not swallow any water, and be careful not to get any in your eyes. If you have open cuts or even if you have shaved in the morning, you will feel some stinging. The magnesium chloride gives the water an "oily" feel. Take a shower with fresh water after leaving the Dead Sea. It is not a good idea to leave the chemicals on your body for too long.

You will see several hotels along the Dead Sea. People from all over the world travel here for the supposed therapeutic effects of bathing in its waters. People afflicted with psoriasis and other skin diseases experience relief. Also, the mud from the floor of the Dead Sea is reputedly beneficial to the skin so cosmetic companies in Israel make skin treatments made from this mud. You will find these preparations on sale throughout Israel.

A town a few miles south of the Dead Sea is named *Sdom* after the Sodom of Gen 18:16–19:29. Guides will even point to a salt formation along the southwestern shore as "Lot's Wife" (see Gen 19:26). Archaeology has not found evidence of the so-called Cities of the Plain mentioned in Genesis 19.

Ein Gedi (H: "the spring of the kid")

"Like a cedar on Lebanon I am raised aloft . . . like a palm tree in Engedi . . ." (Sir 24:13-14).

Ein Gedi is an oasis in the Judean desert fourteen miles north of Masada. The Song of Songs compares Solomon's lover to "a cluster of henna from the vineyards of Engedi" (Cant 1:14). Here the desert's hot climate has combined with the waters of an oasis to provide an environment for tropical plants. Also found in the park are leopards, which stay out of sight, ibex and hyrax, which you will be able to spot easily. Two perennial streams water the area: Nahal David (David's River) and Nahal Arugot (the Arugot River). There is a waterfall of 650 feet and a stalactite cave at the end of the Nahal David. The cave is associated with the story of 1 Sam 24:1-17 as the place where David refused to kill Saul when the opportunity presented itself. The oasis is a marvelous place for hiking. It makes for an enjoyable outing on a day off. But do not go alone; go in groups or better yet, contact the SPNI. It will provide information about guided trips to Ein Gedi oasis. Allow yourself at least three hours to walk the marked trails in the park. Daily 8–4; Summer 8–5. Fee.

Masada

Two and one-half miles west of the Dead Sea is a boat-shaped plateau that rises to thirteen hundred feet above the plain below. This is the fortress of Masada. Though Jewish occupation here was not very long, it has passed into the mythology of Jewish nationalism and it is a symbol of the determination to defend the existence of the Jewish State. During the Parthian invasion of Syria-Palestine in 43 B.C., Herod made use of this solitary mountain refuge along the western shore of the Dead Sea. Parthians were enemies of Rome to whom Herod owed allegiance. Herod hid his family at Masada while he fled to Rome. After the Romans named him king in 40 B.C., Herod built a luxurious winter residence here. A thirteen-foot thick wall with thirty-five towers that were eighty feet high enclosed the summit. Evidently he did not wish to be disturbed. His private quarters comprised a three-tiered palace that clung to the northern slope of the mountain. The decorations of that palace would not offend Jewish sensibilities so in this instance Herod chose to act as an observant Jew. Herod also built a palace on the summit of the mountain for more public functions. He decorated it with mosaic floors, frescos, and colonnades. For his comfort and that of his guests, he built baths. To make life possible in this area, Herod built large storage facilities at the north end of the summit and a water system that had a capacity to capture and store immense quantities of runoff rain water that came down the wadis.

During the First Revolt against Rome, there was a civil war within Jerusalem during the Roman siege. The losers left Jerusalem under the leadership of Eliezer and took up residence on Masada. They sat out the rest of the war. After the fall of Jerusalem, the Romans sought to eliminate any threat of further resistance. They came to Masada and laid siege to it for three years before it finally fell in A.D. 73. One can still see the remains of the Roman siege wall and camps. The wall was almost as long as that surrounding the Old City today. Eventually the Romans built a ramp from their camp to the western wall of Masada. They brought their siege engines to bear against the wall. They broke down the Jewish defenses and captured Masada.

In telling the story of Masada's fall, Josephus tried to portray its defenders as tragic heroes. He has them commit suicide rather than surrender—an act that would win admiration from Josephus' Roman audience. Suicide was not an honorable option for Jews. Josephus' story about the fall of Masada is remarkably like a similar tale he tells about the fall of Gamla, which took place at the beginning of the First Revolt. In any case, Masada passed into Jewish heroic folklore especially with the establishment of the modern State of Israel. A popular Israeli nationalistic slogan is "Masada will never fall again!"

After occupying Masada for a while, the Romans left and the hill was unoccupied until Christian monks established a monastery there for most of the Byzantine Period. The remains of their chapel are on the summit. Eliezer's zealots were on Masada for three years and Christian monks for three hundred! The Muslim conquest of Jerusalem brought an end to Byzantine monasticism and with it Masada's monastery. The summit was unoccupied and its significance unrecognized until 1838 when it was correctly identified by Edward Robinson, who did not climb to the top but simply viewed its northern cliffs through a telescope. It was excavated in the 1960s by Yigal Yadin and the Hebrew University.

There are three ways to arrive at the summit, which is thirteen hundred feet above the shore of the Dead Sea. There is an ascent from the West on the Roman ramp. It is an easy climb but one must set out to Masada from Arad. From the Dead Sea side, one can walk up a snake path that winds up over a two-mile path. It will take about forty-five minutes to climb up by this way. Josephus speaks about the snake path. It was renovated for use in 1954. The easiest way to arrive at the top is to take the cable car, which will let you off near the summit. A short climb up a gentle incline and a few stairs will complete your journey. A hat, sunglasses, bottle of water, and sunblock are essentials if you are going to spend any amount of time on the summit. Daily 8–4; Friday 8–2. Fee.

There is a fee to ride the cable car to and from the top of the mountain. You can choose to walk up the path on the eastern side of the mountain or the Roman ramp on the west side at no charge, but you will have to pay the entrance fee to the site when you get to the top. There is a Sound and Light show at Masada on Tuesdays and Thursdays from April to October.

Qumran (H: Mezah Hasidim "The Fortress of the Pious")

Location. This site is located along the northwest shore of the Dead Sea. It is most famous for the scrolls found in eleven nearby caves in 1948. The Dead Sea Scrolls contain biblical texts, apocryphal and pseudepigraphical texts, and texts composed by the community for its own use. Most of the scrolls are in the Israel Museum's Shrine of the Book. Those fragments that are still not published are in the Rockefeller Museum and are available only to the scholars who are working on their publications. The scrolls have proven invaluable for the textual criticism of the OT and for understanding the Judaism of Jesus' day. Though there have been some fantastic claims about the relationship between the Qumran people and early Christians, these claims are purely hypothetical. The NT never mentions this group. Still, both the early Christians and the Qumran people shared an apocalyptic view of the future. The former, however, looked for the final revelation of God's Reign while the latter waited for the purification of Jerusalem and its Temple and their designation as the Temple's priests.

History. The site was occupied from the eighth century B.C. when it served as an outpost of the Kingdom of Judah. The structure that is visible at the site had some common areas like a dining room where the community shared its sacral meals. There are some work areas visible such as a pottery kiln and workshop. Some also identify one room as a *scriptorium* (a place where texts were copied) although that identification is disputed. The water system and the ritual baths *(mikveot)* that it served provide evidence that maintaining ritual purity was a significant concern for the people of Qumran. Though the settlement's cemetery has been located just east of the buildings, it is not clear where the members of the community lived though it is likely they lived in the many caves to the west of the buildings. The location of this settlement in the Judean desert near the Dead Sea reminds some people of the Christian monks of another age who were attracted to the Judean wilderness for ascetical reasons. The people of Qumran did not come to the desert for such reasons. They came to escape persecution by the priests of the Temple whom they denounced as illegitimate and whose ministrations, they asserted, made the cult of the Temple valueless.

The people who occupied the area from 150 B.C. to A.D. 70 and who produced the scrolls speak of themselves as "the children of light." They have been identified with the *Essenes* mentioned by Josephus and Roman authors. Some scholars have raised questions about identifying the people who lived in the settlement with the people who produced the scrolls. Still, most make this identification. After the end of the First Revolt, the Romans occupied the settlement and turned it into a fortress. Before the scrolls were discovered, the remains

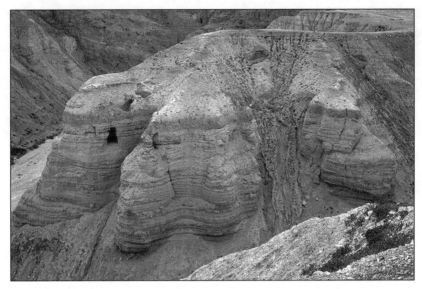

Remains of the Qumran caves where the Dead Sea Scrolls were found.

at the site were considered Roman. After the discovery of the scrolls, the site was excavated by Roland de Vaux, O.P., of the École biblique, and the Jewish presence there was revealed.

The Dead Sea Scrolls. The term "Dead Sea Scrolls" refers to a collection of texts found in caves near the Wadi Qumran beginning in 1947. The Wadi Qumran is a river bed that directs the water runoff to the Dead Sea during the rainy season. The discovery of the first texts was completely accidental. Once the value of these first texts became clear, the local bedouin made a thorough search of caves for every scrap of material, for which they were well paid. The scrolls are now in the possession of the Israeli Department of Antiquities. Though most major documents have been published, there are still many fragments that await reconstruction, deciphering, and publication. The finds were particularly significant 1) because of the paucity of textual material found in Palestine. The dry climate in the Dead Sea region helped preserve the scrolls. 2) The texts revealed the existence of a Palestinian Jewish community that flourished from about 150 B.C. to A.D. 70. This period corresponds to the time that witnessed the ministry of Jesus and the rise of early Christianity. 3) The ideology of this community was apocalyptic in tone with several similarities to Christianity.

The literature found at Qumran falls into three categories. First, there is biblical literature. Several complete scrolls of the Book of Isaiah have been found at Qumran. At least some fragments of every other book of the Hebrew Bible except Esther have been found as well. Comparing the Qumran texts of the Hebrew Bible with the Masoretic text, the surviving Hebrew version of the

Shrine of the Book, Israel Museum, Jerusalem.

OT, reveals no striking discrepancies. What is important to note is that when readings in the Qumran texts differ from those of the Masoretic text, they usually agree with readings from the Septuagint. Before the discovery of the Scrolls, common opinion held that at least some portions of the Septuagint reflected a careless translation of the Hebrew original. Now it is obvious that those who made the Greek translation found in the Septuagint used a Hebrew text tradition different from the one preserved by the Masoretes. This accounts for the differences between the Hebrew Bible and the Septuagint.

A second category of literature found at Qumran is comprised of non-canonical Jewish religious texts. These texts include some books today classified as the apocrypha and pseudepigrapha of the OT. Examples of these texts found at Qumran include the Book of Sirach and the *Testaments of the Twelve Patriarchs*. It is difficult to be certain about the status the people of Qumran accorded these texts. Their presence shows that they helped shape the religious perspectives of the people at Qumran though the rabbis at a later date did not include them in their canon. The third and most important category of texts found at Qumran are religious texts created by and for the community that lived close to the caves where the texts were found. It is assumed that the people living in the settlement produced these texts and that these people were the Essenes mentioned by Josephus, although the word Essene never appears in the texts. These texts include rules that regulate the life of the community, commentaries on biblical texts, and collections of biblical texts with and without commentaries.

It is difficult to overestimate the value of these texts for understanding the religious milieu in Palestine at the time of Jesus' ministry and the rise of Christianity. Analysis of the Dead Sea Scrolls helped to illustrate the diversity that was early Judaism. The texts reveal a community that saw itself as the true Israel. The Qumran community was a group made up principally of priests who believed that the worship in the Temple was hopelessly corrupt because of the moral failures of the priests of the Temple and because of the incorrect calendar used by them. The community of Qumran was waiting for the day when they would be empowered to take over the direction of worship in the Temple and restore it to the authentic service of God. That day would be preceded by a terrible conflict with the powers of darkness. God was going to lead the people of Qumran, "the children of light," to victory.

Analysis of the Qumran commentaries on biblical texts reveals the method of interpretation that was characteristic of the period and which is in evidence in the NT. It is interpretation that pays no heed to the historical circumstances of the text to be interpreted. It shows that the experience of the Qumran community shaped its method of interpretation. Obviously the community looked on itself as composed of outsiders with definite eschatological expectations. The people of Qumran were waiting for God's final intervention in Israel's life since it would vindicate them. The Qumran method of biblical interpretation was based on the experiences of the community and arose from the linguistic possibilities in the actual wording of the text. A similar pattern of biblical interpretation is evident in the NT as it reinterprets OT texts to give expression to its faith in Jesus as the suffering Messiah.

Like other Jews of the period, the Qumran people believed that true piety involved obedience to the Torah. It was the interpretation of the Torah that separated the people of Qumran from other Jews. The people of Qumran believed that only their sages, in particular the Teacher of Righteousness, knew how to expound the Torah and the Prophets correctly. They also believed that God chose each member of their community for salvation. They attain salvation through participation in the community's life. The Qumran community believed that it was living in the final days before God's decisive intervention in Israel's life. They looked forward to this day because they were confident in the correctness of their beliefs and in their eventual salvation.

The relationship of the first Christians to the people of Qumran has been the subject of an inordinate amount of fanciful speculation. After years of study, the consensus is that the Dead Sea Community and Christianity were both reinterpretations of early Judaism's traditions. Their similarities derive from their common origins in the ancestral religion of the Jews. Their differences reflect the diverse experiences of the two groups. No one has successfully proved that Qumran had a direct impact on the development of Christianity's beliefs and practices. Daily 8–4; Summer 8–5. Fee.

CHAPTER SEVEN

Israel: The Negev

THE DESERT TRADITION

"The voice of the LORD shakes the desert . . ." (Ps 29:8).

Most of the Negev and Sinai is a desert receiving two to four inches of rainfall each year. The desert has taken on symbolic value in the Bible and the religious traditions inspired by it though this value is not the same in the Old and New Testaments and in Christianity.

OT. The Hebrew word *midbar* commonly translated as *desert* comes from a verbal root that means "to bring a flock to pasture." During the rainy season and shortly after, the shepherds have their flocks graze in arid and semiarid regions that are not suitable for permanent residence but can support flocks of small animals like goats and sheep. When the resources of a particular area are depleted, the shepherd leads his flock elsewhere. The word *midbar* then is a technical term for the pasture areas adjoining a temporary shepherd encampment. This is the sense one gets from the parable of the lost sheep in Luke 15:4-7. The shepherd leaves the ninety-nine sheep in the *wasteland* to look for the one that has wandered off. The desert then is an out-of-the way place. It is not where people normally live because it is inhospitable and even dangerous. While his flock is in the *midbar*, the shepherd must protect it against predators—animal and human.

For OT traditions that are more town-based, the dangers of the desert are highlighted. God threatens to turn Babylon into a desert where wild animals dwell and where no shepherd nor even an Arab will go (Isa 34:19-22). Edom is promised a similar fate (Isa 34:5-17). By way of contrast, God will transform Israel's deserts into gardens (Isa 51:3). Joel 2:3 contrasts the land of Judah before a certain natural disaster and after by comparing Eden with a desert.

There is also a temporal dimension to the desert motif in the OT. The desert is *before*—before Israelites received the land that God promised to their

ancestors. It was the place where God called Moses (Exod 3:1-5). It was the setting for the making of the covenant (Exod 19–22) or great signs such as the
manna (Deut 8:1-21), the water from the rock (Exod 17:1-7; Num 20:11), and
the victory over Amalek (Exod 17:8-13). But it also was a place of rebellion: the
Gold Calf (Exodus 32), the murmuring against God and Moses (Num 14:1-38;
20:2-6; 21:5), the jealousy of Aaron and Miriam (Num 12:1-8). The desert
marked a time of *transition* when the Hebrew slaves became the people of God.
Once the Israelites came to Canaan, the Promised Land, there was no reason
to go into the wilderness again. Here the wilderness is not presented as a goal
but as a *rite of passage* into the Promised Land.

This is reflected in the way that Second Isaiah and the Qumran people
present the "desert experience." The prophet of the exile sees Judah's second
desert experience as a place of transition from exile in Babylon to restoration
in Jerusalem. Even so the prophet describes a transformed desert. The wilderness will become a place of cultivation and fertility. It will be a place of order
(Isa 40:3-5; 43:18-19; 51:3; see also Isaiah 35 as an editorial transition to Second
Isaiah). Similarly, the Qumran people did not choose to live in the Judean
desert out of any ascetical motivation. They went there to be safe from the attacks of "the wicked priest" and "the sons of darkness" who ruled Jerusalem.
They fully expected that God was going to drive these evil people from Jerusalem so that the Qumran people could take their rightful place in the Temple.
The Qumran covenanters saw the desert as a place of transition and preparation (1QS 9:19-20).

Recent archaeological and historical reconstruction of Israel's origins has
called into question the assumption of Israel's nomadic origins and the ro-
manticizing of the desert that such an assumption sometimes implies. The first
Israelites were not invaders from the desert bringing a new religion with them.
They were peasant farmers oppressed by their Canaanite and Egyptian overlords. These peasants worshiped a God who supported them in their conflicts
with oppressive political powers.

Finally, some prophetic traditions are themselves responsible for romanti-
cizing the desert. To underscore their criticism of Israel's too ready assimila-
tion to Canaanite values and practices, both Hosea (2:14-19) and Jeremiah
(2:2-3) portray the Desert Period differently than other traditions. Still, the
desert—even in these two prophets—is a place of preparation for Israel's life
in the land. During the Exilic Period, Ezekiel has a different interpretation of
Israel's early life (Ezek 16:1-22). Except for Hosea and Jeremiah, the desert experiences of ancient Israel are not portrayed in an altogether positive light in
the OT.

NT. The Greek word usually translated as desert *(eremos)* does not necessarily
mean a desert, but an empty, abandoned place or thinly populated district.
Jesus went to the desert to be alone with God (Mark 1:12; Matt 4:1; Luke 4:1).
The tempter tried to intrude on Jesus' time with God. Jesus went to the desert,
i.e., a place without many inhabitants to get away from the crowds. Paul spent
time in Arabia (Gal 1:17). Some Pauline scholars, however, maintain that Paul
did not live in the desert but in cities like Petra and Gerasa, doing missionary

work. In his allegory on freedom he uses Sinai as an image of slavery and Jerusalem as the image of freedom (Gal 4:22-25). Paul picks up on the OT theme that sees the desert as a symbol of chaos and waste and the city as a place of order and freedom.

Christian spirituality. The image that the desert has in Christian spirituality derives more from the experience of early monasticism than it does from the biblical tradition. It has as its foundation an ascetical ideal that is not characteristic of the biblical tradition. The ascetic joyfully accepts the desert existence and its privations as a prerequisite for the attainment of spiritual delight.

THE SOUTHERN DESERT REGION

According to Num 13:22, the men whom Moses sent to reconnoiter the land of Canaan were to go by way of the Negev. The Hebrew word *Negev* (also spelled *Negeb*) means "south." It is the largest and southernmost region of the State of Israel. Before 1967, it comprised two-thirds of its land resources. The Negev is shaped like a triangle whose base is at the top. It is bounded on the east by the Aravah [see below], on the west by the Sinai, on the north by the Coastal Plain. At the south it ends at the Red Sea. Its main city is Beersheva. Its water resources are limited since all streams are seasonal, i.e., they are dry except following any substantial rainfall during the winter.

Despite its harsh conditions, archaeology has shown that the Negev has been occupied through all historical periods. In antiquity, both major north-south trade routes, the Via Maris and the Kings' Highway passed through it. Effective Israelite control of the Negev was limited to the time of David and Solomon. The Edomites began incursions after the death of Solomon. The Nabateans replaced them in the fourth century B.C. The Romans replaced the Nabateans in the second century A.D. They called the Negev "Palestina Tertia." It was an important link in their eastern empire and it remained so during the Byzantine Period. In the seventh century, the importance of the Negev diminished. It was not until the nineteenth century when Jews began to immigrate to the Negev that its fortunes changed. David Ben-Gurion encouraged settlement in the Negev and made Sde Boker (see below) his retirement home.

Arad

"When the Canaanite king of Arad, who lived in the Negeb, heard that the Israelites were coming . . . , he engaged them in battle and took some of them captive" (Num 21:1).

Location. This tel is in the northeast Negev, twenty-three miles east of Beersheva and seven and one-half miles from the modern town of Arad. The latter's dry heat and elevation (1760 feet above sea level) make it a popular health resort. Also, the modern town is just seventeen miles from the Dead Sea, which also attracts people for its curative properties.

The Biblical Tradition. The Bible remembers Arad in connection with the settlement. The king of Arad prevented the Israelites from entering Canaan from the south (Num 21:1-2). The Book of Joshua lists the king of Arad among the Canaanite kings that the Israelites defeated (Josh 12:14). The relatives of Moses' father-in-law did not accompany the Judahites beyond Arad, but settled in the region nearby this city (Judg 1:16). There are no archaeological remains of a city existing in the LBA when the Israelite tribes were extending their presence in Canaan. There was a MBA and LBA town ten miles away (Tel Malhata). Perhaps the biblical authors had it confused with the Arad of a later period [see below]. Egyptian records list Arad among the cities captured by Shishak during his foray into Judah during the reign of Rehoboam (c. 920; see 1 Kgs 14:25). Arad is one of the cities depicted on the Madaba Map (sixth century A.D.). Records of travelers from both the fourteenth and seventeenth centuries mention a Jewish community at Arad.

Antiquities. Ruth Amiran excavated the city. She uncovered a lower city and a citadel. The **lower city** dates from the Early Bronze Age (2900–2700 B.C.) though there are some remains from the Chalcolithic Period as well. The city was built on a slope to catch runoff rain water. The **well** in the lower city dates from the Israelite Period (ninth to the eighth centuries B.C.). The inhabitants of ancient Arad were involved in agriculture and trade. On the **citadel** is a fortress that dates from the Israelite Period and was in use from the eleventh to the sixth century B.C. Ostraca found here include official correspondence with Jerusalem. Most interesting is the **temple** in the Israelite Period fortress. It is complete with holy of holies and altar of sacrifice. The dating of these structures is still a matter of debate though the citadel was abandoned in the sixth century—probably during the Babylonian invasion. The lower city and the Israelite fortress have been partially reconstructed complete with walls, towers, gates, streets, temples, water system, and houses. Daily 8–4. Fee.

The Aravah

"These are the words which Moses spoke to all Israel . . . in the Aravah"
(Deut 1:1).

The Book of Deuteronomy begins by asserting that it contains the words spoken by Moses in the *Aravah* (1:1). The Aravah is a long (150 miles) and narrow valley that runs south from the Dead Sea to the Gulf of Eilat. It is part of the Rift Valley that extends from Syria to East Africa. The word itself means a dry and desolate area. Water resources here are limited. Agriculture can go on only because of modern irrigation techniques. One resource of the region exploited in antiquity was copper. Its importance came from the trade that passed through this region from the north on its way to the port at Eilat or Etzion-geber (see 1 Kgs 9:26).

Israel did not control this area until the time of David. Solomon built a naval base at the southern end of the Aravah to protect the trade in the Red Sea. When the Davidic-Solomonic Empire split into the two small Israelite kingdoms, the Edomites seized control of the region though Judah managed to displace them at least once (see 2 Kgs 14:22). In the fourth century B.C., the Nabateans replaced the Edomites, who migrated to the Negev. The Romans came to the region in the second century A.D. and built forts to protect the trade and the taxes and tolls they collected from the caravans.

After the Arab conquest, the region lost its importance. It was not until the formation of the State of Israel that settlements began to be established here. The peace treaty with Jordan was signed in the Aravah and both countries are ready to exploit its economic and agricultural potential. There are plans for an international airport in the south of the Aravah to serve both Aqaba (Jordan) and Eilat. Another plan is to run a canal from the Red Sea to the Dead Sea to prevent the Dead Sea from drying up. There is also the possibility that the waters of this canal may generate some electricity as they flow down to the Dead Sea.

Avdat

"Judas Maccabeus and his brother Jonathan crossed the Jordan and marched for three days through the desert. There they met some Nabateans . . ." (1 Macc 5:24-25).

Location. Lying 2100 feet above sea level, the greatest of Nabatean cities in the Negev honors the memory of Obodas II, an important Nabatean king who was buried here. It is about eight miles south of Sde Boker. The Nabateans founded the city in the fourth century B.C. as a stop at the junction of the Petra-Gaza and Jerusalem-Eilat roads. The Romans took control of the Nabatean trade routes and ended their kingdom in A.D. 106. People continued to live through the Roman Period. The city flourished during the Byzantine Period as shown by the Byzantine buildings on the acropolis. It went into a decline after the Arab conquest in the 600s and was abandoned by the tenth century.

Nabateans. These were Bedouin who settled in Transjordan and earned their livelihood as guides for caravans taking the eastern trade routes of Palestine. Their specialty was leading caravans to Mediterranean harbors. They made Petra in Transjordan their capital and built settlements along the trade routes of the Negev and Transjordan. Their language and script were similar to Aramaic and they had a type of Hellenized pre-Islamic Arab culture.

The origins of the Nabateans are unknown. What is clear is that the Edomites began moving into territory of the former Judahite kingdom from just before the Exile, taking advantage of Judah's weakness. For this, the Bible excoriates them (Jer 49:7-22; Ezek 25:12-14; 35:1-10; Joel 4:19; Obad 1-21). Arabian tribes, among them the Nabateans, moved into the territory vacated by the Edomites. By 200 B.C., the Nabateans became an important power because they controlled all trade between Egypt and Arabia.

The Bible makes few references to the Nabateans. According to 1 Macc 5:25 and 9:35, they were sympathetic to the Maccabean revolt, which is not surprising since an independent Jewish state could be a buffer between the Nabateans and the Seleucids. Second Macc 5:5-10 notes that the high priest

Jason fled from Jerusalem and was captured by Aretas, who was a Nabatean king though the text calls him "king of the Arabs" (v. 8). The story of John the Baptist's death (Mark 6:14-29; Matt 14:1-12) offers an indirect connection. Herod Antipas whom the Baptist criticized for marrying Herodias, his brother's wife, was first married to the daughter of the Nabatean king, Aretas IV. Herod divorced the king's daughter to marry his sister-in-law. Aretas took this as a personal affront and invaded Herod's territory and it was necessary for the Romans to save Herod, their client. It was the same Nabatean king who tried to arrest Paul in Damascus (2 Cor 11:32). Evidently Nabatean power extended as far north as Damascus.

The Nabateans founded Avdat the end of the fourth century B.C. to serve a caravan station. They also built a temple here in the first century B.C. and another in the first century A.D. At that time, it became a center for the manufacture of pottery and the breeding of camels, sheep, and goats. Late in the first century the Nabateans began experimenting with agricultural techniques. The Romans annexed this city along with all of the Negev into their *Provincia Arabica* in the second century A.D. The second and third centuries A.D. were times of great prosperity and a town was built along the southern spur of the acropolis. The temples were rebuilt and one was rededicated to *Zeus Abate* whom the Nabateans deified. He was a Nabatean king who ruled from 30–9 B.C. and after whom the town was named. A large catacomb was dug into the southwestern wall. Construction in the area continued until 296. During the reign of Diocletian, Avdat became part of the Roman defense system against Arabic tribes. The Romans built a fortress on the acropolis. When Christianity came to the Negev in the 300s, the temples became churches. The economy shifted as well. It became based on the cultivation of grapes and production of fine wine. The city was abandoned after the Arab conquest in 636.

The Antiquities. Most of the remains visible below the acropolis are Roman Period. This part of the site has not been excavated extensively. You can enter a reconstructed **Roman tower** and walk down the main street of the Roman city. Notice the **drainage canals** and the cisterns so vital for living in this area. At the end of the street is a **wine press** dating from the end of the Roman Period (third-fourth centuries A.D.).

The structures on the **acropolis** come from the Byzantine Period though the Byzantines reused elements from the Nabatean Period. The acropolis served as a **fortress** to which people from the area would flee in time of danger. Located in the fortress are two churches. The **southern church** is called St. Theodore because the martyr Theodorus is buried within it. The church is an apsidal basilica. The sanctuary is two steps higher than the nave. There are five tombs in the church. The **northern church** of Bishop Shachia is the older of the two. It has a baptistery attached to it. These churches were built over Nabatean temples. There are several **caves** beneath the acropolis. The Byzantines cut these caves from the soft stone to store their grain and wine. Some had living quarters at the entrance. There were almost four hundred such dwellings on the terraces beneath the acropolis and this makes the population of the site between two thousand and three thousand. Daily 8–4. Fee.

Desert Farming. From the acropolis one can look to the south and see an **experimental farm** of the Hebrew University. The goal of the work there is to replicate the desert farming techniques of the Nabateans. Obviously, the most important technique in this process was catching and redirecting the runoff following the rains that did fall in the desert. The desert soil was crusted and this prevented the immediate absorption of water. The Nabateans took advantage of this and managed to direct the runoff to the fields under cultivation. Analysis of pollens recovered during excavations shows that the Nabateans cultivated grapes, lentils, wheat, and barley. The wine press on the site confirms that viticulture was a significant part of Avdat's enterprises. The researchers at the experimental farm have been successful in growing these crops using only water gathered, saved, and distributed by the methods developed by the Nabateans.

Beersheva (H: "The Well of the Seven")

"Abraham planted a tamarisk at Beersheva" (Gen 21:33).

This city's name reflects its importance as an oasis in the Negev. Gen 21:22-32 describes a treaty that Abraham made with Abimelech to regulate the use of the well—a treaty sealed by the sacrifice of seven lambs. This is how Israelites of the first millennium explained the origin of Beersheva's name.

This fourth largest of Israel's cities stands on the border between the cultivated fields of Judah to the north and the Negev to the south. It is fifty-two miles southwest of Jerusalem. The city receives about six inches of rain a year and is the demarcation between cultivated areas to the north and desert to the south. It serves as a place where the desert dwellers, the Bedouin, can trade. Each Thursday the Bedouin travel to Beersheva to offer their wares and buy needed supplies. In recent years merchants, noticing how the outdoor "Bedouin market" on the outskirts of the city has attracted many visitors, have moved their goods to this market for sale. This has diluted the original purpose of the market, but a visit to the Thursday Bedouin market is still an adventure.

History. The region around Beersheva has been inhabited from the Chalcolithic Period (4000 B.C.). People were attracted by its water resources. Tel Beersheva is 975 feet above sea level and is situated near the junction of the Wadi Beersheva and the Wadi Hebron a few kilometers from the modern city. There is no evidence of occupation in the MBA (2200–1550 B.C.) that some people designate as the period of the patriarchs, though Genesis associates Abraham with Beersheva. The site was unoccupied from about 3200 to 1200 B.C. From the end of the LBA (1200 B.C.) to the Early Arab Period (seventh–eighth centuries A.D.), Beersheva was almost continuously inhabited. Archaeologists have identified fifteen occupational layers. In antiquity, this city was always a small settlement occupying just three acres at its greatest expanse. For example, the eighth century B.C. population was about one hundred. It was destroyed at the end of that century—probably during Sennacherib's invasion of Judah (701 B.C.). Resettlement took place during the Hellenistic Period. Herod built a fortress and baths here. The population center, however, moved to the west during the Roman and Byzantine Periods (first century B.C. to seventh century A.D.)—in the area occupied by the modern city.

The Biblical Tradition. The ancient town is the setting for some of the patriarchal narratives. It is the place where Abraham and later Isaac make treaties with Abimelech, king of Gerar (Gen 21:32; 26:33). It became Isaac's home and he built an altar there (Gen 26:25). According to Joshua, it was first a city of Simeon (15:28) and then later of Judah (19:2). This probably reflects the absorption of Simeon by Judah during the Monarchic Period. Though there were Israelite settlements south of this city, it became the proverbial southern border of the Promised Land. The formula, "From Dan to Beersheva" occurs several times, e.g., Judg 20:1, as a statement of the extent of Israelite settlement. Beersheva was a premonarchic judicial center (1 Sam 8:2). The NT does not mention this city.

Antiquities. Notice the **walls** and **homes** that have been reconstructed on the tel. The homes are made of mudbrick since limestone is not as common here as elsewhere in Israel. The walls sit on mudbrick foundations. The presence and size of **storehouses** and other administrative buildings lead to the conclusion that Beersheva served as an administrative center during the Israelite monarchy. The city was home to officials from the army, tax collectors, trade regulators, priests, and other royal officials. Still, their number was not large. Among the interesting features of the tel are the **city gate**, the **governor's residence**, the **water system**, the glacis and the **warehouses**. In one of these warehouses well-chiseled stones were discovered which, when reconstructed, formed a horned altar. A copy of this altar has been placed in the assembly area before the entrance to the tel. The original is in the Israel Museum. Evidently, the city had a temple where sacrifices were offered. This, of course, is not in harmony with the cult centralization program of Deuteronomy 12. Outside the city gate is a cistern known popularly as **Abraham's well,** though its presence outside the Iron Age walls is an anomaly. If the cistern was dug in the 1100s, as some maintain, the builders of the walls would have included the well inside the walls. There is a tower on the antiquity site that offers a great view of the region. Daily 8–4. Fee.

Eilat

"King Solomon also built a fleet at Ezion-geber, which is near Elath . . ." (1 Kgs 9:26).

Location. Eilat is the southernmost settlement in Israel, two hundred twenty-one miles south of Jerusalem. It is on the Gulf of Eilat (also known as the Gulf of Aqaba), the eastern branch of the Red Sea. It is at the southern end of the

Arab merchants selling baskets and sea shells near the Gulf of Aqaba.

Aravah, with the mountains of Sinai to the south and west and the mountains of Edom to the east. The latter continue as the Middle Range of Saudi Arabia.

History. In the Bible, the city is known as Eloth or Elath. Both Edom and Judah vied for control of this port (see 2 Kgs 14:22). The Romans called it Aila and stationed a garrison there. It was successively taken by the Byzantines, Arabs, Crusaders, Mamlukes, Ottomans, and British. The Israelis took the city during the 1948 war and founded the modern town in 1951.

Visit. Eilat is an important port facility and a center for tourism. It has beautiful beaches—some with coral reefs. The latter make it a great place for snorkeling. Its temperate climate in the winter makes it a popular international resort. For those who do not want to snorkel but still want to see the coral reef and its marine life in their natural setting, Eilat boasts an underwater aquarium (The **Eilat Coral World**). This city is a center for processing *Eilat Stone.* This is a semiprecious black stone flecked with green malachite, which is oxidized copper. The stones come from the Timna area and they are polished and set in Eilat. **Aqaba** is the twin-city to Eilat, across the border in Jordan. It is the only port that Jordan has. Since the peace treaty between Israel and Jordan, joint ventures between the two are possible. If you decide to visit Eilat by interurban bus, you need to make a reservation for the bus in advance. You can do this at the bus station from which you will depart.

Ein Avdat

"Your southern boundary shall be at the desert of Zin . . ." (Num 34:1).

Location. This is a spring in the wilderness of Zin, four miles southwest of Sde Boker. Its waters flow through a canyon and empty into the Nahal Zin, forming beautiful waterfalls and pools along the way. The canyon is in the central Negev just north of Avdat. It is a delightful place for a pleasant but strenuous walk. Footing can be slippery. Take good walking shoes and be careful. One can see river flora and the ibex that live in the canyon. At one time, the ibex were seen only in the early morning and late evening when they came for a drink. They have become so accustomed to hikers they can be seen almost any time. You will also notice some caves in the canyon; these were hermit dwellings in the Byzantine Period. It is important to take this walk only with an experienced guide.

The Biblical Tradition. This oasis is in the **Wilderness of Zin**, an area that the biblical tradition associates with the entrance of the Israelite tribes into Canaan (Num 20:1; 27:14; 34:3; Deut 32:51). The spies, sent out from Kadesh-barnea, explored the land from this area northward (Num 13:21). This area also ran along the southern border of Judah (Josh 15:1). Here is where Moses committed the offense that prevented him from entering Canaan (Num 27:14: Deut 32:51). It was also where Miriam died and was buried though the tradition does not locate the place of her tomb with any precision (Num 20:1).

Makhtesh Ramon (A: Wadi Ruman, "The Roman Valley")

Seventeen miles south of Avdat, there is a geological formation called a **makhtesh**. There are two others in the Negev to the northeast near Dimona. This one is twenty-nine miles long, six and one-half miles wide, and 1,625 feet deep. There is a small educational center administered by the SPNI in Mitzpe Ramon that explains the geological history of the region. It offers a multimedia presentation and a magnificent view of the *makhtesh*. (Daily 8–4. Fee). The word *makhtesh* is difficult to translate into English since it is used to name a geological formation unique to the Negev. Sometimes the word *crater* is used. Though the *makhtesh* is not a crater, it looks enough like one to justify the use of the word. The Hebrew word *Ramon* is derived from the Arabic name for the area. In Arabic *ruman* means "Roman." There was a Roman road through the *makhtesh* to the Transjordan.

Sde Boker

The name of the kibbutz comes from the Arabic name of a nearby mountain *Shajarat el-Baqqar* ("Rancher's Field"). It also reflects the original aim of the settlers there: to breed cattle in the central Negev. This kibbutz in the Negev hills is thirty-three miles south of Beersheva. When it was established in 1952, it was far from other settlements and had no roads or water supply. The current membership of the kibbutz is less than three hundred.

This is the kibbutz to which David Ben Gurion, the first prime minister of Israel, retired in 1953. He was determined to establish a Jewish state and allowed no obstacle to stand in his path. His personality and drive did not allow him to be remembered with great affection, but his achievements earned him respect and admiration. One of Ben Gurion's goals was to get Israel to turn the Negev desert into a paradise. He went to Sde Boker because he wanted to encourage settlement of the Negev by his personal example. The Negev made up more than half of Israel's pre-1967 territory. Although Ben Gurion returned to public service in 1956, he went back to this kibbutz in 1963, after completing another stint as prime minister. He promoted the Institute of Negev Studies which researches the problems and prospects of agriculture in arid climates like that of the Negev. The kibbutz maintains Ben Gurion's cottage as a museum dedicated to his life and accomplishments. He and his wife Paula are buried on a section of the kibbutz that overlooks the Wilderness of Zin. The view from the burial site is breathtaking. Daily 8–4. Fee.

Timna

"These were the chiefs of Edom: the chiefs of Timna, Alia . . ."
(1 Chr 1:51).

Location. Fifteen miles north of Eilat is a modern copper mining installation named after an Edomite clan mentioned in the genealogy of Esau (see Gen 36:40). Since opening in 1976, the mines have not been in continual operation. Sometimes the world copper prices are too low to make mining profitable. This is also a popular hiking and camping area. The SPNI has an audiovisual program that describes the mining and processing of copper that took place here in antiquity.

History. Copper was already extracted on this site in the Chalcolithic Period (4500–3150 B.C.). Full-scale operations begin in the EBA to the LBA, primarily by Egyptians. The mines were opened again by the Romans who worked them until the second century. It was not until the 1900s that the mines were opened again—this time by the Israelis.

Antiquities. West of the modern mines are ancient ones popularly called **King Solomon's Mines,** but excavation has shown these to be Egyptian works of the Late Bronze and early Iron Ages. Excavation has not only uncovered tools, smelting and casting installations, slag heaps, but also the remains of a **town** where the workers and administrators lived, a **small fort**, and two **temples to the Egyptian goddess Hathor**, the patroness of the earth and of mining. The temples date from 1100–1000 B.C. Also, on the site are rock formations popularly called **Solomon's Pillars.** These are 164-foot sandstone columns formed by erosion caused by wind and rain. There is an ancient **Egyptian inscription** on one of the formations. The erroneous name derives from the view that Solomon had mines here. Daily 8–4. Fee.

CHAPTER EIGHT

Israel: The Mediterranean Coast

In antiquity, the Coastal Plain was the most valuable piece of Canaanite real estate from an agricultural, commercial, and strategic point of view. The area was fertile and well watered. (Today a substantial portion of the area is given to the production of citrus fruit—an important Israeli agricultural export.) The Via Maris passed along the Coastal Plain; controlling this route and taxing the caravans that traveled along it made whoever collected these tolls very wealthy. No doubt Solomon's wealth grew because of his domination of this area. Its strategic importance is obvious in a region that did not have good north-south roads. The coastal region was the path that armies to and from Egypt had to pass and so it was a scene of continual conflict. It was not under Israelite control very much. This is especially true of the southern portion and the cities of Gaza, Ashkelon, and Ashdod that the Philistines dominated.

Acco (G: Ptolemais; A: Tell el-Fukhkhar; French: St. Jean d'Acre)

"We continued the voyage and came from Tyre to Ptolemais, where we greeted the brothers and stayed a day with them" (Acts 21:7).

Location. Acco lies along the Mediterranean coast fifteen miles north of Haifa. Between these two cities is the Valley of Zebulun, named after the tribe that was to "dwell by the seashore" (Gen 49:13). In antiquity, the city's location gave it significant strategic and commercial importance. It was at the junction of the coastal road (the Via Maris) and the inland road that led through Galilee to Transjordan and Syria. Some rabbis in antiquity considered Acco outside the land of Israel; thus pious Jews would not allow themselves to be buried there. Acco's cluster of well-preserved and, in some instances, well-reconstructed mosques, khans, walls, and harbor provide a charming cityscape. It is Israel's most picturesque town after Jerusalem.

History. Acco has been the object of conquest throughout history because of its location, but the Bible says that the tribe of Asher was unable to take it under control of the city (Judg 1:31—the only occurrence of Acco in the OT). Acco is one of the most ancient cities in the world. The Egyptians provide us with the first literary reference to the city in their nineteenth-century B.C. Execration Texts. The fourteenth-century B.C. Amarna Letters mention Acco thirteen times. The Canaanite city of Acco (A: Tell el Fukhkhar) has been under excavation since 1973. The tel is on the road to Zefat, one mile east of the modern city.

While the Israelites were not able to conquer the city, the Assyrians under Sennacherib did in 701 B.C. The city then passed to Babylonians at the beginning of the sixth century and to the Persians at the end of the same century. Alexander the Great brought Acco into the Greek orbit in 333 B.C. Following his death, Acco became part of the territory controlled by the Ptolemies. In 261 B.C., Ptolemy II Philadelphus fortified it, Hellenized it, and gave it a new name: Acco-Ptolemais. He also moved the center of the city closer to the sea. When the Ptolemies lost their Palestinian holdings to the Seleucids (second century B.C.), Antiochus IV renamed the city a second time: Antiochia-at-Ptolemais. The Hasmoneans were not able to wrest this city from the Greeks. It was here that Jonathan was captured and killed in 142 B.C. (1 Macc 13:48). When the Romans conquered Palestine, they made Acco a naval base and called it the Colonia Ptolemais. They also granted the city a measure of autonomy.

It was during the Roman Period that Jews began to settle in Acco. The NT refers to the city by its Greek name (Acts 21:7). Paul's ship put in at Acco from Tyre and he stayed at Acco for one day before continuing to Caesarea. When the Arabs conquered Palestine in the seventh century, the Greek name was abandoned and its Semitic name was restored. The Crusaders arrived in Acco in 1104, built a fortress and a naval base. They gave Acco still another name, *St. Jean d'Acre*. After the loss of Jerusalem in 1187, Acco became the Crusader capital. In a break with their usual policy, the Crusaders allowed Jews to live with them in Acco. Several important Jews, among them Maimonides, visited the city in the Crusader Period. Crusader rule in Palestine ended when Sultan el-Ashraf conquered the city in 1291. He destroyed the Crusader city and Acco became little more than a village until the fourteenth century when Jews returned and rebuilt the town.

Acco regained some of its former importance in 1750 when a Bedouin sheik named el-Amr imposed his rule over Galilee and made Acco his capital. It was not long before the Ottoman Turks regained control over Galilee, but they kept Acco as the capital not only of Galilee, but of their entire province of Syria and Palestine. One of the most famous Turkish pashas (governors), Ahmad, (el-Jazzar, "the butcher"), built the mosque that bears his name, the walls of the city that remain to this day, and an aqueduct that can be seen from the road north to Nahariyah. His most significant achievement, however, was his defeat of Napoleon in 1799. Napoleon wanted to take Acco as part of his grand plan to strip England of India. El-Jazzar frustrated Napoleon's plans and the emperor had to return to France. This was a genuine turning point in history. If Napoleon had taken Acco, the entire Middle East would have been his.

During the Mandate Period, Haifa became the region's main seaport and Acco's importance diminished. The Jews of Acco left the city after the Arab riots of 1936–1939. In 1948, Israeli forces took the city and most Arabs left and the Jews returned. Today's population is mixed: forty thousand of whom about one-fourth are Arab.

Antiquities. As you approach the Old City, the **first wall and moat** you see was built by el-Jazzar in 1799, after Napolean's retreat. The **other wall** is Crusader (twelfth century). The city's **Great Mosque**, built by el-Jazzar in 1781, is the best example of Turkish architecture in the country. Next to the mosque are the tombs of el-Jazzar and one of his successors. Below the courtyard of the mosque are some **cisterns** built to service the Crusader fortress. Across from the mosque is the entrance to the remnants of that fortress. It is currently under restoration, but the most interesting room can still be entered: the **Crypt of St. Jean**. It has been variously identified as a church, a reception hall, a burial site, and a refectory. From the crypt runs a **tunnel** that leads to the medieval **market**. There was an attempt to turn the market into a shopping area for tourists as was done in one section of Jerusalem's Cardo. The project did not enjoy much success. Outside the market is the **municipal museum** that is under renovation. The museum is in a former Turkish Period bathhouse. From the exit of the Crusader fortress, it is possible to walk through the Old City. After reaching the shore, it is a short walk to the reconstructed **Khan el-Umdan** (A: "The Inn of the Columns"). This Turkish Period (1785) caravanserai is easily recognizable by its tall clock tower. The inn served the camel caravans that transported grain and other produce from the Galilee to the port. It was built by el-Jazzar in 1785. The name of the inn derives from the Aswan marble pillars that el-Jazzar acquired from Caesarea to support the building. The lower story housed the animals and goods while people used the rooms on the top floor. From the khan, it is possible to walk along the walls where you can see some of the cannons that repulsed Napoleon's fleet. Eventually this will take you out of the Old City.

Just about one mile from the city is Tell el-Fukhar, the remains of the ancient Canaanite city. Excavation is currently going on though the site has been prepared for visitors. About two miles north of the city, on the road to Nahariyah, there is the holiest spot in the world for the Bahai faith. It is the **Bahai mansion** where Baha'u'llah lived after his expulsion from Persia. This prophet of the Bahai faith died there in 1892 and is buried in the gardens of the mansion. On the road between Acco and Nahariyah to the north, you can see the well-preserved eighteenth-century **aqueduct** built by el-Jazzar, which supplied water into Acco from the Kabri springs to the north. Mosque: Daily 8–5:30. Fee. Bahai Shrine: Daily except Sunday 9–12; Gardens 9–4. Free. Crypt of St. Jean (Knights' Hall): Daily 8–4:45; Friday 8–1:45. Fee. Tell Acco: Daily 8–4; Friday 8–1. Fee.

Ashkelon

"In the houses of Ashkelon at evening they shall couch their flocks . . ."
(Zeph 2:7).

Location. This city is a large seaport town seventeen miles north of Gaza and forty-one miles south of Tel Aviv.

History. Ashkelon was an important Canaanite city-state long before the Israelite tribes achieved dominance in the region. It was an important stop on the Via Maris. With the breakdown of Egyptian and Canaanite control in the 1200s B.C., the Philistines took control of the city (Josh 13:3; 1 Sam 6:4). It remained in Philistine hands until the eighth century B.C. when it came under the control of first the Assyrians, then the Egyptians and finally the Babylonians. At the end of the 400s B.C., the Persians gave the city to Tyre. In the second century B.C., the city placed itself under the protection of Rome to avoid becoming part of the Hasmonean kingdom. Herod the Great beautified the city, probably because of family connections. His grandfather was the high priest of the temple of Apollo and some suggest that Herod himself was born here. Ashkelon did not join in the First Revolt against Rome and so continued to prosper, becoming a center of learning. It finally fell victim to the Crusader-Muslim conflict. It was destroyed in 1270 to prevent it from becoming a Crusader base.

Antiquities. The National Parks Authority have developed the site for tourism. Visitors can see remnants of Bronze Age, Byzantine, and Crusader Period occupations. The Canaanite and Philistine cities are currently under excavation. At the entrance to the site is the city's **wall**. The stone wall is Crusader. The mud brick beneath it is Middle Bronze Age twentieth century B.C. In the center of the site is the Roman Period (second century A.D.) **forum**. There is also a public beach at the site. Excavations are continuing at the site. Daily, 8–6; Summer 8–8. Fee.

Caesarea Maritima
(L: "Caesarea by the sea"; H: Qesaryon; A: Qaisariya)

"Now in Caesarea there was a man named Cornelius . . ." (Acts 10:1).

Location. Midway between Haifa and Tel Aviv stands what was *the* port of Roman and Byzantine Palestine. Now primarily a resort area, Caesarea once served as the capital of Palestine from the time that the Romans replaced Archelaus with a procurator shortly after the death of Herod the Great. The Romans continued to rule Palestine from Caesarea until the end of Byzantine rule in the seventh century. It also was the principal diocese of the region, eclipsing even Jerusalem.

History. The site was an ancient anchorage along the coast—at least from the fourth century B.C. It was known as Straton's Tower. It was a Sidonian possession that cared for ships traveling between Egypt and Phoenicia. The Hasmonean Alexander Yannai acquired it in 100 B.C. It was during this time that Jews began to settle here. Pompey removed the city from Jewish rule in 63 B.C. but thirty years later Augustus gave the place to Herod the Great. Herod built a great Hellenistic city with a port there. Like Herod's other building projects, the construction of Caesarea was contrived by him to immortalize his name as a great king, to secure the loyalty of the Jews who were hostile to his rule, and to provide work for his subjects.

Herod named this city and its port in honor of Augustus. The port was known as *Sebastos*, Greek for Augustus. Caesarea was a Hellenistic city with a theater, amphitheater, a marketplace, a palace, and a temple dedicated to Caesar. Important innovations were his grid street pattern and sewer system, cleaned out each day by the tides. Caesarea became a typical Hellenistic city. It was administered by a city council and magistrates, who were, of course, subject to a military commander appointed by Herod. The Greek-speaking population swelled under encouragement from Herod, who saw Caesarea as a balance to Jewish Jerusalem.

After the ineffectual leadership of Judea by Archelaus, the Romans annexed Judea directly and made it the capital of the Roman Province later known as *Palestina Prima*. Pontius Pilate dedicated a temple to Tiberias while he was prefect of Judea. An inscription to this effect was found in the theater. It was reused during the renovations of the Byzantine Period. Caesarea was the place where the First Revolt broke out. There were tensions between the Jewish and Gentile population and when a synagogue was damaged, the Jews rioted. The Romans put down the riot. Josephus claims that twenty thousand Jews were killed though the city probably had at most forty thousand inhabitants. Since the Romans made no distinction between Christians and other Jews here, the Christian community of Caesarea suffered as well. It did not recover until the latter part of the second century. Following the revolt, the city was a Roman colony with limited self-rule. It was the primary outlet of Roman culture in ancient Palestine. Hadrian visited the city in A.D. 130 and probably had the hippodrome built then. The Romans executed Rabbi Akiva, a leader of the Second Revolt, in the city's theater.

By the end of the second century, both Christians and Jews made a surprising comeback. The lure of the city's economic advantages lured them back. In 195, a local council held that Easter should be celebrated only on Sunday. Origen began his school and library (thirty thousand volumes) here around 250. About the same time, the Jews established a famous rabbinic academy here. The most renowned of Caesarea's bishops was Eusebius (315–339). He was the first to write a history of the Church and a geography of the Bible.

Relations between the city's Christian rulers and the indigenous population, both Jewish and Samaritan, deteriorated in the 400s. The Samaritans revolted in 529 and again in 555 (with Jewish help). The non-Christians sided with the Persians during the latter's invasion in 614. Although the Byzantines made a brief comeback, Arabs took the city in 640. The port silted up, but the area was still agriculturally valuable. The Crusaders took the city in 1101. Louis IX built the fortress in 1251, reusing the seating from the hippodrome and other architectural fragments. Still, the Mamlukes took the city in 1265 after which it was abandoned. The site remained desolate until the 1800s when the Turks settled some Bosnian refugees here. The mosque and minaret date from that period.

Caesarea has an important role in the Church's beginnings as described in Acts. The deacon Philip was the first to bring the gospel here (Acts 8:4-40). It was the home of Cornelius, the first Gentile convert (Acts 10:3-48). His conversion transformed Christianity from a type of Messianic Judaism to a world religion. Paul passed through the port during his missionary journeys (9:29-30) and was imprisoned there for two years (58-60; Acts 23–26) while awaiting his appeal to the emperor.

Antiquities. Caesarea is an enormous antiquity site, covering 235 acres. Systematic excavations have been going on here since 1945 and are continuing. Some of these involved underwater archaeology to explore the remnants of Herod's harbor. Among the important finds at the site are the Roman Period theater, amphitheater, aqueducts, and port facilities; the Byzantine Period hippodrome, esplanade, administrative center, and market; and the Crusader Fortress. Also found were a mithraeum and fifth-century synagogue. Not all remains are available for visitation since excavations and reconstruction are ongoing.

One of the sites you will undoubtedly see is the **Roman theater**. It is famous because of a stone plaque with the name of Pontius Pilate. It is the only inscription from Pilate's tenure in Palestine. It reads [Dis Augusti]s Tiberieum [Po]ntius Pilatus [Praef]ectus Juda[ea]e [fecit d]e[dicavit]. The walls to the north of the theater are part of the sixth-century **Byzantine fortress** that incorporated the back of the theater in the defense of the city. The Israelis have reconstructed the theater and use it for musical and theatrical productions.

The **Crusader castle** dominates the site and one can see remains from the Roman and Byzantine cities that the Crusaders used in building their castle. Notice the glacis. A ten-foot high wall rose above it. It can be entered through the restored eastern gate. Within the castle, one can see some of the **port facilities** from Herod's day, his **temple to Augustus**, and the platform for his **temple to Roma**, later converted to a triapsidal basilica by the crusaders. They abandoned it when the vaults below began to collapse. Just south of the castle, one can see the **Byzantine administrative center and agora**. The **Cardo Maximus** and the **Archive** have not been completely excavated but they represent the governmental and commercial center of the Byzantine city. There are several inscriptions in mosaics there. One inscription asks Christ to protect the officials Ampelios and Musonius. The other is a quotation from Rom 13:3.

Nearer the shore is a **bathhouse**. To the south of this are Herodian **warehouses,** one of which was converted into a **Mithraeum** at the end of the first century A.D. The cult of Mithras was popular among soldiers. This Mithraeum was in use until the fourth century. It is the only Mithraeum found in Palestine. West of the castle, there is an impressive **Byzantine esplanade**. It was built by Flavius Strategius (sixth-century mayor) according to the mosaic. He reused elements from the Roman Period, i.e., the statues. The one in porphyry is Hadrian.

The **hippodrome** is now a cultivated field east of the castle. Built in 130 by Hadrian, it was 1056 feet long and 264 feet wide. There was seating for twenty thousand spectators. The races were world-famous in the Byzantine Period. The Crusaders used the hippodrome to supply building materials for their fortress. All that is visible today are fragments of decorative elements made of Aswan marble. An obelisk lies in the middle of the field.

Remains of Herod's aqueducts, Caesarea Maritima.

Visible north of the Crusader castle are the **aqueducts**. It is possible to climb stairs to the top of the aqueduct along the sea. From there it is clear that what looks like one aqueduct are actually two built next to each other. Herod built the first one, but when the city's population grew, a second was necessary. Along the western face of the aqueduct one can see copies of the plaques left by the tenth Roman legion whose soldiers built the structure. The aqueduct brought water from springs fourteen miles north. Also visible from the top of the stairs is a covered aqueduct just to the east. It dates from the Byzantine Period and brought water for irrigation from the Nahal Tanninim (Crocodile River) four miles to the north. Near the aqueducts are impressive modern villas. The area boasts of the only golf course in Israel. Daily 8–4; Summer 8–5. Fee.

Dor (A: Khirbet el Burj)

"Antiochus encamped before Dor with a hundred and twenty thousand infantry and eight thousand horsemen" (1 Macc 15:13).

Location. Tel Dor is south of the Kibbutz Nahsholim (H: "breakers") along the Mediterranean coast fifteen miles north of Caesarea. In 1949, Jews from Greece founded a settlement here on the lands of an abandoned Arab village named Tantura.

History. The city and its port were probably founded during the reign of Rameses II (1279–1212 B.C.) when trade between Egypt and the Aegean region was flourishing. The port of Dor is mentioned in the *Tale of Wen-Amon* (*ANET*, 26; twelfth century B.C.). Though the Bible says that Joshua defeated the king of Dor (Josh 12:23), the city did not come into Israelite control until the time of David. It became the capital of one of Solomon's administrative districts. It must have been an important district since it was governed by Solomon's son-in-law Abinadab (1 Kgs 4:11). In 732 B.C., Tiglath-Pileser III conquered the city. He made it capital of the Assyrian province of Durru that ran along the region's northern coast from Jaffa to the Carmel Range. It passed to Greek control in the fourth century. According to 1 Macc 15:10-14, Tryphon, the pretender to the Seleucid throne, held out at Dor against Antiochus VII. The Hasmonean, Alexander Yannai, made it part of his Jewish kingdom in the second century. Pompey ended Jewish rule in the city in 63 B.C. and granted the city a measure of self-government. After Herod built the port of Caesarea a few miles away, Dor's importance as a seaport was eclipsed by its neighbor. During the early Byzantine Period, the population was Christian. The city had a resident bishop until the 600s. The Crusaders built a fortress here called Castellum Merle.

Antiquities. The site is still under excavation and has not been prepared for tourism, but it is possible to walk up to the site from the beach at Nahsholim. It is important to be careful when visiting any undeveloped site. Carelessness can harm the visitor and the site. On the eastern edge of the tel is a **residential quarter** from the Persian to Roman Periods. In this area, there are foundations for a wall and tower. Just south of the residential quarter is the **gate area.** Roman and Hellenistic Period artifacts predominate here. The four-room gate dates from the ninth century B.C. Dor of the tenth–eleventh centuries is visible near the south bay. Here one can see houses built on stone foundations with mud brick superstructures. The kibbutz has converted a bottle-making factory to a **museum** on ancient Dor, which highlights the role of the city as a port. The museum offers a video on the techniques of underwater archaeology that is necessary at a site such as this one. Museum: Daily 8–2; Saturday 10:30–3.

Haifa

"Go up to Carmel!" (1 Sam 25:5).

Name and Location. The origins of the name of Israel's third largest city are obscure. Medieval Christians called it "Caipha" believing that Caiaphas, the high priest mentioned in the Passion stories, founded the city and named it after himself. Haifa lies along the Mediterranean coast, fifty-six miles north of Tel Aviv and ninety-nine miles northwest of Jerusalem. It is an important industrial and commercial center, and the country's main port. The city is built partly on an offshoot of the Carmel range and partly on the adjacent coastal plain. During the Mandate Period, Haifa became Palestine's leading industrial and manufacturing center. It was also the region's main port of entry. The city's mixed population of Jews and Arabs do not segregate themselves in separate parts of the city, but live together. The relations between the two groups have been good though tensions make themselves felt occasionally.

Religious Traditions. In speaking about Israel's deliverance, the prophet says: "The desert and the parched land will exult; the steppe will rejoice and bloom. They will bloom with abundant flowers, and rejoice with joyful song. The glory of Lebanon will be given to them, the splendor of Carmel and Sharon . . ." (Isa 35:1-2). Mount Carmel is associated with another prophet, Elijah, who built an altar on this mountain and engaged in a contest with the prophets of Baal to decide which God, Yahweh or Baal, deserved the exclusive loyalty of Israel. The official state policy of the Northern Kingdom, led by Ahab and his Tyrian wife Jezebel, was to promote the worship of both gods. The contest that Elijah set up is described in the familiar story of 1 Kings 18. Elisha, the successor of Elijah, is also associated with Mount Carmel (2 Kgs 4:25). The Song of Songs also reflects this area's reputation for natural beauty (Cant 7:5-6). Jeremiah, on the other hand, uses Carmel as a symbol of strength (Jer 46:18). The beauty and strength of Carmel served the prophets who spoke words of judgment against Israel (Isa 33:9; Amos 1:2; 9:3).

Mount Carmel is a mountain ridge that runs southeast for twenty-one miles until it merges with the central highlands. There are two passes through this mountain. You should visit the one guarded by Megiddo, which oversaw a branch of the Via Maris. There is a small river north of the city: the River Kishon. There the Egyptians had a small port to support trade from Mycenae and Cyprus (fourteenth– thirteenth century B.C.). It went out of use when the Philistines came in the latter part of the 1200s B.C. They preferred Tyre and Sidon as ports. The port near Haifa suffered a cycle of construction–destruction–reconstruction until the Modern Period when it became the most important port of entry into Palestine.

One reason Mount Carmel does not receive much attention in the Old Testament is that it was generally bypassed by armies and caravans that moved up and down the eastern Mediterranean. The Carmel range was a barrier. That is why the Via Maris shifts inland before reaching Mount Carmel. Haifa was not the scene of battles or other dramatic encounters except the one described in 1 Kings 18. The region was one that did not allow large groups of people to move about with ease. The Canaanites consider Mount Carmel to be a holy site long before Elijah in the ninth century. Already some six hundred years earlier Egyptian texts speak of this region as "the holy headland." The veneration of this site continues in the Hellenistic and Roman Periods. Christians and Jews, who both revere the memory of Elijah, honor this place. Later the Muslims joined this veneration calling Elijah, el-Khader. (A: "the Green." Green is a sacred color for Muslims since it was Mohammed's favorite.)

Small Jewish communities lived in the area of the present city in the Second Temple Period. The first time the name Haifa appears in a text from antiquity

The Persian Gardens, as seen from Mount Carmel, Haifa.

is in the third century A.D. rabbinic literature. Arabs settled here after the seventh century A.D. The population grew steadily until the Crusaders came in 1100 and massacred both the Arab and Jewish population, who joined in resisting the Crusader invasion. In 1291, the Mamlukes defeated the Crusaders and destroyed the city.

The Modern City. Haifa is home to the Technion (Israel's MIT), Haifa University, and several museums including the National Maritime Museum and the Museum of Prehistory and Oceanography. A most interesting museum is in the office building of the **Dagon** [H: grain] Company, Israel's grain importer. It is a small museum showing the development of the oldest industry: the cultivation, storage, and distribution of grain. There is a free guided tour of the museum and the grain importing facilities daily at 10:30. Haifa is also home to Israel's only subway, the *Carmelit*, which connects the harbor area to the top of Mount Carmel.

Though the city is not mentioned in the Bible, Jews began to venerate a cave on Mount Carmel's slopes near Haifa as **Elijah's Cave**. The Carmelites who trace their origins to Palestine have a monastery and Church here called **Stella Maris**. Inside the church is a grotto that Elijah used for prayer. The city is the world center for the Bahai faith. Located in the well-kept **Persian Gardens** is the tomb of El Bab, a founder of the faith, its museum, library and archives. The gardens and tomb are open to all visitors. Other buildings are for the exclusive use of Bahais. The tomb is open daily 9–12 and the gardens are open 9–5. Free.

The **Carmelite Church.** The hermits who lived on the slopes of Mount Carmel sought approval from Albert, the Patriarch of Jerusalem for their Order. The Carmelite hermits left Palestine in 1291 when the Muslims took Acco. In the 1600s, they returned to Mount Carmel and lived in a small monastery near the lighthouse across from the present monastery. In the eighteenth century, the Carmelites built the present church over the foundations of a Crusader church. What attracted them here was a grotto in which Elijah is said to have lived. During Napoleon's campaign to take Palestine, the monastery served as a hospital for the wounded French soldiers. After his retreat from the area, the Turks killed the soldiers, who were confined here. They are buried under the pyramid outside the church. The Turks destroyed the church.

In the 1800s, the Carmelites rebuilt their church and monastery again. Pope Gregory XVI honored the church as the basilica of Stella Maris. The statue of Mary is sculpted out of cedarwood from Lebanon. The paintings in the dome were done in the 1920s by a brother from the monastery (Luigi Poggi), and depict Elijah in his fiery chariot, David, the Prophets Isaiah, Ezekiel and Daniel, Saints of the Carmelite Order, and the Holy Family. Below them are the four evangelists. The base of the copula contains OT texts used in the Mass of Our Lady of Mount Carmel. The stained glass window depicts Elijah in the desert and after his ascension in the fiery chariot. Daily 6–1:30; 3–5; Free.

Across from the church is a **cable car** that will take you to Haifa's beach. The ride gives one a unique view of the city. Daily 10–6; Friday 10–1:45; Saturday 10–5:45. Fee.

The Panorama. From the panorama you get a good view of Haifa, its port, and the city of Acco to the north. The city of Haifa is divided into three parts. The lowest part is the port and business center. The grain silo of Dagon is the largest industrial building in Israel, with a capacity of one hundred thousand tons of grain. The middle part of the city is a shopping and residential district and the top of Mount Carmel is the location of the luxury hotels and more exclusive residential areas. From the panorama, you can see the port facilities. Usually there are many ocean-going vessels at anchor. Haifa is a rest and recreation stop for the American fleet that patrols the Mediterranean. Usually you will be able to see some American warships at anchor.

The Muraqah. This site, which overlooks Tel Yokneam, commemorates the contest that Elijah staged with the prophets of Baal to convince the Israelites that they ought to serve Yahweh alone (see 1 Kings 18). From this site in a forested height outside of Haifa, it is possible to look down over the entire Jezreel Valley. The Carmelite Monastery dates to 1883. The name is the Arabic word for "burning" and is probably reminiscent of the biblical story of Elijah's sacrifice in 1 Kings 18. Monastery: Sunday 8–1:30; Monday–Friday 9–1; 3–5; Saturday 8–12; 1–5. Fee.

Jaffa (H: Yafo; G: Joppa)

"(Jonah) went down to Joppa, found a ship going to Tarshish, paid the fare, and went aboard to journey with them to Tarshish, away from the LORD*"* (Jon 1:3).

Location. This city is directly south of Tel Aviv. In 1950, Jaffa and Tel Aviv became a single municipality. The population of Jaffa is primarily Arab while Tel Aviv is Jewish.

History. In antiquity Jaffa was an important seaport. Second millennium B.C. texts from Egypt mention it. Jaffa did not come under Israelite control until the time of David and Solomon. It was to be part of the territory of Dan (Josh 19:40-46). Because Dan was unable to assert its control here, the tribe moved to the north (Judges 18). Jaffa was the port of entry for Jerusalem. Materials imported for the building of the Temple came through this port (1 Chr 2:15). The Book of Jonah naturally names Jaffa as the port where the prophet was going to catch a ship to escape the Lord's commission (Jon 1:3). Taking the city helped the Maccabees consolidate their position against the Greeks (1 Macc 12:24-34). The city is connected with two stories about Peter in Acts. The first is the miracle of raising Tabitha (Dorcas) from the dead (Acts 9:36-43). The other is Peter's vision at the house of Simon the Tanner. The vision ends Christian observance of the dietary laws and, what is more important, it prepares Peter for the inclusion of Gentiles into the Church (Acts 10:9-23). Jews continued to live in Jaffa after the First Revolt and it became an important rabbinic center.

The Crusaders used Jaffa as a port of entry, so the Mamlukes destroyed it in 1268. It was not rebuilt for four hundred years. The city survived on the pilgrim traffic to Palestine. In 1799 Napoleon attacked and destroyed Jaffa on his way up the Mediterranean coast. Because of another spurt of pilgrim traffic in the eighteenth century, Jaffa enjoyed a revival. The rise of Jewish immigration to Israel led to tensions with the Arab population of the city. Riots broke out more than once. During the 1948 war, Jewish forces captured Jaffa and some of its Arab citizens fled. In 1966, a new port was built further south at Ashdod and Jaffa's days as a commercial port ended. Today Jaffa is dependent on tourism. It is an artistic and entertainment center.

Excavations at Jaffa have revealed walls from the LBA and from the Postexilic Period, a glacis from the Iron Age, and a medieval synagogue. Artifacts from the excavations are on display at the small Jaffa museum, which is housed in a former Turkish bathhouse near St. Peter's Church. The museum has a copy of a clay prism from the time of Sennacherib in which he describes his campaign against Jaffa and other coastal cities in 701 B.C.

At the top of the hill in Old Jaffa stands St. Peter's Church. There is not much of a local congregation anymore, but the church serves the Catholics from the diplomatic corps of Tel Aviv in which there is no Catholic church. Since the Vatican has established diplomatic relations with Israel, the residence of the Papal Nuncio will be located in Jaffa near St. Peter's Church. Most countries maintain their embassies in the Tel Aviv area because of the disputed status of Jerusalem.

North of the church, one can see a series of black rocks in the Mediterranean. The Greeks associated these with the story of Andromeda. She was chained to one of these rocks to appease a sea monster and thereby protect the sea voyagers. When the monster approached Andromeda, her lover Perseus, riding on a winged horse, slew the monster, broke Andromeda's chains and saved her. The Romans had on display one of the monster's ribs and Andromeda's chains. The Jews as well had their legends about Jaffa. According to one, all the gold and jewels lost at sea made their way to Jaffa. The sea offered these to Solomon and this was the source of his wealth. Since his death, sunken treasure has been accumulating at Jaffa. It will be apportioned by the Messiah to the righteous in accord with their merits.

Tel Aviv-Jaffa Antiquities Museum. Located a short distance from St. Peter's Church, this small museum houses the small finds from excavations in the area, with an emphasis on pottery. Daily except Friday 9–2. Saturday 10–2. Fee.

The Plain of Sharon

"I am a flower of Sharon, a lily of the valley" (Cant 2:1).

In Hebrew, the definite article always accompanies the name of this region: The Sharon. The name may come from the Hebrew root meaning "level, straight" so the expression "The Sharon" may have meant "The Plain." The Sharon is a region along the central coast of the Mediterranean. Its northern boundary is Mount Carmel (just below Haifa); its southern boundary is the Yarkon River (in Tel Aviv). The Sharon extends eastward as far as the hills of Samaria. In antiquity, the Via Maris ran through its territory. The Sharon was valued for its natural beauty and its agricultural potential (Isa 33:9; 35:2; 65:10; Cant 2:1; 1 Chr 27:29). According to Acts, it was a locus of Peter's early ministry (Acts 9:35). The OT texts convey little information about the Sharon. Most are metaphorical in character. The Acts text, however, implies that the Sharon was an area of considerable population. This may reflect the settlement patterns that developed with the building of Caesarea.

Control of the Sharon was important because the Via Maris passed through it. Before the rise of the Israelite tribes, Egypt dominated the Sharon though the Egyptians governed through local Canaanite rulers. Israel controlled the Sharon from the time of David until the eighth century when it was incorporated into an Assyrian Province by Tiglath-Pileser III in 732 B.C. After Alexander's conquest, the region became thoroughly Hellenized. The Jews considered themselves an oppressed minority in their own country. Jewish resentment grew here until it exploded in A.D. 66 with rioting in Caesarea, the Roman capital of the Sharon, and of all of Roman Palestine. These riots spawned the First Revolt.

After the Arab conquest, the area was depopulated and neglected. What was fertile farm land became a malarial swamp. After the Crusades, the process of transforming the Sharon into an impassable swamp became official Arab policy to keep any invaders from using this region as a beachhead. With Jewish settlement in the nineteenth century, the Sharon was reclaimed. Its agricultural potential is again being exploited. Much of Israel's citrus is grown in this valley.

Rosh HaNiqra (A: Ras en Naqura "top of the crevices")

"(Antiochus) made Jonathan's brother Simon governor of the region from the Ladder of Tyre to the frontier of Egypt" (1 Macc 11:59).

This cliff on the Israeli-Lebanese border at the Mediterranean city is eleven miles north of Acco. Below, there are caverns that have been hollowed out by the pounding of waves. By visiting these caverns you can also see a walled-up railroad tunnel that served the Jerusalem-Beirut line before 1948. There is a **cable car** that takes visitors down to the caves. Looking south from the cliff, one has a good view of Nahariyah, Acco, and Haifa—on a clear day. There is no good view toward the north since military installations at the border are built on the top of the cliff. This area was an important thoroughfare for conquerors in antiquity. Both Alexander the Great (333 B.C.) and Antiochus IV (167 B.C.) entered Palestine from the north by the *Ladder of Tyre*, a mountain range that consists of a series of steps ascending from south to north that begins here. The Romans built a road through this region to connect Acco and Tyre for the benefit of commerce. Daily 8–4; Summer 8–6; Friday 8–3. Fee.

Tel Aviv

Name and Location. The Bible mentions a Tel Aviv (Ezek 3:15) but it has no relation to this city. Tel Aviv is a modern city—the first modern Jewish city in Israel. It was founded in 1908 as a suburb of Jaffa. The biblical Tel Aviv is a city in Babylon where the Judahites were exiled following the fall of Jerusalem to Nebuchadnezzar in 587 B.C. The name of the modern city is taken from the title of a book by Theodore Herzl. He was a Jew from Vienna, sent to Paris to cover the trial of Dreyfuss. This French Jew was falsely accused of spying for Germany in 1894 although the prosecutors knew that a non-Jewish officer was guilty. The trial was marked by eruptions of anti-Semitism and Herzl concluded that a Jewish state was necessary so that the fate of Jews would no longer be in the hands of anti-Semites. Herzl called the first Zionist conference in 1897 in Basel to create a Jewish state in Palestine. He died in 1904 at age 44, but he predicted that a Jewish state would be established within fifty years after his death. The State of Israel was proclaimed forty-four years later. After the state was established, Herzl's body was taken from Vienna and reburied in Jerusalem. One of the books Herzl wrote to encourage Jews to migrate to Palestine and establish a state there was entitled *Altneuland*. When the book was translated into modern Hebrew, its title became *Tel Aviv* (*alt* = old; *tel* = ancient ruin; *neuland* = new land; *aviv* = spring, i.e., the season of new growth). Tel Aviv was the political center of the prestate Israel and the state was proclaimed there on May 14, 1948. After the 1948 war ended, the capital was moved to Jerusalem. Its political importance is still felt since many national organizations, political parties, newspapers, government offices, and embassies are located there. The United States maintains its embassy in Tel Aviv on HaYarkon Street.

Tel Aviv is the economic, cultural, and social center of Israel. It is where most of the country's industry, commerce, and finance are controlled. It is home to the Israel Philharmonic Orchestra and the Israel Opera. Its nightlife is a magnet that draws Israelis and foreigners alike. Jerusalem has little to compare with Tel Aviv's centers of popular culture.

Eretz Israel Museum. An important reason for going to Tel Aviv is to visit the Eretz Israel museum on the campus of the Tel Aviv University. It is a collection of several small museums spread out over thirty acres. The name "land of Israel" museum suggests that it is concerned with subjects that relate to the history, culture, and people of the country. On display are not only the principal artifacts found from antiquity (ceramics, coins, glass, and metal objects) but also the sophisticated audiovisual and sometimes live demonstrations on the techniques used in antiquity for the preparation of these objects. In addition, there are reconstructions of olive presses, a grain mill, an Israelite period house, and a dolmen field. There is a small garden that illustrates Jotham's Fable in Judg 9:7-15.

Within the confines of the museum is **Tell Qasile**. Excavations have shown that the site was occupied from the Neolithic Period to the Mamluke Period. The Philistines founded the city at Tell Qasile in the first half of the twelfth century B.C. on the north bank of the Yarkon River, which one can see from the top of the tell. The city served as an inland port. A short distance from the tell is the Mediterranean Sea. The cultic area is the centerpiece of the exhibit. There are three superimposed temples. The first dates from the end of the twelfth century B.C. and the third from the beginning of the tenth century B.C. Notice the raised mudbrick platform and benches, the pillars, and small rooms at the rear of the temples. The small rooms could be either the "holy of holies" or the treasury of the temples. Next to the earliest temple is a small building with a hearth and two pillars. Besides the temples, the site also displays residential and industrial structures, which have been reconstructed. The remains of the tenth-century Philistine city surrounding the cult area show evidence of having been planned with parallel streets and rectangular blocks of buildings, which is unusual at this time.

Beit Hatefutzot (The Diaspora Museum). Not far from the Eretz Israel Museum on the campus of the University is a museum that tells the story of the Jewish people from the time of the First Revolt (A.D. 70), when the Romans destroyed the Temple, to the beginnings of modern Jewish immigration to Palestine in the 1880s. Daily except Saturday 10–5; Friday 10–2. Fee.

CHAPTER NINE

Israel: The Galilee

"You too were with Jesus the Galilean" (Matt 26:69).

The word "Galilee" derives from the Hebrew root *gll*, which has the meaning of circularity. The name may derive from the location of Canaanite city-states that ringed this region in the pre-Israelite Period. The name of this territory appears seven times in the OT as "Galilee," once as "the land of Galilee" (1 Kgs 9:11), and twice as "Galilee of the nations" (Isa 8:23; 1 Macc 5:15). Its geographical boundaries are the Litani River of Lebanon to the north and the Jezreel Valley to the south, the Coastal Plain to the west and the Jordan Valley to the east.

The OT divides Galilee into subdivisions according to tribal territories. Issachar had the hills southeast of Mount Tabor and the eastern section of the Jezreel Valley (Josh 19:17-23). Zebulun occupied the area surrounding Nazareth to the Beit Netofa Valley on the north and the Jezreel Valley on the south (Josh 19:10-16). Asher's territory was along the Mediterranean coast though its northern and southern extent is not certain (Josh 19:24-31). Naphtali, the largest of the Galilean tribes, had the rest of the region (Josh 19:33-34). Judges 18 describes the migration of Dan, a tribe whose territory was located originally on the central Coastal Plain. After its migration, the tribe was located in the extreme north of Galilee around the city of Laish that was eventually renamed Dan.

Josephus divided Galilee into **Upper** and **Lower Galilee**. The division was based primarily on the difference in elevation. Lower Galilee extends northward from the Jezreel Valley to the Beit HaKerem Valley. Its average elevation is two thousand feet. Upper Galilee, which surrounds Mount Meiron, has an average elevation of three thousand feet. The Mishnah adds a third subdivision: the valley of Gennesar next to the Sea of Galilee. Galilee is still divided into Upper and Lower regions because of differences in climate, vegetation, and agriculture.

Galilee has the highest average rainfall in Israel. In the mountains of the north the annual rainfall can reach forty inches. In the eastern region of Lower Galilee rainfall is much less—about fifteen inches. Because of the high rainfall, there are several perennial streams and many springs in the region. In Upper Galilee the winters can be cold and snow falls on Mount Hermon. The summers are temperate. In the Jordan Valley the winters are mild and the summers hot. This difference in climate in a small geographical area allows for a variety of agricultural pursuits.

History. The early history of the Israelite tribes in Galilee is notoriously difficult to reconstruct. It has recently been suggested that the Israelite tribes served as Egyptian mercenaries guarding the northern border of the region against Hittite incursions. The Book of Joshua locates one of the principal conquest stories in Galilee (Joshua 11) and two stories in Judges take place in the Jezreel Valley: Deborah (Judges 4–5) and Gideon (Judges 7). Both the blessing of Jacob (Gen 40:1-28) and that of Moses (Deut 32:2-29) need to be considered, but their usefulness for reconstructing early Israelite history in Galilee is a problem. The same holds true for the genealogical tables in Genesis 36, 48:8-25, Numbers 26, and 1 Chronicles 1–9.

The biblical traditions have a definite southern bias. After all, Jerusalem was the seat of the monarchy, Temple, archives, and scribes. Events that took place in the far north are hardly mentioned. None of the stories from the period of Samuel and Saul are set in Galilee. When Saul tried to gain control of the Jezreel Valley to enlarge his kingdom to include Lower Galilee, the Philistines defeated him on Mount Gilboa (1 Samuel 31). David, however, was able to include all of Galilee to the Litani River into his kingdom. Both the Bible and archaeology show that Solomon's building activity extended to cities of the Galilee such as Megiddo and Hazor (1 Kgs 9:15).

From the breakup of the Davidic-Solomonic empire (928 B.C.; see 1 Kgs 12:1-20) to Assyrian incursions under Tiglath-Pileser III (732 B.C.; see 2 Kgs 15:29), Galilee was part of the Northern Kingdom known as Israel. Tiglath-Pileser incorporated Galilee into the Assyrian Empire as the Province of Magiddu. When the Assyrian Empire was in decline, Judah, under Josiah, attempted to reclaim the Galilee. One of Josiah's wives was from a town in Galilee (2 Kgs 23:36). There is archaeological and textual evidence (2 Kgs 23:29) that Judah's influence extended to Megiddo, but this was also the site where Josiah lost his life in a battle with Egypt, which was coming to the aid of the Assyrians.

During the period of Persian hegemony (sixth–fourth century B.C.), Acco became an important Persian military and administrative center. The coastal region also became prosperous because of the purple dye trade. The dye was made from a mollusk, native to the northeastern Mediterranean. The main historical question has to do with the cultural and ethnic character of Galilee during the Persian Period. Some maintain that at this period, Galilee was populated by Itureans who were converted to Judaism during the Hasmonean Period. Others hold that there was a continuity of the Israelite population of the region from the Monarchic Period to the Roman Period when the Jewish character of the region is clear.

During the Hellenistic Period, Galilee was the scene of conflicts between the Ptolemies and the Seleucids for control of Syrian-Palestine. Eventually, the Seleucids took control of the territories of the former Israelite kingdoms, including Galilee. During the Maccabean revolt, Galilee was the locus of several battles that the Jews fought against their Seleucid overlords (1 Macc 5:14-23; 1 Macc 11:63; 12:47-49). By the Roman Period, the Jewish character of the region was unquestioned and Pompey appointed the Hasmonean, Hyrcanus II, as ethnarch of the region. Herod the Great began his career as governor of Galilee. Later the Romans recognized him as king of the territories of the former Israelite kingdoms. After his death, however, the Romans divided these territories among Herod's surviving sons. Herod Antipas ruled Galilee as a tetrarch although Mark mistakenly gives him the title of king (6:14). Antipas refounded Sepphoris and made it his capital. He also founded Tiberias and named it in honor of the Roman emperor who was his patron. After the First Revolt, Galilee came under Judean rule. After the Second Revolt, Lower Galilee was administered first from Sepphoris and later from Tiberias. Upper Galilee was under direct Roman rule. In the early Byzantine Period, there was a reorganization of the Roman administration in Syria-Palestine and Galilee became part of a province called *Palestina Secunda*. Also included in this province were the Decapolis and the Golan. Scythopolis (Beth She'an) served as the capital of this new province.

Galilee receives much attention in early Christian and Jewish literature. It was the main locus of Jesus' ministry so it is not surprising that the NT refers to it sixty-two times. Galilee also was the location for Josephus' military activity while he was still on the Jewish side during the First Revolt; consequently, he mentions Galilee in his writings frequently. The Jewish population of Palestine shifted to Galilee after the two unsuccessful revolts against Rome and so it became an important locus of rabbinic activity.

Economy. In the period of Roman-Byzantine rule (first century B.C.– seventh century A.D.), ninety percent of the population was involved in the production, distribution, and preparation of food. Galilee's economic base then was agriculture. The Mishnah speaks about the fruit produced in Galilee: the figs, grapes, and olives. Both Josephus and archaeology testify to the production of cereals as well. There is also some evidence of industrial activity in Galilee. The Sea of Galilee made it possible for the region to be a center for the salted-fish industry. All types of glass and ceramic wares were produced in Galilee though imported wares were common in Galilee as well.

Most Galileans had small farms. There were some larger land owners who probably received land grants from Herod. There were also people who did not own land. The economic circumstances of the latter were trying. In an agricultural economy, people without land were destitute. Because Jesus urged his followers to share their goods with the poor (Matt 19:21; Mark 10:21; Luke 12:33; 18:22), one can assume the existence of an economy in which goods were limited. The parables of Jesus assume an economy in which there were wealthy landowners, share-croppers or tenant farmers, and day laborers (e.g., Matt 20:1-16; 21:33-43).

Major trade routes passed through Galilee. It was the funnel through which Phoenician products made their way south. Similarly, the branch of the Via Maris that went toward Damascus passed along the northern shore of the Sea of Galilee. Some Galileans supported themselves by providing services for the caravans and by collecting tolls from traders as they passed from one area to another.

Galilee and Greco-Roman Culture. Most interpreters agree that a non-hellenized Jew did not exist by the first century A.D. There is just too much evidence to show that the Greek way of life made its influence felt in Galilee. The cities of this region have their theaters, gymnasia, and baths. Upper Galilee Hellenistic cities like Scythopolis (Beth She'an), Tiberias, and Diocaesarea (Sepphoris) facilitated cross-cultural contacts. Even the Gospels present Greeks coming to Jesus for healing (the Syro-Phoenician woman of Mark 7:26) and conversation (see John 12:20). The question that remains is the extent of hellenization. Some believe that the traditionalism of the Galilean peasants resisted Greek influence. Others point to the archaeological evidence that suggests otherwise, e.g., Greek inscriptions in synagogues. Some have even suggested that Jesus and his disciples were bilingual. It is highly unlikely that Pilate knew Aramaic so if Jesus spoke with Pilate, the conversation took place in Greek. It is also likely that Jesus taught in Greek at times. What the archaeology of Galilee has shown is that this region is culturally and economically oriented to the coastal cultures of Phoenicia. Upper Galilee has more trade contacts with the Greek cities of Tyre and Sidon than with Jewish cities in the south, such as Jerusalem. The Greek cities were simply closer geographically and offered more economic possibilities. It is not surprising then that Greco-Roman culture was easily integrated into the cultural mix that was Galilee.

Galilee and the Gospels. Luke believed that both Mary and Joseph were from Galilee. Matthew and Luke agree that Jesus was raised there. Mark places the entire first part of Jesus' ministry in Galilee. The "territory of Tyre and Sidon" (Mark 1:24) could refer to Upper Galilee, which was economically linked with those Phoenician cities, rather than to Judah. It is only in Mark 10 that Jesus and the disciples travel to Judea. According to Matthew, Jesus went to the Jordan to be baptized by John, but following the latter's arrest, Jesus "withdrew to Galilee" (Matt 4:12). Matthew confines Jesus' ministry almost exclusively to Galilee until chapter 19 when he has Jesus leave for Judah. Luke, too, has most of Jesus' ministry take place in Galilee (4:14–9:50), but for Luke, Galilee is the place of beginnings. He does not have the Risen Jesus return to Galilee as the other evangelists do. For Luke, it is from Jerusalem that the gospel will go out to the world. John's Gospel departs from the geographical and chronological scheme of the Synoptics, and he has only a small portion of his story of Jesus take place in Galilee: 1:43–2:12; 4:43-54; 6:1–7:13. According to the Fourth Gospel, most of the ministry takes place in Jerusalem and its environs.

According to Matthew and Mark, the disciples will be reunited with the Risen Jesus in Galilee (Mark 16:7; Matt 28:7). It is on a mountain in Galilee that the Matthean Christ commissions the disciples to go into the world to make disciples (Matt 28:16-20)—though Isa 2:2-4 would lead one to expect that Matthew's predilection for the fulfillment of prophecy would have him place that event in Jerusalem. Similarly, the setting for the final chapter in the Fourth Gospel is Galilee (John 21).

Galilee and Judaism. The remark of Rabbi Johanan ben Zakkai, "Galilee, you hate the Torah," is mistakenly used to support the view that the Jews of Galilee were not observant or that their Judaism was sectarian. Such a view assumes that there was a form of Judaism in the first century A.D. that was "normative." This opinion no longer commands a strong following. Clearly there was a variety of ways to be a Jew until the First Revolt. After that, Pharisaic (rabbinic) Judaism became the dominant form. The rabbi's remark probably reflects Galilee's slow submission to a particular form of rabbinic observance.

After the Second Revolt, Galilee became the center of Judaism in Palestine. The Romans did not allow Jews to live in Jerusalem, so many migrated to the north. Rabbinic academies were established in Tiberias, Sepphoris, and Beth Shearim. Rabbi Judah the Prince compiled the Mishnah at Sepphoris in A.D. 200 and the "Jerusalem" Talmud was a product of Galilean study centers. Most of the synagogues found in Israel are in Galilean towns and villages. In the middle of the fourth century, the Jews revolted against Byzantine rule (Gallus revolt). What prompted this revolt was the growing encroachment of Christians into what had been a Jewish region. The Byzantine legislation that forbade the building of synagogues probably had as its goal diminishing Jewish presence in Galilee. Despite these tensions, Jews and Christians did manage to work out a *modus vivendi* that allowed a measure of coexistence. The imposing fourth-fifth-century synagogue that was built just down the street from "Peter's House" in Capernaum is testimony to that.

LOWER GALILEE

Beth Shearim

Location and History. Excavations on a site in the northwest corner of the Jezreel Valley uncovered a series of catacombs that were hewn out of the soft limestone bedrock of the area to serve as tombs for the pious after the Second Revolt when Jews had no access to Jerusalem and the Mount of Olives. The town originally was part of a Herodian family estate that passed to the Roman emperors following the First Revolt. Emperor Marcus Aurelius made a gift of part of this estate to his friend Rabbi Judah the Prince (H: haNasi). Rabbi Judah was the leader of the Sanhedrin and the compiler of the *Mishnah*, a written compilation of the Pharisaic "oral law."

Rabbi Judah (d. 220 A.D.) chose Beth Shearim as his place of burial. This insured that the town became the preferred burial place for religious Jews because of their reverence for Rabbi Judah. Providing burial services became the main industry of the town. Jews from the Diaspora and Palestine had their bodies shipped to Beth Shearim for burial, keeping the local people busy. After an unsuccessful revolt against Byzantine rule in 352, the town began to decline. By the Middle Ages people forgot that Rabbi Judah was buried there and a tomb in Sepphoris was venerated as his. Archaeologists found the rabbi's tomb there in 1936.

Antiquities. Before arriving at the catacombs, you will pass a fourth-century A.D. **synagogue** and an **olive press**. There are at least two **catacombs** open for visitors. Notice the variety of ornamentation used on the sarcophagi in the catacombs. This shows that there was a variety of ways that religious Jews interpreted the command not to make images. Notice, too, the vaulted chambers, bas reliefs, and frescos that adorn the catacombs. Visit the small **museum**, which will provide more information about the burial industry. Daily 8–5; Friday 8–3. Fee.

Cana

"Jesus did this as the beginning of his signs in Cana in Galilee and so revealed his glory, and his disciples began to believe in him" (John 2:11).

Cana is mentioned four times in the NT: three times in connection with visits that Jesus made to the village (John 2:1, 11; 4:46) and once as the hometown of Nathaniel (John 21:2). Of course, most people remember it as the place where Jesus turned water into wine. Since the nineteenth century, when the Franciscans built a church on the foundations of a fourth-century building, the Arab town of Kfar Kana has become a popular site for Christian pilgrims. It is four miles northeast of Nazareth. Archaeological surveys suggest that the actual site of the first-century village of Cana is Khirbet Qana in the Beit Natofa Valley, eleven and one-half miles north of Nazareth. Daily 9–12; 2–5; Summer 2–6. Free.

Nazareth (H: Natsrat; A: En Nasra)

"He went and dwelt in a town called Nazareth, so that what had been spoken through the prophets might be fulfilled, 'He shall be called a Nazorean'" (Matt 2:23).

Location. Nazareth is a city in the center of Lower Galilee, north of the Jezreel Valley, twenty-four miles southeast of Haifa, and one hundred and five miles north of Jerusalem. The Sea of Galilee is fifteen miles to the east and the Mediterranean is twenty miles to the west. It is about 1,230 feet above sea level and nestles in a circular vale and on the surrounding slopes of the Galilean highlands. The meaning of the word Nazareth is uncertain. The modern Hebrew word for "Christian," *notsri*, and its Arabic counterpart, *nusrani*, are derived from the name of this city. The literal meaning of these words is *Nazarene*.

History. Although archaeological evidence shows that Nazareth was already occupied in the MBA, it is never mentioned in the OT or other Jewish literature before the NT. Archaeology suggests that the village came into existence during the Hellenistic Period and was devoted to agriculture. Excavation shows that during the first century the maximum size of the village was about sixty acres and most of this was open space. Its population in Jesus' day did not exceed five hundred. Nazareth was one of the villages dependent on the city of Sepphoris just three miles northwest.

After the two unsuccessful revolts against Rome, most Jews of Palestine lived in Galilee and apparently Nazareth was a Jewish town. In particular, Nazareth was home to priests from Jerusalem. When Egeria visited it in the fourth century, she says there was no church there, though she did see the cave in which Mary lived. Similarly, neither Eusebius nor Jerome mentions a church in Nazareth. The poems of Eleazar Kalir from about the same time lament the fate of Jewish priests who lived in the city. The anonymous pilgrim from Piacenza (570) says that the house of Mary became a church and testifies that the relations between the Jews and Christians of Nazareth were harmonious.

In 614 the Persians invaded Palestine. The Jews of Nazareth supported the Persians against the Christian Byzantines, whom they regarded as unjust oppressors. After the defeat of the Persians in 628, the Byzantines slaughtered the Jews of Nazareth. Arculf, who came to Nazareth about 664, saw two churches: one where Jesus grew up and another where Mary received the angel Gabriel. When the Muslims came to Palestine at the end of the sixth century, Nazareth became an Arab town. Relations between the Christian and Muslim residents of Nazareth were not good. Christians had to pay a fee to Muslim authorities to pray in the Church of the Annunciation.

The Crusaders took Nazareth in 1099 and made it a Christian town and the capital of Galilee. It became an archbishopric under the Crusaders. This made it necessary to build a larger church. The Mamlukes destroyed the town in 1263. It remained largely abandoned until 1620 when the Druze ruler Fakhr ed-Din allowed the Franciscans to settle there. They built a monastery and churches. Gradually Arabs, Christian and Muslim, began to resettle the city. Today Nazareth is an Arab town of about forty thousand. The nearby Jewish town called *Nazareth Illit* ("Upper Nazareth") was founded in 1957 and has a population of twenty-eight thousand.

Nazareth in the Gospels. Both Matthew (2:23) and Luke (2:51) identify Nazareth as the town where Jesus was raised. Luke also says that it was the home of Mary and Joseph before the birth of Jesus (2:4-5), while Matthew implies that Bethlehem was the couple's home. According to Luke, then, Nazareth was where Mary received the message that she was to be the mother of the Savior (Luke 1:26-38). The Fourth Gospel insinuates that Nazareth did not have a good reputation (John 1:46). Jesus left this village to begin his ministry (1:9). Jesus returned to preach there but was not well received (Mark 6:1-6; Matt 13:57-58; Luke 4:16-30). That Jesus was from Nazareth was common knowledge (Matt 21:11; Mark 14:67) and the charge that Pilate placed on the cross calls Jesus "the Nazarene" (John 19:19).

The Archaeological Record. The current Basilica of the Annunciation went up between 1966 and 1969. Before construction began, Bellarmino Bagatti of the

The city of Nazareth and the Basilica of the Annunciation (upper photo); and the Grotto of the Annunciation.

SBF conducted excavations on the site from 1955 to 1959. The occupational sequence in the area of the church is complicated but put simply it is as follows:

Before the third century A.D.: caves were used for a purpose that cannot be determined precisely but most likely they were used as homes.

Second-third century A.D.: a *mikveh* was cut into the soft limestone. Bagatti suggests that it was used by a Jewish Christian community.

Third-fourth century: the building of a synagogue above the *mikveh* and incorporating the cave—probably the one mentioned by Egeria. Bagatti maintains that this was a synagogue of Jewish Christians as evidenced by the graffiti found on a column now on display in the museum.

Fifth century: the building of a monastery and church that incorporated the cave and the floor of the synagogue. This is the church seen by the Piacenza Pilgrim.

You can see elements from most of these periods in the lower church. Also, in the museum there is a multicolored plan of the site that illustrates this occupational history.

Antiquities. It is not always possible to get a good look at the remains of earlier structures in the basilica because Nazareth is a popular stop for pilgrims. If there is a Mass in progress, you may not be able to see much of the lower church and its archaeological remains. Of course, one must wear proper attire to be admitted to the basilica and the other churches in Nazareth.

Entering the door directly across from the entrance to the **Basilica of the Annunciation** leads one to the **Lower Church**. To the left one can see remnants of the **wall from the Crusader church**. The basilica is built on the foundations of that twelfth-century building. In the center of the lower church is a depression within which there is the **grotto** (18 feet high and 9 feet wide). In front of the grotto are remains from the earlier buildings on the site. You can see the **apsidal basilica** that was the fifth-century church, several mosaic fragments with crosses, the wreath mosaic, and the **mosaic of Conon**. This lower church serves principally as a church for pilgrims though the Franciscan community and the parish use it as well.

Returning to the entrance, go up the staircase to the **Upper Church**, which serves as the parish church for the four thousand Latin Rite Catholics of Nazareth. A unique feature of this church is that images of Mary from twenty countries are found here. Notice the image of Mary from the United States. It is the silver image of Mary along the right side. It portrays the Woman clothed with the sun of Revelation 12. So many countries offered their own portraits of Mary that there was not enough room in the church itself. Outside the upper church is the **baptistery**. It is a gift from the Catholics of Germany. Under the terrace on which the baptistery is found, one can see the caves and cisterns from the early years of Nazareth's existence. Make certain to visit the **museum** but check with the sacristan in the lower church about admittance. After leaving the museum, take a closer look at the **caves** and **cisterns** of Roman Period Nazareth. You will be able to see more of the wall from the Crusader church. In front of the museum are the Franciscan monastery, the parish hall, and the Holy Land High School. Daily 8–11:45; 2–4:45; Sunday 2–5:30. Holy place; modest attire, no shorts. The lower church is a popular place for liturgies. Pilgrim groups use the sanctuary and this makes it difficult to see the antiquities there.

Just beyond the high school is the **Church of St. Joseph**. The present church, built in 1914, was erected on the foundations of a Crusader church, which, in turn, was built over a fifth-century church—one that Arculf mentions. Beneath the church is a cistern and cave that Emmanuel Testa of the SBF maintains is the baptistery from the second century. Pilgrims venerate the Church of St. Joseph as the place of Joseph's workshop. There is no evidence to support this notion. The Greek word that is usually translated as "carpenter" in the English versions of the Gospels can mean simply "skilled worker" or "worker in stone." While Jesus was growing up, Herod Antipas was rebuilding the town of Sepphoris, which was just three miles away. It may be that both Joseph and Jesus worked on that project. Of course, there is no proof of this suggestion.

About a mile from the Basilica of the Annunciation, there is the Greek Orthodox **Church of St. Gabriel**. Here is where the Orthodox commemorate the Annunciation. The eighteenth-century church is built over a still-active spring that leads to an ornate well from the same period which pilgrims venerate as "Mary's Well."

Sepphoris (H: Zippori; A: Saffuriyya)

Location. Sepphoris is in Lower Galilee four miles northwest of Nazareth. It sits on a hill that is 939 feet above sea level. The Hebrew for this ancient city name may come from *zippor,* the word for "bird." The city looks as if it is perched high above the surrounding area. Rabbinic tradition suggests that the city was named for Zipporah, the wife of Moses (Exod 2:21).

History. A spring near Sepphoris attracted settlement in the Stone Age. Ceramic remains from the Iron, Persian, and Hellenistic Ages show that its history extends into the OT period. Still, the city's importance began with the Roman Period. Most of the information about Sepphoris from literary sources comes from Josephus and the Mishnah. The NT never mentions Sepphoris, despite the city's proximity to Nazareth. The Mishnah mentions the city often. It is understandable since Judah the Prince compiled this Jewish religious text here c. A.D. 200. The site is currently under excavation. The results of that will help reconstruct the city's history.

Rome added Palestine to its empire in 63 B.C. In 55 B.C., Gabinus, the proconsul in Syria, located one of the five Roman Synedria of Palestine in Sepphoris —the only one in Galilee. Herod the Great took Sepphoris in 39 B.C. during a snowstorm, after his Hasmonean rival Antigonus left the city. Sepphoris remained Herod's northern headquarters throughout his reign. At his death in 4

B.C., Judah, the son of Hezekiah, led the Sepphoreans in a revolt against Rome. Varus, the governor of Syria, responded vigorously to this threat to Roman rule. The army he sent to Sepphoris burnt the city to the ground and sold its inhabitants into slavery. Perhaps the pacifism of Jesus had its roots in the memory of this event that happened so close to Nazareth. Herod Antipas, who inherited Galilee from his father Herod the Great set about rebuilding the city. He employed craftsmen from villages all over Galilee, which has led to the suggestion that Joseph and perhaps the young Jesus may have found work here. The rebuilt city must have been spectacular since Josephus called Sepphoris "the ornament of Galilee." Antipas paid attention to defense as well as to aesthetics since Josephus also proclaimed Sepphoris "the strongest city in Galilee."

During the late Roman and Byzantine Periods, the city has a mixed population. There were Jews, Christians, and adherents of Greco-Roman religion. Sepphoris was the seat of a bishop who attended the Council of Nicea so it must have been an important Christian center. There were other cities such as Caesarea Maritima that had a similar population mix. What made Sepphoris unique was that diverse population of the city was able to live together in peace.

The Crusaders thought that Sepphoris was the hometown of Mary, the Mother of Jesus. They built a small church there in honor of Joachim and Anna, the parents of Mary according to legend. Byzantine tradition locates Mary's home in Jerusalem. See the Church of St. Anne.

Antiquities. The centerpiece of the archaeological park that displays Sepphoris to visitors is a small building that shelters the most beautiful ancient **mosaic** found in Israel. The mosaic, which depicts legends associated with Dionysus, decorated the floor of a **triclinium**, a formal dining room. The building with the triclinium is behind the ancient city's **theater**. Near the theater is an area with housing. The Jewish character of this area is clear from the number of *mikveot*, Jewish baths. Therefore, the excavators describe this area as **the Jewish Quarter**. Below the city's acropolis is an **agora**. Most of this area is still being excavated. There are many mosaics in the area, the most notable being the **Nile Mosaic**. It is so named because it pictures scenes in Egypt during the Nile's annual inundation. Though the site has been developed for tourism, excavation is still going on. Much of the city's plan has yet to be clarified. Also, there is some disagreement among archaeologists about dating the artifacts that have been discovered. The dates that Parks Authority gives on its brochures and signs represent the view that the city flourished in the Middle Roman Period. Another view dates much of what you see to the Early Roman Period, which would make the site contemporaneous with Jesus. Clarification of these and other problems await the completion of the excavation projects that are continuing at Sepphoris. About a fifteen-minute walk from the site, one can see the partially reconstructed **aqueducts** and **water system** that served ancient Sepphoris.

The Parks Authority has prepared a short multimedia presentation that is shown in the building at the crest of the hill. Daily 8–4; Summers 8–5. Fee.

TIBERIAS AND THE VALLEYS

Belvoir (H: Kochav HaYarden "the star of the Jordan";
A: Kaukab el Hawa "star of the winds.")

Location. Eight miles north of Beth She°an, this fortress is on the eastern edge of the Issachar Plateau, at the top (1,625 feet high) of a scarp that descends eastward into the Beth She°an Valley.

History. As military men, the Crusaders built many of their castles on high ground. Belvoir is no exception. It is set on a height above the Jordan Valley. The Knights of the Order of Hospitallers, who built it, called it Belvoir because of its beautiful view of the valley below. The Hebrew name for the site probably comes from the fact that stones for the castle were taken from the ruins of a nearby ancient Jewish village called Kochav.

Muslim forces began the siege of this fortress shortly after the Crusader defeat at the Horns of Hattin in 1187. The defenders held out for eighteen months, but they surrendered when Saladin's men succeeded in undermining an outer tower. Though the walls had not been breached, the Crusaders knew it was only a matter of time before their enemy would have been inside the fortress. The Muslims gave Belvoir's defenders safe passage to Tyre, which was still in Crusader hands. Saladin's soldiers demolished the chapel inside the fortress, but the rest remained intact. Three statues from the chapel are in Jerusalem's Rockefeller Museum. Local people settled in the castle, turning it into a village. In 1217, the caliph in Damascus decided to tear down all the Crusader castles in Arab hands when he heard rumors of another crusade. When Belvoir was to be demolished, only the upper story was destroyed. The stones from it filled the first story and insured the preservation of that part of the fortress.

Antiquities. The fortress (455 feet by 32 feet) is in the shape of a pentagon with two of its sides facing east, its most vulnerable point. It consists of an **outer fortification** and an **inner keep**. Livestock and supplies that could remain in the open were kept there. It is likely that vegetables were grown in this area as well. A **moat,** sixty-five feet wide and thirty-nine feet deep, encircles the fortress on the sides facing the plateau. It was cut out of the basalt stone that was then used to build the tower and other structures. One can see **cisterns** and **water channels.** Some channels fed the cisterns; others drained dish water and laundry water out of the fortress. The northeastern wing of the outer fortress was the workshop area. The vaults of the outer fortress provided living space for the defenders.

Beth Alpha

"No more shall people call you 'Forsaken' . . . but you shall be called 'My Delight' . . ." (Isa 62:4).

Location. This ancient synagogue is found at the foot of the Mount Gilboa on its north side. Mount Gilboa is the site of the Philistine victory over the Israelites. During the battle both Saul and Jonathan fell—the former by his own hand (see 1 Samuel 28 and 2 Sam 1:17-24). The site is just east of the Jezreel Valley. Two kibbutzim occupy the ancient site: Beth Alpha and Hephizbah. The latter name comes from Isa 62:4. It means "I will delight in her."

Antiquities. In 1928, while digging an irrigation channel for the Hephizbah kibbutz, workers came upon the remains of an ancient structure. E.L. Sukenik from the Hebrew University began excavations and identified the structure as a synagogue. What made this synagogue so unusual was its mosaic floor. It is one of the four Palestinian synagogues with a zodiac mosaic—which is unexpected in such buildings. Not only does the mosaic depict human forms, it also depicts the image of the Greek god Helios and a device associated with divination. All this contravenes traditional Jewish observance. For the prohibition of images, see Exod 20:4 and Deut 5:8. For the prohibition of divination, see Deut 18:9-14.

The Beth Alpha synagogue dates from the fifth century A.D. The mosaic floor with the zodiac was added in the sixth century. The building is an **apsidal basilica**. The **apse** that is against the southern wall orients the building and the worshipers to Jerusalem. In the floor of the apse is a hole covered by a paver. The hole could have served to store the valuables of the community though its function is uncertain. There was a **courtyard** in front of the synagogue, but its contours are not visible since this area is covered by the modern building that protects the interior of the synagogue. A **mosaic** having a geometric pattern decorated the floor of the courtyard. After entering the building, you will walk a few steps down into the **narthex** of the synagogue. You can make out the **triple entrance** to the ancient building. At the main entrance to the prayer hall and just inside the central doorway is an **inscription in Greek and Aramaic**. The Greek inscription reads: "In honored memory of the artists who made this work well: Marianos and his son Aninas." The Aramaic inscription is not intact. It reads: "This mosaic was laid down in the . . . year of the reign of the Emperor Justinus in honored memory of all sons. . . ." The "Justinus" mentioned here may be either Justinian I (518–527) or Justinian II (565–578). This is one of the few synagogues in Israel that can be dated by an inscription. Note also that the inscription makes it clear that the people who worshiped here were bilingual.

The **zodiac** is the centerpiece of a three-panel mosaic floor in the central nave of the prayer hall. The mosaics in the aisles have geometric patterns. The central mosaic is executed in a primitive style. Immediately above the inscription is a panel that illustrates the **binding of Isaac** (Gen 22:1-19). The central panel contains the zodiac. The signs of the zodiac are portrayed in a wheel. Female personifications of the four seasons are found at the corners but not in places that correspond to the proper zodiac signs. The panel at the top shows a **Torah shrine**, two large menorahs, an incense shovel, the lulab, and ethrog—traditional religious symbols.

Jerome Murphy-O'Connor offers the ingenious suggestion that the placement of the zodiac between the two religious panels reduces it to a merely decorative style. The story of the binding of Isaac is an implicit condemnation of

Beth Alpha mosaic.

astrology since it shows that the future is in God's hands. Similarly, the Torah shrine on the topmost panel intimates that the future of the worshipers is decided by their obedience to the Law. Others suggest that the zodiac had something to do with the setting of the time for religious festivals. Still, others maintain that since the battle with idolatry was fought and won within Judaism, representations like the zodiac mosaics are nothing more than artistic embellishments with no ideological content. How the people who worshiped in the synagogue looked upon the zodiac in their place of prayer is not known.

Beth Alpha is just four and one-half miles from the site of ancient Beth She'an that the Greeks refounded as a Hellenistic city in the third century B.C. The city's Hellenistic character continued through the Byzantine Period as recent excavations have shown. Finding evidence of Hellenistic influence at Beth Alpha then is not surprising. A sixth-century chapel from a monastery in Beth She'an also has mosaic floor depicting a zodiac. Daily 8–4; Summer 8–5. Fee.

Astrology and Early Judaism. There is some textual evidence that astrological ideas were assimilated by the Jews despite the Deuteronomic injunction against divination. Texts dealing with such ideas have been found among the Dead Sea Scrolls (4QZodiac). Another text is an encoded series of horoscopes for three individuals whose astrological signs are given. Evidently, the people of Qumran had no problem integrating astrology with their Judaism though they are considered to have been a most conservative group. Important rabbinic sources show a positive view of astrology. For example, the Babylonian Talmud tells the story of Rabbi Joseph bar Hiyya who turned down the opportunity to preside over a rabbinic academy because astrologers predicted that his term would have lasted but two years (Babylonian Talmud, Tractate *Berakoth* 64a).

One reason for the influence of astrology in Judaism was geography. Babylon, the major Jewish religious and intellectual center outside Palestine, had a long astrological tradition. Such influence was felt in Palestine as well because there was a considerable flow of communication between the rabbis of Palestine and Babylon. The nonpolemical tone of the references to astrology in rabbinic texts shows that some rabbis did not consider astrology incompatible with Judaism. This literary evidence is complemented by material evidence uncovered by excavation. It appears then that some Jews from the first century B.C. through the Byzantine Period practiced astrology.

Beth She'an (Beth-Shan; H: "House of [the god] Shan"; G: Sycthopolis "city of the Sycthians"; A: Beisan)

". . . the Canaanites living in the valley region all have iron chariots, in particular those in Beth-shean" (Josh 17:16).

Location. Among the oldest inhabited sites in Israel, Beth She'an is in the center of the Beth She'an Valley, the central and widest part of the Jordan Valley. The city is seventy-five miles north of Jerusalem and twenty-three miles south of Tiberias. The Beth She'an Valley is bounded on the east by the Jordan River and on the west by Mount Gilboa. Its northern end is the Nahal Tavor and the southern end is marked by Wadi Salih. It is blessed with fertile soil and an abundant water supply. What made the site important in antiquity was its location at the junction of two main roads: the east-west road leading from the Jezreel Valley to Gilead and the north-south road that ran through the Jordan Valley.

The Talmud says that if the Garden of Eden was in Israel, Beth She'an was its gate. Its agricultural resources were exploited from the Chalcolithic to the Crusader Period when the effects of the Muslim-Christian conflict led to the disruption of settlement in the valley. This resulted in the growth of swampland and further reduction of settlements here. Jews began to settle here in numbers during the 1930s and have successfully reclaimed the swamps and have exploited the area's agricultural potential. There is, however, an unemployment problem in the city and the Israelis are trying to attract more tourists to the antiquities, hoping that increased tourism will help the local economy.

History. Humans began to live at Beth She'an during the Chalcolithic Period (c. 4000 B.C.). The city became important not only because of its location in an agriculturally important region but also because it was on a spur of the Via Maris and controlled a shallow ford of the Jordan. Because of its commercial importance, the Egyptian presence here was strong during the Middle and Late Bronze Ages. Beth She'an is mentioned in the Egyptian Execration texts (first century B.C.), the lists of cities captured by Tutmoses III (fifteenth century B.C.), and the Amarna Letters (fourteenth century B.C.). A six-foot high stele set up by Seti I in 1318 B.C. was found at Beth She'an. It is on display in the Rockefeller Museum.

The Book of Joshua states that the tribe of Manasseh "was awarded" the city of Beth She'an (17:11), but it was the Philistines who took the city over from the Canaanites. After Saul died on Mount Gilboa (six miles west) following his defeat by Philistines, they impaled his headless corpse on the walls of Beth She'an and placed his armor in the temple of Astarte (1 Sam 31:10). Some suggest that David was successful in adding this city to the Israelite kingdom. Excavation shows that Egyptian influence, and perhaps control, continued until Solomon included the city in his taxation districts (1 Kgs 4:12). Egypt, however, did not give up its claims on the city in Solomon's time. Shishak named it among the one-hundred-fifty cities of Palestine and Transjordan he conquered according to his inscription in the Karnak Temple (c. 926 B.C.; see 1 Kgs 14:25-28).

During the Hellenistic Period, there was an influx of Greek population into the city and its name was changed to *Scythopolis*, "the city of the Scythians." The Scythians were people from what is now southern Russia. They served as mercenaries in Alexander's army. He rewarded them with citizenship in the city named for them. Beth She'an was also known as Nysa. Nysa was the nurse of Dionysus; the Greeks believed her tomb was here. When the Hasmoneans conquered the city, they expelled the Greeks (1 Macc 5:52; 12:40-42; 2 Macc 12:29-31). The Romans, however, allowed the Greeks to return and the city took on a definitely Greek character. It enjoyed a measure of autonomy and was part of the Decapolis, the only one of this federation of ten cities that was west of the Jordan. Its Jewish population increased with the migration from Judah after the unsuccessful Second Revolt.

With the Arab victory over the Byzantines (A.D. 636) in the region, the old Semitic name reemerged as "Beisan" in Arabic and replaced the Greek name in use for a thousand years. This victory is known as "the day of Beisan." The Arabs made Beisan their capital in the north. An earthquake destroyed the city in 749 and so the Arabs decided to move the capital of Galilee to Tiberias. Beth She'an never again enjoyed greatness. The Jewish population that continued to be strong through the Middle Ages began to decline during the Turkish Period. Eventually Beth She'an became an Arab town with a small Jewish community. The Jews left after the riots of 1936–1939. During the 1948 war, the Arabs left and since then Beth She'an has become a Jewish city.

Antiquities. The **Tel** (A: Tell el-Husn). The first systematic excavations in Beth She'an took place between 1921 and 1933 on the tel north of the Roman-

Byzantine city. Eighteen occupational layers have been found. The most significant finds come from the LBA when Egypt controlled the city. There are remains of Egyptian palaces and temples on the tel. Though one can reach the tel by a flight of stairs, the site has not been prepared for tourism. New excavations have begun there recently. The finds from the earlier excavations are on display in the Rockefeller Museum. Most show the dominant Egyptian influence here. The Romans built a monumental temple on the tel but it was an isolated structure. The city moved to the foot of the tel. During the Byzantine and Arab Periods, the tel was resettled and residential quarters have been identified.

The Lower city. In the plain south of the tel were the remains of a Roman Period **theater**. After the site was cleared, a well-preserved eight-thousand-seat theater was uncovered. It is currently under renovation to make it available for contemporary performances. Notice that the theater's exterior is black basalt and its interior is white limestone. This must have been a striking contrast when the building was in use.

The existence of the theater makes it obvious that there were probably other structures from the Roman-Byzantine Period to be found at Beth She²an, but full-scale excavations in the area below the tel did not begin until the late 1980s. These excavations have uncovered a **civic center**, an extensive **bath complex** (there is evidence of six baths there), a **Cardo** and its shops, **temples**, an **odeion**, an **amphitheater**, a **reflecting pool** and **fountains**. There is also evidence that some structures became **churches** during the Byzantine Era. The site is reminiscent of Ephesus.

There has been some criticism that the excavations proceeded too quickly and with too little care for the antiquities. Someone did manage to steal a beautiful small mosaic depicting the Greek goddess Tyche uncovered at the site. After an exhaustive investigation, the mosaic was returned in three bags. The mosaic is now under restoration. One reason for the haste with which the project is going on is due to the desire to make the site a magnet for tourism. Excavation and reconstruction are continuing at the site, which will be spectacular when the project is complete. Daily 8–4; Summers 8–5. Fee.

Capernaum (H: "the village of Nahum"; A: Talhum or Tell Hum)

> *"(Jesus) left Nazareth and went to live in Capernaum by the sea . . ."*
> (Matt 4:13).

Location. Capernaum is on the northwestern shore of the Sea of Galilee. It is three miles north of Tabgha and three miles south of the Upper Jordan River. The name "Capernaum" is a corruption of the Hebrew phrase *kfar Nahum*, i.e., "the village of Nahum." The medieval Jewish association of Capernaum with the biblical Nahum is without historical basis. The OT never mentions Capernaum and archaeological evidence dates its earliest occupation to the second century B.C. so it is unlikely that this "Nahum" was the sixth-century prophet. Capernaum was probably named after the original owner of the land on which it was built, but this is just a guess. Josephus took refuge in this town after he was wounded during the First Revolt (*Vita* 403). Beyond this, Capernaum took no role in that uprising. Talmudic sources assert that there was a Christian community in the town from the second century. The town's prosperity was dependent upon its location on the Via Maris but it also had thriving agricultural and fishing enterprises. It was destroyed in the 500s and never rebuilt. The site, however, was never completely abandoned. In medieval Jewish sources, it is known as Kefar Tanhum or simply Tanhum. Early exploration at the site, beginning in 1838 by the American Edward Robinson, led to theft and vandalism by the local population. When the Franciscan Custody of the Holy Land acquired the site of the synagogue and the surrounding area in 1889, they backfilled the area to protect its antiquities.

Jesus and Capernaum. Matthew says that Jesus moved from Nazareth to Capernaum when he began his ministry (4:13). Such a move is understandable since Nazareth was a small, unimportant village (see John 1:46) while Capernaum was a town with a population of fifteen thousand. The town's size can be explained by its location along the Via Maris. This road serves to connect the region around the Sea of Galilee with the Golan and Syria. Because it was on the border between Galilee and the Golan, Capernaum was a place for the collection of tolls as caravans passed along the Via Maris (see Mark 2:14).

The Gospels mention the town sixteen times and present it as the hub of Jesus' Galilean ministry. While Matthew simply says that Jesus traveled throughout Galilee to teach in its synagogues (4:23), Mark mentions Capernaum's synagogue by name as a place where Jesus taught. The other two evangelists are more specific. Luke identifies the town's synagogue as the site of an exorcism performed by Jesus (4:31-37), and John names it as the location of Jesus' discourse on the bread of life (6:59). Capernaum was the scene of several miracles: the healing of Peter's mother-in-law (Mark 1:29-31), a paralytic (Mark 2:11-12; Matt 9:1-8; Luke 5:17-25), a possessed man (Mark 1:23-28), a leper (Luke 5:12-16), and the centurion's servant (Luke 7:1-10).

Jesus called Matthew [Levi] to discipleship here (Matt 9:9-12; Luke 5:27-32). It was at Capernaum where Jesus said that his disciples were his true family (Mark 3:31-35; Matt 12:46-50; Luke 8:19-21). It was also the setting for Jesus' instruction to his disciples on true greatness (Mark 9:33-37). Despite all this, Jesus did not find much of a positive response to his teaching here. Matthew (11:23-24) and Luke (10:15) say that Jesus cursed Capernaum for its failure to respond to his call for repentance. The Fourth Gospel reports that Jesus lost several disciples following his bread of life discourse (6:60, 66). Capernaum was the site of some of Jesus' greatest triumphs and his greatest disappointments.

Antiquities. The ancient synagogue dominates the site. Recently a modern church was built over the House of Peter. Between these two structures is a group of homes dating from the first century B.C. and in use through the Byzantine Period. Arranged in a courtyard in front of the church are **architectural fragments** from the synagogue. Note the absence of human representations. This shows that the Jews who built the synagogue were conservative in

Fragment of an ark on wheels, Capernaum.

their interpretation of the commandment forbidding images. The decoration uses floral and geometric patterns with a few animal forms though there are depicted some Jewish religious symbols such as the menorah. You will see a six-pointed star. This is not a religious symbol but another geometric pattern. The "Star of David" did not become a Jewish symbol until the Middle Ages. You will also see a five-pointed star. Look for what looks like a temple on wheels. This is probably a representation of the ark found in synagogues. It was on wheels to simplify its movement especially when synagogues were used for purposes other than worship. Later, when buildings were erected for the single purpose of worship, the ark became a permanent feature of the building's interior. Across the courtyard from these architectural fragments from the synagogue, there is an insula that was probably a **work area** for the city. In and around this insula, you can see olive presses, grinders, and other stone tools.

The **synagogue** of Capernaum is still an impressive building a millennium and a half after it was built. It measures 80 feet by 60 feet and is made of limestone ashlars. The stones on the exterior walls were polished to give the appearance of marble. On the interior, their surface was left rough to receive plaster, which was then painted. This gleaming white limestone building stood out from its surroundings since the other buildings of the town were made of basalt, a black volcanic rock that is abundant in the area. The limestone for the synagogue had to be brought in from other parts of Galilee at some expense. This and the delicately sculpted decorative motifs of the building's architectural components show that the construction of this synagogue was a costly project. That the Jews of Capernaum could underwrite such a project is a testament to the community's economic prosperity.

The building is a basilica with a triple entrance in the wall that faces Jerusalem. This required worshipers to make an awkward about-face upon entering the synagogue so that they could pray in the direction of the Holy City. Beside the two rows of columns along the side there is another in front of the north wall. The columns were executed in the simple Attic style while their capitals were in the more ornate Corinthian style. Stone pavers covered the floor and benches lined walls. These were available for people who needed support while sitting, i.e., the sick and the aged. The rest of the congregation simply sat on the floor. One approaches the synagogue by way of a stairway on its southwestern corner. This leads one to a terrace that ran the full length of the synagogue and the adjoining courtyard. This terrace is an open porch paved with large stone slabs. There is another stairway on the southeastern end of the terrace.

Some reconstruction of the synagogue has been attempted though the surviving architectural fragments make it possible to have only a hypothetical image of what the exterior of the synagogue looked like. The façade had a lower story, an upper story, and a gabled roof. The three doorways of the lower story were elaborately decorated. A cornice separated the lower and upper stories. The central feature of the latter was a large arch above the center door. This arch framed a window. There were also windows above the two side doors. A second cornice separated the upper story from the gabled roof covered with ceramic roof tiles. Some archaeologists have suggested that the interior of the building had a second story that served as the women's gallery. Recent work, however, led to the conclusion that the foundation could not have supported a second interior story. In any case, it is likely that the sexes were not separated for worship. Such separation was a thirteenth-century A.D. development within Judaism.

Attached to the east side of the synagogue is a **courtyard with portico** measuring 66 feet by 42 feet. The portico was covered on three sides. The courtyard is not perfectly rectangular but trapezoidal in shape. This area provided an area outside the worship space for the diverse activities that normally took place in the environs of a synagogue: study, the trying of legal cases, communal meals, and other social functions. Travelers could find shelter under the portico.

Directly in front of the synagogue is an **insula of private dwellings**. These date from the first century B.C. and were in use through the Byzantine Period. They are made from basalt field stones. Imagine the contrast between these homes and the gleaming white synagogue. When you see pavement in the insula, this usually suggests an open courtyard between several homes. Usually the homes of relatives were grouped together around a single courtyard. The floors inside the homes were beaten earth. The roof was usually made of mud and sticks matted together by running a roof roller made of stone over this material. Notice the doorways of the buildings and the streets that ran in front of the buildings.

Visiting the **church** can be a problem. Generally it is open only to groups who arrange for Mass or other prayers there. Sometimes the custodian of the church objects to people taking pictures inside. To simplify gaining entry to the church, it is best if the group stays together while one person asks for admittance. From inside the church it is possible to see down into the octagonal structures below. The **mosaic of the peacock** that was in the central octagon has been removed and can be seen near the gate leading to the church. In Christian iconography of the Byzantine Period, the peacock represented resurrection and new life.

From below the church it is also possible to see the three concentric octagons that surround Peter's House. These date from the fifth century. The **outermost octagon** is not complete because an apse and a baptistery were attached to it. The **central octagon** enclosed the worship space and was, in turn, enclosed by a **second octagon**. The octagonal shape of the church shows that it was a memorial church and the presence of the baptistery means that the church also served a local congregation. But if the structure was a memorial church, what event in the life of Jesus did it commemorate? Virgilio Corbo, O.F.M., believes that his excavations below the octagonal church have answered this question. He has concluded that a private home dating from the early Roman Period (63 B.C.–A.D. 70) was rebuilt during the middle of the fourth century as a shrine by Christians who used the building through the fourth century. The transformation of the building involved the enlargement of the room, the reinforcement of the roof, and the plastering of the floor and walls. Clearly this building was no longer a simple home. The absence of domestic pottery from this level of occupation supports this conclusion. The octagonal church replaced this building. From inside the modern church it is possible to see portions of the earlier structures that Corbo has identified as **Peter's House**. Corbo supported his conclusions about the nature of the second-century renovation by more than one hundred graffiti etched on the plaster walls by pilgrims who came to pray in that building. Among the inscriptions in several languages including Latin, Syriac, Aramaic, and Hebrew, Corbo found what he identified as the name of Peter, though the inscriptions are not easy to decipher. Also, Egeria writes that the church at Capernaum was built over the house of Peter.

What archaeology has shown is that a private home built in the early Roman Period was converted into a place of prayer for Christians in the middle of the first century. In the middle of the 400s a splendid octagonal church was built over the same spot. It would be fascinating to know if the house under the octagonal church is the house where Jesus stayed while in Capernaum (see Mark 1:29). Archaeology has not provided a definitive answer though some see that the mass of circumstantial evidence adduced by Corbo points to this conclusion. The first Christian pilgrims to Capernaum scratched their professions of faith on the walls in the belief that they were praying in the very room that Jesus called home at one period of his life. Nothing that archaeology has revealed contradicts that belief.

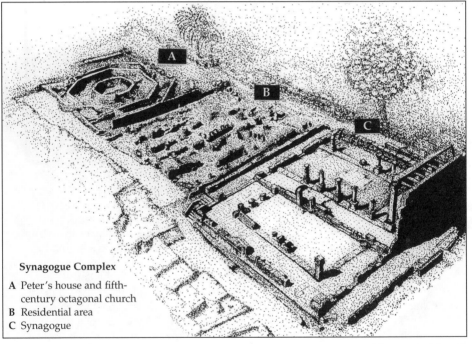

Synagogue Complex

A Peter's house and fifth-
   century octagonal church
B Residential area
C Synagogue

The Capernaum synagogue (upper photo); and a drawing (courtesy of Liguori Publications) of Peter's house and the synagogue complex.

The Synagogue Controversy. In 1838, the American Edward Robinson surveyed the area and correctly identified the architectural fragments that he saw there as belonging to an ancient synagogue. Still, it was not until 1866 that Charles Wilson identified the site as Capernaum. He concluded that the synagogue on the site was the one built by the centurion (Luke 7:5) and the one in which Jesus preached. In 1905, two German biblical scholars, H. Kohl and C. Watzinger, completed an important survey of the synagogues in Galilee. Though they spent only a few days at Capernaum, they concluded that the synagogue came from at least one hundred years *after* Jesus' ministry. After sporadic excavations on the site by the Franciscan Gaudentius Orfali between 1905 and 1926, work began on reconstructing the synagogue from the available architectural fragments. Orfali believed that the synagogue was first century and therefore likely the one where Jesus preached. You will notice that a column in the synagogue bears an inscription honoring Fr. Orfali. Another column has an ancient inscription incised in Greek that translates as follows: "Herdon, son of Mokimos and Justus his son, together with the children erected this column." There is a column with an Aramaic inscription that reads "Halfu, the son of Zebidah, the son of Yohanan made this column. May he be blessed." This column probably stood in the portico.

Between 1968 and 1972, two Franciscans from the SBF in Jerusalem, Virgilio Corbo and Stanislao Loffreda, renewed excavations at Capernaum. Their working hypothesis was that the synagogue was from the second-third century. Because of a vast amount of numismatic evidence, they had to revise their original hypothesis to date the synagogue to the fourth or fifth century. This produced heated controversy. For example, Michael Avi-Yonah considers it unlikely that a magnificent structure such as Capernaum's synagogue could have been built in the fourth or fifth century since the imperial policy, now made by Christians, was hostile to the Jews. The Byzantine authorities forbade the building of new synagogues and even the repairing of old ones. Gideon Foerster dates the building to the second century, based on its architecture. Still, the Franciscans have the coins. How did a fourth century coin end up below a floor laid in the second century?

Corbo and Loffreda have partially excavated the area along the synagogue. You will notice black basalt ashlars beneath the white limestone ashlars on which the synagogue was built. Below and to the west of this platform are field stones like those found in the insula of private homes located between the synagogue and the church. Beneath the nave of the fourth or fifth-century synagogue they found a floor paved with basalt stones. They also maintain that the floor was too large to serve domestic purposes and must be from a public building. Because later synagogues were usually built on the remains of an earlier one on a particular site, they conclude that a structure they found beneath the late synagogue was the synagogue of Jesus' day. This is a hypothesis with no indisputable archaeological proof though Corbo has described the floor plan of what he calls the "Synagogue of the Roman Centurion" (see Luke 7:5). This earlier building is not visible since it is below that late synagogue.

The custodians of Capernaum consider the whole site to be a holy place. No one wearing shorts is allowed inside. Daily 8:30–4:15. Fee.

Chorazin (H: Korazim)

"Woe to you, Chorazin! . . . For if the mighty deeds done in your midst had been done in Tyre and Sidon, they would long ago have repented . . ." (Matt 11:21).

Location and History. At a turnoff on the Tiberias-Rosh Pina Road north of the Mount of Beatitudes is a road that runs to the east, leading to the site of ancient Chorazin. The site, two and one-half miles north of Capernaum, is on a low hill (273 feet above sea level) strewn with basalt stones. In antiquity, the city was noted for its grain (*b. Menah.* 85a). Because Chorazin was so close to Capernaum, it is no wonder that Jesus visited it. But he found its response disappointing. He cursed Chorazin along with Capernaum and Bethsaida for failing to accept his teaching (Matt 11:21-24; Luke 10:13-16).

Antiquities. Evidently Jesus' curse did not have immediate effect. The town thrived into the seventh century A.D. Its population expanded following the general Jewish migration from Judea to Galilee after the Second Revolt. But this site may not be first-century Chorazin since excavations here do not reveal occupation earlier than the second century A.D., though only a part of the site has been excavated. Charles Wilson was the first to excavate here and in 1869 he identified the presence of a synagogue. In 1926, E. L. Sukenik found an inscribed "chair of Moses" (see Matt 23:2) here. It is on display at the Israel Museum. There is an Aramaic inscription on the chair that reads, "In commemoration of the good work of Judah, the son of Ishmael, who made this portico, and its steps. For his work may he share in the lot of the righteous." The inscription must refer to the columns within the synagogue since it had no stoa or portico on the outside. That the chair was an ornamental and symbolic seat for Moses and his successors, the scribes, is inferred. Sustained and systematic excavations took place between 1980 and 1984.

The centerpiece of the site is a beautifully reconstructed synagogue built from the local black basalt. Though basalt is a very dense rock and therefore difficult to work, the synagogue's friezes are beautifully sculpted with geometric, floral, and human forms. The rest of the antiquities are domestic architecture, showing that the town was occupied until the Arab invasion in the 700s. There was another period of settlement in the 1500s and 1600s. One can see a **mikveh**, a **civic center**, an **oil press**, and a **domestic quarter.**

At the left of the site's entrance is a Muslim tomb that someone still maintains by periodically whitewashing it. Recall Jesus' criticism of the religious leaders of his time: *"You are like whitewashed tombs, beautiful to look at on the outside, but inside full of filth and dead men's bones . . ."* (Matt 23:27). Daily 8–4. Friday 8–1. Fee.

Gan HaShelosha
(H: "the garden of the three" also Berekhat Amal "the Amal Pool" from the River Amal in which it empties; A: Sachne, "hot")

"The burning sands will become pools, and the thirsty ground, springs of water . . ." (Isa 35:7).

Near Beth Alpha is a national park at the foot of Mount Gilboa where Saul fought his last battle with the Philistines (1 Samuel 31). It is the site of a natural pool and gentle falls. The pool is fed by warm springs that keep the water temperature at a constant 28°C throughout the year. The water flows into the Amal River and eventually into the Jordan. Though it is principally a recreation area, there is a small archaeological museum on the grounds. The Israelis renamed it in honor of three settlers who were killed by a land mine in 1938. Daily 7:30–4:45; Summer 7:30–5:45; Fridays 7:30–5:45. Fee.

Hamat Tiberias

Location and History. Hamat Tiberias is one and one-half miles south of Tiberias on the Sea of Galilee. Joshua 19:35 lists a town called Hammath in the territory of Naphtali. That this town is to be equated with Hamat Tiberias is doubtful since no artifacts earlier than the Hellenistic Period have been found here. Hamat, which is Hebrew for "heat," is the site of hot springs. Near the hot springs a town developed. Jewish legend credits Solomon with giving the springs its curative properties by changing the area's ordinary spring into a hot spring. He did so by commanding demons to go into the spring and heat its waters. Since they were afraid of Solomon's powers, the demons obeyed. Solomon also made the demons deaf so that they would not hear of his death and stop their work. The Romans exploited the hot springs and one can see the remnants of the Roman Period bath on the site. The spring is still active and you can feel its hot water (140°F). The water is collected and pumped into the spa across from the archaeological site. People with various medical complaints such as rheumatism find relief by bathing in these waters.

Antiquities. Excavations near the spring revealed a **synagogue** and associated buildings. The original monumental building dates from the first century A.D. It was a public building that was converted in the third century for Jewish worship alone. The mosaic floor was added one hundred years later. This makes it the oldest zodiac mosaic found in Israel. In its fourth-century phase, the synagogue was a broad house. The wall of orientation was the southern broad wall. Entrance was possible through three doors in the northern wall. Fifth-century remodeling covered over the mosaic. In this phase, the synagogue received an apse that oriented the worshipers to Jerusalem. The fifth-century building was destroyed in the first half of the 600s. When rebuilt, the new synagogue followed the lines of its fifth-century predecessor though the apse was no longer used. A mosaic with geometric forms graced its floor.

In one of its phases (fourth century), the synagogue's floor was decorated with a beautiful mosaic that depicts traditional Jewish religious motifs in its upper register. Its middle register, however, shows a **zodiac** with the god Helios riding his chariot across the sky in the center. The lower register contains an inscription naming the synagogue's benefactors. The significance of the zodiac in a synagogue is debated. (See the entry on **Beth Alpha.**) It is clear what a later generation of Jews thought about it. When the synagogue was rebuilt in the fifth century, following earthquake destruction, foundations for a floor were laid atop the zodiac mosaic, hiding it from view and defacing it.

At the southern end of the fourth-century building, you can see an entrance to a raised room. This may be the site of the synagogue's permanent **Torah shrine**. In a departure from the usual pattern, the interior space of this synagogue was divided into four areas by three rows of columns. The area between the two westernmost rows served as the **nave** since it was the widest space. A mosaic covered the floor. East of the nave the pattern was strictly geometric. Remnants of the floor west of the nave suggest the same. The nave section has the zodiac. The section of the mosaic that was closest to the place for the synagogue's Torah shrine depicted such a shrine flanked by a lit menorah on each side. Surrounding the menorahs are a lulab, shofar, ethrog, and incense shovel. The mosaic provides a frontal view of the Torah shrine pictured as a rectangular cabinet topped by a gabled roof with a conch shell in the pediment. A curtain knotted in the middle hangs in from the shrine's closed doors. Below this patently Jewish panel is the zodiac with Helios in the center and pictures of the four seasons personified as women in each corner. The third panel contains a Greek inscription naming benefactors. The eastern aisle contains two inscriptions naming benefactors: one in Greek and one in Aramaic, suggesting that the people who worshiped here were bilingual. The Greek inscription is "the pupil of the most illustrious patriarch . . . to the members of the Sanhedrin located in Tiberias." Another Greek inscription credits Profuturos with the building of a porch. The Aramaic inscription refers to the site as a "holy place," i.e., a synagogue. The entrance to the site is through a small building that gives historical and scientific information about the hot springs. It is sponsored by the spa across the road. It also contains a few artifacts found during excavations. Daily 8–4; Summer 8–5. Fee.

The **Tomb of Rabbi Meir**. Tombs of revered rabbis are places of pilgrimage for religious Jews. Rabbi Meir Ba'al-Hannes, i.e., "the wonder worker," was a rabbi of the second century A.D. who received his sobriquet because he miraculously secured the release of his sister-in-law from the Romans. His tomb is the building with the two white domes on the hills above the synagogue.

Hazor (A: Tell el-Cheetah)

". . . Joshua, turning back, captured Hazor . . . for Hazor formerly was the chief of all those kingdoms" (Josh 11:10).

Location. Hazor is the largest tel in Israel. It is 130 feet high, 1,950 feet long and 650 feet wide. The excavations of Yigal Yadin in the 1950s and '60s provided the setting for James Michener's novel, *The Source*. Michener builds his story around the more than twenty occupational layers that Yadin identified at Hazor. The tel is on the Tiberias-Qiryat Shemona Road 23 north of Tiberias, opposite Kibbutz Ayelet Hashachar (H: Morning Star), which operates a small **museum** of the finds from the area. In antiquity, the site controlled the northern spur of the Via Maris. Standing on the tel shows that it commanded the Jordan and Hula Valleys through which the caravans traveled. Both Egyptian and Assyrian texts mention Hazor because of its strategic location.

The Biblical Tradition. The Bible describes two conflicts with Hazor. According to Josh 11:10-13, the Israelite tribes captured the city, killed its king, and burnt it to the ground. Archaeology has revealed a violent destruction at Hazor in the Late Bronze Age. Unfortunately, excavation has not shown who was responsible for that destruction. According to Judg 4:1-2, Jabin, who ruled at Hazor, oppressed the Israelites. Led by Deborah and Barak, they defeated Jabin's army led by Sisera (Judges 4–5). By the beginning of the Monarchic Period, Hazor became an Israelite city. Solomon fortified it along with Megiddo and Gezer (1 Kgs 9:15). These and later fortifications did not stop the Assyrians from taking this city in 732 B.C. and incorporating it into the Assyrian provincial system (2 Kgs 15:29). Jeremiah's oracles reflect the sixth-century B.C. situation when Hazor was no longer under Israelite control (Jer 49:28, 30, 33). During Jonathan's campaign against Demetrius, the Jewish army passed through Hazor (1 Macc 11:67).

The Antiquities. Excavators have recovered a great array of material from domestic pottery to monumental architecture. Finds include examples of Canaanite, Egyptian, and Israelite artifacts. Some are on display in the small museum opposite the site. Many more are in Jerusalem's Israel Museum. At the tel, you can see remains of the city's **walls and Solomonic gate, storage facilities**, and some **private dwellings**. Also, you can walk into the city's **water system** completed during the reign of Ahab in the 500s B.C. The site is currently under excavation again. Take care when approaching the excavation area. It is best to stay on the paths. Heed all warning signs so that you will not endanger yourself or the antiquities. The part of ancient Hazor open for visitors is the upper city that covers approximately thirty acres. A much larger, lower city covering 175 acres has been partially excavated but is currently under cultivation. Occupation here was from the eighteenth to the thirteenth century B.C. Here were found houses, fortifications and gates, temples. Daily 8–4; Summer 8–5. Fee. Visit the small museum across from the tel first.

The Horns of Hattin

Six miles west of Tiberias is a dormant volcano the summit of which looks like a pair of horns. It is 1,050 feet above sea level. There are remains of a fortress and a wall at the summit, but the area has not been systematically excavated. Surface sherding gives evidence of occupation from the Bronze Age through the Hellenistic Period. This is to be expected because the Via Maris ran through this area. The most noteworthy event to take place here was the battle between the Crusaders and the Arabs led by Saladin in 1187. The crushing defeat suffered by the Crusaders was the moment when Crusader rule in Palestine began its decline. Though Acco, the final Crusader stronghold, did not fall until 1291, the victory of Saladin was the harbinger of the total Muslim victory over the Europeans. This is one of those battles that affected the course of history. If the Crusaders had been victorious, the history of the Middle East would have been very different.

On April 25 of each year, the Horns of Hattin provides the backdrop for Druze ceremonies in honor of Shueib, the Druze name for Jethro, the father-in-law of Moses. The Druze have great veneration for Shueib, who is their principal patron.

The Hula (Huleh) Valley

On most maps of ancient Israel, you will see a lake north of the Sea of Galilee. This is Lake Hula (Huleh) of which only a small area remains today. It is the smallest of the three bodies of water in the Jordan Rift. The Sea of Galilee and the Dead Sea are the other two. In the Middle Ages, people thought that the lake was "the waters of Merom," the scene of a conflict ancient Israel had with the Canaanites over control of the region (Josh 11:5). The area once covered by the lake is now among the richest agricultural land in the country. Its northern and western boundaries are the mountains of Upper Galilee. The Golan is its eastern boundary while the mountains of the Galilee and the Golan plateau form its southern boundary. Its length from north to south is seventeen miles; its average width is about six miles.

The three sources of the Jordan enter the valley at its northern end and emerge as a single river as they leave the valley. Although this valley was a fertile area in antiquity and therefore exploited by farmers, the wars of the Crusader Period destroyed many farming villages. This led to the deterioration of the area into a malarial swamp. Large-scale drainage projects began in the 1950s. These made large tracts of land available for cultivation again. Swamps that developed at the southern end were drained by straightening and deepening the Jordan River channel. This, in turn, helped the river's drainage into the Sea of Galilee. It also reduced the size of Lake Hula to a little over one thousand acres, part of which is a nature reserve. This small lake and the surrounding valley serve as stations for migrating birds. The birds cause problems for farmers—especially those engaged in fish farming. Pelicans and other migrating fish-eating birds have themselves a feast at the expense of these farmers.

When the Turks controlled Palestine from the 1500s to the beginning of the 1900s, they exploited the land's natural resources. In particular, the trees that grew on the mountains of Galilee were harvested and no seedlings were planted to take their place. Goats and sheep ate the few seedlings that sprouted naturally so that the mountains were denuded of vegetation and massive erosion resulted. The Israelis have been at work reforesting the mountains, but you can still see evidence of the erosion on some that have not yet been reforested. The soil is almost completely gone and limestone bedrock is visible. The soil from these mountains was washed off by rain into the Hula Valley and is, in part, the source of its fertility. In some places the first-century level of the valley is seven feet below the current level because of the buildup of eroded soil in the valley.

Kursi

"(Jesus and the disciples) came to the other side of the sea, to the territory of the Gerasenes" (Mark 5:1).

Location. Tel el-Kursi is found on the eastern shore of the Sea of Galilee at the mouth of the Wadi es-Samak. This is the site where the Byzantines commemorated the expulsion of the devils in Gerasa (Mark 5:1-17) or Gadara (Matt 8:28-34) or the country of the Gerasenes (Luke 8:26-39). The name "Kursi" is an Arabic corruption of Chorazin, which some thought was located here.

Antiquities. The building of a new road in the Golan in 1970 brought to light a site that was previously unknown. Four years of excavations revealed a sixth-century **monastic complex.** A 390 feet by 455 feet **wall** encircled the monastery. The wall was made of dressed basalt stones that were covered with plaster. The main entrance was in the west. It will be the one through which you will enter the site. At the entrance were a **gate** and a **watchtower.** A **street** with basalt pavers leads to the **monastic church** that was in the center of the settlement. The church, which is an apsidal basilica, had an **atrium, narthex,** and a **main hall** with two rooms flanking the **apse.** The southern flanking room was converted into a **baptistery,** suggesting that this monastic church also served a congregation. The floor was decorated with **mosaics** but only those in the aisles survived, though it was defaced in antiquity. The mosaic has floral and faunal motifs. The animal heads were defaced though the perpetrators are not known. Some Christians and all Muslims objected to art depicting animal or human forms. There is an **oil press** in the northern wing of the church and a **burial crypt** in the southern wing. On a slope six hundred fifty feet southeast of the monastery is another **chapel** built onto a natural cave. It was this cave and chapel that led excavators to identify the site as commemorating the gospel narrative about the swine. They maintain that the topography of the site matches the description in the Gospels. One can walk up to this cave to view the reconstructed chapel. Daily 8–4; Summer 8–5. Fee.

Megiddo (A: Tell el-Mutesellim, "the tell of the Governor")

"On that day the mourning in Jerusalem shall be as great as the mourning of Hadadrimmon in the plain of Megiddo" (Zech 12:11).

Location. This tel is at the junction of the Haifa-Jenin Road with the Hadera-Afula Road. It is twenty-two miles southeast of Haifa and seventeen miles southwest of Nazareth. The site covers fifteen acres and rises to 195 feet above the Jezreel Valley.

History. Megiddo's location made it a very important city during the Bronze and Iron Ages. It controlled the agriculture in and commerce through the Jezreel Valley. The Via Maris turned northeast from the coast through a narrow pass, the Nahal ᵓIron at Megiddo. Because of Megiddo's location at the edge of a valley that allows for the maneuvering of troops and chariots, Megiddo and its environs have been a battlefield throughout history. It was there that in 1918 British Forces defeated those of the Ottoman Empire, insuring Allied control of the Middle East during World War I.

Historians have reconstructed Megiddo's story by combining knowledge gained from literary sources (the Bible and other ancient Near Eastern texts) and material remains revealed by archaeology. The first systematic excavation at the site took place from 1924 to 1939. It was a project of the Oriental Institute of the University of Chicago. John D. Rockefeller, Jr. financed the project. Jerusalem's Hebrew University has mounted more recent investigations of the site between 1960 and 1967. Archaeologists have uncovered over twenty-five distinct occupation layers on the tel.

Megiddo's spring and its location next to a fertile valley make it obvious why this site was occupied already in the fourth millennium B.C. The first time the city is mentioned in a literary source is in a fifteenth-century B.C. Egyptian text (*ANET*, 245–248). It tells the story of the conquest of this city by Tutmoses III (1490–1436) of Egypt. In 1468, he came to Megiddo to secure Egyptian control of Canaan and Syria. He faced a coalition of local rulers arrayed against him. He defeated them and laid siege to Megiddo. The city held out for eight months before finally surrendering. In the site's museum, there is a multimedia display that describes Tutmoses' victory at Megiddo.

For most of its history, Megiddo was an important military and prosperous commercial center. As expected, it has a very high level of material culture and the site yielded many significant and beautiful artifacts. Many are on display in the **Rockefeller Museum** in Jerusalem that was originally built to house them.

The Biblical Tradition. The Book of Joshua lists "the king of Megiddo" among the thirty-one kings defeated by the Israelite tribal army (see Josh 12:7-24, esp. 21). There is, however, no archaeological evidence of Israelite presence at the site before the Monarchic Period. Judges 1:27 affirms that the tribe of Manasseh in whose territory Megiddo was located could not subdue the city (see Josh 17:11). The Song of Deborah mentions the "waters of Megiddo" as the site of a battle with the Canaanites (Judg 5:19). Megiddo probably passed into Israelite control only during David's reign. When Solomon consolidated his control by dividing his kingdom into twelve districts, Megiddo was an administrative center for one of these (1 Kgs 4:12). To protect his kingdom from external threats, Solomon fortified several cities—Megiddo among them (1 Kgs 9:15). It also became the headquarters of one of Solomon's chariot armies (1 Kgs 10:26). After the breakup of the David-Solomonic Empire following Solomon's death, Egypt tried to regain control of Syria-Palestine. The Bible mentions only Shishak's attack on Jerusalem (1 Kgs 14:25-27), but on a relief that Shishak had carved on a wall of the Karnak temple, he lists one hundred fifty towns of the

Israelite kingdoms that he attacked and destroyed (c. 920 B.C.). One of these was Megiddo.

The kings of the Omride dynasty restored Megiddo to its former glory. King Ahaziah of Judah was visiting King Joram of Israel, the last of the Omride dynasty, when the Jehu revolution broke out (see 2 Kings 9). Though Ahaziah tried to escape the ensuing bloodbath, he was caught and killed at Megiddo (2 Kgs 9:27). Later in the sixth century, Aram tried to extend its control over the territory of the Northern Kingdom. In 815 B.C., Hazael, king of Aram, attacked and destroyed Megiddo as part of that attempt. Israel was able to hold off the Arameans and during a period of peace and prosperity under Jeroboam II (786–746), Megiddo was rebuilt. But as Hosea and Amos warned, that prosperity was short-lived because it was built, in part, on injustice and oppression. In 733 B.C., Tiglath-Pileser invaded Israel, took the Galilee, and incorporated it into the Assyrian Empire as the province of Magidu with Megiddo as its capital.

When the Assyrian Empire was disintegrating at the end of the sixth century, Josiah of Judah wanted to prevent the Egyptians from helping the Assyrians against the Babylonians so he fought Pharaoh Neco at Megiddo. The Egyptians preferred a weak Assyria to a strong Babylon. Josiah wanted to end Assyrian hegemony in Palestine because he wanted to reclaim former Israelite territories that Assyria had annexed. Josiah also recognized that Babylon was in the ascendancy and wanted to support it against Assyria and its allies. His political insight did not translate into military victory. Josiah fell at Megiddo (2 Kgs 23:18-28; 2 Chr 35:22). Egypt, however, was not able to prevent the fall of Assyria and the rise of Babylon. Like the rest of Israelite and Judahite territory, Megiddo became part of the Babylonian Empire. While Megiddo continued to have some political importance during the Persian Period, its days of glory were past. It was abandoned in the Hellenistic Period and remained so until the site was excavated earlier in this century. In the Roman Period, the Second and Sixth Legions guarded the Nahal ᵓIron pass. These Roman legions encamped at Kefar Othani, a village about one mile south of the tel. Early travelers mistakenly identified the ruins of the Roman village as Megiddo.

Zechariah 12:11 mentions the city in connection with the eschatological events that involve Jerusalem and the Davidic dynasty. Megiddo, or at least a Greek corruption of the Hebrew words *har megiddo,* "the mountain of Megiddo," appears once in the New Testament as *Armageddon* (Rev 16:16). This summary of Megiddo's history makes it clear why the seer of Revelation considered it the ideal location for the final battle of good against evil.

Antiquities. Entrance to the site is by way of a small **museum,** which has displays that clarify the pre-Israelite history of Megiddo, highlighting the battle fought here by Tutmoses III. There is also an excellent model of the city that helps visitors have some idea of its complex history of occupation. A short walk from the museum is the **northern gate** of the city. Here gates from the pre-Israelite and Solomonic Periods are visible. One can see remains of **palaces,** a **granary,** and the **homes** located within the wall. There is one area identified as the **stables.** This identification suggested itself because the structure bears some resemblance to stables, and 1 Kings 10 notes that Solomon built stables at Megiddo. This structure is probably like a **warehouse**. The first excavators identified the structure as "Solomon's Stables." Later stratigraphic excavation revealed that the structure in question dates from the ninth century, probably from the reign of Ahab. Also, examination of the building makes it clear that it would have been unsuitable for the housing of horses. A most impressive site is the EBA and MBA **temple complex**. From the vantage point above the temples, one can look all across the Jezreel Valley and see its wide expanse. To the northeast, Tabor is clearly visible. One can even recognize the Church of the Transfiguration on its summit. One leaves the site by passing through the tunnel cut into the limestone, leading to the spring that supplied water to the city. The shaft leading to the tunnel is 195 feet deep and the tunnel itself is 390 feet long.

There are no shady spots on this site, which is extensive. It is important to wear a hat and have a supply of water. Take your cameras because Megiddo offers many good photo opportunities—especially of the Jezreel Valley. It is important to stay on the marked paths for your own safety and for the preservation of the site. This is one of the best reconstructed Bronze and Iron Age sites in Israel. It is well worth a visit. Daily 8–5; Friday 8–3. Fee.

The Mount of Beatitudes
(H: Har HaOsher, "the mountain of wealth" also Har Nahum, "Nahum's mountain")

"When (Jesus) saw the crowds, he went up the mountain . . . (and) he began to teach . . ." (Matt 5:1).

Four miles north of Capernaum on the Zefat-Tiberias road, there is a turnoff that leads to the Mount of Beatitudes, the summit of which is four hundred feet above the Sea of Galilee but still 227 feet below sea level. The site has a pilgrim hospice, a convent, and an octagonal church. The latter was built in 1937 to commemorate the episode narrated by Matthew 5–7, the Sermon on the Mount. Its shape imitates the octagonal form used during the Byzantine Period for churches built at places associated with an event in Christ's life. Egeria tells of visiting a cave on the mountain where Jesus gave the Beatitudes. There is such a cave beneath a sixth-century monastic church further down the hill. This church is just three hundred yards and across the modern road from the Church of the Multiplication of Loaves and Fishes across the modern road. The church was a small (31 feet by 14 feet) apsidal structure with no columns but with an atrium in front of its entrance. The Persians destroyed the monastery and its church in 614. These buildings were never rebuilt. The location chosen for the modern church offers an extraordinary view of the Sea of Galilee. Its well-kept gardens offer a beautiful setting for reflecting on Jesus' teaching. This is a holy place and you will need to wear appropriate clothing if you wish to visit the church and the gardens. No shorts allowed. Daily 8–12; 2:30–5. Free.

Church of the Beatitudes, overlooking the Sea of Galilee.

Mount Tabor

". . . Jesus took Peter, James, and John his brother, and led them up a high mountain . . . and he was transfigured before them" (Matt 17:1-2).

Location. This mountain (1,850 feet above sea level) that stands alone at the northeastern edge of the Jezreel Valley is twenty-two miles southeast of Nazareth. The summit is a plateau measuring 3,250 feet by 1,300 feet. From it one can see most of the Jezreel Valley, Mount Carmel, Mount Gilboa, and Mount Hermon.

The Biblical Tradition. Though most visitors come to Mount Tabor because the church at its summit commemorates the Transfiguration (Matt 17:1-8; Mark 9:1-7; Luke 9:28-36), the NT never mentions Mount Tabor by name. This mountain became associated with the Transfiguration because after coming down from "the high mountain," the first town Jesus enters, according to Matthew (17:24) and Mark (9:33) is Capernaum. A "high mountain" near this town is Tabor. Another mountain associated with the Transfiguration is Mount Hermon because just before the Transfiguration, Jesus and his disciples are in Caesarea Philippi (Matt 16:13; Mark 8:27; Luke does not give a location for Peter's confession in 9:18-22). The "high mountain" near Caesarea Philippi (Banias) is Mount Hermon.

  The OT mentions Tabor as the scene of the decisive encounter between several Israelite tribes led by Deborah and Barak, and the Canaanites led by Sisera, a general in the service of Jabin that Judges calls the "king of Canaan" (4:2). The story of that battle is told in narrative form in Judges 4 and in what some believe to be among the oldest surviving Hebrew poems in Judges 5. Whatever the historical basis of these accounts may be, the control of the Jezreel Valley was decisive in the Israelite tribes' attempt to gain hegemony over Canaan. The valley's agricultural potential could support a larger population and its commercial importance as a trade route was an important source of economic power. If various Canaanite city-states had maintained control of the valley, the Israelite tribes in Galilee would have been cut off from those in the central region. It is doubtful that any national identity could have developed in that case.

  Tabor is at the convergence of the territories assigned to three tribes: Zebulun to the west, Issachar to the south, (Deut 33:18-19 mentions a mountain where Zebulun and Issachar "shall offer right sacrifices." This may be a reference to Tabor.) and Naphtali to the north. The Song of Deborah commends all three tribes for participation in the battle (Judg 4:14,18). Tribes like Reuben, Dan, and Asher, which were not immediately affected by the Canaanite control of the valley, did not participate in the conflict and are criticized for this (Judg 4:16-17). In the prose account, the forces led by Barak are made up of Zebulun and Naphtali. Tabor and the immediate vicinity have been the scene of battles before and after the one that took place between Israel and Canaan according to Judges 4–5. The plain below the mountain makes it possible for chariot forces to maneuver and control the outcome of any battle. The

Interior of the Basilica of the Transfiguration, Mount Tabor.

poetic account of Deborah's victory notes that the Israelites attacked after a rain storm (Judg 5:4). The mud caused by the rain would have rendered the chariots useless. The Israelites could then face the Canaanites on more equal terms.

Excavations have shown that the summit of the mountain was occupied during the Monarchic Period. In his critique of Israel's leadership, Hosea accuses them of being "a net spread upon Tabor" (5:1). Some commentators have taken this to be a criticism of a form of worship there that the prophet considered not authentically Yahwistic. Jeremiah 46:18 and Ps 89:13 include it among the great mountains of the region.

Antiquities. The tradition that identifies Tabor as the mount of the Transfiguration is attested by the fourth century. The Byzantines built a **church** on this site in the sixth century and the Crusaders another in the twelfth. North of the church are the remains of a **Benedictine monastery** from the Crusader Period. The Crusaders also built a fortress here in 1213. Muslim armies destroyed it fifty years later. Parts of the **wall** surrounding the fortress still stand. The road to the church passes under **a gate of the Crusader wall**.

The Shrine. When the current church was built in 1921, elements from the earlier buildings were incorporated into it when possible. The apse that encloses the sanctuary is from the sixth-century church. Trap doors in the sanctuary open and reveal the top of the mountain. The Greek Orthodox Church controls the northern half of the summit. Their church, built in 1911, honors Elijah the Prophet. There is also a cave on their property that they identify with Melchizedek, the king of Salem mentioned in Genesis 14.

The Ascent. Tour buses are not able to reach the summit of Mount Tabor. Those who travel to Tabor on buses leave them at the village of Daburiya. There will be a slight wait while taxis shuttle pilgrims up and down the mountain. It is possible to go to the summit by private car. The site is a holy place and appropriate attire is necessary. There is a rest house near the church. One can buy refreshments and have a meal if arrangements are made in advance. Daily 8–11:30; 2–5:30. Holy Place: modest clothes, no shorts.

The Sea of Galilee (H: Kinneret)

Some derive *Kinneret*, the Hebrew name for the Sea of Galilee from *kinnor*, "harp," because the shape of the lake resembles that of a harp. It is the largest expanse of water in the Rift Valley and it separates the Galilee from the Golan. The surface of the Kinneret is 682 feet below sea level. It is twelve and one-half miles long and its greatest width is seven miles. It is four and one-half miles from Tiberias to the eastern shore. The circumference of the lake is thirty-two miles. Its deepest point is about 159 feet. Springs feed the lake, but it also receives water from the Jordan. That river flows into the lake at the north and continues its descent to the Dead Sea at the Kinneret's southern end. The waters of the lake are clear, fresh, and warm. From antiquity, the lake has supported a fishing industry. Today there is extensive fish farming by settlements in the Galilee since the lake itself cannot supply the current needs.

The Biblical Tradition. The OT mentions the Kinneret just three times: Num 34:11; Josh 12:3; and 12:27. Each time it is mentioned as a boundary marker. The Gospels use several names for this lake. John 6:1 and 21:1 call it "the Sea of Galilee" and "the Sea of Tiberias" though the lake was known by the latter name only after Jesus' ministry. Matthew and Mark call it the "Sea of Galilee" (Matt 4:18; Mark 1:16) or simply "the sea" while Luke calls it the "Lake of Gennesaret" (5:1) or simply "the lake" (8:22). Josephus calls it "the Lake of Gennesar," "the Lake of Tiberias," or simply the "Lake of Gennesaret" and notes that some people call it the "Lake of Tarichaeae" after a town on its shore.

Jesus' Galilean ministry took place almost entirely in the towns in the lake region. The call of his first disciples takes place along its shores (Mark 1:16-19; Matt 4:18). One time Jesus taught from a boat just off the lakeshore (Mark 3:7-9). From the immediate area of the lake, Jesus "toured all of Galilee" (Matt 4:23). Many of Jesus' miracles took place in towns on the shores of the Kinneret, e.g., the healing of a paralytic at Capernaum (Mark 2:12), the healing of a blind man at Bethsaida (Mark 8:22-25), the healings at Gennesaret (Mark 6:54-66). Some miracles took place on the lake itself, e.g., the miraculous catch of fish (Luke 5:1-11), the calming of the storm (Matt 8:23-27; Mark 4:35-41), and the walking on the water (Matt 14:22-23; Mark 6:45-52). Though usually calm, the waters of the lake can become very treacherous. Even moderate winds become fierce when channeled through the gaps in the heights to the east and west of the lake. Though the Gospels note the fishing industry connected with the lake (Mark 1:16-20; Matt 4:18-22; 17:27; Luke 5:1-10; John 21:1-11), Jesus' parables do not exploit it; rather, Jesus derives his imagery from farming and other commercial activity.

Kinneret as a Boundary. The lake served as a border between Jewish territory to the west and non-Jewish territory to the east. The fishing, farming, and other commercial activities of the area surrounding the lake led to a dense population of the regions on both sides. Many of these settlements became cosmopolitan in the Hellenistic and Roman Periods. There were contacts between the Jewish and Greek populations as is clear from the similarity of their material culture. Also, the presence of Greek inscriptions in Jewish areas shows that the Jews were bilingual.

The First-Century Boat. Israel takes much of its water for both drinking and irrigation from the Kinneret. In the 1980s, there were several years of abnormally low rainfall. This brought the lake's level down so much that a first-century boat that had been under water was discovered in the mud of the receding shore line. Two members of the Kibbutz Ginosar, Moshe and Yuval Lofan, came upon the boat in the mud in 1986. The clay of the lakebed protected the boat and prevented its deterioration. It was removed after careful excavation and has been undergoing chemical treatments to prevent deterioration. The boat is on display at the Yigal Allon center of the Kibbutz Ginosar, which is four miles north of Tiberias. The boat is about twenty-five feet by six feet and contains seven different types of wood. It was used for fishing and transport in the first century A.D. The center offers a short film on the discovery of the boat, its excavation, and the process involved in its preservation. Enterprising members of Kibbutz Ein Gev had several boats similar in design built in Egypt. These boats now ply the waters of the lake ferrying pilgrims from Ein Gev to Tiberias. The center also offers a sound and light show about the Galilee. Daily 8–5: Friday 8–1; Saturday 9–5. Fee.

Tabgha (G: Heptapegon; A: Tabgha is a corruption of the Greek word; H: En Sheva; "seven springs")

"When (Jesus and the disciples) had finished breakfast, Jesus said to Simon Peter, 'Simon, son of John, do you love me more than these?'" (John 21:15).

"Then taking the five loaves and the two fish and looking up to heaven, (Jesus) said the blessing, broke the loaves, and gave them to (his) disciples to set before the people . . ." (Mark 6:41).

Location. Two miles south of Capernaum, there is an area that the Greeks called *Heptapegon* because of the seven springs there. In the Byzantine Period, it was the site of three churches, two of which have been rebuilt in modern times. The Byzantine Church of the Beatitudes (see Matt 5:1-11) was not rebuilt though a new church was built on the summit of the hill across the road from Tabgha (see **Mount of Beatitudes**). The two other churches are the Church of the Primacy (see John 21) also known as *Mensa Christi* ("The Lord's Table") and the Church of the Multiplication of Loaves and Fishes (see Matt 14:15-21; Mark 6:35-44). Appropriate attire is necessary for entrance to both churches.

The Church of Peter's Primacy. The fourth-century pilgrim Egeria mentions that near Capernaum was "the stone on which the Lord placed the bread which has now been made into an altar." At one time, it was believed that Egeria was referring to the stone under the altar in the Church of the Multiplication of the Loaves and Fishes just a few yards to the south. Stanislao Loffreda of the SBF believes that the rock Egeria was speaking of was enshrined in the fourth-century church that commemorated not the multiplication of loaves but the story found in John 21 (See also Wilkinson's hypothesis below). According to that post-resurrection story, the Risen Christ prepared a meal of fish for his disciples who were fishing (John 21:1-14). After the meal, Jesus speaks with Peter and commands him: "Feed my sheep" (vv. 15-19).

The Franciscans built the present church in 1933. Its walls stand on the foundation remaining from the Byzantine structure that enclosed the rock that

Egeria mentions. Before the first church was built, there was a quarry on the site. One can see "steps" on the south side of the church. Loffreda observed the characteristic cuts made by stone masons when freeing limestone blocks. Among the artifacts discovered in the area were tools used by masons quarrying stone. In front of these steps are several "heart-shaped" column bases. These bases supported columns found at the corners in basilicas. Their shape allowed them to bear weight in two directions. What they are doing here is unknown though over the years guides have come up with explanations that satisfy the pilgrims' curiosity. In the fifth century, the church that Egeria saw was enlarged and the stone became its focal point. The walls of that church were especially thick, suggesting that the ceiling was vaulted. When Arculf visited the area in 670, he did not mention this church, probably because the Persians destroyed it during their invasion of 614. The Church of the Primacy is too small for many pilgrim groups so an altar was built in front of the church to accommodate them. To the right of this altar is a modern bronze sculpture of the scene described in John 21:15-19. Daily 8–12; 2–5. Free. Holy Place—modest dress required.

The Church of the Multiplication of Loaves and Fishes. John Wilkinson has suggested that the Tabgha site originally commemorated the events narrated in John 21. Since the story mentions bread and fish (John 21:9) and since the site was a small grassy plain, it also became associated with the feeding of the five thousand (Mark 6:41). Another church just a few yards south of the Church of the Primacy was built at the end of the fourth century. It was not oriented directly to the east as most churches were but was set off by some twenty-eight degrees. During the latter half of the 400s, this church was remodeled and enlarged. An apse oriented worshipers directly to the east. The enlarged building contained the church, an atrium, and a hospice for pilgrims. The building has a trapezoidal shape because it had to avoid running into a branch of the Via Maris that ran right alongside its northern wall. Another unusual feature of the building was that it had a rectangular transept. Its exterior was made of crudely cut basalt stones. This did not make for a very impressive exterior, but the church's interior more than made up for it. A colored mosaic with geometric patterns and motifs of animal and plant life covered the nave's floor. The mosaic on the floor of the transept depicted flora and fauna from the Nile plus a nilometer (a device to determine the depth of the Nile River.) Two Greek inscriptions are set into the floor. One names Saurus as the creator of the mosaic and the other Martyrios, a Patriarch of Jerusalem from 478-486, as its patron. Martyrios lived in Egypt as a young man and this may explain the Egyptian motifs. The Martyrios inscription reads as follows: "To the memory and the repose of the sponsor, the holy patriarch Martyrios." This helps date the mosaic that was obviously completed after the death of Martyrios in 486. When Arculf visited, he saw only a few columns on this site. Evidently the Persians also destroyed this church.

The site was abandoned and forgotten until part of the mosaic was discovered by accident at the beginning of this century. The site was cleared in

Mosaic of the miracle of the loaves and fish, Tabgha.

1911. Excavations were conducted in 1932 and 1970. In 1980, the Benedictines, who are the guardians at this site, built a new church here on the foundations and according to the style of the fifth-century building. The Benedictines request that visitors treat the church as a house of prayer. They ask that all explanations be given outside the church before visitors enter to preserve a quiet atmosphere in the church. They have prepared a fine slide presentation on Tabgha and its church shown on request in one room of the cloisters that surround the atrium. Daily 8:30–5. Free. Holy Place—modest dress required.

Tiberias (H: Teveriya)

"Other boats came from Tiberias near the place where they had eaten the bread when the Lord gave thanks" (John 6:23).

Location. Tiberias lies along the center of the Kinneret's western shore. It is about one hundred eight miles north of Jerusalem and nineteen miles northeast of Nazareth. It is 682 feet below sea level and its climate is subtropical, which means very hot and humid summers and mild winters. To the west are steep hills and to the east is the Sea of Galilee. Two miles north was Magdala and one mile south was Hamath. The center of the city is the "old town." Many older buildings are of black basalt stone that is common in the region. In the last ten years several large hotels have been built in the center of the city. Besides foreign tourists, their guests include many Israelis who travel to Tiberias for the weekend.

History. The town was built by Herod Antipas in A.D. 18 to replace Sepphoris as his capital. Antipas named it in honor of the Emperor Tiberius, who allowed him to rule as tetrarch of Galilee in accordance with the will of his father Herod the Great. When the city was being built tombs were discovered, so observant Jews would not live in it. Many of the Gentiles who lived in Tiberias were freed slaves. The Bible mentions Tiberias only once: John 6:23. According to this text, boats from Tiberias were carrying people who were looking for Jesus. During the First Revolt, the people of the city supported the revolt and Josephus made it his headquarters before his defection to the Romans. When Vespasian and his armies appeared, the Tiberians thought better of resistance. They surrendered to the Romans and begged for mercy. The Roman legions did not destroy their city.

At first, the rabbis regarded the city as ritually unclean because of the tombs inside its limits. But following the failures of the Jewish revolts against Rome and the migration of Jews to Galilee, Rabbi Shimon bar Yohai declared the city to be ritually clean. Rabbinic etymology derived the name of the city word *tavur*, "navel." This etymology suggested itself because of the importance that this city had in early Judaism. After the destruction of Jerusalem, Tiberias became one of the centers of the Jewish world. It was the seat of the Sanhedrin after its move from Sepphoris. Also, Tiberias was the site of the rabbinic academy where a good portion of the Jerusalem Talmud was completed. One system used to insert vowel indicators into the vowelless Hebrew Bible was developed here. This development was necessary when Hebrew was no longer a spoken language and its correct pronunciation became a problem. Semitic languages are not written with vowels though, of course, vowels are necessary for pronunciation.

A convert from Judaism named Joseph built a church here in the early fourth century. He received authorization from Constantine since the city became overwhelmingly Jewish in the years since the Jews from the south came to resettle in Galilee. In 383, Egeria notes that she saw where the house of James and John stood. In 527, Justinian banned Jews from serving in the government so Christians took over political control of the city. During the Persian invasion of 614, the Jews of Tiberias sided with the Persians against the Byzantine rulers of Palestine. When the Byzantine authorities regained control in 628, the Emperor Heraclius first pardoned but later executed the Jews of the city—even those who converted to escape punishment.

At the eve of the Arab conquest of the Galilee, Tiberias became the most important Christian center of Palestine after Jerusalem. After all, there were many Christian shrines in the area. Tiberias surrendered to the Arabs who came in 636. They made it the capital of the province of al-Urdun (Jordan). Jews in some numbers returned to the city in the early Arab Period. The Crusaders took the city in 1099 and it became a popular pilgrimage site because Christians of that period believed that Jesus lived in the city, though the Gospels do not state this. The Crusaders made it the capital of the "principality of

Galilee" and held on to it for one hundred fifty years. Tiberias was destroyed in 1187 after a great battle between the Crusaders and the Arabs and remained abandoned until 1560. In that year Suleiman the Magnificent allowed a Jew named Don Joseph Nasi to rebuild the city. He did so and Jews returned to the city they regarded as holy. These Jews were primarily Jews whom Queen Isabella expelled from Spain. Most were Cabbalists, i.e., Jewish mystics.

In the middle of the 1700s, a Bedouin sheikh, Daher el-Omer wrested control of the Galilee from the Turks. He ruled the region as a semi-independent province from Tiberias. The remnants of black basalt walls and a tower that can still be seen in the center of town were originally built by the Crusaders and reconstructed by el-Omer. He invited Jews to settle in Tiberias. In 1777, a group of Hasidic Jews accepted his invitation and laid the foundation for the present Jewish population of the city. In 1837, a great earthquake destroyed the city, but the Jews rebuilt it. Since the 1967 war diminished the threat from the Syrians on the Golan Heights across the lake, the city has grown and become a center for tourism in the Galilee.

Since the Gospels mention this town only once, no Christian shrines were built there except by the Crusaders. They built a church in honor of St. Peter. The Franciscans rebuilt the church at the beginning of this century. Its apse is shaped like a boat to remember Peter's original occupation. The church once served a local congregation, but now the population of Tiberias is entirely Jewish. The church is in the center of town near the shore.

Religious Jews hold the city in such high regard, in part, because it is the burial place of so many great rabbis. Among those buried in Tiberias are Maimonides, Yohanan ben Zakkai, and Akiva. Maimonides (d. 1204) is also known as Rambam, a word made from the initials of the full name: Rabbi Moshe ben Maimon. He lived most of his life in Egypt and is renowned as a philosopher and rabbinic scholar. Yohanan ben Zakkai was the leading rabbi at the time of Jerusalem's fall in A.D. 70. He founded the rabbinic academy at Yavneh (Jamnia). Near him are buried several of his important disciples. Another important rabbi whose tomb is in Tiberias is Akiva, who lent his support to the Second Revolt. A few years after that unsuccessful uprising, the Romans captured Akiva and executed him in Caesarea's theater as a warning to all would-be revolutionaries.

Antiquities. Tiberias has several archaeological sites either within the city or in its immediate environs. Unfortunately little has been published of the excavations that have taken place there. You should visit the ancient synagogue of **Hamat Tiberias** (see above). Further south along the western side of the lake is **Tel Rakkat**, which is probably the Rakkath mentioned in Josh 19:35. The site was occupied from the EBA into the Byzantine Period. The highway cuts into the tel. Within Tiberias itself is **Hurvat Bet Maʾon**. It is currently under excavation. Surveys show that there was occupation on the site in the Biblical Period though most remains come from the Late Roman and Byzantine Periods. The latter two sites have not been prepared to receive visitors. As you travel north from Tiberias, you will see the site of ancient **Magdala**; it also has been excavated but has not been reconstructed for tourists. Magdala is next to the lake and east of the highway. West of the highway, you can see some sarcophagi that have eroded from the original places in the limestone caves above.

Yardenit

"Then Jesus came from Galilee to John at the Jordan to be baptized by him" (Matt 3:13).

At the southern end of the Sea of Galilee where the Jordan River begins its descent to the Dead Sea, there is a picturesque spot called "the baptismal site." Christian pilgrims recalled Jesus' baptism by John at a site about six miles south of Jericho. The Greek Orthodox have a monastery there in honor of the Baptist. After the 1967 war, this area was closed by the Israeli military because of its proximity to the Kingdom of Jordan. There was a fear of infiltration by terrorists. The Israelis allowed Christians access to the site only rarely. Because this original baptismal site was no longer accessible, Christians found another. Evangelicals used to come to the place where the Jordan leaves the Sea of Galilee to commemorate Jesus' baptism and to celebrate baptism of converts and "rebaptisms" of the pious. Soon enterprising members of a nearby kibbutz built changing rooms for those to be baptized, ramps leading into the water, refreshment and souvenir stands. This is a contemporary example of a phenomenon that happened more than once in antiquity. When a site commemorating a particular event becomes inaccessible, pilgrims do not stop commemorating the event. They simply move the site of their commemoration as happened in Jerusalem with "St. Stephen's Gate."

The baptismal site offers a beautiful spot for lunch. A specialty of the kibbutz is honey made from dates. The members of the kibbutz make samples available to visitors. Daily 8–4; Summer 8–5. Free.

UPPER GALILEE AND THE GOLAN

Banias (NT: Caesarea Philippi; G: Paneas "[The city] of Pan")

". . . Jesus and his disciples set out for the villages of Caesarea Philippi" (Mark 8:27).

Location. The ancient city of Caesarea Philippi is located in the Banias nature reserve along the Hermon River (sometimes known as the Banias River), one of the sources of the Jordan. It is thirty-three miles north of the Sea of Galilee and two and one-half miles from Dan. It is at the southwest foot of Mount Hermon.

History. Although there is no certain evidence, the site may have been a cultic center in the Canaanite and Israelite Periods. The place names *Baal-gad* (Josh 11:17; 12:7; 13:5) and *Baal-hermon* (Judg 3:3; 1 Chr 5:23) were located in the general area. Some suggest that the placing of Peter's Confession here was deliberate because of the site's cultic connections. Banias certainly was a cult center in the Hellenistic Period. The Greeks built a shrine here to the god Pan, the god of woodlands and caves. Caesar Augustus gave Paneas to Herod the Great in 20 B.C. In gratitude, Herod built a temple to Augustus near the cave. Following the death of Herod the Great, the Romans confirmed his son Philip as tetrarch of the Golan, the region Luke calls Ituraea and Trachonitis (see Luke 3:1). To express his thanks to the emperor, Philip renamed Banias "Caesarea." To differentiate it from the Caesarea built by his father along the Mediterranean coast, this city became known as "Caesarea Philippi," i.e., Philip's Caesarea. This is how the NT refers to it (Matt 16:13; Mark 8:27). Looking at the escarpment above Pan's cave, one understands why the metaphor of "the rock" suggested itself to Jesus.

Agrippa II, the last Jewish king to rule the region, enlarged the city and named it "Neronias" in honor of Nero (c. A.D. 53). The name by which the town was usually known, however, was Caesarea Panias. In A.D. 70 the Romans celebrated games here to mark Titus' capture of Jerusalem and the end of the First Revolt. In the Late Roman and Byzantine Periods, "Caesarea" drops out of the town's name and it becomes simply "Panias." The Crusaders built a fortress here, calling it "Belinas." The name "Banias" is an Arabic corruption of the Greek name for the city. Since Arabic has no "p" sound, the "b" sound takes its place.

Antiquities. Across from the entrance to the nature reserve, excavations are currently in progress. If the gate is open, one can enter. It is important to be careful in walking through the site to protect it and oneself. The archaeological site has not been prepared for tourism. Keep on the paths and off and out of the structures. What one sees here are **medieval fortifications**—evidence of the Crusaders' presence here and **monumental vaulted building** from the Roman Period, which the Crusaders repaired.

Upon entering the park and its popular picnic area, one's attention is drawn to the **cave of Pan**. Inside the cave was a shrine with a statue of Pan playing a flute. The niches with Greek inscriptions dedicated the shrine to Pan. Herod's **temple to Augustus** has been revealed under rocks that have fallen at the entrance of the cave. The spring that feeds the Hermon River is inside the cave. The water is melted snow from Mount Hermon that has percolated through the limestone. To the west of the cave is a path that leads up a slope to a terrace. On the terrace was a **platform** that supported either another temple or a palace from the time of Herod, the Great. Above that is the **tomb of Sheik el Khadr**, the Arab title of the prophet Elijah.

The River Walk. There are several hiking paths in the nature reserve. Take the one that follows the river until you come to a footbridge. After crossing it, you will follow a path that will lead past some **Roman** and **Crusader walls**. You will approach an old **grain mill** that used the river's current to turn its grinding stone. Usually there are some Arabs there, making and selling the flat Bedouin bread filled with sweet cheese or jelly. After a short walk you will cross the river again and see the remnants of the pool built by the Syrians. The icy waters of the river fed the pool, but it has fallen into disrepair and is no longer in use. Continue following the path along the river that begins to cut a valley as it descends toward the Sea of Galilee. You will hear the river, but will no longer be able to see it. Finally, after a walk of almost one kilometer, you will cross the river again, backtrack a bit, and come upon beautiful falls and a small lagoon. Do not go into the water because the current is very swift. Daily 8–4; Summers 8–5. Fee.

Baram

"The king loved Esther more than all other women . . . So he placed
the royal diadem on her head and made her queen . . ." (Esth 2:17).

Location. The village of Baram is along the northern slopes of the Meiron massif. It is seven miles northwest of Zefat and just a few miles from the frontier with Lebanon. According to Jewish tradition it is the burial spot of Queen Esther. Neither the Bible nor other ancient Jewish sources, except travelers' diaries, mention the site.

The Synagogue. This site boasts of one of the best-preserved synagogues in the country. Another rarity is that this synagogue is among the few that bear an inscription. It is on the window sill on the east side of the façade. The Hebrew inscription reads as follows: "Built by El'azar son of Yudah."

The synagogue's façade faces the south, i.e., toward Jerusalem. There was a covered porch in front of the triple entrance. This feature sets this synagogue apart from others in Israel. Several columns that supported the roof of the atrium have been replaced on their bases. The building interior is divided into a central nave and two aisles by two rows of six columns each. There is also a row of four columns in front of the back wall, and an entrance in the eastern wall. Notice the decoration of the synagogue reflects a conservative approach. The motifs are floral and geometric. There are no animal or human forms in evidence. There is some dispute about the dating of this synagogue and the accuracy of its reconstruction. Some date it to the third century on architectural grounds. This is unreliable. There needs to be stratigraphic excavation that can provide more reliable dating and more evidence regarding its interior architecture.

There was another synagogue in the village, but little has remained from it except some architectural fragments which are on display behind the reconstructed synagogue. One of these is a lion's head. Apparently those who built the second synagogue did not share the scruples about images that characterized the builders of the reconstructed synagogue. There was also a Hebrew inscription on the lintel of the second synagogue. It read: "May there be peace in this place and in all the places of Israel. Jose the Levite, the son of Levi, made this lintel. May blessing come upon his deeds. Shalom."

The Arab Village. South of the synagogue, there is a path that leads to the parish church of Baram, which is about fifty yards from the antiquity site. Before 1948, Baram was a Christian Arab (Maronite) village. During the 1948 war, the Israeli army did not want any concentration of Arabs near the border of Lebanon because of the fluid military situation. The people of Baram did not resist the Israeli forces, but they moved five miles south to the village of Gush Halav with the promise that they could return after the end of hostilities. The Israeli government has not fulfilled that promise. Still, families originally from this village will return to this small church for weddings, funerals, and baptisms. They have not given up the hope of one day returning to their village. Daily 8–4; Summer 8–5. Fee.

Dan (A: Tell el-Qadi)

". . . [the Danites] attacked Laish . . . and destroyed their city . . . The Danites then rebuilt the city, which was in the valley . . . and lived there. They named it Dan after their ancestor Dan . . ." (Judg 18:27-28).

Name and Location. Dan is a Hebrew word for *judge* (see Gen 49:16). The Arabic word *qadi* means the same thing. The Arabic names for places in Israel often preserve the ancient Semitic name in some way. The biblical formula "From Dan to Beersheva" (1 Sam 3:20; 2 Sam 3:10; 1 Kgs 5:5) marks this city as the northernmost in ancient Israel. Dan is one hundred forty miles north of Jerusalem, but it is no longer the northernmost city of Israel. Metulla has that honor. The tel and the surrounding area are part of a nature reserve along the Dan River, the most important of the three sources of the Jordan. There are marked trails leading through the reserve to the antiquity site.

The antiquity site covers some fifty acres and it rises sixty-five feet above the surrounding plain. This site was occupied in the Neolithic Period about 5000 B.C. There is a gap in evidence of later occupation until the EBA almost twenty-five hundred years later. It was not until the second millennium B.C. that the city came into its own when a system of defensive walls was built around the settlement. The most remarkable feature is a mud brick gate in the southeast corner that has survived to this day. The gate dates to the first century B.C. A fire destroyed the city in 1100 B.C., but it was immediately rebuilt. Dan was fortified heavily in the ninth century, possibly by Ahab who was protecting his northern flank from the Arameans. You will see part of the ninth-century wall. The eighth century was a time of prosperity for Dan as it was for all Israel during the long and peaceful reign of Jeroboam II (786–746). There is no destruction level from the time of the Assyrian crisis (c. 734 B.C.). Apparently the city was peacefully incorporated into the Assyrians' provincial system. The houses of the sixth century are well built and reflect continuing prosperity. Though the archaeological record for the city's history after the Babylonian Period is not complete, there is evidence that the sanctuary continued to be in use. It was modified and expanded during both the Hellenistic and Roman Periods. A dedicatory inscription in Aramaic and Greek was found on the site. It reads: "To the god who is in Dan." Apparently, the sanctuary stopped functioning during the Byzantine Period.

The Biblical Tradition. Genesis mentions the city of Dan as the place to which Abraham pursued four kings whose forces kidnapped his nephew Lot (Gen 14:14). According to Deuteronomistic tradition, calling this place Dan was anachronistic because it did not have that name until after the Settlement Period (Judg 18:28). The story of the tribe of Dan and its search for a place to settle is an illustration of how difficult it is to reconstruct the history of early Israel from the Bible alone. According to biblical tradition, the territory assigned to Dan was along the Mediterranean coast near Jaffa (Josh 20:40-47). The Bible tells us the people of Dan eventually settled elsewhere, but the tradition supplies two different reasons for the move. The Book of Joshua asserts that the territory assigned to the Danites was too small so they attacked the city of Leshem. They took the city, renamed it Dan, and took its territory for themselves (Josh 20:47-48). The Book of Judges, however, offers another explanation. First, it says that the Amorites prevented the Danites from claiming the territory assigned to them (Judg 1:34). Later in the book, there is the story of Samson, a Danite, living in the territory assigned in Joshua but having conflicts with the Philistines who want to have that territory for themselves. Eventually Samson falls while bringing down a Philistine temple at Gaza (Judges 13–16). Finally, in Judges 18, the Danites are looking for a place to settle because "they had received no heritage among the tribes of Israel" (Judg 18:1). They went to the city of Laish, which they destroyed. The Danites built a new city on the ruins of Laish, which they renamed Dan, in honor of the ancestor (Judg 18:27-29).

The Hebrew text of Judges provides an interesting footnote to the story of the taking of Laish. It says that the Danites set up an idol for themselves and a grandson of Moses served as its priest. A pious scribe copying this text was so scandalized that Moses' grandson was associated with idolatry that he tried to insert another letter into the name of Moses to make it read Manasseh (see Judg 18:30). The attempted insertion has become part of the Hebrew text of Judges. The association of Dan with illegitimate worship appears later in Kings. After the David-Solomonic Empire split into the two Israelite kingdoms, Jeroboam, the first king of the Northern Kingdom (Israel), built a temple there (1 Kgs 12:28-29). The author of 1 Kings told the story of the building of that temple to discredit Jeroboam's efforts. In fact, the expression "the sin of Jeroboam" became a refrain in Kings to discredit all the kings of Israel and their religious rituals.

Antiquities. Excavations have shown that the people of Dan did not accept the Deuteronomic perspective on the centralization of sacrificial worship. Dan remained a cult center into the Roman Period. At the high point of the tel, excavators have found the place where religious rituals were performed. They found a 22.5 feet by 61.5 feet **rectangular platform**, but not the foundations of the temple mentioned in the Bible. Also, excavations have revealed a rampart, a sixth-century **city gate** with seats for the elders outside it, a thirteen-foot thick **city wall**, an area of private homes just inside the gate. A most striking find is the thirteen-foot high MBA **city gate** made of mud brick. You can still see flecks of the lime whitewash that had to be applied annually before the onset of the wet season. Without this preventive maintenance, the mud brick wall would have disintegrated during the rains. The Dan area can receive almost forty inches of rain during the wet season. Excavations are continuing at Dan. Though you can visit the site of the excavations, you need to remember that they have not yet been fully prepared for visitors. You must be very careful to endanger neither the site nor yourself.

Nature Walk. The SPNI administers this site. There is a lovely path along the river and through the woods and underbrush that offers a delightful alternative to the maintenance road for those wishing to reach the antiquity site. The path along the Dan River is well marked but good walking shoes will help make the walk safer and more enjoyable. Shorts and sandals are not recommended for this short hike because of the underbrush and the slippery footing. Daily 8–4; Summer 8–5. Fee.

Gamla

Location. Gamla is in the southern Golan, ten miles due west of the northern end of the Sea of Galilee. The ancient city is at the summit of a hill shaped like a camel (H: *gamal*). The hill rises from a valley that leads to the Sea of Galilee, which is plainly visible from the site.

Excavations. Gamla, known previously as Tel Salam, was surveyed after Israel occupied the Golan Heights after the 1967 war. The first to suggest this as the site of Gamla described by Josephus (*Jewish Wars* 4:2) was Y. Gal. In 1976, excavations began on behalf of the Department of Antiquities. Shmaryahu Gutman, who led this project, is certain that this is the Gamla described by Josephus. Murphy-O'Connor rejects this identification. No inscriptional evidence has been found to support Gutman. Earlier identifications for Gamla include Tell el-Husn (the hill of Sussita) and Tell ed-Daraʾon in Jordan.

The site's location on a steep hillside makes excavating here complicated. Erosion over the centuries has made stratigraphic digging very difficult. Many artifacts simply washed down the side of the hill and collected in the structures there. Reconstructing the history of this site is tentative because financial problems have forced the cancellation of the excavations begun in 1988. Only preliminary reports on the results of eight seasons of work are available. Much of the following comes from Josephus and assumes that the site is the Gamla he describes. According to preliminary excavation reports, the site was occupied in the EBA. There was no further settlement at the site until the first century B.C. In 23 B.C., Herod the Great took control of the Golan and wanted to establish permanent settlements to pacify it because the area had been a refuge for bandits and revolutionaries. Gamla probably benefited from this policy. When the First Revolt began in A.D. 66, the Romans were intent on protecting their eastern flank against any possible support coming to the Jews of Palestine from their co-religionists in Babylon. Gamla was on that eastern flank. Also recognizing the strategic importance of the city, Josephus, while he was still loyal to the rebellion, fortified the city. In the spring of 67, the Romans first sent their client Agrippa II, the last Jewish king, to take Gamla. He failed so Vespasian, later to become emperor, attacked the city in September of 67. The city fell in a matter of weeks. The Romans destroyed the city and the site was never occupied again.

Antiquities. After turning off the highway to the entrance of the site, you pass through a **dolmen** field. A dolmen is a burial chamber made from large unworked stone slabs. They look like large tables. The word *dolmen* is a Breton word meaning "stone table." Two stones form the walls and one or more horizontally laid stones form the roof. They are found on land that has little agricultural value except for grazing. Their builders probably erected them on slopes because this allowed the large stones to slide into position. This was easier than lifting them or sliding them up ramps. Most are found in a narrow strip along the Rift Valley from Aleppo to the Dead Sea. Since grave robbers looted these tombs in antiquity, dating them is a problem. Most agree that they were already in use at the beginning of the EBA. Whether they were still being used in the MBA and LBA is debated. At one time, archaeologists suggested that the dolmens were tombs for nomads. This is unlikely. Since a nomad did not need a house during his lifetime, it is doubtful that he thought one was necessary after his death. It is more likely that they were used by sedentary farmers. Still, it must be significant that the geographical distribution of dolmen fields shows them to be found where the two life-styles (nomadic pastoralism and sedentary agriculturalism) meet. There are nearly two hundred dolmens in the area.

At the entrance to the site, the SPNI has prepared a display that illustrates the Roman siege techniques that were probably used in taking Gamla. The display also describes the area's flora and fauna. Particular attention is devoted to the vulture since the cliffs above Gamla are home to the largest concentration of vultures in Israel. The vultures can be seen atop the cliffs about the Gamla River with its 167-foot waterfall.

Reaching the site from the plateau above it requires a strenuous walk that includes steep descent down steps made from the basalt stones found in the area. Since these steps are irregular, having a sturdy pair of shoes will make the walk more comfortable. Sandals are not recommended. The walk down to the site will take about thirty minutes; the walk up slightly longer. There is no shade or water available at the site. Take a hat, sunglasses, and water. Along the way to the site, there are in Hebrew and English, bronze plaques with Josephus' account of Gamla's fall. It reads like his account of the fall of Masada. The similarities show that one goal of Josephus' work was to present the Jews as noble opponents who preferred death to defeat.

After passing the archaeological expedition's camp, you will see the **wall** of the town that begins at the height of the northern slope and continues to the steep drop on the south. The east side of the town was the only side requiring a wall since the other parts of the town were protected by deep ravines. At the north end of the wall, the excavators have reconstructed the **tower** to its original height. Inside the wall is a **basilica** that the excavator identifies as a synagogue.

If this identification is correct, this building is the oldest synagogue found in Palestine. There is neither an inscription nor any Jewish religious symbol in the building or on any of the associated architectural fragments that confirm the identification. The basilica was a public building used for various purposes, one of which may have been public prayer. It probably was built under the sponsorship of Herod when he was trying to encourage settlement in Galilee. Near the synagogue is a **mikveh**, which prompted the excavator to identify the basilica as a synagogue. Below the basilica are some **private homes** that have been excavated. Gamla's location required the houses of the town to be terraced down the steep hillside. The roof of one house provided a balcony for the house above it. The floors of these houses were beaten earth as was usual in the first century. Other structures reveal some industries of Gamla including the production of pottery and olive oil. An **olive press** has been reconstructed at the west end of the town. The site used to be strewn with **ballistae**, round stones catapulted into the town during the siege, and arrowheads that show the intensity of the conflict there. They are now in the **Golan Archaeological Museum** at Katsrin where many other artifacts found at Gamla are on display. Allow about two hours for the visit to Gamla. Daily 7:30–4; Summer 7:30–6: Friday 7:30–3:45. Fee.

The Golan

"The clans of the Gershonites received from the half-tribe of Manasseh: Golan in Bashan with its pasture lands . . ." (1 Chr 6:56).

The Golan refers to an area of Transjordan bounded on the north by Mount Hermon, on the south by the Yarmouk River, on the west by the Jordan Valley, and the east by Nahal Raqqad. It is a basalt plateau formed by volcanic activity. The basalt stone of the region and several cones of extinct volcanoes are evidence of this. These heights (the highest peak is 3,960 feet above sea level) rise above the eastern shore of the Sea of Galilee.

According to biblical tradition, this area was part of the inheritance of that part of Manasseh that lived east of the Jordan River. The Bible credits Moses with its conquest (see Josh 12:1-6). The Bible subdivided the Golan into a northern region called Maacah and the southern region called Geshur (Josh 12:1-6; 13:11-12; Deut 3:13-14). David brought this area into his kingdom by marrying Maacah, the daughter of the king of Geshur (2 Sam 3:3). During most of the Monarchic Period, Aram controlled the region (1 Kgs 20:24) and it does not play a significant role in biblical narratives. Little is known of this region before the fourth century B.C. Most of the structures built during the Hellenistic Period were fortresses built by the Seleucids to control lines of communication. The Hasmonean Alexander Yannai was able to incorporate the Golan into his kingdom, which passed under Roman control in 63 B.C. Under Herod the Great, there was a significant influx of Jewish population to the Golan. Several of these Jewish settlements joined in the First Revolt, the most notable being Gamla.

Rusting remains of the 1967 War in the Golan Heights.

Archaeological surveys showed a more dense Jewish population in the Golan than expected for the Byzantine Period. Apparently the heavy taxation of Jews in Galilee led them to abandon their settlements there in favor of the Golan. The Byzantines were probably trying to encourage this. More than one hundred seventy settlements from this period have been identified. From the quality of material remains it was a period of great prosperity. The Golan's population was mixed: Jewish and Christian. There are at least twenty-five sites with synagogues and twenty-two with churches. There were three towns that had bishops: Hippos (Sussita), Afeca, and Khisfin.

The Arabs swept through the Golan in 636 on their way to Damascus. In 637, they fought a decisive battle with the Byzantines near Yaqusa in the southern Golan. The Arab victory there marks the end of Byzantine control in Palestine. During the early Arab Period, the Golan suffered a significant depopulation. During the Turkish Period, the region was home primarily to Bedouin groups. Attempts at Jewish settlement in the first century failed. After the first World War this region was part of the Mandate that the League of Nations gave to France. It then became attached to Syria. The Golan Heights command the Hula Valley and its agricultural settlements that are north of the Sea of Galilee. Until 1967, these came under regular bombardment and missile attacks from the Syrians. During the 1967 war, Israel gained control of the Golan Heights and most of the Arab population fled. Jewish settlements were soon established and the settlers in the Golan oppose returning the region to Syria, though the Syrians demand the return of the Golan Heights before any normalization of relations with Israel will be considered.

Among the sites that you should visit in the Golan are Banias, Kursi, Katsrin, Nimrod's Castle, and Gamla. The Golan is also home to a significant part of Israel's Druze population. Their villages are along the slopes of Mount Hermon.

Gush Halav (H: block of milk)

Location. This Arab-Christian town is a mile north of Meiron.

History. There is archaeological evidence that the site was occupied in the Late Bronze Age. The first reference to the city comes from Josephus in the first century A.D. The Greek name of the town was Gischala. It was the home of the Jewish revolutionary, John (Yohanan) of Gischala, a leader in the First Revolt against Rome. Jerome asserted that Paul's parents came from this town although he located it in Judea rather than Galilee. The basis of the town's prosperity was the highly prized olive oil that came from Upper Galilee. The site was abandoned in the Byzantine Period, probably because of economic pressures brought on by high taxation. Today the town is populated by Christian Arabs some of whom come from Baram. The Arabic name of the town is Jish, an abbreviated form of its ancient Greek name.

Antiquities. Excavations have uncovered a Middle Roman Period synagogue. It was damaged several times by earthquakes and abandoned in the sixth century A.D. after significant earthquake damage. It was not rebuilt as Jews left the region because of high taxation. Look for the lintel which has the image of an eagle carved on it. The presence of the eagle is a particular puzzle since it violates the command against making images and the eagle was the symbol of the hated Romans and Byzantines. From the synagogue, look to the east and notice the large blocks of white limestone bedrock visible across the wadi. These limestone outcrops probably inspired the town's name. Daily 9–4: Friday 9–1. Fee.

Katsrin (variants: Qazrin, Qasrin, and Qatsrin)

Location and History. This reconstructed Byzantine Period Jewish village is in the central Golan about one-half mile from the modern town that bears its name. There is a spring at the site that supplied water for the ancient village. Although there are ceramic finds in the area from the Bronze Age, buildings appear in the late third or fourth century A.D. when the village prospered because of the olive oil trade. A synagogue was built in the fourth or fifth century and reconstructed in the 500s. The village was abandoned immediately after the Arab invasion in the seventh century, though shortly after squatters returned. In 749, an earthquake destroyed the synagogue. In the 1400s–1500s, Arabs settled in the village and converted the synagogue to a mosque. The bedouin, who settled here in the first century, regarded the mosque/synagogue as a holy place.

Antiquities. The village has been partially reconstructed and its buildings fitted with the tools and implements used for everyday life in the Roman-Byzantine Period. You can see some private homes and their furnishings, the town's water system, and its synagogue. You also can observe the methods and tools the ancient builders used in putting up these buildings. Note that the houses here consist of a large multipurpose room, a storage room separated from the larger room by a wall with a series of windows, an upper story (for sleeping) above the storage area, and an outdoor courtyard.

The fifth-century **synagogue** was a square structure with its main entrance in the north. It had benches and six columns. In the sixth century, the synagogue was enlarged—eight columns were necessary to support its roof. A platform for the ark was along the south wall. A mosaic covered the floor and panels of painted plaster decorated the walls. Because of faulty foundations, the floors cracked and it was necessary to replace the mosaic with pavers. Retaining walls were necessary to support the structure. The reconstruction of Katsrin makes it possible for visitors to have a good idea of how ordinary people lived in the Golan during the Byzantine Period. Visitors can walk into the homes, industrial and work areas, and in the synagogue. Going up a small tower gives a panoramic view of the whole site. This is well worth a visit. The **Museum of the Golan** is in the modern town of Katsrin. Most of the artifacts come from the excavations at Gamla. Village: Daily 8–4; Summers 8–5. Museum: Daily 8–4; Fridays 8–1; Saturdays 10–4.

Meiron

This small moshav, seven miles from Zefat, is an important pilgrimage center for Hasidic Jews. They come here to visit the tomb of Shimon bar Yochai, the author of the *Zohar,* a book of Jewish mysticism. There are several other tombs of ancient rabbis in the region. These too attract pilgrims. Above Shimon's tomb is a third-century **synagogue**, which is among the largest in Israel. Notice the absence of any animal forms or floral pattern decorations. The people were very strict in their interpretation of the commandment forbidding images. Below the synagogue was the **ancient village**. You can see both a residential and an industrial quarter. These were excavated in the late 1970s, but the site has not yet been developed for tourism. The size and construction of homes in the residential quarter make it clear that some wealthy people lived here. The town was abandoned during the early part of the Byzantine Period, probably for economic reasons. The site may be overgrown, though it is still worth a visit.

Nimrod's Castle (H: Mezudat Nimrod; A: Qalat Nimrud and Qalat es-Subeiba "the castle of the cliffs.")

"Cush became the faith of Nimrod, who was the first potentate on earth. He was a mighty hunter . . ." (Gen 10:8-9).

The local population named this Crusader-Era fortress in honor of Nimrod (see Gen 10:8-9) who was a giant according to Muslim tradition. People assumed that this fortress had to have been built by someone who had superhuman strength. Arabic tradition holds that Nimrod could sit on the top of the fortress and reach out his hand to the Banias River for a drink of water. This magnificent fortress is situated on the border of the Golan with Mount Hermon. It rises on a narrow ridge that is 2,650 feet above sea level. Deep wadis surround it and give it an air of impregnability.

This fortress controlled both the route to Damascus and the Hula Valley and it stood at the border between the Crusader and Muslim forces. When and by whom it was built is not precisely known. There are several inscriptions in the fortress and they are all in Arabic. The earliest one dates to 1228. Its construction does not reflect that typical of the Crusaders, but it is similar to Arabic style. It does not appear to have ever been held by the Crusaders though they tried to take it in 1253. After the fall of Acco in 1291, the Crusader threat to Muslim rule in Palestine ended and it became unnecessary to man and maintain Nimrod's fortress. Under the Mamlukes, it became the seat of a local governor.

Antiquities. This site has never been systematically excavated. The National Parks Authority has developed the site for tourism primarily because of its view. One enters the site from the west. Along the western wall, there is a series of **towers**. The main **fortress and keep** are at the eastern end. The fortress' water supply was maintained by a series of **cisterns**; the most impressive is below the tower at the southwest corner of the fortress. Daily 8–4; Summer 8–5. Fee.

Zefat (A: Safed)

"A city set on a mountain cannot be hidden" (Matt 5:14b).

Location. Zefat rises on the slopes of Mount Canaan, which is 3,150 feet above sea level. The city itself is 2,660 feet above sea level and the highest in Israel. It is one hundred forty-five miles north of Jerusalem and forty-six miles east of Haifa. Though it is only twenty-two miles from Tiberias, reaching Zefat requires a climb of almost 3,500 feet. Viewing Zefat from Tiberias or especially from Meiron at dusk is an excellent illustration of Jesus' saying about a city built on a hilltop (Matt 5:14-16). Viewing the Sea of Galilee from Zefat at night allows one to see the many settlements that ring the lake.

History. Along with Hebron, Jerusalem, and Tiberias, Zefat is considered a city holy to the rabbis. A curious religious tradition holds that the name Zefat is an acronym for *tsitsit* (the fringes on prayer shawls), *pe'yot* (the side curls worn by the Orthodox), and *tefillin* (the phylacteries worn during morning prayer). The consonants of Zefat and the initial consonants of these three words are the same in Hebrew. Still, Zefat cannot compare with the Hebron, Jerusalem, and Tiberias when it comes to antiquity. This city is a relative newcomer. Neither the Bible nor early rabbinic literature mentions it. It came into prominence during the Crusader Period (twelfth century).

Because of its high elevation, Zefat was one of the chain of towns beginning with Jerusalem that lit signal fires to mark the new moon and festival days so that observant Jews could celebrate the festivals at the right time. Josephus says that he fortified the region in preparation for a Roman attack during the First Revolt. Like the rest of Galilee, Zefat received Jews driven from Jerusalem by the Romans after the Second Revolt. The tombs of several early rabbis are venerated in the area around Zefat. The Crusaders exploited its position in their attempt to control the road to Damascus. Remnants of the Crusader fortress built in 1140 are found on the "citadel." In 1266, the Mamlukes captured Zefat. After Spain expelled the Jews in 1492, many settled in Zefat and augmented the Jewish community already there. By the 1500s, Zefat became a popular pilgrimage center for Jews who came to pray at the tombs of revered rabbis located near the city. One of those tombs is that of Shimon bar Yochai located in Meiron just six miles from Zefat. This second-century A.D. rabbi is the reputed author of the *Zohar* (H: the brightness), which is a basic work of Jewish mysticism called Kabbalah (H: reception, tradition). The city became a magnet attracting the Kabbalists. The first printing press in Palestine began operation here to disseminate the work of the town's religious scholars. The first book printed in Palestine, *Shulhan Aruk* (H: the arranged table), a book of Jewish religious rituals, was printed here.

The town went into a decline in the seventeenth–eighteenth century. There were power struggles between the Druze and the Arabs for political control. Two terribly destructive earthquakes in 1738 and 1837 caused much damage. An epidemic in 1812–1814 led to the decline of the Jewish population. By 1948, there were seventeen hundred Jews and twelve thousand Arabs in the town. Still, during the 1948 War the greatly outnumbered Jews, augmented by one hundred twenty young volunteers, routed the Arabs who fled the city. Today the town is totally Jewish and has a population of sixteen thousand.

Visit. The old part of town is quite picturesque with its medieval synagogues and its artist quarter. The former mosque of the city is now a gallery that displays the works of the city's many artists. Jewish artists began settling in Zefat in numbers beginning in the 1930s. The exhibition, which serves some fifty artists and sculptors, changes regularly. Some artists welcome visitors to their own workshops and galleries. From the center of town, one can look down to the valley below and see a cemetery. According to Jewish tradition, this is the burial place of a Jewish mother and her seven sons who refused to abandon their ancestral religion at the time of the Maccabean Revolt (See 2 Maccabees 7). It is possible to visit some of the town's medieval synagogues. Entrance is free though you will be asked for a donation. Modest dress is required. Men must cover their heads.

CHAPTER TEN

The Palestinian National Authority

Since 1993 when the State of Israel recognized the Palestine Liberation Organization (PLO) as the representative of the Palestinian people, negotiations have been taking place between Israel and the PLO regarding the political status of the Palestinian people and their relationship to Israel. The goal of these negotiations has been to bring the blessings of peace upon the Israeli and Palestinian peoples. The final shape of the political solution to the problems standing in the way of peace is still not clear. It is best to leave these matters to the parties involved in them. What others can do is offer their support and encouragement as the peace process goes forward.

There are several important historical, archaeological, and religious sites in the region that are the subject of negotiation. These will be included in this section though their inclusion does not imply support for or opposition to any decisions made by the principal parties in the peace process. What everyone hopes for is a solution that ensures lasting peace between the Israelis and the Palestinians and one that enables visitors access to the historical and religious sites in the entire region.

The last and most difficult step in the peace process will be negotiations over the status of Jerusalem. In 1967, the Israelis annexed the Old City and East Jerusalem. These had been part of Jordan since 1948. The united Jerusalem serves as the capital of the State of Israel. The Palestinians also wish to make Jerusalem the capital of a Palestinian state. For the convenience of those who will use this book, all sites in Jerusalem are located in the Israel section of this book. Again, this does not imply support or rejection of any political position. The matter will be decided by the Israelis and Palestinians in a future round of negotiations. People of good will everywhere wish them well in their efforts to conclude the peace process successfully.

Names. Palestine is the name the Romans gave to the homeland of the Jews that became part of the Empire in 63 B.C. The name continued in use until the Modern Period and is the name the Arabs of the region prefer. The land that is the subject of negotiations between the PNA and the Israelis goes by several names. The **Gaza Strip** refers to land along the southern Mediterranean shore that borders on the Sinai (Egypt) and Israeli territory. It was controlled by Egypt between 1948 and 1967 when it passed to Israeli control. It extends over just one hundred and thirty square miles but has a population of eight hundred thousand. Since 1994, it has been under Palestinian control.

The **West Bank** refers to the land west of the Jordan River that was under Jordanian control until it was occupied by the Israelis following the 1967 war. Complicating the negotiations between Israel and the PNA are the Jewish settlements in this area, which are also known as the **Occupied Territories** or simply the **Territories**. Israeli nationalists who want Israel to annex this area tend to call it **Judea and Samaria**. They maintain that the region is the heartland of the ancient Israelite kingdoms, having been promised by God to Abraham and his descendants forever. The West Bank covers 5,900 square miles and has a population of about 1.2 million Arabs and about one hundred thousand Israelis. Jericho came under the control of the PNA in 1994. Negotiations have led to Bethlehem, Ramallah, Tulkarm, Nablus, and Jenin coming under Palestinian control as well. Negotiations are continuing. Certainly the question of Jerusalem will be the most difficult. After the 1948 war, the city was divided with the Old City and East Jerusalem under the Jordanians and West Jerusalem under the Israelis. After the 1967 war, Israel annexed the Old City and East Jerusalem, making the united Jerusalem its capital. The Palestinians want Jerusalem to serve as the capital of the national state that they hope to establish.

History. Nomadic Arab shepherds like the Bedouin and traders like the Nabateans have been part of the population mix in the Eastern Mediterranean for thousands of years. Because of its geographical position, this land bridge between Asia and Africa has attracted a mixed population. At the end of seventh century A.D., the region's local population, both Jew and Christian, resented their Byzantine masters and welcomed the Arabs as liberators. The Arab population in the region grew dramatically following the fall of the Byzantine Empire. The victories of the Arab armies, which were intent on spreading Islam, brought to Palestine the Arabic culture, language, and religion. Most of the local population accepted these and became Arab. Even those who remained Christian became Arab in culture and language, if not religion. The number of Jews decreased although the Muslims tolerated both Christians and Jews. This enabled small Jewish and Christian communities in Palestine to survive.

As the center of power in the Arab world moved from Damascus to Baghdad to Cairo, Palestine was subject to a succession of new masters but each was Arab and Muslim. Beginning in the 1100s, there were a series of wars, known as the Crusades, with European powers. As the European threat to Muslim hegemony in the Middle East ended, Arabs were no longer in control of Palestine. Power passed to the Ottoman Turks. These people were Muslims but they were not Arabs. They were a nomadic people from Central Asia who managed to displace the Byzantines in Anatolia and then extended their rule into Europe, Asia and Africa. In the 1500s, Palestine became another province of the Ottoman Empire.

The Ottoman Empire was among the defeated Central Powers in World War I. This empire did not survive the victory of the Allies, who dismantled it. In 1920, the League of Nations entrusted Palestine as a Mandate to Britain until a final determination could be made regarding the future of the region. The Arabs of Palestine expected Britain to reward them for their opposition to their Ottoman masters, but they were disappointed. At the time, Palestine's population was about seven hundred thousand of whom fifty-six thousand were Jews and the rest Arabs, though seventy-four thousand of these were Christians.

What made Britain hesitate to establish a Palestinian Arab state in the Mandate was, in part, due to the Zionist Movement started in 1875 by Theodore Herzl. The goal of this movement was to establish a national homeland for the world's Jews. After some debate, the Zionists decided that this homeland should be in Palestine. In 1917 Lord Balfour, the British Foreign Secretary, issued the "Balfour Declaration" that gave the support of the British government to the goals of establishing a Jewish state in Palestine. Of course, the Arabs of Palestine opposed this policy, the practical effect of which was to increase Jewish immigration to the region. There were anti-Jewish riots in several cities of Palestine and Jewish agricultural settlements were attacked.

In 1939 the British government reversed its policy and restricted Jewish immigration to Palestine. This led to Jewish political and armed resistance. These included terrorist acts such as the bombing of the King David Hotel in Jerusalem and the massacre of the Arabs at Deir Yassin. The escalating conflict over the future of Palestine led Britain to surrender its Mandate over Palestine to the United Nations. In 1947, the UN decided to divide the territory of the Mandate to form two states: one Jewish and the other Arab. Jerusalem was to be an international city. Following the departure of British troops in May of 1948, Jewish leaders in Palestine proclaimed the establishment of a Jewish state in the territory allotted to it by the UN. The Arabs rejected the arrangement and armies from several neighboring Arab states entered Palestine with the intention of ending the existence of the Jewish state.

To the surprise of almost everyone, the armed forces of the new Jewish state defeated those of the Arab states and a cease-fire was negotiated by the UN in 1949. The State of Israel ended up controlling seventy-seven percent of Palestine. Egypt controlled the Gaza Strip and Jordan annexed the West Bank, an action that was not recognized by the UN. No Arab state was established in Palestine. Again Palestinian aspirations were frustrated.

In 1964, the Palestinian Liberation Organization was established. Its stated aim was to destroy the Jewish state and replace it with an Arab one. The Palestinians began a war of attrition against Israel that involved terrorist activities against Israelis in Israel and abroad. In 1967, Israel launched a preemptive strike against Egypt and Syria. When Jordan joined the war, Israel attacked it as well. After just six days, Israel had crushed the armed forces of these three Arab states. It occupied the Gaza Strip, the Golan Heights, and the West Bank to use as bargaining chips in peace negotiations. When the Arab states refused to negotiate peace treaties, Israel began its occupation of these new territories. Military occupation was followed by civilian settlement. The possibility of establishing a Palestinian state seemed more remote than ever.

In October 1973 Syria and Egypt attacked Israel. They failed to achieve the destruction of the Jewish state. Israel retained control over the Territories so Palestinian hopes were dashed again. But the tide of international support for Israel was waning for several reasons and in 1974, the UN granted the PLO observer status and Yasser Arafat addressed the General Assembly. This, however, had no real practical effect in advancing Palestinian political aims and PLO terrorism continued. In 1977 Egypt struck a severe blow to Palestinian hopes when it made peace with Israel. Five years later Israel invaded Lebanon with the goal of destroying the PLO. International pressure made it impossible for Israel to achieve this aim so it allowed the PLO leadership to relocate in Tunisia. Many PLO fighters were killed by the Lebanese in the Sabra and Shatilla refugee camps while the Israelis were supposedly guaranteeing their security. With the PLO leadership in Tunis and the PLO guerilla forces depleted, the young people of the Territories responded with what has been called the *Intifada*. This spontaneous uprising began on December 8, 1987 and consisted of general strikes, the harassment of Israeli troops in the Territories, the execution of collaborators, and terrorist acts against the Israeli civilian population. Though the PLO leadership did not inspire the *Intifida*, it soon co-opted it.

In December 1993 the United States and the Soviet Union convened the Middle East Peace Conference to begin a process that could lead to a settlement of the issues between the Israelis and their Arab neighbors. A delegation of Palestinians was among the parties at this conference. A year later, the Labor Party in Israel came to power after pledging to move the peace talks ahead. Yitzhak Rabin became the prime minister. In September 1993 Rabin and Arafat exchanged letters that led to the establishment of the Palestinian National Authority and the PLO's recognition of Israel's right to existence.

An Israeli religious nationalist assassinated Rabin in 1995. Continued terrorist acts against the Israeli populace led some people to question their government's policies toward the PNA and the PLO. This reassessment led to the election of Benjamin Netanyahu of the Likud Party as prime minister. He has pledged to proceed with the peace process at a more deliberate pace and has chosen to continue Jewish settlement in the Territories. Still, the peace process continues and there is some hope that Palestinian aspirations will find fulfillment.

Archaeology and the Territories. The West Bank has many important archaeological sites, the most famous of which is certainly Qumran. Still, there are several others that are significant. The excavation of ancient Shechem (Tel Balata) by G.E. Wright was important not only because of the site's significance, but because a whole generation of Palestinian archaeologists were trained there. Among other important sites in the Territories are Jericho, Mount Gerizim, the Herodium, Tel Ai (Deir Dibwan), Samaria (Sebaste), Tel el-Farah (Tirzah), and the monasteries of the Judean desert. The pace of archaeological projects tapered off following the 1967 war because of the protocols of excavating in occupied territories. Of the projects that did continue, only a few have been prepared to receive visitors. What follows are sites that have been developed. Hopefully, once the status of the Territories is settled, a priority will be making the archaeological sites of the region accessible to visitors.

Bethlehem

"But you, Bethlehem-Ephrathah, too small to be among the clans of Judah, from you shall come forth for me one who is to be ruler in Israel . . ." (Mic 5:1).

Location. The city where Jesus was born is just a short bus ride from Jerusalem. It is little more than five miles away. The main focus of any visit to this city is **Manger Square** and the **Basilica of the Nativity**. The town is geared toward serving pilgrims. There are many tourist shops and some restaurants in the Manger Square area. You will also meet some street vendors selling souvenirs. As part of the interim peace accord between Israel and the Palestinian Authority, the town of Bethlehem is under the administration of the Palestinian Authority.

There are several sites on the way to Bethlehem that deserve mention. About two miles from Jerusalem, south on the Hebron Road, stands the **Ecumenical Institute** (Tantur). This place of study was founded at the initiative of Paul VI following his trip to the Holy Land and the conclusion of Vatican II. The pope envisioned scholars of various Christian churches coming together to study the Word of God in the Holy Land. The institute provides a conducive place for scholars spending a sabbatical for study in Israel. Tantur also runs sabbatical programs for pastoral ministers.

About a mile and a half from Bethlehem is **Rachel's Tomb**. According to Gen 35:19, Rachel died giving birth to Benjamin and was buried in Bethlehem (See also Gen 48:7). Another tradition locates her grave in Ramah in the territory of Benjamin (see Jer 31:15; Matt 2:18). Pregnant Jewish women pray at this tomb for a safe delivery. Free. Sun.–Thurs. 8–6; Fri. 8–1. Just past this tomb is a fork in the road. To the right is the road to Hebron; to the left is the road to Bethlehem and Beit Sahour, the site of **Shepherds' Fields**. The total distance between Jerusalem and Bethlehem is six and one-half miles. You will probably visit Bethlehem with your tour group. If you want to return for another visit, you can take public transportation. Buses no. 22 and 47 from the Arab Bus Station on Suleiman Street stop in Bethlehem. You can also ride in a shared taxi. Make certain you agree on the fare before you begin the trip. Bus service stops at dusk, but taxis will continue to be available.

Biblical Tradition. The Old Testament mentions Bethlehem several times besides naming it as the place of Rachel's burial. It was also the home of the Levite whom Micah hired as priest for his shrine (Judg 17:7-13). It is the home of Naomi to which Ruth follows her and becomes the wife of Boaz and the great-grandmother of David (Ruth 1:19; 4:1-22). It was the home of Jesse,

Manger Square and the Basilica of the Nativity, Bethlehem (upper photo); and the shrine of the nativity, where tradition says Jesus was born.

David's father. Samuel went there to find David and anoint him as king (1 Sam 16). Micah proclaims that a ruler for Israel is to come from this city (See Mic 5:1 that Matt 2:5 cites; see also John 7:42). The Philistines occupied it (2 Sam 23:14) and later Rehoboam fortified it (2 Chr 11:6). Despite its association with David, Bethlehem never plays any significant role in the history of Israel. It always remained a village whose principal claim to fame was the wheat grown in nearby fields. A popular etymology of the name Bethlehem is "house of bread." In Jesus' day, Bethlehem was an unassuming village dwarfed by its larger neighbor, Jerusalem.

The Byzantine Period. Bethlehem's fortunes changed with the coming of the Byzantines. Constantine built a great basilica there over the caves that earlier Christians honored as the birthplace of Jesus (Matt 2:1-18; Luke 2:1-21). To discourage Christian veneration at the site, the Romans built a sanctuary to Adonis there. Still, the tradition about the caves as the place of Jesus' birth persisted and Constantine built his church there in 326. Justinian wanted to outdo Constantine so he enlarged the basilica and adorned it with striking mosaics. (You can see evidence of the Constantinian building where the Justinian floor was removed. Lift up the trap doors in the floor and you will see the Constantinian mosaics.) When the Persians invaded Palestine in 614, they did not touch this church because the mosaic on its façade depicted the Magi dressed in Persian garb. When the Muslims arrived in 638, they used the southern transept as a place of prayer because they honored Jesus as a prophet. Because of this, the church was not harmed during the reign of Hakim in the eleventh century when Christian churches all over the country were systematically destroyed.

The years have not been kind to the church, but what we see is essentially the building erected by Justinian. It is the one church building in Israel that has survived from the Byzantine Period. The interior mosaics are nearly all gone. Looters removed the marble facing of the walls. (That is one reason the front door has been almost entirely walled up—to make it more difficult for looters to take anything else from the church.) Other walls were added, obscuring the original lines of the structure. The lines of the building's interior architecture have also been obscured by altars and other liturgical items. The impressive façade of the church is all but hidden by a monastery and buttresses. Still, enough remains of the building to help one visualize what a monumental structure it was.

The place venerated as the site of Jesus' birth is a cave beneath the basilica's sanctuary. There are stairs that descend into the cave from either side of the sanctuary. The cave is small and can be crowded when several groups are there for a visit. Your patience will be rewarded when you see a silver star on the floor beneath a small Greek altar. This star marks the site that pilgrims honor as the birthplace of Jesus.

St. Jerome settled in Bethlehem to learn Hebrew so that he could translate the OT from its original language into Latin. Other people, including Paula and her daughter Eustochium, joined in the caves to live a life of penance and prayer. Eventually two large monasteries were needed to house Jerome and his followers. The caves served as the burial places for Paula and Eustochium according to Jerome, whose tomb is also found here. The entrance to these caves is in St. Catherine's Church.

Bethlehem Today. The town is home to **Bethlehem University** founded by Cardinal Pio Laghi, who was the Apostolic Delegate when Paul VI visited the Holy Land in 1964 and suggested that a Catholic university be established in Palestine. The Christian Brothers administer the University. Most of the faculty are Palestinians. This institution aims to provide training in professions that Palestinians can practice in their homeland. The exodus of so many Palestinian Christians alarmed the pope. Doctors, lawyers, dentists, and other professionals who found that there were few opportunities for them there left for America and other countries. The pope believed that if this trend were not checked, the Holy Land would be left without a living Christian community. A principal emphasis at Bethlehem University is education for the tourism industry.

The mainstay of Bethlehem's economy is the tourist trade. Local artisans specialize in preparing souvenirs inlaid with mother-of-pearl. Of course, one can buy an olive wood nativity scene of almost any size there. Bethlehem also has a *suq* that many Israeli bargain hunters preferred to the one in the Old City. Since the Intifada, Israelis avoid Bethlehem for the most part. The people of Bethlehem hope that the negotiations between the Israeli government and the Palestinian Authority will bring peace to their town, which has felt the effects of political unrest in recent years.

The Greek Orthodox, Armenian Orthodox, and Roman Catholics all have rights in the basilica that each group jealously guards. It is fortunate that each group celebrates Christmas on a different day (Romans: Dec 25; Greeks Jan 6; and Armenians Jan 19) otherwise the chaos of dueling liturgies would be overwhelming. The Latin Rite Catholics do not celebrate midnight Mass in the basilica, but in the adjoining Church of St. Catherine of Alexandria as required by the *Status Quo*. Church of the Nativity: Daily 6–6. Free. St. Catherine's Church: Daily 5–12; 2–6. Free. Shepherd's Field: Daily 8–11:30; 2–5; Summer 2–6. Free.

Gibeon (A: Jib)

Name. The name of an Arabic village near the antiquity site preserves the first syllable of the Hebrew name Gibeon. Jar handles found on the site were inscribed with the name.

Location. The ancient site is found in a fertile plain six miles north of Jerusalem. The site itself is a rocky outcropping in the plain. Building the town here did not take up agriculturally valuable land.

History. The earliest remains are LBA. The biblical tradition remembers that the people of Gibeon were able to conclude a treaty with the Israelites which precluded any violent confrontations between the two groups (Joshua 9). Saul, however, violated this treaty and massacred many Gibeonites (2 Sam 21:1). Years later the Gibeonites retaliated by executing seven of Saul's descendants (2 Sam 21:1-9). Other traditions associate Gibeon with other bloody affairs. David's forces defeated those of Abner in what appears to be a ritual military contest (2 Sam 2:12-17; 3:30). It was also the place where Joab killed Amasa (2 Sam 20:4-13).

Gibeon was an important shrine in the early years of the Israelite monarchy. According to Chronicles, it was the place where the Israelites kept the Tent their ancestors used for worship in the desert (1 Chr 16:39; 21:29; 2 Chr 1:3, 13). The importance of Gibeon's shrine is clear from the city's presence on the list of Levitical cities (Josh 21:17). After Solomon succeeded David, he went to the shrine at Gibeon. There he had a dream in which he asked God for wisdom (1 Kgs 3:4-5; 2 Chr 1:5-13).

The earliest extrabiblical reference to Gibeon is in the tenth-century B.C. list of cities captured by Sheshonk I (=Shishak, see 1 Kgs 14:25), the pharaoh who led a military campaign in Israel following Solomon's death. Gibeon has no role in biblical narratives after 1 Kings 3. Jeremiah mentions the city as the home of his rival Hananiah (Jer 28:1) and as a place where an attempt was made on the life of Ishmael, the assassin of Gedaliah (Jer 41:12). Nehemiah 7:25 lists Gibeonites among those who returned from exile in Babylon. Josephus notes that the Romans took Gibeon in A.D. 66 as the beginning of the First Revolt.

Antiquities. Though Gibeon was excavated more than thirty years ago, it has not been developed for tourism. Much of the excavated area is overgrown but two features of the site can still be seen. Evidently, the area around Gibeon mass-produced wine since sixty-three **wine cellars** have been discovered. One can see the entrances, which are round holes cut into the bedrock. The cellars date to eighth century B.C. More impressive are the remains of the city's water system. Clearly visible is the **pool** cut into the bed rock, with steps that allowed people to get to the water chamber. Below ground are two **tunnels** that were used more regularly to allow people access to the water.

Herodium

Location and History. Located about six miles east of Bethlehem is one of a string of fortresses built by Herod the Great between 24 and 15 B.C. It is the flat-top mountain that is visible from many vantage points in the Jerusalem and Bethlehem region. This palace is supposedly Herod's burial place though no tomb has yet been found. The zealots who fought the Romans sought refuge here until the place fell to their enemy in A.D. 71. It was an important center for another generation of revolutionaries. Some suggest that the Herodium may have served as a headquarters for Bar Kochba, the leader of the Second Revolt. During the Byzantine Era, the site became a monastic settlement.

Antiquities. You should visit both the palace at the foot of the mountain and the fortress at the top. The palace complex included a pool, a garden, and bathhouse. The fortress had living quarters, a dining room, Roman baths, and a *mikveh.* Notice the four towers that guarded the structure. The excavators suggest that those who used this fortress during the Second Revolt converted the Herodian dining room to a synagogue by adding benches along the walls. There is no inscription nor Jewish religious symbol in evidence to support this suggestion. It remains debated. Getting to the fortress requires a short uphill walk. Sturdy walking shoes are recommended. Daily 8–4; Friday 8–3. Fee.

Hebron

". . . Abraham buried his wife Sarah in the cave of the field of Machpelah, facing Mamre (that is, Hebron) in the land of Canaan" (Gen 23:19).

Location. This city lies on the crest of the central highlands about 3,350 feet above sea level. It is nineteen miles southeast of Jerusalem. Arab intercity bus number 23 runs regularly between Jerusalem and Hebron.

History. Excavations have shown that people have lived in Hebron for four thousand years. The Bible associates this city with Abraham (Gen 13:18). It was also an important town in the tribal territory of Judah. David was king over Judah following Saul's death and ruled over that tribe for seven years before the other tribes accepted him as their king as well (2 Samuel 2, 5). Absalom, David's rebellious son, began his insurrection here (2 Samuel 15). The Book of Joshua named it a city of refuge (21:3) where someone guilty of accidental killing could find protection until the matter was settled. The city did not fare very well during the closing years of the Kingdom of Judah. It was not until Herod the Great began building a monumental structure over the **cave of Machpelah.** Did Herod do this to ingratiate himself to his Jewish subjects or because of a genuine reverence for Jewish tradition? While we cannot be sure of the answer, the structure built by Herod remains almost intact and gives the visitor a hint of what the temple area must have looked like before A.D. 70. The cenotaphs placed over the tombs date from the eighth to tenth centuries A.D. The wall surrounding the tombs is Herodian. Other structures within the wall date from the Crusader Period.

Control of the structure has passed from Jew to Christian to Arab to Christian to Arab and to Jew. It has been a synagogue, a mosque, and a church. Currently, the city of Hebron is a flashpoint in Israeli-Palestinian relations. Visits to this site should not be made without consulting local authorities.

Jericho

"Then Joshua . . . secretly sent out two spies . . . saying, 'Go, reconnoiter the land and Jericho'" (Josh 2:1).

Location. The name of this city is related to the Hebrew word for moon. It may be that this city was originally named for the moon god. Jericho is an oasis in the Aravah Valley six miles northwest of the Dead Sea and seventeen miles east of Jerusalem. It is just east of the Judean highlands. At 821.5 feet below sea level, it is lower than any other city on earth. This site shows evidence of human occupation from the Mesolithic Period (9000–8700 B.C.) to the Babylonian Period. The site grew around a spring known as Ain es-Sultan or Elisha's Spring (see 2 Kings 19–22), the latter name was given to the spring in the Middle Ages. It is the spring that makes this site habitable. The tel is 1.6 miles northwest of the modern city. Jericho gets little rain during the wet season. The town has mountains to both the east and west. Combined with its "elevation," this makes for a tropical climate during the dry season and a mild wet season. The spring provides enough water to irrigate the rich alluvial soil and almost any crop will grow here.

The Biblical Tradition. Jericho is best known as the first site conquered by the Israelites after crossing the Jordan. Before crossing, the Israelites encamped across the river from Jericho (Num 22:1; 26:3). Joshua sent two spies to the city who were saved from discovery by Rahab (Joshua 2). The sending of the spies is an anomaly since the Israelites took Jericho by a miracle after engaging in a liturgical rather than a military exercise (Josh 5:13–6:23). The city was in Benjamin's territory (Josh 16:1, 7; 18:12, 21), but by the time of the Judges it is in the hand of the Moabites (This assumes that the "City of Palms" of Judg 3:13 is Jericho.). In the 800s B.C., the city was home to prophetic bands (2 Kgs 2:4-5, 15). After the fall of Jerusalem, King Zedekiah was captured near Jericho. After seeing his family executed, the Babylonians blinded him and took him off to exile (Jer 39:5-7). The Greeks built a fortress here during the Maccabean Period (1 Macc 9:50). Simon and his son were lured to Jericho and then assassinated (1 Macc 16:11-17). Sirach uses the rose of Jericho as metaphor for wisdom (Sir 24:14). In the NT it was the scene of Jesus' healing of a blind man (Matt 20:29-34; Mark 10:46-53; Luke 18:35-43). It was also the home of Zaccheus (Luke 19:1-10). Local people will point to the very sycamore tree into which Zaccheus climbed to get a better look at Jesus. The author of Hebrews uses the biblical story of Jericho's conquest as an example of faith (Heb 11:30).

Old Testament Jericho (A: Tell es-Sultan). Excavation uncovered homes, tombs, some monumental buildings, but these are difficult to locate because the site has not weathered very well. Also, the excavations took place forty years ago before more modern methods of reconstruction and preservation were developed. Most of the structures that can be identified are walls from the Bronze Age. The earliest structure you will see is a **tower** dating from 7000 B.C., the Neolithic Period. It is among the oldest artifacts that you will see on this trip. The tower is solid except for a stairway in the middle that provides for access to the top from inside the tower. At this time, the Stone Age inhabitants built a wall for defense. Some suggest that the wall and tower mark the transition from a food-gathering culture to a food-producing culture. The latter needed to defend the fruits of its labors. Also visible are **mud brick walls** from the EBA (2650 B.C.). An important defensive innovation in evidence (in the northeast part of the tel) is the MBA **glacis**. This is an artificial slope at-

Remains of Tell es-Sultan, Jericho.

tached to the wall. It was covered with plaster made from lime. A glacis forced attackers to completely expose themselves but it allowed defenders the luxury of cover behind the walls. It also made it impossible to undermine the walls. About 1560 B.C., the occupation of Jericho came to a halt because the city was destroyed by a great fire.

There is no evidence of fortifications at Jericho during the LBA. There are also meager material remains at the site and this suggests that the settlement was small and poor. This, of course, does not correspond with the biblical account in Joshua 2–6, which describes the destruction of a large walled city. At the time the Israelite tribes were taking control of Canaan, Jericho had no walls and few inhabitants.

Jericho was not reoccupied to any great extent until the ninth century B.C. The Bible suggests that this is due to the curse placed on the city by Joshua (Josh 6:26). A certain Hiel from Bethel fortified the site during the reign of Ahab (see 1 Kgs 16:34). One explanation for failure of Jericho to attract a new population after the MBA was that continuous occupation from 9000–1600 B.C. led to the pollution of the spring. The text asserts that the water of Jericho was bad (2 Kgs 2:19-22). It was not until the seventh century that nature was able to overcome completely the damage caused by human beings. There was extensive reoccupation of Jericho at the time and it was inhabited until the time of the Exile. There are no remains on the tel from after 587 B.C. except encampments.

Besides its historical and biblical importance, Jericho is significant in the development of archaeology in Palestine. In 1953, Kathleen Kenyon modified a method of excavation used by Mortimer Wheeler on classical sites. The results of her work introduced the method of stratigraphic archaeology into excavations in Palestine. Stratigraphic archaeology seeks to excavate a site stratum by stratum to clarify the occupational history of the site. The contents of each stratum (the pottery in particular) are used to date the stratum or occupational layer. Still, visible on the site is the probe trench cut by Kenyon to help control her excavation at Jericho. Her systematic excavation made it clear that at the time usually given for the entrance of the Israelite tribes into Canaan, Jericho was a village with no protecting walls. Her work helped clarify the account of the capture of Jericho in Joshua 2–6. This account is not a historical description of an Israelite attack, but probably developed from rituals celebrating the Israelite control of the region. Daily 8–4; Summer 8–5. Fee.

Hasmonean and Herodian Jericho (A: Tulul Abu el-Alayiq). Jericho was important agriculturally and militarily during these periods. It provided food and medicinal plants popular at that time. It guarded the eastern flank of Judea. The people no longer built in the area of the tel but elsewhere along the oasis. In the Hasmonean and Herodian Periods, the settlement moved to the plain at the end of the Wadi Qelt. This is sometimes called Herodian Jericho or NT Jericho. Excavations have revealed Herodian fortifications and palaces, but the area has not been developed for tourism. What these excavations have shown is that Jericho became a winter resort for Jewish aristocracy. Besides the palaces, Jericho had a theater, hippodrome, and amphitheater.

The Synagogue. About a kilometer north of Tel es-Sultan, you can see the floor of the Byzantine Period synagogue. On this floor, there is a mosaic with a menorah. Below the menorah there is a Hebrew inscription that reads "Peace upon Israel." You will find this menorah and inscription reproduced on souvenirs. This is your chance to see the real thing. The visit will not take long since nothing beyond the floor of the synagogue has survived. Daily 8–4; Summers 8–5. Fee.

Hisham's Palace (A: Khirbet el-Mafjar). This site is one mile north of Jericho. Though the structures here clearly date from the Omayyid Period, there is no reference to them in ancient literature. What you can see here is a partial re-

Artistic remains of Hisham's Palace, Jericho.

construction of a magnificent winter palace built in the eighth century A.D. An earthquake destroyed the palace in 747, shortly after it was built. The rubble from the earthquake protected the beautiful mosaics found on the site. This place is an invaluable site for appreciating Arabic architecture and art. Its most fascinating features include the window that has been set up in the middle of the central courtyard, the pool, baths, mosques, and beautifully executed mosaic floors. Also important to note is that some of the palace's ornamentation does not reflect the Islamic avoidance of images. Besides the more orthodox floral and geometric patterns, artistic motifs here include both animal and human forms.

The **palace** was a two-story square building planned around an unroofed **courtyard**. One room on the south side of the palace served as a **private mosque** for the caliph. The rooms on the first story were storage and guest facilities. The principal living quarters were probably on the second story. There was a **bathing area** on the west side of the palace. The largest element of this bath was its *frigidarium* or cold pool. It covers 97.5 square feet. Though its floor was completely covered by mosaics, only a small portion has been left for viewing. The intended effect of this mosaic was to make it appear as if rugs covered the floor of the pool. Domes and vaults covered the entire bathhouse. Behind the cold pool, one can see the heating installations that were necessary for the *caldarium,* the hot pool. There also are some **toilets** near the hot pool. At-tached to the bathhouse was a *diwan* (A: reception room). Its mosaic floor is a masterpiece as is the stucco decoration. East of the bathhouse is a large **public mosque**. Finally, east and south of the mosque is a fifty-two square-foot shal-low **pool with a fountain**. This area was the forecourt of the palace. Daily 8–4; Summer 8–5. Fee.

The Jordan River (H: HaYarden)

". . . Jesus came from Nazareth of Galilee and was baptized in the Jordan by John" (Mark 1:9).

There is a debate about the origins of the name "Jordan." Some suggest that it comes from the Hebrew root *yrd,* "to go down." The name then means, "the descender." Others view this as a popular etymology. The name may not even be Semitic. The element *den* may reflect the Indo-Aryan root *don,* i.e., "river" and *yar* the Indo-Aryan word for year so that *yarden* means *perennial river.* Hebrew often uses the definite article with the name, i.e., the Jordan. This suggests that originally *yarden* may have been a common noun rather than a proper name.

Running south from Mount Hermon to the Dead Sea, the Jordan is the longest river in Israel. It is two hundred eight miles in length. The distance be-tween the Sea of Galilee and the Dead Sea is sixty-five miles, but the river meanders for almost two hundred miles. Its journey involves a descent of about half a mile. On medieval maps, the name Jordan is composed of Jor and Dan, the names of the two sources of the river. Actually, the Jordan has three sources: the Hermon (also known as the Banias River), the Dan, and the Senir (also known as the Hasbani). As it flows to the Dead Sea, many small streams feed it, the largest of which is the Yarmouk River that flows into the Jordan from the east just below the Sea of Galilee.

The first time the Jordan appears in a literary text is in an Egyptian text that discusses how best to cross the river (*ANET,* 242). The Jordan is one of the most famous place names in the Bible. It appears 181 times in the OT and fif-teen in the NT. Its first appearance in the Bible is in the story of the separation of Lot and Abraham (Gen 13:10). The Israelite tribes experienced the fulfill-ment of God's promise and they follow Joshua over the Jordan into Canaan (Joshua 1–4) though God did not allow Moses to cross (Deut 34; Num 20:10-13; Deut 32:48-52). The Jordan provided boundaries. It marked the western boundary of the kingdoms of Og and Sihon (Deut 1:4). The upper Jordan was the eastern border for Naphtali (Josh 19:33-34) while the lower Jordan was the eastern border for the Issachar (Josh 19:22), Ephraim (16:7), Benjamin (16:7), and Judah (15:5). Judges fought alongside the river (Judg 3:28; 6:33; 7:24; 8:4; 12:5-6). David crossed the river several times (2 Sam 10:17; 16:14; 17:22-24; 19:15-18, 31-34). Elijah crossed the Jordan to the east at God's command during a drought (1 Kgs 17:1-6). It provided the backdrop for two of Elisha's miracles: the cure of Naaman (2 Kings 5) and the recovery of the lost axe (2 Kgs 6:1-7). The Jordan is part of several prophecies (Jer 12:5; 49:19; 50:44; Zech 11:3). It is also the place where John was baptizing Jews who responded to his message of repentance (Matt 3:13-17; Luke 3:21; John 1:28). It was also the scene of Jesus' baptism by John (Mark 1:9-11; John 1:19-34).

The river is both a natural boundary and a vital source for water. It is little wonder then that it is a source of contention between the State of Israel and its neighbors, Jordan and Syria. Water is a precious commodity in the Middle East. The one item that held up the peace treaty with Jordan was the problem of Israel's diversion of water from the Jordan. Agreement was reached to build a dam on the Yarmouk that will make more water available for Jordan. The Palestinian Authority also claims rights over the river.

The Jordan Valley (H: Aravah)

"Then we left behind us the Aravah route . . ." (Deut 2:8).

The Jordan Valley is part of the four-thousand-mile Great Rift that runs from Turkey to East Africa. This fault developed twenty million years ago when the subsurface plates beneath the continents created a fracture in the earth's surface. The Jordan Valley developed two million years ago by additional faulting. The two plates on either side of the fault are moving away from each other creating the potential for earthquakes. The region experiences serious earthquakes every one hundred fifty years.

The Jordan Valley divides the region into two parts: Cisjordan (the area west of the river) and Transjordan (the area east of the river). The valley extends from Mount Hermon in the north to the Dead Sea, a distance of about one hundred and forty miles. It is also constantly descending. The difference in elevation between north and south is about 2,356 feet. There are four principal subdivisions of the Jordan Valley. At the far north is the Upper Jordan Valley or the Hula Valley (fourteen miles by five miles). South of this is the Sea of Galilee basin (four miles wide). Next is the Middle Jordan Valley ending with the Beth She'an Valley. The southernmost subdivision is the Lower Jordan Valley ending on the Plain of Jericho (fifteen miles wide). The use of the term "Jordan Valley" is sometimes restricted to the Middle and Lower Valleys and sometimes only the Middle Valley. The area has been continuously inhabited since the Stone Age because of its agricultural potential. Except for the Jordan and its tributaries, the valley is dry. Rainfall in the north is about twenty-two inches per year while in Jericho it is usually less than four inches per year. Its summers are hot, but its winters mild.

After the 1948 War, the Kingdom of Jordan annexed the Lower Jordan Valley. Since 1967, it has been occupied by the State of Israel. Jordan has given up claim to the area west of the river to the PLO. Currently, there are negotiations with the Palestinian Authority about its future political status.

Samaria - Sebaste (A: Sebastiya)

Name. The Bible says that Omri, the king who made Samaria his capital in 876 B.C., named it after Shemer, the person from whom he bought the land (1 Kgs 16:24). The site's topography suggests another explanation for the name. The

Hebrew root *šmr* means to watch or guard. Set on a hill that is three hundred feet above the surrounding valleys, Samaria "guards" its environs. In first century B.C., Herod the Great rebuilt the city and named it after Augustus Caesar, his patron. Sebaste is the Greek equivalent of the Latin Augustus. The Arabic name preserves the Greco-Roman name. This is unusual since most often the Arabic name of a site will preserve its Semitic name.

Location. Like the two other capitals of the Northern Kingdom, this one, too, is in the central highlands, but unlike them it has a clear view to the west. Omri moved his kingdom to the world that lies outside the central highlands. He succeeded and this eventually brought economic prosperity, military power, and political strength to the Kingdom of Israel. The city was located near roads that went between Shechem and the Jordan Valley and between Megiddo and Jerusalem.

History. Like Jerusalem, Samaria was a royal city, i.e., it was the possession of the monarchs and not part of the common Israelite heritage. The prophets represent the latter and so Amos and Hosea strongly condemn the royal establishment that made its home in Samaria. For example, Amos contrasts the fine homes of the aristocracy (3:15; 6:4) with the humble houses of the poor. Amos preached during the reign of Jeroboam II (786–746 B.C.) when Samaria enjoyed its greatest economic prosperity. This prosperity was short-lived because of military pressure brought to bear by the expansionist Assyrian Empire that annexed the whole of the Northern Kingdom into its provincial system by 721 B.C. The city passed to the control of the Babylonians in the early part of the sixth century B.C. Toward the end of that century, it became part of the Persian Empire. Apparently the governors of Samaria also had some control over Judah during the Persian Period, explaining Judah's hostility toward its neighbor to the north. During the Hellenistic Period, the city was refortified because of the growing power of the Hasmoneans to the south. John Hyrcanus succeeded in taking the city in 108 B.C. The whole of Palestine fell into the hands of the Romans in 63 B.C. It was partially rebuilt by Gabinius in 57 B.C. Herod the Great rebuilt the city on a grand scale in 30 B.C. and dedicated it to Augustus his patron. The NT references to "Samaria" refer not to this city but to the region of central Palestine that was known by the same name. Some suggest that the "city of Samaria" visited by Philip in Acts 8:5 was Sebaste. The city became a Christian pilgrimage center in the Byzantine Period because tombs in the area were identified as those of John the Baptist, and the prophets Obadiah and Elisha. A sixth-century tradition located the beheading of the Baptist here though Josephus has it taking place at Machaerus (*Antiquities* 18.119). The city prospered during the Byzantine Period but it began to decline in the sixth century after a devastating earthquake.

Antiquities. Perhaps the most famous find here took place in 1910 when sixty-six potsherds with ink inscriptions were found by G.A. Reisner. They comprise the earliest body of ancient Hebrew writing that exists. The **Samaria Ostraca** are housed in the Archaeological Museum of İstanbul. Antiquities that can be seen on the site come primarily from the Roman Period. The most impressive remains belong to the time of Septimus Severus (A.D. 193–211). He modified the **temple to Augustus** that Herod built two hundred years earlier. One can see the temple's **monumental staircase** leading to the altar. Also visible on the site are a reconstructed **stadium** (197 feet by 755 feet) and a **colonnaded street** that is 2,625 feet long. Almost six hundred columns that lined the street have survived. There is also a **theater** and a **basilica** from the Roman city.

Shechem (A: Nablus)

Name. This is one instance when the Arabic name of a city preserves not the ancient Semitic name but the Roman one. Nablus is an Arabic corruption of the Latin "Neapolis" ("New City") which is the name given to the place near ancient Shechem where veterans of the Roman legions settled.

Location. Ancient cities in Canaan were usually located near important roads, close to a reliable water supply, and on a height that made defense easy. Shechem enjoyed all three advantages. It was in the central highlands with perennial springs nearby and it controlled the only east-west pass in the area. This made communication with the Via Maris and other important commercial highways easy.

History. There is evidence of occupation in the Chalcolithic Period (4000 B.C.). It was an important city in the Middle Bronze Age (nineteenth century B.C.). Deuteronomy remembers the important liturgical role the city had at the beginning of Israel's history (see Deut 28:11-13; Shechem is located between Mount Ebal and Mount Gerizim). Shechem was the place where the first and unsuccessful attempt was made to establish an Israelite monarchy. Abimelech, Gideon's son, had himself proclaimed king of Shechem. The attempt ended with his assassination (Judges 9). After Solomon's death, the elders of the Israelite tribes met here to negotiate with Rehoboam regarding conditions for his succession to the throne (1 Kgs 12:1-11). When Rehoboam refused to negotiate, all but his own tribe of Judah offered the kingship to Jeroboam, establishing a second national state (1 Kgs 12:20). Shechem served as the capital of the Kingdom of Israel (1 Kgs 12:25) until the capital was moved to Tirzah (1 Kgs 15:33) and then Samaria (1 Kgs 16:24).

Relations between the two Israelite kingdoms were sometimes bad and other times good, but all this changed following Judah's Exile. The Judahites who returned from exile in Babylon did not consider the people who lived in the territory of the former Kingdom of Israel to be authentic Israelites but the products of intermarriage with foreign settlers. The Judahites also considered the religion practiced by these people to be an inauthentic version of the ancient Israelite religion (see 2 Kgs 17:24-41, esp. v. 34). They believed the cult practiced in Jerusalem to be the only divinely approved worship (cf., Deuteronomy 12). When the people of the North offered to help the Judahites rebuild the Temple of Jerusalem, their help was refused (Ezra 4:1-3). Thus began a rift that grew ever wider.

Rebuffed by the Judahites, the people of the North built their own temple on Mount Gerizim. When the Jewish kings of Hasmonean dynasty came to power in Judah following their victories over the Seleucids (164 B.C.), they incorporated the northern territories into their kingdom. In 128 B.C., John Hyrcanus destroyed the temple on Mount Gerizim. So the animosity between the Jews and the people of the North, which the Bible calls the "Samaritans" after Samaria, the capital of the Kingdom of Israel, was hardened. The conversation between Jesus and the woman at the well in John 4 reflects this controversy. John 3:23 locates the place where John baptized in a village four miles from Shechem. Acts 8 describes a successful mission to the Samaritans.

In the Roman Period, veterans from the Roman legions that suppressed the First Revolt settled here. They named their city "Neapolis," i.e., "the new city." The Romans built a temple to Zeus on a nearby height in the second century A.D. and a seven thousand-seat theater at the foot of Mount Gerizim. Despite this Roman presence, the Samaritans continued to follow their ancestral traditions. The Byzantines built churches here at the site of Jacob's Well and on Mount Gerizim. This helped make the Samaritans bitter enemies of the Byzantine rulers. In 529 B.C., the Samaritans revolted and the Byzantines snuffed out the revolt with ferocity. It is not surprising that the Samaritans regarded the Arabs who came about one hundred years later as liberators.

Sites. The only site that is prepared to accept visitors is **Jacob's Well** (see Gen 33:18-20). You can enter the garden of a Greek Orthodox church where you will see the remains of an unfinished reconstruction of a Crusader church. You can enter the crypt of that church to view the well. The spring that feeds the well still produces water. Nearby is **Joseph's Tomb**, a pilgrimage site for religious Jews. According to Muslim tradition, Joseph is buried in Hebron with the other patriarchs and their wives.

The Bronze Age city (**Tel Balata**) has been excavated but the site is fenced off to protect it since it has not been prepared to receive visitors. Sometimes, if the guide knows the guardian of the site, it is possible to have a look at the excavations. In Nablus itself, one can see parts of the Roman Period city that have been unearthed but the excavations have not been preserved well and are not worth a visit. There has been significant archaeological work on **Mount Gerizim**. Access is possible but it is best to go with a guide.

Among the structures that one can see at the summit is the second-century B.C. **sacred area**, which was part of the Samaritan temple. One can also see the foundations of an **octagonal church** from the fifth century. The Muslims destroyed the church in the 700s.

CHAPTER ELEVEN

Jordan

Introduction

Roughly four times the size of Israel, Jordan has been the neighboring country with closest ties to Israel by reason of both geographical and historical affinity, Jordanian political claims to the West Bank (the Territories), and the fact that both countries have substantial Palestinian populations and a common problem of the fate of Palestinian refugees. From north to south, the length of the country is about 358 miles. To the northeast is a corridor about 133 miles long and 67 miles wide, stretching to the Iraqi border. Since Jordan is a landlocked country except for a narrow opening onto the Gulf of Aqaba at its seaport, Aqaba, and since its neighbors are Syria, Iraq, Saudi Arabia, and Israel, it has since 1948 served as a buffer zone and important bridge of communication between Israel on one side and some of its bitterest enemies on the other.

General Information. There are direct flights from the U.S. to Jordan, arriving at the international airport in Amman. One can also cross into Jordan from Israel at the Allenby Bridge, the Husseni Bridge, and at Eilat/Aqaba. It is also possible to take a ferry from Nueiba in the Sinai to Aqaba. United States passport holders are required to have a visa obtainable at any Jordanian embassy or consulate for $20. It is also possible to obtain a visa at border crossings but having a visa upon arrival speeds up the entry process. The local currency is the Jordan dinar, which is divided into one thousand fils. Traveler's checks and foreign currency can be exchanged at banks, money changing offices, and at hotels at rates fixed by the government. Direct-dial telephone service is available to the U.S. Consult your long-distance carrier for the access numbers.

Politics. When the victorious European powers carved up the former Ottoman Empire after World War I, the country of Transjordan, extending from the Iraqi border to the Jordan river, was set up in 1923, under the protection of England. In 1946 Abdullah, who had long been the key player on the Arab side, was proclaimed king in a fully independent country. After the 1948 war with the newly independent State of Israel, Jordan held the West Bank, which it annexed in 1950. A disgruntled subject who thought that Abdullah did not do enough to defeat Israel assassinated the king outside Jerusalem's Aqsa Mosque in 1951. Abdullah's son was mentally ill, so his grandson Hussein emerged as sole ruler at age seventeen and is still a very popular king, with his younger brother Hassan as crown prince. The constitution of 1952 established a constitutional monarchy with a bicameral representative assembly. The king has broad authority over it and most of the government. King Hussein died in 1999 and was succeeded by his son Abdullah.

The population of Jordan without the West Bank is just more than three million, with more than one million concentrated in the capital city of Amman. About ninty-two percent are Sunni Muslims, about six percent Christians, and the rest are small groups of Shiʾite Muslims and Druze. Most of the Christians are Greek Orthodox, though there are also small numbers of Latin Catholics and several other Orthodox communities. Arabic is the official language but English is spoken widely since it is taught in all schools as a second language.

Between 1950 and 1967, there was free movement of Palestinian refugees from the new State of Israel across the Jordan. In 1964, the Palestine Liberation Organization was formed. After Israel captured the West Bank during the Six-Day War in 1967, Palestinian migration into Jordan again surged. In 1974, the PLO plotted to overthrow Hussein. The plot was crushed and the Jordanian army began to move against the PLO, which remembers this event as the Black September. Many Palestinian supporters of the PLO then moved to Lebanon.

Today, estimates of the percentage of Palestinians in the Jordanian population range from fifteen percent to sixty percent. Understandably, the Jordanian government does not want to know exactly how many, much less to publish it. Many Palestinians settled in, became Jordanian citizens (a right extended to them immediately), and are well integrated into Jordanian economic and political life. There are also about forty thousand Bedouin. A small number continue to live the traditional nomadic life; most have settled down to become agriculturalists instead of pastoralists; and some have integrated fully into the social and economic life of the country.

Geography. The climate in most of Jordan is similar to that in most of Israel: hot and dry, with a short, wet winter. If the West Bank is not included, eighty percent of Jordan is a desert. Jordan has four geographical regions, if the West Bank is included, as it traditionally is: the West Bank, the Jordan Valley, the East Bank, and the desert. The central spine of the country, the highland plateau and the hilly region that run north and south includes the country's major population centers: Amman, Irbid, Madaba, and Kerak. To the west is the Aravah that runs the length of the country and includes the Jordan Valley and the Dead Sea.

Jordan and the Middle East Problem. In 1988 King Hussein renounced Jordan's claim to the West Bank (Territories), so its status as territory occupied by Israel, of which some towns have now been turned over to the Palestinian

Authority, is even more ambiguous than before. Its heartland was the ancient Samaritan center, and it contains some very important biblical sites, like Shechem, Mount Gerizim, and Hebron, all of which currently, because of the tense political situation, are not favorable for tourist visits. Bethlehem, too, is in the West Bank, as is Qumran, but because of proximity to Jerusalem and outstanding value to pilgrims and tourists, Bethlehem is usually accessible, and Qumran is located in an uninhabited area. Since December, 1995, Bethlehem is under the control of the Palestinian Authority. East Jerusalem was also, of course, part of the original West Bank territory taken from Jordan in 1967. Israel now claims sovereignty over this area.

Jordan's neighbor Iraq has been a major trade partner, especially through the Jordanian port of Aqaba. Jordan has no petroleum sources of its own, and depended heavily on Iraq for oil. During the Gulf War in 1991, like any small, resource-poor country squeezed between two powerful antagonists, Jordan tried to remain neutral, but its refusal to enforce the blockade against Iraq made it appear to the West and the Gulf states that Jordan was pro-Iraq. Another source of income came from Palestinian and Jordanian workers in the Gulf states, most of whom were expelled because of the failure of Jordan to support the blockade. Jordan was therefore one of the big economic losers of the war.

The peace between Jordan and Israel in 1994 is given mixed reviews by Jordanians. Many welcome it for the economic boost that it will give the country. In one year, tourism increased by twenty-seven percent. Joint projects between the two countries are in the planning: a common Dead Sea resort area, for instance. Other Jordanians feel that the country is "selling out" on Arab solidarity against the oppressor of the Palestinians, and resent Israel's superior economic and military power. One of the sticking points is sharing of the most precious resource: water.

Biblical History. The land now known as Jordan was never united as a political entity before this century. Recent archaeological work has shown that Stone Age humans lived in the region as far back as a half million years ago. Villages and mud brick houses from 8000 B.C. have been found. Urban life in the area began in the EBA (c. 3200 B.C.). From the third millennium B.C. Assyrians, Babylonians, and Amorites were among the conquerors. The Asiatic Hyksos occupiers of Egypt added it to their empire (from 1700 B.C.), and Egyptian control was paramount until the Hittite conquest, completed about 1300 B.C. By the time of the Israelite conquest, the territory was divided among three groups familiar from the Bible, with whom the Israelites had close connections: the Ammonites to the north, east of Samaria, with their capital at Rabbath Ammon, the Moabites to the south of them, across the Dead Sea from the northern Negev, and the Edomites to the far south. The area just along the Jordan River was also known as Gilead.

The Bible remembers the relations between Israel and Edom as difficult. It presents the problem as beginning with the Edomite refusal to allow the Hebrews to pass through Edom on the way to Canaan (Num 20:14-21). Saul and David fought the Edomites (1 Sam 14:47; 2 Sam 8:12-14) and the latter incorporated their territory into his empire. Once the Davidic Empire disintegrated following Solomon's death, the Edomites reclaimed their independence and contended with the Kingdom of Judah for control of the south of Palestine. The prophetic oracles against Edom testify to this rivalry (see Amos 1:11-12; Isa 21:11-12; Jer 49:7-22; Ezek 25:12-14; Joel 4:19; Obad 1:1-14). Under pressure from the Nabateans, the Edomites moved west into the Negev. During the Maccabean Period, the Jews retook control of the Negev and forcibly converted the Idumeans to Judaism. The Romans named the Negev after ancient Edom, calling it "Idumea." Antipatris, the father of Herod the Great, was an Idumean.

The Moabites were thought to be descendants of Moab, son of Lot, Abraham's nephew. Because of the refusal of the Edomites to give the Israelites safe conduct through their territory, they came around through Moabite land. The response of the frightened Moabites was to hire Balaam to curse the Israelites and so get rid of them—but of course, Balaam's donkey had a thing or two to say about that (Numbers 22–24). Intermarriage of Israelites and Moabites is frequently mentioned, e.g., Num 25:1, and Ruth and her sister-in-law Orpah were Moabites married to Israelites (Ruth 1:1-4). David incorporated Moab into his empire, but it regained its independence following the death of Solomon. Moab then began a rival of the Kingdom of Israel for control of central Palestine. The Moabite Stone, also known as the Mesha Stele, describes the achievement of Mesha, king of Moab, in overcoming Israelite hegemony over the territory east of the Jordan. In the New Testament Period, the region was known as Perea.

For Israelite involvement with the Ammonites, see below under **Amman**.

The area was extensively hellenized by the foundation of a number of Greek cities, and after the Roman conquest under Pompey in 64–63 B.C. A league of ten hellenistic cities known as the **Decapolis** was formed in the north. Of these, nine were east of the Jordan. Herod the Great's sphere of influence extended into Nabatean territory, where he built his fortress of **Machaerus** about forty-one miles southwest of Madaba. Though the gospel accounts in Matt 14:1-12 and Mark 6:14-29 do not give the location for the death of John the Baptist, Josephus places the incident at Machaerus (*Antiquities* 18.119) and the church historian Eusebius follows his account (*Church History* 1.11.6). Excavation of this fortress began in 1968 by Virgilio Corbo, O.F.M., of the SBF. Today the project is under the control of the Jordanian Ministry of Tourism and Antiquities.

Another significant location is the city of **Pella** (in Arabic, Fahl), one of the Decapolis cities situated twenty-five miles south of the Sea of Galilee and about five miles east of the Jordan River. According to Eusebius, the Jewish Christian community of Jerusalem fled here at the time of Vespasian's siege of the city during the Jewish uprising (*Church History* 3.5.3) though some contemporary historians and archaeologists maintain that a sizeable Christian community remained in Judah and Galilee during and after the revolt.

When Trajan annexed the kingdom of the Nabateans in 106, their territory became the Roman province of Arabia. Later, sometime between A.D. 285 and 311, Diocletian divided this province, so that the southern portion was united with the province of Palaestina, of which the greater part lay west of the Jordan River. Eusebius, writing about 313, refers to places south of the Dead Sea as being in Palestine, designating the area by the political name at the time.

Amman

Location. Amman is situated in the Transjordan plateau east of the Jordan Valley. The city was a small town until after World War II, but today it is a modern city of 1.4 million people, the capital and largest city in Jordan. The American Center of Oriental Research is a major archaeological center, from which they are active at a number of sites, including the newly discovered church at Petra.

History. The Rabbath Ammon or Rabbah of the Old Testament, capital of the Ammonites, has been continuously occupied since the Bronze Age (Deut 3:11; 2 Sam 11:11; 12:26-27; 17:27; Jer 49:2; Ezek 21:20; Amos 1:13). The uncommonly large iron bed of King Og of Bashan was on display there as a tourist attraction (Deut 3:11), apparently taken as spoil in some previous battle. Though the Ammonites had previously been friendly to the Israelites, the relationship soured under David, and Joab besieged and captured Rabbah. Meanwhile, back at the palace, David was noticing Bathsheba at her bath. Her husband Uriah the Hittite was then sent to die in the front lines at the battle of Rabbah. David arrived in time to take possession of the captured city and put its inhabitants to forced labor (2 Sam 10–11; 12:26-30). This does not seem to have finished off the Ammonites, however, for Amos (1:13-15), Jeremiah (49:1-6), and Ezekiel (25:1-7) later prophesied oracles of doom against a still powerful city.

In the Hellenistic Period it was refounded and renamed Philadelphia in honor of Ptolemy Philadelphus (285–246 B.C.) and was soon one of the commercial centers of the Decapolis, conveniently located on the King's Highway, a major trade route between Egypt and Damascus. In Roman times the city was grandly rebuilt and expanded, and in the Byzantine Period it was a center of a bishopric.

Antiquities. The **citadel**, the acropolis or highest point of the city, is the site of ancient Rabbah, but the remains there are mostly Roman and Byzantine. There is a small church of the sixth or seventh century, a second-century temple of Hercules that is under restoration, and a large Omayyad building of the eighth century, whose use is uncertain. The **National Archaeological Museum**, also located on the acropolis, is small but inclusive of many historical periods. It contains a copy of the Mesha Stele.

The great ancient attraction of Amman is its Roman **theater** probably of the second century, now in a park in the center of the city. With a seating capacity of six thousand, it has extremely steeply banked rows. From the top of the theater, a good view is had of the citadel and vice versa. In the wings of the theater are two museums, of Folklore and Traditional Jewels and Costumes. Contrary to the title, the latter also contains mosaic church floors from the area, most notably from Madaba. Nearby is a heavily reconstructed **odeion** or small theater.

Aqaba

Location. One popular entry point into Jordan is at Aqaba, the country's only seaport, just across the border from Israel's Eilat. The body of water on which both sit is called the Gulf of Aqaba or the Gulf of Eilat, depending on which side of the border you are. Each town is clearly visible from the other along the same coast. The two towns are so close to each other that a few years before the peace between the two countries, a horse escaped from Aqaba and swam ashore at Eilat, where it was promptly arrested as a suspected terrorist. After several days of inspection, it was finally determined that the horse was not carrying anything dangerous or subversive, and it was amicably returned to its Jordanian owner across the border.

History. Like Eilat, Aqaba is a popular resort and a major commercial port. It has been a port for many centuries, for Solomon's Ezion Geber, on the Red Sea shore (1 Kgs 9:26) was a naval and shipping center in the vicinity, perhaps at what is now called Tel al-Khalifa, about two and one-half miles to the west of modern Aqaba. At that site, now just on the Jordan-Israel border, there is evidence of copper smelting from the tenth to the fifth centuries B.C., probably of products of the copper mines in the Aravah like those at Timnah. In the Roman Period, a major road built under Trajan came from Damascus and Amman (Philadelphia) via Petra to Aqaba (then called Aila), then turned west in two routes to Egypt and Palestine. In the seventh century A.D. the city had its own bishop. The area was occupied by Muslims, then Crusaders in the twelfth century. The Crusaders fortified an island about six miles offshore, then called Ile de Graye, now called Pharaoh's Island. Saladin controlled the area by 1170. The fort and town dwindled into a quiet fishing village until it was captured by the British in World War I and became a nerve center for the flow of troops and equipment from Egypt.

Visit. Aqaba is a popular spot for those looking for sun and beaches. The Gulf of Aqaba has one of the most beautiful and accessible coral reefs in the world. Snorkeling is a year-round activity here. Equipment can be rented. Be sure to wear beach shoes when snorkeling since the coral is sharp and can do serious damage to unprotected feet. The fortress on Pharaoh's Island is now a museum.

Jerash

Location. About an hour's ride north-northwest of Amman lies the magnificent archaeological site of **Jerash**, or ancient Gerasa.

History. Jerash was founded probably by the Seleucids sometime in the second century B.C. under the name Antioch on the Chrysorhoas (River) as one of the ten hellenistic cities in the territory known as the **Decapolis** (Matt 4:25; Mark 5:20; 7:31). All of these cities were to the north and east of the Jordan River with the exception of Scythopolis (Beth She'an) on the west side. The names of the cities are: Philadelphia (Amman), Gerasa, Pella, Scythopolis (Beth She'an), Gadara, Damascus, Hippos (on the hill just above present Ein Gev), Canatha, Dion, and Raphana. Contrary to popular belief, they probably were not in any kind of formal league. The Hasmonean rulers of Jerusalem controlled their territory for most of the second century B.C., and when Pompey took Palestine and Syria in 64–63 B.C., they became part of the Roman province of Syria. At this time the name of this Antioch was changed to Gerasa, and it was remodeled into a Roman city, the basic plan of which is still visible today. After Trajan absorbed the Nabatean region into the Roman sphere, the southern Decapolis cities were split off into the Roman province of Arabia. Jerash was at its height in the first to third centuries A.D. as a Roman city, with some continuing Nabatean influence. It continued to prosper later as a Christian Byzantine city, with episcopal representation at the Councils of Seleucia (359) and Chalcedon (451). Its many early churches (at least thirteen) attest to its Christian prosperity; seven are known to have been built during the reign of Justinian alone (527–565). For Jerash as for the other cities of the region, the Persian conquest came in 614 and the Islamic conquest in 636. By the middle of the eighth century, when the church of St. Stephen at Umm er-Rasas was just being built, Jerash had gone into decline, though there continued to be some occupation until about the thirteenth century. The site was rediscovered in 1806, and the modern town dates from 1878. Much of the site was previously buried under debris, which helped preserve it. Nearly all excavation dates from this century.

Antiquities. Jerash is, like Ephesus, one of the archaeological gems of the Greco-Roman past because of its high state of preservation. Everything preserved dates from no earlier than the Roman era. Like Ephesus, the fact that it was not continually built over and inhabited has saved much of its earlier material intact. The site is enormous and takes at least two hours for a barely adequate visit.

Entrance from the south was by way of a monumental **Gate of Trajan**, erected for his visit to the city in A.D. 129–130. The gate can be seen on the left next to the hippodrome as one approaches the site. In the modern ticket office building through which one enters the site, there is a large model of the city that gives the visitor an overall view and sense of proportion.

Entry into the city is by way of the south gate in the city wall, which was built in the 70s of the first century A.D. From there, one enters immediately the famous **oval forum**, a unique design for a Roman city. Ionic columns line the edges, and in the center is a base that probably held a dedicatory statue. To the left are the stairs that led up to the **Temple of Zeus** (first or second century A.D.), of which a few walls have been restored. Constructed on the site of a previous temple, it originally had an altar at the lower level. Just behind the temple is the **South Theater**, with one restored level of the *scaena frons* or backdrop to the stage. It was originally at least two stories high. Seating capacity

Jerash. Remains of the Temple of Artemis (upper photo); and the *cardo*.

was about five thousand. Take the time to climb to the top of the theater seats. From there can be had the best view (and best photos) of the oval forum and the layout of the city.

After leaving the theater, the visitor crosses the forum and begins the walk down the *cardo*, or main north-south street, which in Jerash is oriented slightly to the northeast, so that it aligns perfectly with the entrance to the Zeus Temple. The street runs 1,665 feet to the north gate of the city. To the left on the way is an unusually shaped octagonal market area identified as a meat market. The cardo was intersected by two *decumani*, or major east-west cross streets. At each of the two intersections of a decumanus stood a **Tetrapylon**, or four-based ornamental structure. The southern one was made into a circular area in the third century. The southern decumanus continued to the east down the hill and across the river into what is now the modern town.

One next approaches on the left the so-called **Cathedral**, an impressive church even though there is no real evidence that it was an episcopal one. This church was in use in the mid fourth century, an indication of the early and large Christian presence in the city. It is built in classical basilical style, with rectangular nave, apse on the eastern end, roof supported by two rows of columns that create two side aisles, and entrance through three doors from an atrium to the west. From the cardo one ascended through a monumental gateway up a flight of stairs. These structures cover the site of an earlier temple that was perhaps dedicated to a Nabatean god. Though the church is to the west of the cardo, still the architects preserved the early Christian custom of orienting the church with its apse to the east, so that worshipers facing the altar would face the rising sun. This means that at the top of the stairs, one arrives not at the entrance to the nave, but at the back of the church, behind the apse. A walkway on either side enabled worshipers arriving from the cardo to traverse the length of the nave on the outside, and so enter the church through the atrium on the west side. The atrium contained a fountain in the middle, and so is often known as the **Fountain Court**. At the end of the 300s, the church historian Epiphanius of Salamis in Cyprus reported that he knew some travelers who had drunk from the fountain, whose waters changed to wine annually for the commemoration of the miracle at Cana!

At the end of the 400s the **Church of St. Theodore** was built just above the cathedral to the west. Its apse actually cut into the atrium of the cathedral, the new church also being oriented with apse facing east. This new church, dated to 496, also had its own atrium further to the west, and a baptistery on the south side. Immediately behind the Church of St. Theodore is the triple church complex of **Sts. Cosmas and Damian, John the Baptist, and George**, all built together about 530. They share a common narrow atrium and connecting doors. All had fine mosaic floors, some of which can be seen in Sts. Cosmas and Damian from a vantage point further up the hill.

Back on the cardo, the next building to the north is the monumental **nymphaeum** or fountain, a two-story building of the late second century. The empty niches were filled with statues, and the water ran out into a pool below. The next thing on the left is the entrance to the massive **Temple of Artemis**, patron of the Roman city. To the right at this point is the **Viaduct Church**, built in the sixth century. Its nave was originally part of a colonnaded passageway leading from the east side of the city to the temple. On the left or west, an imposing gateway from the cardo leads up a flight of stairs to a plaza with the foundations of the altar. Another flight of stairs leads to the entrance of the temple. The temple was built on a platform constructed of vaulting, 131 feet long, 74 feet wide, and almost 14 feet high. It was built in classic style with an inner walled cella containing the statue of the goddess, surrounded on all sides by columns, here of the Corinthian order. Many of the columns are still standing, but precariously. Guides encourage visitors to insert a narrow object or even a finger in the cracks between a base and column to actually feel the movement of the column as it sways in the wind. Like most Greek temples, the opposite of Christian churches, the temple is oriented to the west, so that the approach is from the east and the rising sun could illumine the inside and the statue of the goddess that stood at the west end.

Beyond the Artemis Temple are the remains of the **North Theater** to the west (left) of the cardo, the **West Baths** to the east or right (the **East Baths** were still further to the east in the modern town across the river), and the **North Tetrapylon** at the intersection of the north Decumanus.

Kerak

Location. About one and one-half hours north of Petra on the King's Highway is the town of **Kerak** or **Karak**, dominated by its Crusader Fort. The site stands forty-four hundred feet above the Dead Sea, of which it commands a magnificent panorama.

History. Kerak was located in the ancient land of Moab under the name of Kir Heres, Kir Hareseth, or Kir of Moab. In the Bible the city is best known for the gruesome story in 2 Kings 3, in which, about 850 B.C., King Jehoram of Israel, King Jehoshapat of Judah, and the King of Edom set out together to conquer King Mesha of Moab, who had revolted from paying tribute to Judah. When only the city of Kir Hareseth remained to him and was under siege, he sacrificed his firstborn son as a burnt offering on the wall of the city. The sight so shocked the besieging army that they withdrew—exactly the intended effect of the sacrifice.

In the Byzantine Period the city was the seat of a bishopric under the name of Characmoba, by which it is known on the Madaba map. The Crusaders made it the capital of their kingdom of *Oultre Jourdain* and constructed the fort in approximately 1133. It held out against invaders until taken by Saladin in 1188, its most famous commander having been Renaud de Chatillon, who was killed by Saladin for his treachery in 1187 after the battle of the Horns of Hattin. The usual story told about Renaud is that of his habit of killing conquered enemies by throwing them off the castle wall into the valley below, with wooden boxes around their heads so they would not lose consciousness until they hit the bottom. The strategic location of the city continues to attract commanders. After World War I, it was a British administrative center and is still the capital of the Karak Governate of Jordan.

Antiquities. The castle is partly restored but not as completely as Belvoir in the Jordan Valley. It has the usual vaulted corridors, dark passageways, cisterns, and dungeon. The museum contains a copy of the famous **Mesha Stele** found a few miles away near Dhiban in 1868. The original, largely intact until deliberately destroyed in a local quarrel that year, is reconstructed in the Louvre in Paris. The stele recounts the exploits of King Meshah of Moab, the same one who sacrificed his son on the city wall. Understandably, he does not mention this event in his memoirs, but rather brags of his victories, mostly over the kings of Israel.

Madaba

Location. Just northwest of Umm er-Rasas, on the ancient King's Highway, is the town of **Madaba** (ancient name Midaba). It is most famous today for the **Madaba Map**, a late sixth-century church mosaic floor that depicts the extended area of the Holy Land. With one exception, it is the oldest existing map of the area. The city is also the headquarters of the Franciscan Archaeological Institute, which coordinates the archaeological activities of the SBF in Jordan.

History. Known as Medeba or Midaba, the town is mentioned in Josh 13:9 as part of the territory allotted to Reuben and Gad, and in Isa 15:1-2, along with Kir (Kerak), Nebo, and Dibon (Dhiban) as a destroyed city of Moab (also Num 21:30). The name also appears on the Mesha Stele of c. 850 B.C.

Antiquities. The famous mosaic map was made sometime between A.D. 542 and 614. It shows in Jerusalem the Nea Church built by Justinian in 542, and it is assumed that a church such as this one in Madaba could not have been built after the turmoil that accompanied the Persian and Islamic conquests in 614 and 636. The map was discovered at the end of the last century when Christians of the area were given permission from the Ottoman authorities to build a church only where one had previously stood. This prompted archaeological efforts that resulted in the discovery of this and other ancient churches. The map is now in the little Church of St. George.

The original map must have covered most of the area of present Syria, Lebanon, Israel, Jordan, and northern Egypt. The remnants that remain run from the Nile delta up the coast north, past the north end of the Dead Sea, into southern Samaria and the beginning of the Jordan Valley, across the river into western Jordan. All place names are of course in Greek, and reflect sixth-century usage, so they have to be pointed out by someone who knows the map well, or figured out painstakingly with a guidebook. Because of the usual rush of people trying to get in, there is little time for that. A detailed guidebook that includes a large full-color map with explanations can be purchased at the back of the church.

The most famous part of the map is its depiction of Jerusalem. The semicircular plaza with its column inside Damascus Gate (still called "Gate of the Column" in Arabic) can be clearly seen. The next time you step inside Damascus

Gate, stop and look around, and you will see the extent of the plaza, where the buildings begin and the streets divide. On the sides, the buildings have encroached on what was then open space. The two diverging streets are also clear, one to the left toward the Temple Mount (el Wad St.) and the other slightly to the right (Khan es-Zeit St.) past the Church of the Anastasis (Holy Sepulchre) and continuing on to the Nea on the south side of the city. Both roads were colonnaded the whole way; excavations in the Jewish Quarter have brought to light some of this Byzantine pavement and colonnade. The main north-south street of a Roman/Byzantine city is called the *cardo*. In this case, there were two. Besides Damascus Gate, St. Stephen's Gate to the east and Jaffa Gate to the west are visible. To the trained Byzantine specialist, many more of the monuments of Byzantine Jerusalem and the Holy Land are to be seen on the map, which is a priceless witness to early Christian topography.

Mount Nebo

Location. Just seven miles and a few minutes' ride northwest from Madaba lie the pilgrimage center and antiquities of **Mount Nebo**. Though the mountain that today bears this name is about three kilometers to the southeast, the place to visit is popularly known as Mount Nebo, but its real name is **Siyagha** (Aramaic "monastery"). The mount is located on the western edge of the highlands that run down the center of the country. Immediately to the west, the land begins its steep decline toward the Dead Sea. Siyagha perches on the edge, twenty-four hundred feet above sea level and more than three thousand feet above the Dead Sea. On a clear day, the view is magnificent, all the way across the Aravah to Jericho, the Judean hills and the top of the Mount of Olives. At night, the lights of Jerusalem and Bethlehem can be seen.

History. According to Deut 34:1-6, Moses went up Mount Nebo in the land of Moab to see the Promised Land which he was not to enter. From there he was shown the vast expanse of the land across the Dead Sea. Afterwards, Moses died and was buried in a secret place nearby on the plains of Moab. The intrepid pilgrim Egeria visited the site in the late fourth century, and was shown, inside a relatively small church, a raised memorial, identified by the local guides as the tomb of Moses, who had been buried by angels. She was then taken to the porch of the church for the view, and every possible biblical site was pointed out to her by the holy men (monks or hermits) who lived nearby. By the late fifth or early sixth century, the smaller church that Egeria saw must have been replaced, for another visitor, Peter the Iberian, was shown a large church surrounded by monasteries. In 1217, a crusader named Thietmar visited the site and spent the night with a group of Greek monks living there. In 1864 the French Duc de Luynes visited the site which was then called Jebel Mousa because local lore had it that this was the site of the death of Moses. Several other exploratory visits were made in the late 1800s by Europeans and Americans. The extensive ruins were excavated by the Franciscans of the SBF in the 1930s under the direction of Sylvester J. Saller, O.F.M. In recent years, another Franciscan archaeologist, Michele Piccirillo, has continued the excavation and restoration of the site. The project accepts volunteers for a four-to-six-week season in June and July.

The original small building, probably Egeria's small church with the tomb of Moses, was in a tripartite shape called a **cella trichora**, with three equal apses in a cloverleaf pattern and a small nave, all encompassed within a rectangular outer wall. Within the area of this church there were five tombs in the floor. Both the style of the building and the coins found in one of the tombs suggest a mid-fourth-century date for this first building. By the late fifth century, visitors to the area describe something else: a large church surrounded by monasteries. The earlier church may still have been standing at this time, and in fact, was probably changed into a basilica by the addition of a nave to the west.

The area of the earlier church formed most of the sanctuary of this second, larger church. At the end of the sixth century, this second church was destroyed, probably by an earthquake. It was immediately rebuilt, and two mosaic inscriptions date this rebuilding to 597 A.D. This is the church whose foundations can be seen today. The sanctuary, however, was completely changed. In the previous church, the triple apse, older small church had served as the sanctuary. With the rebuilding, this structure was replaced with a single apse and a square room to each side. According to the custom of Eastern churches, one would be the **prothesis** where the eucharistic gifts were prepared, and the other the **diakonikon**, or sacristy. Between the nave and the sanctuary can be seen both the low pillars that connected the original chancel screen and the column bases of the taller and more elaborate colonnade, a kind of separation between nave and sanctuary that came into vogue in the late sixth century. In the basilica itself, the mosaics depict geometric patterns with occasional birds, and a vine motif that frames the aisles. An occasional dedicatory inscription can be seen. This church continued in use until the eighth century, when it collapsed and was abandoned. Upon these foundations, after the excavations, were built, following the same ground plan, the walls of the church that can now be visited. In the meantime, however, a visitor in 1564 saw only ruins, and during the 1800s the area became a cemetery.

On either side of the basilica are other smaller chapels: to the north, or left of the entrance, is a long rectangular room in which there is a splendid mosaic featuring hunting scenes, the work of artists Soelos, Camas, and Elias in A.D. 531. To the south or right are two smaller chapels. The first on the right is known as the **Theotokos Chapel**, and the second was the **baptistry**. Entrance to all three is only by means of the basilica.

Baptistry. The baptismal font sits within an apse at the end of the baptistry. It is made of a single piece of stone, over a meter wide and almost a meter deep. Its design is a quatrefoil: four semicircles in a cross-shaped pattern, each with a seat or step below the surface. Two sunken panels in the stone bear the names of Bishop Sergius and religious superior Martyrius. The font is surrounded by mosaics of birds, trees, and animals repaired, and there is a mosaic medallion immediately to either side. A single inscription continues from one to the other: "With the help of our Lord Jesus Christ, the work of the church with the baptistry was finished under the most reverend Bishop Sergius and

Martyrius, beloved presbyter and hegumen (superior) in the 15th indiction of the year 492" (of the Roman province of Arabia) = 597 A.D. The figures of the animals were mostly defaced, and later repaired—an indication that the church was still in use beyond the Iconoclastic Period of the early eighth century. The foundations of a chancel screen set off the baptismal area from the rest of the room, where stone benches lined either side of the nave.

The **Theotokos Chapel** was also built in basilical design, with apse at the end separated from the nave by a chancel screen. At a later date, the chancel screen was replaced by taller columns to form a colonnade. The chapel is so named because of a dedicatory inscription just outside the chancel screen which identifies the chapel by the name of Theotokos ("God-bearer," the title given to Mary by the fifth century), completed under bishop Leontios, who dates from the end of the sixth or beginning of the seventh century. Such dedications to Mary as Mother of God are common after the Council of Ephesus (A.D. 431). Most of the animals in the mosaic between apse and chancel screen have been defaced. In the center of their panel, however, is a building thought by the excavators to be the representation of the Jerusalem Temple. Within a large arch are an entry courtyard at the bottom, flames on an altar, and an inner sanctuary. Within the mosaic, in two pieces to either side of the structure, are the words of Ps 50 (51):21: "Then they will place calves upon your altar." The nave of the chapel was lined with stone benches, and an altar stood in the sanctuary.

Petra

Location. Petra is located about eighty-three miles northeast of Aqaba, near the ancient trade route (and today's more scenic route) from the Gulf north to Amman. It is hidden in the Wadi Musa, a deep valley that winds for several miles through the desert.

The crown of any visit to Jordan is the red sandstone city of the Nabateans, hidden deep in a valley, with its monumental tombs and spectacular scenery. The city is popularly called "rose-red" after Dean Burgen's poem *Petra* (the "rose-red city half as old as time"), but even Burgen himself, once he had seen the locale, admitted that the color of the stone is mostly of a deeper hue, in many places ribboned with yellow, gray, and other tones.

History. There is evidence of occupation in the area from Neolithic times and in the Iron Age. The Nabateans were Arab tribes from Saudi Arabia who migrated into this area and the southern Negev about the sixth century B.C. and set up an empire by banditry and taxation along the trade route from India that passed through their territory on the way to the Mediterranean coast. The city flourished in the Hellenistic Period under the Nabateans. In 63 B.C. the Roman general Pompey took control of Syria-Palestine, but the Nabatean king Aretas III was able to negotiate an economic incentive to Pompey to leave his territory alone. In A.D. 106, the Nabateans were finally overpowered by Rome, after which Petra continued as a Roman city in the new Roman province of Arabia.

Both the new province and the new Roman road built by Trajan that came down from Damascus began to be advertised on imperial coinage in A.D. 111. Petra had been the Nabatean capital, but the Romans moved theirs further north and east to Bostra. Petra was designated a metropolis, therefore an important city even if not the capital, and it then began to be built up in Roman design with baths, stoas, etc. In 129–130, Trajan's successor Hadrian visited Petra and conferred upon it an additional name, Hadriane. As Palmyra to the north grew into a larger commercial center and as other ports were developed, Petra's influence declined. But it was still large enough to be the seat of a Christian bishop and to build impressive churches. It was known to the first Muslim invaders and to the Crusaders, who occupied it briefly. Then the city was forgotten by all except the local Bedouin for five hundred years.

The rediscovery of Palmyra to the north in 1751 spurred European exploration of the area. Apparently the locals were not at all eager to reveal the site. In 1812 the Swiss explorer Johann Ludwig Burckhardt followed up on some rumors he had heard from the Bedouin and managed by a ruse to sneak a few surreptitious glances at the lost city in the Wadi Musa. He then reported to the West that Petra had been found. Since then, a steady stream of adventurous travelers have made their way there. Only recently has the area been developed for tourism, and the stream of visitors is now becoming a flood that threatens the preservation of many of the monuments on the site.

Antiquities. All visits begin with the dramatic walk down the Siq, a narrow passageway about fifteen feet wide, whose walls are as high as six hundred feet in some places. Until recently, it was possible to ride a rented horse through the Siq, but the increase of traffic has now made this impossible. Beyond the ticket office, a ten-minute walk or a very brief horse ride takes the visitor to the entrance to the Siq, which was marked by a Nabatean arch destroyed in an earthquake in 1837; remnants are still visible. The distance of the Siq is little more than one mile and the way is dotted with antiquities, especially some of the less spectacular tombs, among which is the **Obelisk Tomb** (A.D. 71) on the left. In some places along the way the Nabatean water channel can be seen. The Wadi is subject to flash floods in season. The gorge grows narrower and narrower, until suddenly one catches ahead a glimpse of the **Khazneh** or **Treasury**, the best known and most impressive of the Petra tombs. This is where the end of *Indiana Jones and the Last Crusade* was filmed. The light is best on it in the morning, but in the late afternoon the rock takes on a hue that is closest to "rose-red" of any of the monuments. The one-hundred-twenty-foot high façade is elaborately carved in Greco-Roman style, while the inside consists of one large and one small empty room, with others to either side of the entrance. At the threshold is a hole for libations that empties into a drain on the right side. The exact date of construction is disputed, and it is not even certain whether it comes from the Nabatean or Roman Period.

After the Treasury, the road turns to the right and opens into a wider passageway, in which tombs in various states of preservation can be seen on both sides. Soon on the left the **theater** appears. Its observable size indicates a capacity of three thousand, but excavation has revealed that it was actually

Khazneh (or Treasury), Petra.

much more extensive, for a capacity closer to eight thousand. Its location is puzzling, for it is surrounded by tombs, and is therefore not likely to have been used for ordinary drama unless all the tombs postdate it. Possibly the theater was intended for some kind of religious rituals connected with burial or commemoration of the dead. Ancient athletic competitions originated as funerary celebrations in honor of prominent deceased persons. This is perhaps the connection. It has also been argued that at some period many of the surrounding spaces hollowed out of the rock were not tombs but houses.

After the theater, the wadi becomes wider and one sees to the right an impressive series of tombs known as the **Royal Tombs**. A short moderate climb takes one first to the **Urn Tomb**, not the most noticeable on the outside, but with a large inside room whose strands of color are some of the best. Next to it is the **Corinthian Tomb**, with poorly preserved Greco-Roman sculptured façade. The third is the enormous, three-story **Palace Tomb**. Still further is the tomb of the Roman **Sextius Florentius** (A.D. 130). Inside some of these tombs and others, especially the **Monastery**, you will see crosses on the walls, an indication that later in the Christian Period they were used as churches.

Back down on the wadi floor, the road continues to a **colonnaded street** or stoa of second-century Roman construction. Many of the paving stones are preserved. The street goes against the usual Roman custom of aligning the main street, the cardo, in a north-south direction; this one goes east-west. But given the nature of the terrain, this is the only possible way. A fountain or **nymphaeum** on the right and a market or **agora** on the left are poorly preserved. The street passes through a monumental gateway that marked entry into the temenos, or sacred area, of the temple that lies just beyond. The path ends at this large building on the left, a Nabatean **temple** of about 30 B.C., perhaps to the Nabatean god Desire, probably converted to a temple to Isis and Serapis by the Romans, and now called the **Qasr al Bint Faroun** or Castle of Pharaoh's daughter. Major portions of the walls are still standing, and the building is impressive not only for its size and state of preservation, but also because it is one of the few known freestanding buildings in the city.

The museum located nearby is small but interesting, housing especially a number of small artifacts from the site. Heading back in the direction from which you came, across the way and up the hill is the **Temple of the Winged Lions**, recently excavated and probably dedicated to Atargatis, sometime consort of Dushara. A little further on, also on your left, is a **Christian church**, a large structure that at the time of this writing was not yet open to the public, but its size and general contour can be seen from outside the protective fence. It is being excavated and restored. In a lower level room of the church were found about one hundred and fifty papyrus scrolls so tightly wrapped that they were not completely destroyed by the fire that swept through the room, probably at the time the church was destroyed. They are now being read and published. All the scrolls date to the middle of the sixth century. Most are legal documents dealing with land ownership and inheritance. When published and studied, they will yield valuable social information about Petra in an age from which very little such information has so far been available.

If there is time and you are willing to do some climbing, there are a number of surrounding sites with spectacular monuments and views over the valley. The closest but least interesting, except for the view, is the **Crusader Castle**, reached by steps that start behind Qasr al-Bint Faroun. Another climb of about one-half hour is to the **High Place** from a marked set of steps just south of the theater (on the left if you are facing it). Do not stop at the plateau where there is a little obelisk, but keep going up to the very top, where you are rewarded with a view of the whole valley and a flattened area in which is still visible the base of an altar with channels for the flow of blood of sacrificial animals. If you have time, instead of returning the way you came, you can descend from the back of the plateau down the back of the mountain, passing several monuments, including a badly eroded **Lion Fountain** and the **Tomb of the Roman Soldier** with **Triclinium** opposite for annual funeral banquets. Some of its interior decoration is still preserved. Continue across the Wadi Farasa where the city's rubbish dumps were located, to the **Pharoun Column**, remnant of another temple. Continuing on the path, you will find yourself behind the Qasr al-Bint and near the museum. But this full itinerary will take one and one-half to two hours.

Still another climb is to the **Monastery** or **Deir**, between thirty and sixty minutes each way, but not a hard climb. The path begins near the museum. The tomb façade is similar to that of the Treasury but considerably larger. The doorway is twenty-four feet high and the whole monument is one hundred and fifteen feet tall. A path to the left leads up behind it to the top.

There are many more areas that can be explored, but it would take days to do it. If you have time, it is certainly worth doing some exploring on your own. But gauge your time well. Remember, you have to go out through the Siq the way you entered, and the way is gradually but steadily uphill; it will be the end of a long day, so it will take longer than when you entered.

Umm er-Rasas

Location. About fifty miles northeast of Kerak, and halfway between the King's Highway and the Desert Highway, is the little town of **Umm er-Rasas**, "mother of lead" or "mother of bullets." (Ancient name, Kastron Mefaa.)

History. The site was a Nabatean administrative center, and inscriptions in the vicinity include those in Nabatean and Arabic. It was occupied in the Roman Period, and was, under Diocletian (A.D. 285–305), an outpost against the Persians and the Bedouin.

Antiquities. In 1986, an exquisitely preserved mosaic church floor began to be excavated there. The Church of St. Stephen is in a covered building on a hillside surrounded by the ruins of other Byzantine structures. There are actually two churches, both consisting of an apse and a nave with two side aisles. The principal church also had an atrium before the entrance. The inscription in its apse dates the completion of the apse mosaic to March, 756 under Bishop Job of Madaba, an otherwise unknown figure, done by two hitherto unknown mosaicists, Staurakios, son of Zada, and Euremios. The date of construction means it was built more than a century after the Arab conquest, under the Abassids of Baghdad, an indication of the good relationship of Christians and Muslims at that time. Another inscription just below the apse dates the completion of the nave floor to 785 under Bishop Sergius II, another otherwise unknown bishop. Another inscription just below this one commemorates several officials of the church, including Alafa, son of Constantine, "protopresbyter" (highest official under the bishop) and Peter, son of Isaac, "archdeacon." Other memorial inscriptions are in four medallions in the area to the left of the apse. Here the central medallion, having contained a human form, has been defaced as have been most of the other human depictions in the mosaic. There are other commemorative inscriptions elsewhere.

It is not the inscriptions that immediately catch the eye of the visitor, however, but the almost perfectly preserved depictions of the major churches of the region that line the area between the column bases on both sides. On the right side they are all in the Transjordan, with two exceptions, running from north to south on Trajan's road. From closest to the apse they are: Kastron Mefaa (Umm er-Rasas), Philadelphia (Amman), Midaba (Madaba), Esbounta (Hesbon, Josh 12:2), Belemounta (Bet Baal Maon, Num 32:38; Josh 13:17), Areopolis (Ar Moab, Isa 15:1), and Charachmouba (Kir Hareshet or Kerak, 2 Kgs 3:25; Isa 15:1; 16:7-11). On the left side are churches of Palestine. Beginning nearest the apse: Hagia Polis (Jerusalem, Isa 52:1; 1 Macc 2:7), Neapolis (Roman city near Shechem, present Nablus), Sebastis (Samaria, capital of the kingdom of Israel, 1 Kgs 16:24, renamed Sebaste by Herod the Great in honor of Augustus), Kesaria (Caesarea Maritima), Diospolis (Lydda, present Lod), Eleutheropolis (present Beth Guvrin in the Shefala), Askalon (Ashkelon on the Mediterranean coast), and Gaza.

Inside the stylobate is a black border filled with aquatic images that is meant to suggest the Nile. Within it are representations of Egyptian cities along the Sinai coast and in the Nile Delta. From top left, moving clockwise: Tamiathis (Damietta on the east branch of the Nile delta), Panaou (an unknown city named after the god Pan), To Pelousin (Pelusium, another delta city), Antinaou (probably Antinoupolis, city founded by Hadrian in honor of his "favorite" Antinous in the Thebaid), To Heraklion (Herakleopolis in the Delta), Alexandria (the metropolis of Egypt), To Kasin (city on the coast of the Sinai peninsula), Thenesos (Tennis, a port city), Kynopolis (Koinopolis), and Pseudostomon ("false mouth," another Delta city).

What looks like a side chapel to the left of the main church is probably really the original church on the spot, since its dedicatory inscription in the apse is dated to the time of Bishop Sergius I (575–602), specifically in the year 587. It is thus roughly contemporaneous with the Madaba church of St. George. The inscription immediately in front of the apse is a quotation from Ps 86 (87):2: "The Lord loves the gates of Zion more than all the tents of Jacob."

CHAPTER TWELVE

Egypt

"Do not be afraid to go down to Egypt" (Gen 46:3).

There are six hundred thirty-two references to Egypt in the Bible—more than to any other of ancient Israel's neighbors. The Bible's attitude toward Egypt is ambivalent. It remembers Egypt as a place of oppression (Deut 26:5-7) and a place of refuge (Matt 2:13-15). It remembers Egypt as an ally (1 Kgs 3:1) and an enemy (1 Kgs 14:25). It commands the Israelites not to hate the Egyptians (Deut 23:8) but contains severe oracles of judgment against them (e.g., Ezek 29:1-16). Anyone fascinated by the Bible will find that fascination intensified by a visit to Egypt. It is a country whose ancient monuments can transport your imagination into the world of antiquity more quickly than almost anywhere else in the Middle East. It is possible to see temples and tombs that were standing a thousand years before the time of David. Ancient Egypt's material culture far outclassed that of ancient Israel. Viewing even the remnants of ancient Egypt's material culture is breathtaking. Egypt offers visitors an abundance of interesting and beautiful sites to visit. What follows describes the most basic of visits to Egypt.

GENERAL INFORMATION

Currency. Note that Israeli currency is not accepted in Sinai or Egypt. You will need to use American dollars or Egyptian currency: the Egyptian pound (EP) which is divided into one hundred piasters. In Egypt, one can change currency at banks and hotels. Banks usually give a better rate. Some banks maintain offices at major hotels, the airport, and border crossings. Shopkeepers and people on the street will offer to change money. Their rates sound more attractive, but one must be very careful about changing money on the street to avoid being short-changed. You will have less trouble exchanging traveler's checks. Agents of banks will not accept torn or defaced American currency. They are wary of counterfeit currency and sometimes hesitate to accept currency in large denominations such as $100 bills. While banks will exchange American currency, individual clerks will decide whether to accept a particular note. When changing money at a bank, you will receive a receipt. If you have Egyptian pounds that you wish to change back into dollars at the end of the journey, you will need to present that receipt. The Egyptians use paper money for all denominations. There are some coins in circulation, but one rarely sees them. Having a supply of small denominations is convenient when tipping.

Food and Water. The Egyptians can drink their tap water; most visitors cannot. You should drink only bottled water while in Sinai and Egypt. It is readily available and cheap. The food is safe—except fruits and salads that may be washed in water. It is best not to buy food off the street. Food in restaurants is safe except for raw fruits and vegetables. It is important to pay special attention to these matters.

Egyptian Souvenirs. Your Egyptian guides will take you to visit places where the most popular Egyptian souvenirs are manufactured and sold. For example, part of any trip to Memphis is a visit to a "rug factory." What you will visit is not the factory where the rugs are made but a place where the process of weaving is demonstrated and where you may purchase the final product. You will see children weaving rugs by hand. Their skill and agility are matched only by the beauty of the rugs—especially the ones made from silk. Prices vary according to the material (cotton, wool or silk), the intricacy of the design, and the size of the rug. A small woolen rug will cost about $30 and a nine-by-twelve-foot silk rug will cost upwards of $10,000. The guides will assure you that the children are not exploited but do this work "after school" to supplement their families' income.

Another popular souvenir is papyrus. Your guide will take you to a "papyrus factory" where you will see a very brief demonstration of how papyrus is made. Then you will have the opportunity to purchase papyrus painted with various pharonic and coptic themes. The price of the painted papyrus varies with the size of the papyrus and the picture painted on it. A small piece of papyrus four inches by six inches may cost about $5; the largest piece may run above $200. While you wait, an artist will paint your name in hieroglyphics on a papyrus for a few dollars. If you buy a papyrus, make sure you examine it to be sure that you are satisfied with its quality before you pay for it.

Other popular souvenirs are silver and gold cartouche pendants. A cartouche is the name given to the oval enclosed space in which the pharaoh's name was written in Egyptian texts. One can buy these ready-made. They will replicate actual pharonic cartouches. Also, one may special order a cartouche with a name to be spelled out in hieroglyphs. The price will depend on the size and metal used. Silver cartouches can cost about $25. Gold ones will be considerably more expensive. Buying anything made of gold requires care. Unless one is an expert in appraising jewelry, it will be necessary to rely on the merchant's attestation that the weight and purity of the gold are as claimed.

Alabaster is another popular Egyptian souvenir. Alabaster is sculpted into objects of different sizes and shapes. One must take care that polished limestone is not substituted for genuine alabaster. The latter is translucent while the former is not. Sometimes merchants will display some of their alabaster items with electric lights behind them to show their translucent character. When you visit Luxor, your guide will probably take you to an alabaster factory to see the process used in manufacturing these items. Of course, there will be an opportunity to purchase some as well.

Egypt is also famous for its leather and cotton goods. A particularly Egyptian example of the latter is the *galabia*. This is the comfortable long robe that is the traditional clothing of the countryside. They have been modified as sleep wear and evening wear for women. You will also be invited to "perfume factories." Here offered for sale is "the essence" of popular fragrances like jasmine, geranium, roses, violets. These can be dissolved in alcohol: 1:9 for perfume, 1:30 for cologne.

One can shop for the Egyptian souvenirs in the lobbies of the major hotels in Cairo and Luxor. Another venue is the **Khan Khalili,** an immense outdoor market in the center of Cairo. To shop here successfully, it is important to engage the merchant in bargaining. Most merchants employ "runners" who try to direct you to specific shops.

Travel within Egypt. It is necessary that foreigners travel in organized groups as they move about in Egypt. The language, cultural, and political barriers make going off on one's own imprudent. A popular way to travel from Cairo to Luxor and Aswan is by overnight train. The trains that tourists use have sleeper cars that are clean and modern. Meals are served in your compartment. One can also fly to Luxor and Aswan, and there are ferries that travel up and down the Nile. This is the most luxurious form of travel in Egypt. It is for people with time and money. The best way to get around the cities such as Cairo, Aswan, and Luxor is by taxi. Make certain that you and the driver agree on the fare *before* you get in the taxi. At the end of your trip, the driver may ask for more money. Simply give him the amount agreed upon and leave the taxi. There are buses in Cairo but one must be familiar with the system and be willing to be packed in like a sardine to use the system. In Luxor horse-drawn carriages ply the streets along the river. Most hotels will post the fares to each of Luxor's major attractions.

AN OUTLINE OF EGYPT'S HISTORY

The dates that follow will serve to give you a general framework for understanding the history of Egypt that extends for more than five thousand years. The priests of ancient Egypt kept a list of pharaohs. The one that has survived is that of Manetho (c. 300 B.C.). Since he wrote during the Greek Period, the names he gives are Greek equivalents of the Egyptian names. Since the decipherment of the ancient Egyptian language, it is possible to give the names of pharaohs in their own language. For example, the great pyramid of

Giza was built by Khufu, who is sometimes known by his Greek name "Cheops." Here the Egyptian names for the pharaohs will be used. The Greek equivalent will be given in parentheses. Manetho is also responsible for breaking up Egyptian history into thirty-one dynasties from Mena (Menes; 3000 B.C.) to Alexander the Great (332 B.C.). The chronology of the pharaohs before the Ptolemaic Period is still a matter of dispute. The dates given here provide a general frame of reference. You may find different dates given in other sources.

The Old Kingdom [Dynasties 1–6] (Memphis)	**3000–2270 B.C.**
The Step Pyramid of Zoser	2700
The Pyramids of Giza	2600–2200
The First Intermediate Period [Dynasties 7–10]	**2270–2100**
The Middle Kingdom [Dynasties 11–13] (Thebes)	**2100–1700**
The Second Intermediate Period [Dynasties 14–17] Hyksos	**1700–1555**
The New Kingdom [Dynasties 18–20]	**1555–1090**
Canaan under Egyptian Control	1550–1150
Amarna Period [Akhnaten]	1361–1325
Tutankhamen	1333–1325
Rameses II	1279–1212
Merneptah [Israel] Stele	1207
Canaan/Philistines/Israelites independent	1150
The Late Age [Dynasties 21–26]	**1090–525**
Shishak invades Israel (1 Kgs 14:25)	930
Persian Period [Dynasties 27–31]	**525–332**
Greco-Roman Period	**332 B.C.–A.D. 395**
Alexander conquers Egypt	332 B.C.
Ptolemaic Period	305–30
Cleopatra's death—Egypt a Roman Province	30 B.C.
Byzantine [Coptic] Period	**395–640**
Arab (Islamic) Period	**640–1800**
Cairo founded	969
Saladin builds Citadel	1171
Modern Egypt	**1800–**
Mohammed Ali	1800–1848
Suez Canal	1869
A British Protectorate	1914
Republican Revolution	1952
Aswan Dam	1971
Peace Treaty with Israel	1979

Egypt of the Pharaohs. At the beginning of Egyptian history, there were two states between the First Cataract of the Nile (Aswan) and the Mediterranean Sea. One was north and the other south of a boundary that was about forty miles south of Cairo. Mena (Menes) united these two states and became the first pharaoh of Upper and Lower Egypt. The capital of united Egypt was at Memphis. The pharaohs of this early period mined the turquoise and copper of the Sinai. The pharaohs of the third and fourth dynasties were responsible for building the great pyramids at Giza to serve as their tombs. Other pharaohs of the Old Kingdom built pyramids at Subsir and Saqqarah. The latter place was also where nobles prepared tombs for their burial.

In the twenty-third century B.C. the power of the nobility began to threaten the authority of the pharaohs. The central authority became irrelevant and Egypt was divided, for all practical purposes, into several states, each led by local nobles. This period of decentralized authority is known as the First Intermediate Period. In 2100 B.C., the princes of Thebes were able to assert their authority over all Egypt and the country was united again. It was a time when art, architecture, and literature flourished though the problems caused by the disorder of the First Intermediate Period had continuing effects on the Egyptians. It seems that their self-assurance was affected. Even their views about death and their relationships with the gods changed. For example, note the way the tombs at Saqqara are decorated. On the walls are depicted scenes from the deceased's ordinary life. Evidently the first Egyptians saw death as simply a transition from one form of life to another. Life will go on and the deceased will enjoy their social position, wealth, occupation, and favorite diversions in the next life as in this one. After the First Intermediate Period, the theme of tomb decoration changes. Scenes of judgment predominate. Death is a dangerous transition from this life to the next. The prayers, incantations, rituals depicted on the walls of the tombs are to help the deceased survive this difficult transition.

Unfortunately, the great artistic explosion during the Middle Kingdom ended with the invasion of the Hyksos from the East. The Hyksos ruled Egypt from Avaris, a city in the Delta for almost one hundred fifty years. Many monuments of earlier periods were destroyed. While it was an artistically unproductive period, the Hyksos contributed something to Egypt that made its empire possible. They introduced the horse and chariot into Egypt. These were previously unknown. The Egyptians had the implements they needed to begin their own wars of conquest. In 1550 B.C. Ahmose (Amosis; 1552–1527) drove the Hyksos from Egypt and founded the New Kingdom. His descendants began aggressive military campaigns to the north. They conquered Canaan and moved up the eastern Mediterranean coast to Lebanon and Syria. They eventually reached the Euphrates where they met another aggressive power intent on establishing an empire—the Hittites. The pharaohs of the New Kingdom rebuilt the temples destroyed by the Hyksos. They also built new temples such as those of Karnak and Luxor. All these projects were financed by the booty and tribute taken from the subject peoples of the Egyptian empire.

Egypt was distracted from its imperial concerns by an internal controversy initiated by Amenhotep IV (Amenopis; 1361–1340 B.C.). He wanted to break the economic power of the priests of Amun, who controlled a vast amount of land and its produce. He transferred his capital from Thebes, the sanctuary of Amun, to Amarna, the sanctuary Aten. He changed his name to Akhnaten ("the Spirit of the Sun") and tried to make Aten the god that all Egyptians worshiped. The priests of Amun saw Akhnater's policies as threats to their position and power so they probably had the pharaoh assassinated. Eventually, the priests were able to put an eleven-year-old boy named Tutanknaton (King Tut, 1333–1325 B.C.) on the throne. They had him move the capital back to Thebes, the city of Amun. They also convinced him to change his name to Tutankhamen. The priests of Amun were back in control. During this period of religious and political controversy, Egypt's attention was distracted and it paid little attention to its empire. This caused a period of near anarchy in Canaan as is clear from the Amarna Letters, written by local Canaanite rulers to their Egyptian masters. These letters were filed but apparently never answered.

Egyptian imperial power reached its height under Rameses II (1279–1212) who ruled for sixty-seven years. He solidified Egyptian hegemony in the eastern Mediterranean region by making peace with the Hittites. Then he began to glorify his rule through monuments that still can be seen all over Egypt. He ordered so many that the artisans could not keep up so they sometimes just effaced the names of earlier pharaohs and chiseled in Rameses' name on monuments. He moved his capital to the former Hyksos capital in the Delta and had it renamed "the House of Rameses." The Bible has the Hebrew slaves building two supply cities in the Delta: Pithom and Rameses (Exod 1:11), though it does not mention the name of the pharaoh who put them to work. After Rameses' long reign, Egyptian power continued for a while but eventually the inevitable decline began. After the loss of its empire, the country began an economic decline. In the Late Period the power of the pharaohs dwindled and that of the Amun priests grew. Eventually Nubian kings conquered Egypt and ruled as pharaohs. Egypt also had to contend with the rise of Assyria, another aggressive military power bent on adding Egypt to the Assyrian Empire.

After the collapse of Assyria in 621 B.C., there was a minor renaissance in Egypt. The achievements of this Late Period were no match for those of the Old Kingdom. Its military prowess was not what it used to be. Egypt relied on mercenaries, like the Jewish colony at Elephantine Island, to protect it. Egypt fell to the Persians in 525 B.C. and then to Alexander the Great in 332 B.C. The Greeks remained in control until the Romans made Egypt a mere province of their empire in 30 B.C. The Greek dynasty who ruled Egypt, the Ptolemies, adopted Egyptian customs and acted as though they were the heirs of the ancient pharaohs. They built beautiful temples like the one at Philae Island near Aswan. The Egyptians were not fooled by all this and rebelled several times. Perhaps that is why the Romans ruled Egypt through a prefect who acted in the emperor's name. The Roman emperor was given the titles and status of the pharaohs and is depicted as such in temples constructed at this time.

The Coming of Christianity. Christianity came to Egypt soon after the death of Jesus. Eusebius asserts that Mark the Evangelist founded the Church of Alexandria. Eusebius asserts that in A.D. 68, Easter was celebrated on the same day as the feast of Serapis. The devotees of Serapis were angered by the Christian feast and arrested Mark. They dragged him around the city of Alexandria until he died. Two Venetians stole the body of Mark from its tomb in 838 and interred it in the cathedral of Venice. In 1968 Paul VI ordered that the relics of Mark be returned to Egypt. Despite the Roman persecution, Christianity took a firm hold in Egypt.

In 389 Emperor Theodosius proclaimed Christianity the religion of the empire and ordered all ancient temples to be closed. The last of the Egyptian temples to cease operations was that of Philae. Justinian the Great ordered it closed in 553. With that the Pharonic Period of Egypt ended. The Egyptians, after having accepted Christianity, abandoned ancient beliefs, converted some old temples to churches, used the Greek alphabet to write their language, and adopted Byzantine artistic forms in place of the pharonic ones. The passion with which the Egyptians embraced Christianity is clear from three different phenomena. First, the Egyptians showed themselves willing to die as martyrs. Second, monasticism developed in the Egyptian desert. Third, the Egyptians participated in the christological controversies that shook the Church in the Byzantine Period. Because of these religious controversies, the Egyptians elected their own patriarch to assert their independence from Constantinople. At this time, they began calling themselves *Copts*, a name derived from *Qibt*, the name of Egypt in the old language. The Greek and Latin words for Egypt come from this name, as does the English word. The Semitic word for Egypt is completely different. The Bible calls Egypt *mitzraim*. Arabic has a similar word: *Misr*, but used *qibti* to refer to the Christians of Egyptian descent.

More than anything else, the Coptic Church reflects the problems that the first Christians had in understanding the person and work of Jesus. In the mid-first century, Docetism appeared which held that the human form of Jesus was a mere illusion. Later Gnosticism became important in Egypt (The Nag Hammadi manuscripts now in the Coptic Museum. They are Coptic translations of Greek Gnostic texts). The Gnostics believed that personal knowledge of God was reserved for an elite who came to this knowledge through participation in rituals and incantations. To combat these problems a theological school was established in Alexandria in the late second century. Some of its alumni were Clement of Alexandria (190) and Origen (250). Another alumnus was Heraclas, who became patriarch of Alexandria in 230, and assumed the title *pope* several hundred years before the bishop of Rome did. The Coptic patriarch of Alexandria uses the title "pope" to this day. The Roman emperor, Septimus Severus, authorized the first persecution of Egyptian Christians in Egypt in 188. Persecution continued and became most intense during the reign of Diocletian, beginning in 284. So horrific was his persecution that the Copts begin their calendar with the accession of Diocletian. They call their calendar the "Martyrs' Calendar." The Coptic year begins on September 11 of the Gregorian calendar.

The peace that came with Constantine's legitimation of Christianity made it possible to resume the christological debates. Arius was a priest of the Church of St. Mark in Alexandria. He maintained that Jesus was of the same essence as God, but because he was begotten, Jesus was not equal to God. Athanasius, the Egyptian secretary of the patriarch of Alexandria, was the Greek

Arius' chief opponent. Athanasius argued that Jesus and God were of one, indivisible essence. The Greeks supported Arius while the Egyptians supported Athanasius. Constantine tried to mediate the dispute and eventually called the Council of Nicea in 325 to settle the matter. The emperor had Arius exiled, but his followers kept his doctrine alive. Constantius II was an Arian and Athanasius found himself in exile during his reign.

In the fifth century, Nestorius, the Patriarch of Constantinople, refused to call Mary the "Mother of God." He preferred the title "Mother of Christ." His chief opponent was Cyril of Alexandria. The Council of Ephesus seemingly settled the matter in 431, but again Nestorius' disciples continued to spread his teachings and these were influential in certain churches of the East. During the second Council of Ephesus (449), Dioscurus, the patriarch of Alexandria, presided over the deposing of Flavian, the patriarch of Constantinople whom Pope Leo supported. Two years later the Council of Chalcedon reversed the decision of Ephesus II, deposed Dioscurus, and made Constantinople second only to Rome. The Egyptians rejected the decision of the council. The Copts were dismissed as "monophysites" (from the Greek, meaning one nature) though they never denied the two natures of Christ that they saw as mystically one. The emperor appointed a new patriarch for Alexandria whom the Egyptians rejected in favor of one they elected. They dismissed the appointee of the emperor as a "Melkite" (*mlk* is the Semitic root for king. A *melkite* then is a *king's man*). Several emperors tried to heal the rift between Alexandria and Constantinople but without success. The persecution experienced by the Copts led them to welcome the Arabs in the seventh century as liberators. After Vatican II, dialogue between the Copts and Rome led to the settling of the christological issue, which was more a misunderstanding than anything else. The main problem now between Rome and the Copts is papal (i.e., Roman) primacy.

The Muslims. In A.D. 640 Amr ibn el As, a general in the army of Omar, the caliph who defeated the Byzantines in Jerusalem, entered Cairo. He was welcomed by the native Egyptians who had no love for their Byzantine rulers. Most Egyptians assimilated with the conquering Arabs. Those who remained Christians preserved their Coptic language and their religious art, but they, too, gradually assimilated the language and customs—but not the religion—of the Arabs. Today about ten percent of the Egyptian population is Christian. From 640 to 1517, eleven Arab dynasties ruled Egypt directly or indirectly. The Ottoman Turks ended Arab rule in 1517. Egypt remained part of the Ottoman Empire until 1805. Napoleon occupied the country from 1798 to 1801 under the pretext of protecting Ottoman rule. Napoleon wanted to cut English communications with the East—in particular India.

Modern Egypt. Mohammed Ali founded the modern state of Egypt in 1805. While he acknowledged the sovereignty of the Ottoman sultan, Mohammed Ali was the *de facto* ruler of Egypt. In the mid-1800s both France and Britain considered Egypt in their sphere of influence. By 1901 the two European powers agreed that Britain would make Egypt a "protectorate." Egypt did not enjoy full sovereignty until 1921 and Sultan Fu'ad assumed the title of king. Parliamentary government was established in 1923. In July 1952 following the loss of the 1948 war with Israel and other internal difficulties, army officers under Gen. Mohammed Naguib staged a *coup d'etat*. In June 1953 the monarchy was abolished and Egypt declared a republic. General Adb al-Nasser assumed the presidency in 1954 and then nationalized the Suez Canal. Nasser expelled all British military personnel in June 1956. This led to an attack on Egypt by Israel, Britain, and France in October 1956. A UN cease-fire was ordered in November and UN peacekeepers took positions in December, allowing the canal to reopen. Nasser died two years after the disastrous Six-Day War in 1967. He was replaced by Anwar Sadat who launched the Yom Kippur War on October 6, 1974. Five years later he was the first Arab leader to make peace with Israel. Many Egyptians have found it difficult to be reconciled with their former enemy. Military officers who opposed the peace assassinated Sadat in 1981. The current president in Hosni Mubarek.

Muslim fundamentalism is sweeping the country and is trying to undermine its stability. Egypt is still committed to peace with Israel though relations are correct but not cordial. Egypt is a developing country with a burgeoning population. Its resources are stretched to the limit and it is dependent upon aid, much of which comes from the United States.

THE CULTURE OF ANCIENT EGYPT

"Blessed be my people Egypt . . ." (Isa 19:25).

Upper and Lower Egypt. Ancient Egypt saw itself as a union between two distinct regions: *Lower Egypt* (the Delta, represented by the lotus, vulture, and white crown) and *Upper Egypt* (the Nile Valley, represented by the papyrus, cobra, and red crown). The union of the two was the achievement of Pharaoh Mena (Menes), who ruled toward the end of the fourth millennium. Despite the political union, memories of the distinction between Upper and Lower Egypt remained. Many artistic and decorative motifs reflect this distinction.

Geography. Ancient Egypt's geographical position protected it from invasion until the Hyksos Period (seventeenth-fifteenth centuries B.C.) and allowed for a distinctive culture to develop. Egypt is protected by vast deserts to the east, west, and south, and by the Mediterranean Sea in the north. Though Egypt covers a vast territory in the northeast corner of Africa, the area that could support human habitation in antiquity was limited to the Nile Valley, a narrow strip of land on either side of the river. Egypt was known as the "Gift of the Nile." That river gave the land its fertility through the river's annual inundation. It also made irrigation possible during the hot and dry season that ran from April to October.

Society. Egyptian society was highly stratified. At the top was the pharaoh. He was the god Horus personified. At death, he became one with the god Osiris, the god of the underworld. Next in importance were the priests whose economic power was significant. Temples owned and priests controlled almost eighty percent of the arable land in Egypt. When one pharaoh, Akhnaten, tried to break the power of the priests of Amon by promoting the worship of Aten, he was assassinated and the religious and economic power of Egypt returned to the priests of Amon. The nobles were responsible for provincial government. At the end of the Old Kingdom Period (2270–2100 B.C.), these nobles who governed the provinces or nomes ended the centralized political power of the pharaoh. The nobility of Thebes (Luxor) succeeded in imposing its rule over Egypt around 2100 B.C. and a centralized political system reemerged. Scribes formed the next class. They were the administrators of government, commerce, and large estates. They were able to read, write, and keep accounts —skills limited to a few. The vast majority of ancient Egyptians were farmers and artisans.

Architecture. Egyptians used mud and reeds for their earliest buildings. Since it rarely rains in Egypt, shelter could remain simple. When larger homes began to be built, reeds were lashed together to provide support for the roof. Interlaced palm fronds were fashioned into a "wall" surrounding the house. Domestic buildings were constructed of mud brick like the houses that one can see in villages today. The homes of the wealthy were made of the same material, but were set within gardens. Even palaces were made of mud brick, though they were much larger than private homes and were decorated with painted walls. None of the pharaohs' palaces has survived to the present because of the materials used in their construction.

While mud brick served for the homes of people, the Egyptians used only stone for their temples since the latter were to last forever. There were two types of temples: the state temple (the house of the chief god of a particular region) and the mortuary temple (the place where the deceased pharaoh was worshiped). The temples had an ornamental entry way or *pylon,* which led to a colonnaded courtyard, a *hypostyle hall* (a hall of columns that looked like bundles of reeds), one or more vestibules, and then to the sanctuary proper. Bas-relief that described the rituals of the temple or the military victories of the pharaohs decorated the walls and columns of the temples. The walls, columns, and reliefs were painted. Usually statues of pharaohs stood guard at the entry ways into the temples. There was also a sacred lake or well where priests underwent purification before their service. Other structures included storerooms and places for sacrifice. A mud brick wall surrounded the whole complex.

Art. Egypt has the raw materials for the development of sculpture: limestone, alabaster, granite, and diorite. The first statues were small objects but soon full-sized figures appeared. The latter were always part of the architecture decoration of a temple or tombs. Thus, they served a religious purpose. Colossal statues did not become popular until the New Kingdom. There is some debate whether statues were meant to be portraits; more than likely they were idealized images. Some statues were painted to represent living persons. Royal figures could be sculptured alone or with their wives. The statue shows the pharaoh walking or seated with his hands on his knees.

Temples and tombs were decorated with reliefs. Most often these were bas relief, i.e., the background was cut away. There are some examples of sunken reliefs. The latter are easier and therefore cheaper to produce. Almost all reliefs from the time of Rameses II were sunken reliefs. Like sculpture, reliefs were integrated as decorative elements of monumental buildings. The reliefs were supposed to be painted though this was not always done.

Painting developed as a still quicker and cheaper decoration than sunken reliefs. Egyptian paintings are not frescoes since they were done on dry surfaces. First, a master artist made an outline of the picture in red. Then other artists would fill in the painting by using colors made of natural materials. Egyptian painting usually does not reflect perspective when depicting the human form. People are depicted in profile rather than in full form. The Egyptians never developed ceramics into a true art form as did the Greeks. Egyptian pottery is utilitarian with little stylistic variation.

Religion. The people of ancient Egypt were very religious. It is important to remember that most inscriptions found from ancient Egypt are religious. The monuments that have survived to the present are religious in nature. They are either temples or tombs. Most of the latter were built for the pharaohs who were considered living gods. On the other hand, it is also important to remember that the public did not take part in the daily rituals of Egyptian religion. These took place *inside* the temples to which ordinary people had no access. Temples were the domains of the pharaohs and priests.

Daily Temple Rituals. The day for the temple priests began with a purification ritual. The priest dressed in the appropriate garments, took water from a sacred lake or other source, and approached the door to the shrine. He broke the seals placed there the night before. He removed the linen covering the statue and washed the statue before placing new linens on it. The priest lit the incense and placed offerings of food and drink before the god. He then withdrew and resealed the room. Additional purification rituals took place at noon and in the evening. Priests removed the previously set-out meal before placing a new one before the image. The priests ate those meals that were removed. The purpose of these daily rituals was to insure that the forces of chaos could not overcome those of order. The Egyptians believed that the ordered way of life was established only with great difficulty. The gods maintained the order established by them. The goal of rituals was to maintain the divinely established order in the world. The temples were built of stone because it was the hardest material known to the Egyptians and it protected the gods from the powers of chaos.

Festivals. While the public did not participate in the daily rituals in the temples, it did view the great processions that were part of the festivals. Each temple had its calendar of feasts. They may have lasted from a few days to as many as thirty. They were agricultural feasts connected with fertility of the fields and flocks. During these feasts, priests carried the image of the god usually housed in the temple in procession around the town or to a neighboring temple. While in these processions, the gods gave oracles replying to questions that could be answered with a yes or no. The directions for the celebration of the processions were inscribed on the walls of the temple.

Priests. The people charged with the service of the gods in the temple were the priests. At first, nobles and state officials served as priests, but later the priesthood became a professional class with several grades. Women served as priests to several female deities such as Isis, and as singers for male gods.

Mythology. Egyptian religion had its sacred texts, but not the idea of an initial revelation. There were several complicated creation myths that served as the basis of Egyptian religion. The Egyptians had no problem with several variations of these myths. What follows is one variation, which originated in the temples of Heliopolis. From the watery chaos, there emerged a mound of earth like the mounds that appeared when the Nile inundation receded. On this first mound appeared Atum (the original sun god who was later identified with Re). From Atum came Shu (air) and Tefnut (moisture, clouds, dew). From these came Geb (the earth) and Nut (sky). The union of the latter two produced Osiris, Seth, Isis, and Nephtys. These four generated other gods and then human beings. There are many local variations on this basic theme.

Gods. Perhaps the most perplexing side of Egyptian religion is the multiplicity of deities and the depiction of many of them in animal form. Despite appearances, Egyptian religion was monotheistic at its core since it believed that the universe was the conscious creation of one, supreme deity. But the act of creation resulted in the complex world of human experience. The world is infused with divinity. The principles and laws that govern the world and keep it in order are simply aspects and functions of the one divinity. Egyptian religion has given a name and an image to each of these functions—these are the "gods" of Egypt. Animals were chosen to image some of these functions. For example, the jackal was chosen to portray that aspect of the divinity that guards over the dead and leads them to the next world. Jackals inhabited the places where the Egyptians built their tombs and they came to regard the jackal as the guardian of those tombs. The following is a list of some other aspects of divinity as understood and portrayed by the Egyptians:

a. the Hapi, the gods of the Nile represented by the lotus (the feminine of the pair) and the papyrus (the masculine of the pair);

b. Bast, killer of snakes represented by the cat;

c. Taueret, fertility and motherhood, represented by the hippopotamus;

d. Bes, also a god of motherhood, represented as a dwarf;

e. Maat, the god of wisdom, represented as a woman with a feather on her head;

f. Thoth, the god of the scribes, represented by the ibis;

g. Buts, the god of Lower Egypt, represented by the cobra;

h. Nekhebet, the god of Upper Egypt, represented by the vulture;

i. Osiris, the god of the underworld, represented by the mummy of a man;

j. Horus, the living pharaoh, represented by the falcon;

k. Amun, the sun god, represented by a ram;

l. Hathor, the goddess of the sky; represented by a cow.

Isis. Egyptian religion—especially the cult of Isis—became popular in the Greco-Roman world. Originally Isis was part of an Egyptian version of the myth of fertility. Isis was the wife of Osiris. He and his brother Seth were in conflict over kingship. Seth imprisoned Osiris in a chest loaded down with lead and threw him into the Nile to drown. The chest moved up the Nile and the Mediterranean coast to Byblos where Isis found it. Before she could do anything for Osiris, Seth took the body and cut it into pieces that he scattered about. Isis found the pieces and reassembled them. She became impregnated by Osiris with Horus. Horus fought Seth for hegemony on the earth and defeated him. Osiris then became the god of the underworld. In the Greco-Roman Period, the Isis cult became one way in which people tried to survive death. Isis became identified with various Semitic, Greek, and Roman deities. Through the participation in the rituals of this cult, the individual could enjoy a new life in another world. Even after Christianity became the official religion of the empire, the Isis cult survived. It was not until the sixth century that Justinian succeeded in suppressing it. Christianity borrowed much of the iconography connected with Isis to depict Mary, the mother of Jesus.

Death. One might get the impression that the Egyptians were obsessed with death, but they were devoted to life. They could not imagine anything better than the continuation of life in another world where they could carry on the activities that gave meaning to their life in this world. One key to the continuation of life in the next world was the preservation of the body. Where did they get this idea? In the pre-Dynastic Period (before 3000 B.C.), people were simply buried in baskets or linen shrouds and placed in the sand. Their bodies were remarkably well preserved because of the dry climate. In the hot sands in which they were buried, bodies desiccated before putrefaction set in. When the Egyptians started building tombs, they had to duplicate what happened naturally in sand burials. In the artificial atmosphere of the tombs bodies deteriorated.

The word mummy comes from the Arabic word *mummiya* (bitumen), a liquid used in a later process of preserving the body. At first the process was a dry one. After death, the soft parts of the body except the heart were removed. The brain was taken out through the nostrils and then discarded since the Egyptians were unaware of its functions. The lungs, intestines, liver, and stomach were placed in jars. These have become known as canopic jars after the mistaken identification with characters in Greek mythology who were portrayed in the form of jars with heads on them. These were the sailors of Menelaus' fleet who died in the city of Canopus. The jars used by the Egyptians had heads of minor deities on them; therefore, the identification made during the Hellenistic Period. Next natron (sodium carbonate), a naturally occurring drying agent was applied to the body cavity to clean and dry it. After the body desiccated, it was stuffed with cotton to preserve its shape. Then it was covered with linen strips. Amulets that would help the deceased make the transition to the next world were placed on the body before burial. The process of mummification took about seventy days to complete.

For burial the body was placed in one or more caskets before being placed in the sarcophagus of the tomb. A few weeks after burial, priests returned to the tomb to perform the "opening of the mouth" ritual. This involved a symbolic opening of the deceased's mouth so that it could benefit from the offerings and food and drink brought to the tomb. Following this ceremony, the tomb was permanently sealed. Subsequent rituals took place in mortuary temples located near the tombs.

EGYPT AND THE BIBLE

"Then Israel came to Egypt, and Jacob sojourned in the land of Ham"
(Ps 105:23).

Humans have lived in Egypt since 10,000 B.C. In the fourth millennium B.C., Egypt became the first national state. It was a great civilization for more than two thousand years before the rise of the Davidic monarchy in Israel. The pyramids were standing for fifteen hundred years when Solomon began to build the Temple. The social, political, and cultural achievements of Egyptian civilization are beyond calculation. Still, the influence of Egypt on other ancient peoples, including ancient Israel, was not commensurate with these achievements.

One reason for the surprising meager influence that Egypt had over ancient Israel was the geographical isolation of Egypt. The settled area of Egypt is a strip of arable land ranging between three and five miles wide on either side of the Nile. Deserts separated Egypt from other cultural centers though it did develop commercial ties with the coastal cities of Phoenicia north of Israel. Also, Egypt's political influence and military dominance over the eastern Mediterranean was strong at times. Under Tutmoses III (1502–1448 B.C.) Egypt gained control over Canaan, though it controlled the region through local rulers. It was the breakdown of Egyptian hegemony in Canaan in the thirteenth century B.C. that helped make possible the rise of the Israelite tribes there. Culturally Israel was oriented toward the East and the Semitic civilizations of Mesopotamia.

For the biblical tradition Egypt is a paradox. The core memory of this tradition centers on the liberation that Israel's ancestors experienced from slavery in Egypt. The first victory that Yahweh won for Israel was over Pharaoh and his army at the Red Sea (Exodus 15). Still Deuteronomy admonishes, "You shall not abhor any of the Egyptians, because you were an alien in his country" (23:8). Perhaps the reason for this ambivalence was that Egypt served as a place of refuge. Abraham (Genesis 12:10-20) and Jacob's families (Genesis 46) go to Egypt in time of famine. After the fall of Jerusalem, some Judahites who could not accept the Babylonian hegemony went to Egypt (Jer 41:11-18). There was a Jewish colony at Elephantine and another at Leontopolis. The Ptolemaic Period witnessed significant Jewish settlement in Egypt with Alexandria having a sizeable Jewish population. The Gospel of Matthew has Joseph taking Mary and Jesus to Egypt to avoid Herod's plot against the child (2:13-15).

The most important area of Egyptian influence in ancient Israel was in the wisdom tradition. Prov 22:17–24:22 is a reworked version of an Egyptian sapiential text entitled "The Wisdom of Amenemope." The conduit for this text and other Egyptian wisdom material may have been the Egyptian scribes that helped set up the royal administration of David and Solomon. At least one of Solomon's officials bears an Egyptian name (1 Kgs 4:3).

A most significant aspect of Egyptian religious belief was its notion of the afterlife. No other ancient civilization had such an elaborately developed belief in life after death. The Egyptians believed that survival after death depended on the preservation of the body so they perfected the process of mummification. How extensive was belief in a life after death among the ancient Israelites is still a matter of study. The two explicit statements of that belief in the Hebrew Bible (Isa 26:19 and Dan 12:2) are texts from as late as the second century B.C. The origins of ancient Israel's belief in resurrection, however, do not seem to have roots in ancient Egypt's belief. Egyptian religion was a complex system involving many deities though this multiplicity was understood as the manifestation of a single divine principle. Probably for political and economic reasons, Amenhotep IV (Akhnaten, 1377–1358 B.C.) tried to simplify it by promoting the worship of a single god, Aton. He was unsuccessful. After his death, the Egyptians reverted to their traditional patterns of worship and attempts were made to obliterate Amenhotep's name from all records. Some scholars have tried to relate the monotheism of early Judaism with the beliefs and practices promoted by Amenhotep IV. This is unlikely. Monotheism is a late development in the religion of ancient Israel. When it does emerge unambiguously in the sixth century B.C., it is clear that Egypt has little to do with the development of monotheism in Israel.

THE SINAI

After the 1967 war, the Israelis controlled the Sinai. They developed several oil fields in the south. They also developed the area's potential for tourism —especially along the seashore. To accomplish this the Israelis had to put in a modern infrastructure for the Sinai. Along with all this came a few Israeli settlements. Israeli archaeologists began surveying the Sinai and excavating where warranted. To the surprise of almost everyone they found no artifactual evidence to support the Bible's description of the Exodus. Though the archaeologists found remnants of campfires from the Stone Age, evidence of a mass migration in the Late Bronze Age did not emerge. One result of Israel's 1979 peace treaty with Egypt was the return of the Sinai to Egyptian sovereignty.

Taba

This is where it is possible to cross the Egyptian border from Israel into Sinai. The precise location of the border was not settled by the 1979 Israel-

Egypt Peace Treaty. The dispute continued for several years. It centered on the control of the luxury hotel built close to the border but supposedly on the Israeli side. The governments of Israel and Egypt agreed to international arbitration to settle the disagreement. Arbitration favored Egypt, which now controls the hotel.

Border Crossing. Travel into Sinai is popular among Israelis who enjoy the new resorts along the gulf. Of course, pilgrims and tourists want to see Mount Sinai. As a result, formalities at the border can take some time. First, you will pass through Israeli passport control. Have your passport ready and the small white card you received at the airport filled out completely since you are leaving Israel for Sinai, which is Egyptian territory.

Once these formalities are completed, you will walk to the Egyptian side of the border, taking all your luggage with you. Keep your passport handy and be ready to fill out the Egyptian entry forms. You will receive a visa for the Sinai here. The Egyptian border police will check your passport several times. After passing through Egyptian border control, you will be ready for the trip to Sinai and Jebel Musa.

Note: To simplify the process, listen carefully to the instructions you receive from the Israeli and/or Egyptian guides, the Israeli border police, and your guide. Make sure you have a supply of water and patience. The water in Sinai may not be safe for drinking so it is best to buy bottled water that is readily available. Payment in Egyptian pounds or American dollars is acceptable. Israeli currency is not accepted in Egypt. A supply of single American dollars will serve you well and will obviate the need to buy Egyptian pounds.

Coral Island. Eight miles into the Sinai, stop for a view of Coral Island, which was a Crusader fortress built in the twelfth century. It marked the southernmost extension of the Crusader Kingdom. Saladin seized it at the end of the twelfth century.

The MFO. You will notice vehicles with a logo bearing the letters MFO. This stands for *Multinational Force and Observers*. The members of MFO can be distinguished by their orange berets. They are American military personnel who monitor a demilitarized zone of the Sinai into which the Egyptians are not allowed to bring tanks, artillery, or other heavy equipment. The MFO is part of the Camp David Agreement between Israel and Egypt brokered by Jimmy Carter in 1979.

The Sinai Peninsula

"Mountains trembled in the presence of the Lord, the One of Sinai . . ."
(Judg 5:5).

The Sinai is a peninsula between Israel and Egypt. North is the Mediterranean Sea. Its sides are washed by two branches of the Red Sea. To the east is

The rugged terrain of the Sinai desert.

the Gulf of Eilat and to the west is the Gulf of Suez. It is the southwestern tip of Asia and its bridge with Africa. The Sinai Peninsula is divided into three sections. In the north is a well-traveled road from Israel to Cairo. This coastal road is separated from the rest of Sinai by almost impassible **sand dunes**. The middle third of the Sinai is known as *al-Tih*, the Plateau. It receives little rain and there are few water sources so there are little vegetation and population. There are some mineral deposits and a few oases where there will be some groves and orchards and where the bedouin will get water. The southern third of the Sinai has high **granite peaks**. Jebel Musa (A: "the Mountain of Moses;" Mount Sinai is nine thousand feet high). It has enough water sources to support settlements and this is probably why the Byzantines decided to build a monastery in the south.

Routes through the Sinai. While the Torah gives a prominent place to the story of the Israelites' move from Egypt to Canaan, there is no consistent way the details of the move through the Sinai peninsula are presented. This is not surprising since the narratives describe how a later generation thought their ancestors must have proceeded on the trip through the Sinai. While these traditions were taking shape and by the time they achieved written form, there were several ways the trip between Egypt and Palestine could be made. One followed the coast of the Mediterranean. It was known as *The Way of Egypt*. A second route followed a road through the center of the Sinai with its terminus as Kadesh-barnea at the edge of the Negev. This route was known as *The Way of Shur*. A third approach took a more southerly route from the Gulf of Suez to Elath. Its name was *The Way of the Wilderness*. Those who told the story of Moses and the Hebrew slaves he led from Egypt assumed that they took one of these routes. What follows uses the documentary hypothesis to help untangle the geographical details of the various stories found in the Torah.

The Elohist [E] and the Deuteronomist [D]. Neither gives a complete itinerary. Some scholars combine the details each gives to produce a single itinerary. What is common to the two traditions is that both refer to Sinai as *Horeb*. According to the combined narratives the Israelites cross the Sea of Reeds, arriving at the Way of the Wilderness (Exod 13:18). They follow that route to Mount Horeb (Exod 17:2-3). From Sinai they follow another route, the Way of the Amorites, to reach Kadesh-barnea (Deut 1:9). From there spies leave for Canaan. The Israelites, however, refuse to act on the spies' report and threaten revolt. This leads to a return to the desert by the Red Sea Road (Deut 1:20–2:1). The tribes wander in the desert for a long time (Numbers 13–14) until God bids them to travel through Edom. They move through Elath and Edom on their way to the mountains of Moab, which are just east of the land that God is planning to give to the Israelites (Deut 2:2-15). Thirty-eight years were spent in wandering in the wilderness after the departure from Kadesh-barnea.

The Yahwist [J]. After the Israelites cross the Sea of Reeds, they go by the Way of the Wilderness of Shur to Sinai (Exod 15:22-25a, 27). After reaching Sinai, they go to Kadesh-barnea (Num 10:29-36). From there they try to enter Canaan through Edom (Num 20:14-21) but are rebuffed.

The Priestly Account [P]. The Israelites travel by the Way of the Wilderness (Num 33:1-49). The text lists forty stopping points but none of these can be identified with any certainty. From Etzion-Geber they go to Kadesh by way of the Sea of Reeds (Num 33:36). From there, they cross Edom and Moab going by way of sites along the King's Highway.

Neither archaeology nor the Bible can provide the type of data necessary to attempt a reconstruction of events assumed by OT tradition. The confusion about the Sinai continues in the NT. Paul believed that Sinai was located in Arabia (Gal 4:25). What the Bible does is reflect ancient Israel's self-understanding as a people freed by Yahweh and given the land of Canaan as an inheritance. The story of Exodus-Sinai is the celebration of a people set free.

The Sinai tradition in the OT is a significant one, but it has little to do with the Sinai's location in the desert. Some hold that the Exodus-Sinai tradition is *the* central theological affirmation of the OT (see Deut 10:19; 15:15; 16:3, 12; 24:22). The Bible affirms that the Exodus was God's doing and that there was a divine purpose in the freeing of the Hebrew slaves. To emphasize the divine purpose and divine activity, the miraculous is accentuated, and historical or realistic details are few, e.g., the pharaoh responsible for the oppression and the pharaoh at the time of the Exodus are not mentioned by name. The story of the Exodus is more of a religious meditation expressing itself poetically rather than an historical, objective account of events.

The Sinai tradition is an election tradition that needs to be seen in contrast to the other principal election tradition in the OT: the Davidic tradition. Sinai stands for a theological and cultural legacy that views God as one who expects a response from human beings—not just a passive acceptance of God's gifts. It views the human person as responsible—not determined. It views others as people with rights that must be respected. People cannot be manipulated or used. The revelation of Sinai is that the divine/human relationship is simply a by-product of just and humane intersocietal relationships. This perspective forms the fundamental theological stance of the prophetic tradition.

The David-Zion tradition underlies texts such as 2 Samuel 7, Nathan's Oracle about the eternity of the Davidic dynasty. Here the emphasis is on the gracious choice that God made and the eternity of that choice. Here David is a microcosm of the entire people of Israel. Their very existence as a people and their possession of the land as an inheritance from God are God's gifts. All Israel can do is humbly and gratefully receive them. This perspective forms the fundamental theological stance of the royal and priestly traditions.

These two election traditions stand in tension with one another, but they are not mutually exclusive. In the David-Zion tradition, the emphasis is on divine activity, i.e., what God has done for Israel. In the Sinai tradition, the emphasis falls on Israel's responsibility—its obligation to respond to God's goodness by creating and maintaining a society based on justice.

Archaeology. During the Israeli occupation of the Sinai between 1967 and the implementation of the Camp David Accords, the Israelis had an unprecedented opportunity to excavate in the Sinai. Obviously there was the hope of finding some evidence from the Exodus Period. The biblical stories about the journey of the Hebrews do not provide a coherent picture of that journey (see above). The Israelis hoped that excavations could provide a clearer picture.

Surveys and some full-scale excavations in the northern Sinai explored one hundred fifty settlements from the New Kingdom Period or the Canaanite LBA. These surveys revealed the well-planned and organized system of fortresses and caravan stations that secured and eased travel on what the Egyptians called the "Way of Horus." This was the main line of communication between the Egyptian homeland and territories the Egyptians controlled in Canaan and beyond. No one was surprised when no evidence of the Hebrew presence emerged in this region. The density of Egyptian military presence here made it unlikely that escaped slaves would have chosen the "Way of Horus" as their escape route.

It was hoped that excavations in southern Sinai would yield different results. Because of the area's geographical structure, mild climate, and water sources, it was a prime candidate for the setting of the Hebrews' journey in Sinai. What became clear is that there was a wave of migrants in the southern Sinai during the Bronze Age, but these were Canaanites who traveled to the southern Sinai to settle there. No evidence of the Hebrews was discovered. It is interesting that the article on Sinai in the *New Encyclopedia of Archaeology Excavations in the Holy Land* ([N.Y.: Simon & Schuster, 1993] IV: 1384–1403) never mentions the Exodus. Archaeology has not uncovered any data relating to the biblical stories of the Hebrews' journey in the desert following their liberation from slavery in Egypt.

Mount Sinai.

Mount Sinai

"The Lord spoke to Moses on Mount Sinai . . ." (Num 3:1).

The mountain rises above the monastery of St. Catherine. Its summit is 7,362 feet above sea level and 2,349 feet above the monastery. A small chapel and a mosque are at the top, along with some refreshment stands. The way to get to the top of Mount Sinai is to hike, although one can ride a camel most of the way. It will take a minimum of three hours to climb to the summit. The Egyptian government is planning to build a cable car that will take visitors to the summit, but that is probably a long way off. You need to wear a sturdy pair of walking shoes rather than sandals. Be sure to have a supply of water and

Greek Orthodox chapel at the top of Mount Sinai.

some hard candy or snacks. It is a good idea to climb before the sun rises to avoid the heat and to see the sunrise from the top of Jebel Musa. It is prudent to do most of the climb while it is still dark. Your eyes will adjust to the dark if you do not use a flashlight. Take one along in case it is needed. Though people will walk at different paces, it is helpful for groups to stay together. No one should walk alone. It is also good to take an extra top or shirt. You will perspire if you walk up and it will feel good to have a dry shirt available once you finish the climb.

Jebel Musa and Mount Sinai of the Bible. The monastic settlements in the southern region led to the preference for the southern route for the Exodus and the identification of Jebel Musa as Sinai. This identification dates from the Byzantine Period though some scholars favor a southern route for the Exodus. The Bible does not provide evidence necessary to make a completely satisfactory conclusion (see above). Southern Sinai could support many monks because of its water supply. Although only about two to four inches of rain fall in Sinai each year, the runoff from the granite mountains of the south makes it the equivalent of twelve to sixteen inches. The runoff from the mountains goes into the valleys and remains there because of the granite bedrock. Carefully placed wells will recover it.

FROM JERUSALEM TO CAIRO

If one combines a visit to Egypt with a visit to Israel, the least expensive way to get to Egypt is by bus. It is also possible to fly from Tel Aviv to Cairo. Flight time is about thirty minutes. A bus trip from Jerusalem to Cairo is an all-day affair, but it gives visitors an opportunity to see more of both Israel and Egypt. You will leave in the morning from Jerusalem and arrive in Cairo around 5 or 6 p.m. Getting to Cairo involves traveling from Jerusalem or Tel Aviv to the Israel-Egypt border, passing through Israeli and Egyptian passport control and security, transferring to a second bus for a trip through the northern Sinai, crossing the Suez Canal by ferry, and then continuing from the canal to Cairo. Make certain you have water, snacks, your journal, and reading material with you in the bus. Also, do not pack your passport in your luggage. You need to have it on your person when you cross the border.

Part I: Jerusalem to Rafah. The Israel-Egypt border at Rafah (H: Rafiah) is eighty miles from Jerusalem. It will take about two hours to reach the border once you get out of the city. You will travel southwest in the direction of Ashkelon and then pick up the main coastal highway to Rafah. You will pass near Gaza, which is about fifteen miles south of Ashkelon.

Gaza (H: ʿAzza)

"Then the angel of the Lord spoke to Philip, 'Get up and head south on the road that goes down from Jerusalem to Gaza . . .'" (Acts 8:26).

Gaza was an important city in antiquity because of its location on the Via Maris. It was one of the most important Philistine cities. When the Philistines went to the region from the Aegean area (probably Mycenae), they sought to take over Egypt. Rameses III repulsed them in 1190 B.C. He then engaged them as mercenaries and settled them along the southern coast of Canaan. In 1150 B.C., the Philistines defeated Rameses VI and expelled the Egyptians. They then formed a confederation and began expanding into the rest of Canaan. They were the dominant military force in the region until David was able to defeat them. After their defeat by David, the Philistines never again were a dominant force in the region. The Babylonians eliminated them in the sixth century B.C. Still in the second century A.D., Hadrian named the territory of the former Israelite kingdoms after the Philistines, calling it *Provincia Palestinae*. This was probably a studied insult to the Jews of the region who twice revolted against Roman authority. This name survives as *Palestine*.

Gaza's most famous biblical association is with the story of Samson (Judges 13–16). The men of Gaza tried to capture Samson when he went there to visit a prostitute, but they were unsuccessful (Judg 13:1-3). Later, the Philistines were able to capture Samson because Delilah betrayed him. They took him to Gaza and he died in bringing down the city's temple of Dagon upon himself and the assembled Philistines (Judg 16:21-30). The prophet Amos condemns Gaza's treatment of prisoners of war (Amos 1:7). Zephaniah announces divine judgment on the city (Zeph 2:4). Gaza did not come under Jewish control until Alexander Yannai took it in 96 B.C., though the Book of Joshua lists it among the cities belonging to Judah (15:47). After Herod's death, the city was placed directly under the control of the Roman proconsul of Syria. In the Byzantine Period, the Jewish population grew. Jews continued to live there when the Arabs replaced the Byzantines and when the Crusaders replaced the Arabs. Jewish population diminished by the eighteenth century. The few Jewish families left Gaza during the anti-Jewish riots of 1929. Gaza and the strip of land between it and the Egyptian border were taken by Egypt in the 1948 war. Israel captured it in the 1967 war. Since 1994 it has been part of the territory administered by the Palestinian Authority. Gaza has been a center for Arab nationalists and lately of Muslim fundamentalists. Security reasons will have you skirt this area on your way to the border.

Rafah (H: Rafiah)

This city lies just on the Israeli side of the border with Egypt. Like Gaza, it was an important commercial and strategic center in antiquity because of its location on the Via Maris. It, too, remained outside the control of the Israelite kingdoms. It was not until Alexander Yannai that it passed under Jewish hegemony. Pompey granted the city autonomy in 63 B.C. During the Byzantine Period, it had its own bishop. This ended with the Arab conquest in 634. Jews returned to Rafah after that time. The city flourished until it was destroyed in the thirteenth century—a victim of the Crusader-Muslim wars.

Part II: Rafah to the Suez Canal. The trip across the Sinai along the northern route is about 167 miles. You will be traveling along the Mediterranean coast. After thirty-eight miles you will reach El-Arish, the largest town in the Sinai and the capital of the province of Northern Sinai. This is a popular vacation spot. You will continue toward the west and the Suez Canal. To the south are the sand dunes of the northern Sinai. After another hundred miles you will be ready to cross the Suez Canal. Here there is a rest stop. There will be a chance to purchase some refreshments before boarding the bus for the short ferry ride across the Suez Canal.

Work on the **Suez Canal** began in 1859 and the canal opened ten years later. Britain opposed the project but the French engineer Ferdinand de Lesseps was a friend of the Turkish Pasha (governor) of Egypt and convinced him to support the project. At first, the canal was considered impossible to complete since faulty calculations led to the conclusion that the water level of the Red Sea was lower than that of the Mediterranean Sea. Though this proved to be wrong, the construction was still very complicated and dangerous. Thousands of laborers died because of construction accidents.

The canal opened with great splendor in 1869. The Mena House Hotel in Giza was built to accommodate European dignitaries that included the wife of Napoleon III, Empress Eugenie, and the Prince and Princess of Wales, Edward and Alexandra. Though the British opposed building the canal, they soon realized its potential. The British government bought the shares owned personally by Pasha Ishmaʾil, who found himself in great debt. With other purchases the British owned forty-four percent of the canal. It quickly became a vital link between Europe and the East and soon the canal was earning profits beyond the expectations of investors. Unfortunately, almost none of the profits stayed in Egypt, but went to financial houses in Europe. After the 1952 officers' revolt that ended the Egyptian monarchy, Nasser nationalized the canal. England, France, and Israel invaded the Sinai in 1956 to retake control of the canal from Nasser, but they were not able to consolidate their success since the U.S. and UN demanded that they withdraw their forces. The canal was closed between 1967 and 1980 because of the Six-Day and Yom Kippur wars (Note the Egyptians refer to the latter as the October 6th War) when its channel was clogged with sunken ships. Since the treaty with Israel, the canal has reopened and is still a vital commercial link between Europe and the East.

Part III: The Suez Canal to Cairo. After crossing the Suez Canal near Ismaʾiliyyah, you will be on the highway to Cairo, which is southwest of the crossing point. Most of the road will pass by military installations with their checkpoints until you approach the Cairo International Airport, which is ten miles from the city. From there it is another seven miles to Heliopolis, an affluent suburb. This is a modern city founded in the twentieth century. The ancient city of Heliopolis was three miles east. Once you arrive in Cairo, it will take a while to get to the hotel. Cairo is a very congested city of more than fourteen million. The streets in the city center and Giza are overcrowded both day and night. Because this is a constant of life in Cairo, Egyptians do not need the personal space that westerners do. Some foreigners find the crowds discomforting at times. It is important to keep your wallet or purse where petty criminals will have a difficult time reaching because most petty crimes are crimes of opportunity. Always keep your passport secure.

CAIRO AND VICINITY

Cairo (A: al-Qahira) is not an ancient city like many others in Egypt. It was founded in A.D. 969 by Gawhar, a Sicilian general who converted to Islam. He was in the service of the Fatimid caliph, al-Muez. Cairo has been the largest city in Africa for centuries. Though Cairo itself dates to the tenth century A.D., it encompasses many earlier cities and their monuments from the pyramids of the pharaohs to the Citadel of Saladin. The city's skyline mixes minarets and modern art deco villas. The Nile flows through the center of the city. It should be no surprise that with its population, Cairo is very congested. It also suffers from serious air pollution. It serves as the capital of Egypt and the headquarters of the Arab League.

The Citadel and the Mohammed Ali (Alabaster) Mosque

Saladin (the person who defeated the Crusaders at the Horns of Hattin) built a fortress on the Moqattam Hills, the only high ground in Cairo. A Kurd born in what is now Iraq in 1137, Saladin displaced the Fatimid dynasty and

Mohammed Ali Mosque, Cairo.

ruled Egypt from 1174. He completed the Citadel in 1182 and left Egypt for Palestine where he died in 1193 after effectively ending the Crusader Kingdom. The Citadel never had to defend Cairo from outsiders though it was the scene of several internecine conflicts. The view from the Citadel gives a panorama of both Cairo and the pyramids of Giza.

There are several mosques inside the Citadel, but the most magnificent is that of Mohammed Ali. It is among the largest mosques in Egypt and is used primarily on special occasions when a larger number of worshipers are expected. Construction began in 1830 and was not completed until 1857. The main construction material is limestone though the lower story is faced with alabaster so it is also known as the Alabaster Mosque. The clock in the forecourt was presented to Mohammed Ali by King Louis Philippe of France in 1845. Mohammed Ali gave the French monarch the obelisk that now stands in Paris' Place de la Concorde. The interior is massive and is crowned with a large central dome surrounded by four half-domes. Alabaster panels face the walls to a height of thirty-six feet. To the right of the entrance is the tomb of Mohammed Ali.

Giza

This is the site of the three most famous pyramids in Egypt although there are seventy others near Cairo. The Giza plateau is solid rock. It was necessary to build the pyramids here because of the support necessary for the tremendous weight of three pyramids of pharaohs of the fourth dynasty (2620–2480). The three main pyramids are those of **Khufu** (Cheops): it is the largest, made up of 2.3 million stones. It is 481 feet high and faces north. The entrance used by visitors who want to see the burial chamber was cut by the Caliph Mamum to rob the tomb; **Khufra** (Chefren) the son of Khufu: it is ten feet shorter than Khufu's pyramid although it appears larger because it was built on higher ground; and **Menkaure** (Mycenerius), the smallest of the three at just two hundred feet.

The visit to Giza should include a walk inside a pyramid. While it is not an easy walk because of the small size of the passage ways and their steep incline, the distance is not great. Near the pyramids is the **Sphinx,** which depicts the pharaoh's head on a lion's body. The Sphinx was to guard the causeway of Khufu's pyramid/temple complex that connected his valley temple with the funerary temple that stood immediately before his pyramid. The Sphinx is carved out of living rock. In antiquity, the sands covered it and people forgot about it until the time of Tutmoses IV c. 1413. The Sphinx is sixty-six feet high and two hundred and twenty feet long. Its mouth is seven feet and seven inches long. Currently the Sphinx is under restoration. Your visit should also include **Khufu's Valley Temple**, which is a short distance from the Sphinx.

After dark, there is a sound and light show at Giza near the Sphinx and the pyramids. This is a dramatic presentation dealing with the pharaohs who built the pyramids and their reasons for this project. Check with your guide for the schedule of shows.

Old Cairo

The **Roman Period fortress** known as *Babylon* (A: Qasr al-Sham "The Fortress of the Beacon"). The early history of the site is unknown. There was a fortress here before the Roman Period. Some suggest that it may date from the Assyrian (eighth century B.C.) or the Persian (sixth-to-fifth-century B.C.) occupations. Trajan had the fortress rebuilt (c. A.D. 98). During the Arab invasion, the Byzantine patriarch and governor, Cyril, held out here for some months before finally surrendering. Most of the fortress was still standing in the 1800s when the British began dismantling it. Only part of the towers remains. The northern tower is almost completely rebuilt. The western half of the southern tower is gone and it is possible to see various layers of construction in the hollow circular structure.

The **Church of the Virgin.** Just south of the tower is the Coptic Church of the Virgin. The history of the church is a matter of conjecture. It is first mentioned in the middle of the ninth century. During the reign of Hakim the Mad (eleventh century), it became a mosque. After his death, it was returned to the Christians. The present structure was extensively rebuilt in the 1800s. The church is known as *al-Muʾallaqah* ("the hanging church") because it is built on top of the Roman Period gates to the fortress.

The **Coptic Museum**. This museum has the finest collection of Coptic antiquities in the world, including illuminated manuscripts, icons, liturgical

The limestone Sphinx (upper photo) near the pyramid complex of Pharaoh Khufu, Giza; and the alabaster sphinx, Memphis.

vessels, instruments, and vestments. Although it was built with private funds at the beginning of the twentieth century, it is now a state institution. Included in the display of manuscripts are portions of the Nag Hammadi Codices (room 10).

The **Church of St. Barbara**. The church, built in 684, was originally dedicated to Sts. Cyrus and John. When the relics of St. Barbara were brought here, the church was renamed in her honor. Barbara was converted to Christianity by Origen and executed by the Romans for propagating the faith.

The **Church of St. Sergius and St. Bacchus** (fifth century). The crypt is where pilgrims are shown the site of the Holy Family's place of refuge. Because of the rising water table, visitors can no longer enter the crypt. The Coptic patriarch was elected in this church from the ninth to the twelfth centuries. It is a basilica with a nave and two side aisles. There are twelve Corinthian columns on each side of the nave.

The **Ben Ezra Synagogue**. This building was a church until the time of Hakim the Mad who closed it. Cairo's Jewish community bought the building after Hakim's death. During the nineteenth century, the structure was extensively remodeled and the synagogue's *genizah* (a storage room for worn and torn Torah scrolls, prayer books, and other religious articles) was found. It contained several hundred old Hebrew manuscripts. Among these were portions of the Hebrew Ben Sira and Aquila's translation of the Hebrew Bible. The synagogue was in disrepair until the peace treaty between Egypt and Israel led to increased Jewish tourism. The tourists financed the renovation of the synagogue which serves a Jewish community of about one hundred individuals.

The Egyptian Museum. This museum, built in 1900, houses the artifacts made in or imported into Egypt to the sixth century A.D. except items relating to the Coptic culture, which are housed in the Coptic Museum. The highlight of the museum is the Tutankamun gallery, containing the contents of his tomb in the Valley of the Kings. Your guide will take you through the museum and point out significant exhibits with the emphasis on the Tutankamun galleries. These galleries are generally crowded with groups. The press of so many visitors sometimes causes problems. The best way to minimize these is to keep up with the guide. If you have the opportunity, you may want to return and visit the museum at a more leisurely pace.

Of great interest to students of the Bible is the **Merneptah stele**, sometimes called the "Israel stele." The guidebook to the Egyptian Museum calls it the "Israel defeat stela." This stele contains a series of hymns celebrating Pharaoh Merneptah's victory over the Libyans in the fifth year of his reign (1207 B.C.). It was found in the pharaoh's mortuary temple in Luxor in 1896. The last of the hymns deals with Palestine in addition to Libya. That stanza contains the only mention of early premonarchic Israel outside the Bible. The significance of the stele for the reconstruction of early Israel's history is enormous. The stele is located on the Ground Floor, section 13 East. Its exhibition number is 599. The hieroglyphic of Israel is illuminated. It is toward the bottom of the stele, about in the center. You will be looking at an artifact that predates David by at least two hundred years. It should not be missed.

Memphis

"Pack your baggage for exile, capital city of daughter Egypt; Memphis shall become a desert, an empty ruin" (Jer 46:19).

Location and History. Eleven miles from Cairo lies the ancient city of Menufer (Memphis). This city was the capital of Egypt from its founding in 3100 B.C. by Menes or Mena, the first king of the First Dynasty, until the capital was relocated to Luxor during the Middle Kingdom. Although it was no longer the political center of Egypt, Memphis remained an important city until the Muslim era. There is little left of the ancient city and its temple to Ptah. A high water table, intensive agriculture, and the current population in the area have limited the possibilities of excavation in the region.

Antiquities. The highlight of a visit to Memphis is a **colossal limestone statue of a young Rameses II.** It is lying on its back in a small museum built to protect it. The statue shows excellent technique though water damage is evident on its feet and back. Outside the museum one can see granite statues of Rameses II found in the area. There are other stone objects and sarcophagi in the enclosure next to the museum. The most impressive of these is an eighty-ton alabaster sphinx. It is uninscribed though it is probably from the time of Amenhotep II (1450–1425 B.C.). Other artifacts are displayed in a small archaeological garden.

Saqqarah

This name is an Arabic corruption from the name Sokar, the green god with the hawk's head, who is a god of the netherworld. At little more than a mile west of Memphis is the vast (4.5 by .9 miles) necropolis of Saqqarah. The Step Pyramid of Zoser dominates the site. There are many tombs in the area that are worth a visit, but the amount of time available means that choices must be made.

Antiquities. The **Step Pyramid of Zoser** (2667–2648 B.C.) is the most impressive monument in the area and should not be missed. Its architect was Imhotep whom the Greeks deified as Aesclypius. The pyramid and the associated buildings were the first large construction in stone. Note that none of the stone blocks is very large because Imhotep was experimenting with the tensile strength of stone. The whole complex of structures is surrounded by a great limestone wall with fourteen entrances, only one of which is a true entrance. This is a stone representation of the king's palace, which was made of mud brick. Note how the ancient Egyptians expended more effort and expense at building temples and tombs than at building homes or palaces.

After entering the single entrance, one passes through a series of engaged columns that look like bundles of reeds. The columns support a roof that was of stone made to look like logs. These stone structures imitated the look of the more modestly made buildings that people actually lived in. The columns were not freestanding because the builders of this first stone building did not realize the strength of the limestone in supporting a stone roof. After entering the enclosure itself, you will see two B-shaped altars that stand in an open area before the pyramid. The pyramid began as a *mastaba* (A: bench). These were rectangular structures that served as tombs for the nobility. To this original mastaba, Imhotep added four more of decreasing dimensions, one on top of the other to form a step pyramid. The core of the structure was local limestone, and finer imported limestone served as facing. The pyramid stood over a twenty-foot square shaft sunk almost one hundred feet into the bedrock. A granite plug weighing three and one-half tons sealed the tomb. This did not prevent tomb robbers from finding the burial chamber and other galleries and removing all the treasures buried with Zoser. Behind the pyramid is Zoser's mortuary temple, which is under reconstruction. Next to the temple is a small doorless room facing the pyramid with a seated statue of Zoser. One can view a replica of the statue. The original is in the Egyptian Museum in Cairo.

East of the pyramid/temple complex is a reconstructed building used during the *Heb-Sed Festival* (the Festival of the Tail) ceremony. This festival took place after thirty years of a pharaoh's reign. During the ceremony, the pharaoh ritually proved his strength to carry on and then received the allegiance of the officials of Egypt. One test involved subduing a bull by grasping its tail; hence, the name of the festival. The **Heb-Sed Court** is to the right of the enclosure. It is almost entirely rebuilt. The buildings are full-sized models of the originals, but they cannot be entered. The buildings and the ritual have been reconstructed based on scenes portrayed in First Dynasty tombs in Abydos. The reconstruction of the buildings is not yet complete.

The **Mastaba of Meruka**. Near the Step Pyramid is the mastaba of Meruka, the vizier and son-in-law of Teti (c. 2345 B.C.). Teti's pyramid, which is in a state of collapse, is nearby. The building, a family tomb, looked like a large bench to the Arabs and that is what they called it. Meruka's is the largest mastaba in Saqqarah, containing thirty-two rooms. The bodies of both Meruka and his wife were found in their tombs. They were middle-aged when they died. Meruka's son Meri-teti was also to be buried here, but his rooms were not completed. What is most intriguing about this tomb is its decoration. Scenes from the life of a well-to-do Egyptian covered the walls of the tomb. There are scenes of hunting, goldsmiths at work, furniture-making, the domesticating of animals, and boat-building. There are no judgment scenes in these tombs. The early Egyptians apparently thought of death as the natural continuation of life. It was only when their society experienced social and political dislocations that the Egyptians' self-confidence was shaken. The passage to the next world then became problematic. One had to pass through a judgment that determined whether one was worthy of the next life. A person would be buried with religious texts that helped him to make it through this judgment. In the tomb's chapel, the roof of which is supported by six pillars, there is a beautiful statue of Meruka.

The **Serapeum**. Also, a short distance from the Step Pyramid is the so-called Serapeum. What you will visit is the burial place of the Apis bulls that were sacred to the Egyptians who considered them as representations of the soul of Ptah. The term Serapeum properly refers to the temple of Serapis that stood above the tombs of the bulls. The Ptolemies introduced the cult of this god to Egypt from Europe. They hoped that the Greeks and the Egyptians would both worship this god. The priests chose a single bull on the basis of particular markings that set it off as sacred to Ptah. It would be killed before the effects of age set in. After mummification, it was buried in an enormous sarcophagus. Then another bull was chosen in its place. The new apis would be recognized by the star-shaped patch of white hair on its forehead. There are twenty-four bull sarcophagi (sixteen by nine feet) set in galleries carved out of rock. The tombs date from the Ptolemaic Period. Almost all of the sarcophagi were robbed in antiquity. The treasures from the one sarcophagus that was found intact are in the Louvre. Niches at the entry of the Serapeum were for stelae, also in the Louvre. These commemorated visits to the temple and stood above the tombs.

LOWER EGYPT

Alexandria

Location. Alexandria is Egypt's second largest city and its principal port. It is in the northwestern part of the Nile Delta and lies on a narrow strip of land between the Mediterranean Sea and Lake Mariut (Mareotis). It is linked to Cairo by two major highways, the railroad, and an express bus route. It is a popular resort with nearly one hundred seventeen miles of beaches along the Mediterranean.

History. As its name implies, Alexandria's origins lie with the Greeks. In 332 B.C., Alexander the Great ordered his architect Diocrates to build the city on the site of an old Egyptian village named Rhakotis. The city flourished in antiquity, becoming an important cultural, intellectual, political, and economic metropolis. It was the Ptolemaic capital of Egypt and was the site of a lighthouse that was numbered among the Seven Wonders of the World. It fell into the harbor during an earthquake about six hundred years ago. Recently, divers have found it on the floor of the Mediterranean. There is some talk of raising it to the surface and reconstructing it in the harbor.

Antiquities. Pompey's Pillar was actually built more than three hundred years after Pompey. It is an almost seventy-five feet high granite pillar erected to honor the Emperor Diocletian in A.D. 297. The pillar is the most prominent Roman-Period landmark in the city. The **Roman Amphitheater** was discovered in the 1960s during the digging of a foundation for a new building. It is a very well-preserved structure with twelve marble tiers. It is the only Roman theater to be found in Egypt. The **Catacombs of Kom al-Shoqafa** is the city's largest Roman Period cemetery (second century A.D.). It was cut into existing rock and has three levels. Its decoration blends pharonic and Roman art forms. The **Tombs of Al-Anfushi** are five Ptolemaic tombs from the third century B.C. The **Fort of Qaitbay** is a medieval fortress built on the site of the ancient lighthouse. Its design reflects medieval architecture and the layout of the lighthouse. In the fortress is Egypt's Naval Museum. The **Mosque of Mursi Abul Abbas** is the largest Muslim place of worship in Alexandria. The building dates to this century and was built on the site of an earlier mosque. It has four domes and a minaret. The **Al-Montazah Palace** was the summer residence of the modern royal family of Egypt, deposed in 1953. The palace complex has several buildings, gardens, and woods. There are also restaurants, a museum, beaches, and a tourist center.

Wadi Natrun

Location. The Wadi Natrun is fifty-four miles north of Cairo. It is a natural depression that runs from southeast to northwest for thirty miles between Cairo and Alexandria. It is 16.5 feet below sea level. The region has been a center of monasticism for seventeen hundred years. Currently it is home to four Coptic monasteries. Monasticism in Egypt has enjoyed a renaissance in the last twenty years. The monks welcome visitors and lead them on tours of the monasteries, informing the guests about the Coptic Church and their monastic way of life. Two monasteries that tourists find especially interesting are ones dedicated to St. Mecarius and St. Bishoi.

The Monasteries. One monastery is named for **St. Mecarius** (d. 390), a disciple of St. Anthony of the Desert, who came to the Wadi Natrun area in 330. Others followed his example and a community of hermits, who met together on Sunday and important feast days, developed. In time, some monks lived permanently within the community while others continued to be hermits. In the ninth century, raids by Bedouin forced the monks to build walls around their monasteries. All the monasteries have the same basic design: a high wall surrounds several churches, living quarters for the monks, and rooms for pilgrims and guests. Many monks today are professional men who have chosen to devote their lives to the pursuit of the monastic ideal. Their experience, knowledge, and dedication have led to improving the life of their neighbors in the Wadi Natrun. Not only have they made the desert bloom, they provide their fellow Christians with inspiration and hope in a land where they are a small minority (about ten percent). The increase of Muslim fundamentalism and the economic disadvantage of being a Christian in a Muslim country makes their contribution essential to the survival of Christianity in Egypt.

A second monastery in the region is named after a disciple of Mecarius, **St. Bishoi**. There are five churches in the monastic complex, which is a popular pilgrimage site among the Copts. The main church dates from the ninth century. Its last renovation took place in 1957.

UPPER EGYPT

Aswan

"See, some shall come from afar, others from the north and the west, and some from the land of Syene" (Isa 49:12).

In pharaonic times, Aswan was on the border with ancient Nubia (now known as Sudan). It is near the Tropic of Cancer and just above the First

Cataract of the Nile, which was the natural border between ancient Egypt and Nubia. The modern city is one hundred fifty miles north of the current border with the Sudan. The ancient Egyptians called the city *Abu* (elephant). The Bible knows this city as *Syene* (Isa 49:12; Ezek 29:10 and 30:6). The Greeks called it *Elephantine*. *Aswan* is an Arabic corruption of the Coptic word for island: *Sawan*. Some derive the name Aswan from the Coptic word *swenet* that means trade.

Inhabited from the third millennium B.C., Aswan was an important commercial center for ancient Egypt. Through it passed gold, ivory, slaves, and exotic animals from the south into Egypt. The first cataract of the Nile made it difficult to attack Egypt from the south, but it also required that cargo going north to Egypt had to be unloaded and carried by smaller boats that could traverse the rapids or be transported around the rapids by land. All this cargo passed through Aswan. It was the site of a Jewish military garrison and a Jewish temple from the fifth century B.C. The existence of this temple shows that not all Jews supported the Deuteronomic attempt to centralize all sacrificial worship in Jerusalem (Deuteronomy 12). The city has regained its importance in the last twenty-five years, primarily because of the High Dam.

The **West Bank**. A pleasant way to visit the west bank of Aswan is to take a felucca there. A felucca is a sailboat that was once the mainstay of travel on the Nile. Now it is used primarily as a ferry for visitors. On the way one passes **Elephantine Island** (1.6 by .4 miles). The ancient Egyptian city of Abu was at the south end of the island. The antiquities are under excavation by a German team of archaeologists. Of most interest to biblical studies and the history of Judaism is the Jewish settlement on the island that began in the fifth century B.C. Some Jews who wanted to escape the unsettled conditions in their homeland following the Exile came to Egypt and became mercenaries in the pharaoh's army. Some were assigned to Aswan. The Egyptian authorities allowed them to build a temple to their ancestral God. Several Aramaic papyri from this Jewish settlement have been found. These help profile the life of a Jewish community outside Israel. Also on the island is a Nilometer used to calculate the height of the flood. These calculations predicted the effects of the inundation on the crops and was used to set tax rates on Egyptian farmers.

There are two Egyptian temples on the island. One was dedicated to Khnum, the ram-headed god, who was the god of the first cataract of the Nile that was just south of Aswan. It dates to the fourth century B.C. though its builder Necbatano II (360–343 B.C.) reused stones from earlier structures. A second temple is that of Satet, the female counterpart of Khnum. She is depicted as a woman wearing the white crown of Upper Egypt with horns. Though her temple dates from the New Kingdom, there is evidence that she was worshiped here from the First Dynasty.

After passing Elephantine Island, the felucca lands on the west bank that is the site of the villa and **tomb of Agha Khan III** (1877– 1957). The Agha Khan is the spiritual leader of the Ishmaʾili Muslims. This is a branch of the Shiʾite movement in Islam. (Egyptian Muslims are Sunni.) Most of the Ishmaʾili are found in India though there are some in east Africa and elsewhere in the world. Agha Khan III was educated in Europe and spent most of his time

Sailing down the Nile on a felucca.

there. He was extremely wealthy. His followers contributed to his wealth on his diamond jubilee in 1945 when they gave him his weight (also legendary) in gold and diamonds. He retired to Aswan because of its lack of humidity. He found relief here from the debilitating effects of his arthritis. After he died in Switzerland, his widow honored his request to be buried in Aswan. His widow returns to the villa for a few months each year.

North of the Agha Khan's tomb are tombs of nobles from the Old and Middle Kingdoms. These are cut into the side of the hill and their entrances are visible from the river. The sandstone is of poor quality and the tombs have poorly executed carvings. These inscriptions provide data regarding the commercial traffic between Egypt and Nubia. Because of the difficulty in reaching these tombs and the poor quality of their execution, you may not wish to visit them but the feluccas will pass by them on the way back to the east bank.

Before returning to the east bank, you may want to stop on Plantation or **Kitchener Island**. This island contains specimens of trees and shrubs that are native to tropical Africa. At one time, Lord Kitchener of the British Army lived here following his successful campaign in the Sudan.

The East Bank. The **High Dam**. Gamal Addul Nasser, who was president of Egypt from 1954 to 1970, wanted to dam the Nile at Aswan to control its annual flooding and to generate electricity. He asked for help from the United States. When it was not forthcoming, he turned to the Soviet Union, which was happy to have this inroad into the Middle East. Work began in January 1960, and the dam was completed eleven years later. The dam allows for year-round irrigation, produces two million kilowatts of electricity, and makes possible cultivation of large tracts of land that otherwise would be desert. A large lake (Lake Nasser) was created behind the dam. The government stocked it with fish, providing an important food source for local consumption and export. Unfortunately, the lake is so large that it has even altered the weather patterns in Egypt. Moisture from the lake evaporates and returns to the earth as rain. Before the dam was built, it hardly ever rained in Egypt. Now rain is not as infrequent as it once was. The lake also threatened to destroy some pharonic monuments. At Abu Simbel, the Temple of Rameses II was moved to avoid being inundated. Near Aswan, the Temple of Isis had to be taken down and moved from Philae Island and reassembled at Agilqiyyah Island. The dam was completed in 1971, and the Philae Temple was reconstructed on its new site in 1980. Unfortunately, many Nubian and Christian monuments were not saved. The dam has changed the level of the water table along the banks of the Nile. Parts of Old Cairo, for example, have high-water problems. Also the soil around the lake is becoming too saline because of the concentration of salts in the lake. This salinity is beginning to spread down the river.

Just south of the high dam, one can see the impressive **Temple of Kalabshah**. Its original location was about forty-one miles south of Aswan. It was moved to the present site in 1970. The foundations of the temple date to the sixteenth century B.C. It was dedicated to Marul, a Nubian fertility god. The building was reconstructed during the Ptolemaic Period and renovated by the Romans, but it was never finished.

The **Temple of Isis** (Philae). To see this temple, you will take a motorized ferry to Agilqiyyah Island. The Temple of Isis takes up about one quarter of the island. Most of the components of the sacred area date from the Ptolemaic and Roman Periods when the cult of Isis was popular. The Egyptians regarded a nearby island as the burial place of Osiris, the husband of Isis. The first pylons lead to a forecourt with colonnades on each side. There is a second set of pylons that open onto the hypostyle hall. Behind the hall is the temple proper. East of the Temple of Isis is the *Kiosk of Trajan*, a small Roman Period temple. The cult of Isis continued here until the fifth century A.D. since Aswan was among the last areas of Egypt where Christianity penetrated. After Aswan accepted Christianity, it became a monastic center from which missionaries were sent to Nubia to the south. This temple, originally located on Philae Island, had to be dismantled and then reassembled at its current location on Agilqiyyah Island. Philae Island is now completely under water. This is another effect of the High Dam.

The **Unfinished Obelisk**. Aswan marble was famous in antiquity. Its pink and black colors are unique. Herod the Great imported this marble for his building projects. You can see examples of this Aswan marble in Caesarea and elsewhere in Israel. You can visit an ancient quarry to see how this stone was quarried. The highlight will be an examination of a stone that was being quarried to serve as an obelisk until the stone cracked and was abandoned by the quarriers.

Luxor

". . . *Thebes shall be breached and its walls shall be demolished*" (Ezek 30:16).

The name of this town in the ancient Egyptian language was *Waset* (scepter). When the Greeks conquered Egypt, they gave it the name *Thebes*, the name of an important royal city in Greece. The Romans called it *Diospolis Magna* (the great city of God). *Luxor* is the Arabic name for the town. It comes from the word "palaces" (*al-Uqsur*) since the Arabs who came here in the seventh century believed that the temples they saw were royal palaces. Luxor is a city in the Nile Valley four hundred nineteen miles south of Cairo. The ancient and modern cities are along the east bank of the river. The west bank of the river was the site of the ancient city's necropolis. The capital of Egypt moved from Memphis to Thebes at the beginning of the Middle Kingdom Period (c. 2100 B.C.).

The Necropolis. To reach the necropolis, you will take a short ferry ride across the Nile. From the landing, you will go by bus to see some highlights of the west bank. Among the sites that you should visit are:

The **Valley of the Kings**. Because the pyramids did not protect the tombs of the kings buried in them, but pointed out the burial places to tomb robbers, the pharaohs of the Middle Kingdom later chose to be buried in tombs in a valley below the limestone hills of the area. It was a secluded area that they

Statue of Ramses II, Karnak Temple, Luxor.

Avenue of the ram-headed sphinx, Luxor.

thought could protect their tombs from the robbers. The top of the hill nearest the valley looks like a pyramid. Time will permit you to visit just a few of the tombs. Notice some techniques used to confuse the tomb robbers and the way these tombs were prepared and decorated. The efforts made to preserve the royal tombs intact were for nought. All were robbed except that of King Tutankhamen. The debris left when an adjacent tomb was being prepared may have hidden the entrance to his tomb. The burial chambers are found at the end of a long, inclined corridor cut into the rock. Sometimes there are side rooms for storing goods or to confuse robbers. The decoration is primarily religious in theme and usually shows the king in the presence of the gods. Also, religious texts are illustrated in some tombs. The best preserved of the tombs is that of King Tut. Entering it usually requires a short wait and an extra fee. Tutankhamen's mummy rests in the tomb. All the other tombs are empty. Usually tourists visit three or four other pharonic tombs in the Valley of the Kings.

The **Colossi of Memnon**. These statues are all that remain of the funerary temple of Amenopis III (1417–1379 B.C.) who built the temple of Luxor to Amun. The Greeks gave these statues their current name. According to the *Iliad*, Memnon was the son of Aurora and Tithon who was king of Egypt and Ethiopia. He went to fight for Troy and was killed by Achilles. His mother Aurora asked Zeus to resurrect him once a day. The Greeks noticed that each morning these stones made noises and they concluded that these statues were of Memnon who was coming back to life in the morning. The cause of sound is the heating of the stone by the morning sun. As the stone warms in the morning sun, it vibrates, causing the sound.

Deir el-Bahri. This is the unfinished funerary temple of Hatshepsut (1503–1482 B.C.), the woman who ruled as a pharaoh. It hugs the rock cliff of the Valley. The temple's decorations depict Egypt's commercial and international relations during Hatshepsut's reign and describe her conception and birth as the daughter of Amun and her expedition to Punt. In the Christian era, it became a monastery. (*Deir* is the Arabic word for monastery.) This helped preserve the structure. It is currently under excavation and reconstruction.

Deir el-Medinah. This is the city of workers who built and maintained the monumental structures of the Valley of the Kings. These tombs of the lower classes mimicked the royal tombs though they are much smaller. One tomb that tourists regularly visit is that of **Senedjem**. The increase of light and moisture that comes with the visits of tourists are threatening the tombs. The government will have to take more aggressive and expensive restoration measures if the delicate tomb paintings will survive.

The **Ramesseum**. This is the funerary temple of Rameses II. On the inner face of the first pylon is depicted the battle of Kadesh. Rameses fought the Hittites there for control of Canaan. While the pylon's inscriptions depict a great Egyptian victory, the battle ended without a decisive victory for either side. In the second court of the temple is the head from a statue of a seated Rameses. According to some estimates the statue weighed one thousand tons.

The **Temples of the East Bank.** The temple to the south is the **Luxor Temple** built by Amenopis III around 1405 B.C. It is a place to celebrate creation and the fertility aspect of Amun. The image of Amun from the Karnak temple was carried in procession to the Luxor Temple during the second and third months of the Nile inundation to mate with the goddess Mut. The hierglyphs on the walls of the temple describe this procession and ritual mating. An avenue of ram-headed sphinx (the ram represents Amun) ran between the Luxor and Karnak temples. Akhnaton (Amenopis IV 1361–1340 B.C.) erased Amun's name from the inscriptions of the temple because he wanted Egypt to worship the Aten represented by the solar disc. Rameses II (1279–1212 B.C.) added pylons. The Greeks and Romans also added elements to the temple. During the Christian Era, it became a church. The apse of the church and some of the painted plaster on the walls are visible in front of the room for the cult statue of Amun built by Alexander the Great who is depicted in Egyptian costume on its walls.

Two and one-half miles north of the Luxor temple is the **Karnak Temple**. The area is a forty-acre complex of structures built over a long time principally to the Theban triad of Amun-Re (sun), Mut (cobra), and Khonsu (moon). Pharaoh Shoshenk I (the Shishak of 1 Kgs 14:25) inscribed the story of his victories in Palestine on the walls of this temple (c. 930 B.C.). He invaded Palestine during the reign of Rehoboam, the son and successor of Solomon. The temple was never completed as a look inside the outermost pylons makes clear. The story of the temple, its builders, and its religious significance is told during a sound and light show that is well worth a visit. If you wish to see the Karnak Sound and Light Show make certain that you make a reservation for a time when the presentation will be made in English since the show is presented in several languages on alternate evenings.

CHAPTER THIRTEEN

Greece

GENERAL INFORMATION

Travel Documents. Visitors from the United States and the European Union do not need a visa for stays shorter than three months. All others should inquire about visa requirements at a Greek Embassy before leaving for Greece.

Arrival. The airport at Athens is divided into two sections. All Olympic flights use the west terminal while all other airlines use the east terminal. From the Olympic terminal one can get connecting flights to the Greek islands. There is an airport bus that will take you to the city center for a reasonable fare. There are also taxis but one needs to be careful because drivers sometimes take advantage of tourists. Make certain you agree on a fare before you get into the taxi. You can find out the current fare to the city center at the information booth in the airport.

Currency. The currency in Greece is called the *drachma,* which is not divided into small units. All prices will be quoted in drachmas. It is very easy and convenient to change money in Greece. Banks maintain exchange services in the airports, tourist offices, and in some post offices. You may also change money at your hotel, but the rate will not be as favorable. Banks and other exchange facilities are not open on Sundays.

Postal Services. You can buy stamps for letters and postcards at your hotel. There are also post offices throughout Greece. In Athens, you can find post offices in both Omomia and Syntagma Squares.

AN OUTLINE OF GREEK HISTORY

Stone Age

Caves in the Louros Valley	40000 B.C.
Neolithic farming villages in Thessaly and Macedonia	6000 B.C.
Earliest settlement on the acropolis of Athens	3500 B.C.

Early Bronze Age	**2800–2000 B.C.**
Early Minoan culture (Crete)	c. 2600 B.C.
Invasion by Hellenes	2200 B.C.
Middle and Late Bronze Ages	**2000–1100 B.C.**
Invasion by Ionians	2000 B.C.
Minoan culture	2000–1400 B.C.
Mycenean (mainland) culture	1450–1200 B.C.
Unification of Attica under Athens	1259 B.C.
Dorian invasion	1200 B.C.
Dark Age following Dorian Invasion	1200–800 B.C.
Hellenic City-State	**1100–27 B.C.**
Geometric Period	900–725 B.C.
Archaic Period	800–500 B.C.
Solon's Laws; democracy in Athens	594 B.C.
Classical Period	500–338 B.C.
Battle of Marathon	490 B.C.
Sack of Athens by Persians	480 B.C.
Age of Pericles	461–429 B.C.
Peloponnesian War [Athens vs. Sparta]	431–404 B.C.
Plato	428–347 B.C.
Execution of Socrates	399 B.C.
Hellenistic Period	**338-146 B.C.**
Philip of Macedonia defeat Athens	338 B.C.
Death of Alexander the Great	323 B.C.
Greco-Roman Period	**27 B.C.–A.D. 330**
Achaea, a Roman Province; Athens, a free city	27 B.C.
Paul in Athens	A.D. 50
Hadrian rebuilds Athens	120–128
Early Christian (Bzyantine) Period	A.D. 300–600
Theodosius I bans Olympic Games	393
Edict of Theodosius II closing all temples	
or converting them to churches	429
Justinian closes schools of philosophy	529
Dark Age	650–850
Arab Invasion	early 600s
Athens breaks from the Latin Church and becomes	
dependent on Constantinople	733
Arab occupation of Crete	823
Iconoclastic movement	726–843
Parthenon becomes cathedral of the Abp of Athens	857
Middle Byzantine Period	850–1100
Liberation of Crete	961

Crusader Period	1200–1300
Sack of Constantinople [Fourth Crusade]	1204
Latin Kingdom	1204–1261
Late Byzantine Period	1300–1460
Turkish Period	1460–1830
Parthenon becomes a mosque	1546
Venetian Bombardment	
and explosion of the Parthenon	1687
War of Independence	1821–1830
Modern Greek State	
Greek Monarchy established	1833
First Modern Olympic Games in Athens	1896
Nazi Occupation	1941–1944
Greek Republic Proclaimed	1973

ANCIENT GREECE AND BIBLICAL STUDIES

Until the time Alexander the Great entered the territory of the former Israelite kingdoms, the Israelite region was oriented culturally and commercially to the East. Linguistically and culturally it was related to Mesopotamia. Akkadian and Hebrew are both Semitic languages. The influence of the mythological and sapiential literature of Mesopotamia on ancient Israel is well known. The trade routes that ran through Israel facilitated exchange between Egypt, Mesopotamia, and the East. From the eighth to the fourth centuries, Israel was politically dependent upon eastern empires: Assyria, Babylonia, and Persia. Alexander's victories at Issua in Asia Minor (333 B.C.) and Arbela (331 B.C.; see 1 Macc 1:1-4) led to a process of reorienting the lands of the eastern Mediterranean region to the West. This process is known as Hellenization.

At first glance, there appears precious little that the Greek and ancient Israelite cultures shared. The Greeks thought of the Persians as destroyers of civilization. The Bible looks upon them as great liberators and benefactors. Isaiah refers to Cyrus, the king of Persia, as "the champion of justice" (41:2), "my (God's) shepherd" (44:28), and "my (God's) messiah" (45:1). The Books of Ezra and Nehemiah speak about the Persian Empire's concern over the rebuilding of the Temple and the normalization of affairs in Jerusalem (See Ezra 1:1-4; Neh 2:1-9). For the Bible, Greek culture was the principal threat to the integrity and the very existence of Judaism (see 1 Maccabees). As Athens was experiencing a renaissance following the Persian wars, Judah was just about surviving as a subprovince of the Persian Empire. Judah's golden age was long past. Athens and Greece were headed for a new golden age under Alexander the Great. Jerusalem rebuilt its Temple in 539 under the sponsorship of the Persians. Those who remembered the Temple of Solomon regarded the Second Temple as "nothing" (See Hag 2:3). A century later, in 438, the Greeks completed the Parthenon whose beauty and architectural achievements still inspire wonder.

Alexander the Great was not averse to the cultures of the ancient Near East. He admired them. His dream was to unite the best features of the old cultures with the new (Greek). He advanced this project on several fronts. First in importance were the political and military fronts. The ancient world and the Greek world were united under one political system. This provided the setting for the unification of their cultures. Alexander also encouraged the members of his army to settle in the lands that they had conquered. This not only pacified those territories, but led to intermarriage that furthered the cultural interpenetration. On an institutional level, Alexander fostered the development of the *polis*, the self-governing city. Because such cities had political and economic advantages, people sought to have their cities achieve this status. But this required that the city be "refounded" by the addition of Greek cultural institutions like the theater, gymnasium, city council, and temple. These institutions were the practical and painless ways of disseminating Greek culture among the people of Palestine. The people of Jerusalem even sought the advantages of having their city achieve the status of a polis. In 180 B.C., the high priest Jason (note his Greek name) established Jerusalem as a polis and renamed the city "Antioch-in-Jerusalem" (see also 1 Macc 1:11-14). Finally, economic considerations served to advance Hellenization. Greek became the language of commerce. It is likely that many people in Palestine became bilingual. They spoke their native Semitic language, Aramaic, and the language of the Greeks who ruled their land. Of the one hundred sixty-eight second-century Jewish ossuaries with inscriptions, one hundred fourteen were inscribed in Greek. Jews began to charge interest on loans, which was contrary to tradition (Lev 25:35-36) but an acceptable Greek business practice.

Alexander was content to allow the Hellenization of Palestine to go ahead slowly, peacefully, but methodically. However, he died in 323 B.C. just ten years after his victory at Issus. His generals divided his empire among themselves. Judah came under the hegemony of Ptolemy who ruled from Egypt. The Hellenization of the Jews continued peacefully under the Ptolemies. The Jews took an interest in Greek ideas and culture. A large Jewish community developed in Alexandria, one of the largest Greek cities in the world. The religious needs of this community required the translation of the Hebrew Bible into Greek because many Jews of Alexandria no longer understood Hebrew. This is the origin of the *Septuagint* (c. 250 B.C.). The success of Hellenization among the Jewish community is evident from a book that found its way into the Septuagint: the Book of Wisdom. Written sometime in the first century B.C. in Greek, it combines the religious traditions of Judaism (see chaps. 11–15) with Greek literary style and motifs (see especially chaps. 1–5).

Seleucus, Alexander's general who ruled in Mesopotamia, always believed that the territory of Judah belonged to him rather than to Ptolemy. In 198 B.C., the Seleucid king Antiochus III wrested control of Judah from the Ptolemies. With his own appetite for conquest, Antiochus IV decided to take control of Egypt from the Ptolemies (1 Macc 1:16-19; Dan 11:25). A preliminary campaign was successful. To insure economic, political, and military support in Judah for his second Egyptian campaign (See Dan 11:29; 2 Macc 5:1, 11), Antiochus IV thought it wise to proscribe the practice of Judaism (1 Macc 1:20-62) and impose Greek religious practices upon the Jews. The great symbol of this foolish policy was the setting up of a statue of Zeus in the Temple—what the Bible calls "the abomination that makes [the Temple] desolate" (1 Macc 1:54; Dan 9:27; 11:31). After the Romans frustrated Antiochus' designs for Egyptian conquest, he turned his fury on Judah and Jerusalem (2 Macc 5:11-26).

Antiochus' actions provoked a revolt led by Mattathias and his sons, who were popularly known as the Maccabees ("the hammers"). Surprisingly, the Maccabees were able to defeat the Seleucid armies. First, they liberated Jerusalem and rededicated the Temple (1 Macc 4:26-61). Eventually, with the support of Rome and Sparta, they were able to reestablish Jewish rule first in Judah (1 Macc 14:16-49). Later the descendants of the Maccabees ruled over a larger part of the territories of the former Israelite kingdoms. In gratitude for their deliverance, the Jews proclaimed Judas Maccabee their "permanent ruler and high priest" (1 Macc 14:42). This was the origin of the Hasmonean dynasty, which derived its name from Hasmon, Mattathias' great-grandfather. This dynasty restored Jewish rule in Palestine from 142 to 63 B.C. Alexander Yannai (103–76 B.C.) also assumed the title of "king." This was the catalyst for opposition to the Hasmoneans, which became a Hellenistic dynasty (e.g., their coins had Greek inscriptions). Both the Pharisees and the Qumran community emerged as opponents to the Hasmoneans in the second century B.C. This opposition, however, was not able to dislodge the Hasmoneans until Herod did so by intrigue and murder. Herod continued the policy of Hellenization espoused by the Hasmoneans. His additions to Jerusalem (e.g., the theater) reinforced its Hellenistic character. He rebuilt the Temple of Jerusalem, in part, to assuage the feelings of his more conservative Jewish subjects. He built Caesarea Maritima as a totally Hellenistic city.

An intriguing question is to what extent was Jesus "Hellenized." Did Jesus, for example, speak Greek? First, no first-century Jew could help but be Hellenized to some extent. Second, Jesus grew up just a short distance from Sepphoris, a Hellenistic town built by Herod Antipas. It has a theater, and some students of the New Testament submit that Jesus' use of theatrical vocabulary suggests he was familiar with this Greek institution. (The word *hypocrite* [lit. mask-wearer] comes from the theater in which actors wore masks appropriate to their roles.) On the other hand, some hold that Jesus himself was anti-Hellenistic. He rejected the authority of the Hellenized Jewish religious leadership (Mark 8:15; 12:13; Luke 13:31-33) and died as a messianic revolutionary. Of course, the evangelists show that Jesus did not see himself as a militant revolutionary.

The Acts of the Apostles presents the origin of Hellenistic Christianity as a new moment in the life of the Church. The mission to the Greeks was not the result of careful planning, but was controversial and divisive. Some problems described in Paul's letters reflect tensions between the Jewish-Christian tradition and the Hellenistic-Christian mission. The development of this mission reflects a similar phenomenon in cults like that of Isis which tried to attract a following throughout the world. Still, there was not general acceptance of a mission to the Gentiles. Galatians describes a compromise in which Peter was to preach to the Jews and Paul to the Gentiles (Gal 2:8-9). One effect of this was to separate Jewish Christianity from Gentile Christianity. It was not long before Christianity became a predominantly Gentile religion, though there was a small number of Jewish Christians in Palestine.

ATHENS

"People of Athens, I see that in every respect you are very religious . . ."
(Acts 17:22).

Location. The name of the eastern part of central Greece is Attica. In the center of this region is the city of Athens. It is located on a large plain that is surrounded on three sides by mountains and on the fourth by the Saronic Gulf. East of Athens is the Hymettus mountain chain. To the northeast is Mount Pentelicus (the site of the quarry from which the Athenians took their marble, viz., Pentelic marble), to the north is Mount Parnes, and to the west is Mount Aegaleus. This mountain separates the Athenian Plain from that of Eleusis.

Getting Around in Athens. Many tourist hotels are located in the center of Athens. It is convenient to be within walking distance of the Acropolis, the Plaka (the old market), the National Museum, the Byzantine Museum, and other sites of interest. You can get a map of Athens and other information at the Government Tourist Office at 2 Karayeoryi Servias in the National Bank of Greece building in Syntagma Square. There is another office in the General Bank building at 1 Ermou St., also in Syntagma Square. Athens has a fine public transportation system, but if your hotel is in the center of the city, you will probably be able to walk to most sites of interest. There is a subway line that runs to Pireus, the port of Athens. You can catch ferries from Pireus to the Greek islands. There is a shortage of taxis in Athens. It is difficult to catch one on the street. If you have your hotel call for one, you will be charged extra for the pick up. Make certain you find out from your guide or from the concierge the approximate fare to the destination and pay only that amount.

City Center. Dominating the area is **Mount Lycabettos**, the highest peak in the Athens area. At the southern end of the **National Gardens** are the **Temple of the Olympian Zeus** and **Hadrian's Gate [Arch]**. The emperor Hadrian (117–138) built a new Athens just as he built a new city of Jerusalem.

The **Temple of Zeus**. Antiochus IV (the enemy of the Jews in Maccabees and Daniel) began the temple in the second century B.C. He never completed it and it remained unfinished until Hadrian completed it in A.D. 132. This temple is among the largest built in the Greco-Roman Period. It had one hundred four columns of the Corinthian order. They stood almost fifty-six feet high in a double row along the sides and a triple row in the back and front of the building, which measured 351 feet by 133 feet. Its cella had statues of both Zeus and Hadrian.

Hadrian's Gate. Though constructed as a Roman triumphal arch, this structure served as a gate leading to Hadrian's new Athens. It is made of Pentelic marble with Corinthian pilasters and columns. Above the arch and facing old

Athens, there is a frieze with the following inscription: "This is Athens, the former city of Theseus." On the other side, facing the Temple of Zeus, is another frieze with the following inscription: "This is the city of Hadrian, and not of Theseus." Hadrian called his new city: *Hadrianopolis* (the city of Hadrian) or *Novae Athenae* (New Athens). This new district covered a large area and consisted primarily of villas with large gardens.

Syntagma Square. At the northern end of the National Gardens stands the *Old Palace,* which now serves as the parliament building. Before it is a monument to those who fell in Greece's wars. Honor guards, known as *Evzone,* stand before the monument around the clock. On Sunday, members of the honor guard dress in colorful, traditional Greek military uniforms. The changing of the guard, which takes place hourly, is worth seeing. Across Amalias Street, west of the parliament building, is **Syntagma** (Constitution) **Square**. In the area around the square is one of Athens' principal upscale shopping areas. In Syntagma Square, you can find the Greek Tourist Office, banks, a post office, and several restaurants and pricey cafes.

Continuing north on Venizelou Street is the **Cathedral of St. Dionysus** (Denis). It serves the small Roman Catholic population of Greece. About ninety-seven percent of Greece's people belong to the Orthodox Church. You will see several Orthodox churches as you travel around the city. The monumental buildings north of the cathedral belong to the **University of Athens**. At the north end of the campus is the **National Library** of Greece.

Omonia Square. A fifteen-minute walk from Syntagma Square is Omonia Square which is surrounded by hotels, shops, banks, and restaurants. Here you will find the **Neon Cafeteria**. This is a convenient place for lunch. The selection is great and the prices are moderate compared to some tourist traps of the Plaka. Beneath the square is a subway that will take you to **Pireus**, the port of Athens, from which you can catch a ferry to the island of **Aegina**.

From Omonia Square, walk south on Athinas Street and you will arrive at the **Plaka**, one of the oldest sections of the city. It is now a tourist area with shops and restaurants that cater to the many tourists that visit Athens. West of the Plaka is Athens' **Flea Market** where Athenians shop. There are also shops for tourists but the souvenirs are not as upscale as in the Plaka.

Antiquities. Both the agora and the acropolis are archaeological parks. Entrance fees are required for both. Only licensed Greek guides can offer explanations here. Before your visit check with the tourist office or your hotel concierge about the hours that these sites are open as they are not open every day. The agora is spacious and one usually does not experience it as crowded. The acropolis is one of the world's most frequently visited sites and it can be very crowded at times. Be sure to wear a hat and sunglasses. Take some water.

The Agora and Acropolis. The Monastiraki district is at the edge of the Plaka and Flea Market. In this area is the last subway stop before the light rail train that goes to Pireus begins traveling above ground. It was during the excavation of the rail-bed for this light rail system that the ancient *agora* was discovered. It is interesting that the flea market of modern Athens is so close to its ancient counterpart.

Most of the archaeological sites in the agora and acropolis area were occupied over a long time. The structures that have survived or have been reconstructed do not always come from the same period. For example, the Temple of Hephaistos was built in the middle of the fifth century B.C. while the stoa of Attalus II date from the middle of the second century A.D. The most striking feature of the Acropolis is the Parthenon, a temple dedicated to Athena. It comes from the middle of the fifth century B.C. There was a temple to Athena on the acropolis from the Mycenaean Period (c. fourteenth century B.C.). Some buildings constructed in one period were enlarged or rebuilt in another. For example, the *bouleuterion* (city council chamber) was first built in 500 B.C. In the 300s B.C., a new building was erected over the old one. Archaeological sites can sometimes be confusing because of the remains that are visible from different periods. Your guide at each site will be able to date the structures you will see.

The **Agora** (L: forum; E: marketplace). From the fifteenth to the seventh centuries B.C., this area served as a cemetery. During the early part of the sixth century B.C., some shops went up north of the Areopagus hill. Over time, more shops were built. Since the market is a convenient gathering place, buildings for the civil administrators, theaters, and temples were erected here as well. The area also became the administrative and political center of Athens. The agora also had shrines to Apollo and Zeus. The order of a visit to the agora can vary. What follows is a description of some sites you can see.

On the *Kolonos Agoraios* hill overlooking the agora stands the **Temple of Hephaistos.** It is the best-preserved temple in Athens. Called the *Hephaisteion,* the temple of Athena and Hephaistos dates from 449 B.C. Metal workers built it to honor the patron deity of the city and the patron deity of their guild. During the Byzantine Period (seventh century A.D.), Christians used this temple as a church. At one time, it was identified as the sanctuary of Theseus because reliefs on a frieze about the columns depict the exploits of Theseus. It is, however, certain that this is the temple of Hephaistos that Pausanias (second century A.D.) describes as situated above the agora. The temple is built of Pentelic marble. The columns, which are of the Doric order, are not completely vertical but lean inward slightly to counteract the eye's perception that "sees" long straight lines as concave. Without this correction, you would "see" the columns as falling outward. Within the temple is the *cella,* which contained the statues of Athena and Hephaistos. The statues are lost, but the marble pedestal on which they stood has survived.

From the Kolonos Agoraios one can see a long, low hill to the southwest. This is the **Pynx,** which was the place where the assembly met after the establishment of democracy in Athens. Members of the assembly either stood or sat facing the **bema** or orator's podium. Today this hill is the place where visitors to the Acropolis Sound and Light Show sit. Below the temple is the **bouleuterion** (the city council chamber), built about 500 B.C. After the Peloponnesian War, another structure was built for the council's use. It was a great assembly hall with the seats arranged in a semicircle. West of the bouleuterion is the **tholos** (circle). Its circular shape gave rise to its popular name. Built in 465 B.C., it was a dining and rest hall for those who served on the council.

The agora was a place for statuary. Opposite the bouleuterion one can see foundations for the statues that honored the patrons of Attica's ten tribes, known as the **eponymous heroes**. The platform that rested on the foundations supported the statues. The sides of the platform served as the city's official "bulletin board." Here were posted indictments, draft notices, and proposed legislation. On the platform, there is an artist's rendition of the area when it was in use.

One of the agora's most impressive features is **Odeion of Agrippa** built in 15 B.C. Theatrical and musical productions took place here. It was made entirely of marble in the Corinthian style. Its auditorium held one thousand people. In the middle of the second century A.D., the roof collapsed. During the repairs, there were some modifications. For example, the seating capacity was reduced to five hundred. West of the Odeion was a building that housed Athens' inspectors of weights and measures. Here were kept the standard weights and measures that officials used to regulate those used by merchants in the market.

The most impressive of all structures on the agora is the **Stoa of Attalus**. King Attalus II of Pergamum in Western Asia Minor (Turkey) built a great stoa on the eastern side of the agora in the second century B.C. It was a two-story building that had forty-five Doric columns in the front and twenty-two Ionic columns in the interior. It was about three hundred and eighty feet long. It had twenty-one small rooms in the rear that were probably shops. This building has been reconstructed by the American archaeologists who excavated in the agora in the 1950s and 1960s. It houses a small museum that contains the small finds uncovered during the excavation. It is also a good place to rest before climbing up to the acropolis.

To reach the acropolis from the agora, you will walk up the **Panathenaic Way**. This was a processional road that ran diagonally across the agora up to the acropolis. This road was the site of the procession that took place during the Panathenaic Festival. The purpose of the festival was to present Athena with a new woolen garment that adorned her wooden statue, the Athena Polias, that stood on the acropolis. The garment was woven by the women of Athens and taken in procession from the city to the acropolis. The festival, which began in 556 B.C. and took place every four years, also included athletic contests. Winners received amphorae filled with oil and impressed with the figure of Athena.

Midway between the agora and the acropolis stands the **Areopagus** hill ("the hill of Ares"). On its summit met the Areopagus Council, the highest criminal court of the city. Later it became the seat of the city council. In the Roman Period, it was an area for public assembly. It was the scene of Paul's address to the Athenians (Acts 17:16-34). Here he tried to adopt his preaching style to fit the penchant of the Greeks for philosophizing. His failure led him to abandon such attempts and to preach Christ crucified (1 Cor 1:18-25). The text of Paul's speech is inscribed on a bronze plaque at the base of the Areopagus.

You can climb to the top of this low hill, but the climb is treacherous. You should have a good pair of walking shoes and a good sense of balance. The limestone has been buffed by the many tourists who walk up every day. This has made the hill slippery, especially when wet. The view from the top of the hill is exquisite, but be very careful as you walk up and down the hill.

The Acropolis ["Upper City"]. In the middle of the Athenian plain is a group of low hills, one of which is the Acropolis that is about two hundred ninety-two feet above the surrounding land. Its top is a level plateau measuring 878 feet by 507 feet. It is not the highest hill in Athens; Mount Lycabettos is higher. People lived on this hill in the Stone Age. Later a settlement was established below the hill. It grew into an unfortified town. In times of attack, people sought the safety of the hill, which was the seat of kings who dominated the region. This hill was the site of a sanctuary whose service was the responsibility of the royal family. When Athens became a democracy in 510 B.C., the acropolis was reserved for the gods. The palace became a sanctuary for Athena.

Athena became the patron deity of Athens after a dispute with Poseidon. Each offered the Athenians a gift. Poseidon's was a well of salt water from the depths of which one could hear the sound of the sea. Athena offered an olive tree. The Athenians took the olive tree and chose Athena as their deity. The Acropolis was the site of several temples to Athena, the **Parthenon** ([the temple of the] Virgin, i.e., Athena) is the one that has survived to this day. Its construction began in the latter part of the fifth century. Its foundations were laid and its columns were being set up when the Persians attacked Athens in 480 B.C.

Visitors enter the acropolis by a gate house called the **Propylaea**, originally built in 485 B.C. Be careful of the steps. They are steep and slippery. The Persians destroyed it and the Athenians rebuilt it in 437. Its construction was never completed. From inside the acropolis one can still see the projecting bosses used for holding the ropes used to hoist the stones into place. The actual gate to the acropolis was concealed by a monumental building that was intended to provide a magnificent entrance to the holy area. In antiquity many statues stood both outside and within the Propylaea. This monumental entrance does not face the façade of the Parthenon, which is slightly to the southeast. This allows one to have a view, not just of the front of the Parthenon, but of its entire northern side and provides a spectacular panorama. When the ancient Athenians walked through the Propylaea, they saw a twelve-foot high statue of Athena Promachos (the champion), the goddess of war.

To the south of the Propylaea is a small temple in honor of **Athena Nike** (Athena, the Victorious) built to commemorate the victory at Marathon over the Persians (490 B.C.). Its four columns are Ionic in style. Above the columns is a frieze depicting an assembly of the gods with Athena in the center. There are also scenes from the battle of Marathon. The frieze slabs on the east and north sides are originals; the others are castings made from the originals now in the British Museum.

After walking through the Propylaea, you will approach the **Parthenon**, the temple to Athena that Pericles had built in 447 B.C. After nine years' work, the building received its roof and the statue of Athena was placed in the *cella*. The entire building was completed in 432 B.C. It is made of Pentelic marble. It is built in the Doric style, having seventeen columns along its length and eight columns on its front and back sides. There are several temples in Greece that are larger, but the Parthenon is famous for its striking visual effect. This is due to its dominating location on the plateau, the sculptures on its exterior, and,

The Parthenon (upper photo); and the porch of *Korai*.

most importantly, the harmony and perfection of its architecture. Its columns incline slightly inward to achieve the effect of perfect perpendicularity. The corner columns are a little thicker than the others. This was necessary to insure that they would "look" like the others. Similarly, the steps leading up to the temple are concave to overcome the eye's tendency to see long straight lines as convex. Thus the steps "look" perfectly straight though they are not.

The friezes above the columns all depict battle scenes. Some are still *in situ*; others were removed by Lord Elgin in 1801 and are in the British Museum. The pediment on the east side of the temple depicted the birth of Athena from the head of Zeus. (The east side was the "front" of the Temple.) The pediment on the west displayed the conflict between Athena and Poseidon over Athens. (The western end of the temple was its treasury.) Inside the temple was a colossal statue called Athena Parthenos. Its core was wood, but plates of gold and ivory covered the wood. Its marble pedestal was almost ten feet high. The statue itself was about thirty-five feet high. Athena wore a helmet and held a spear and shield. The statue disappeared in antiquity but several ancient copies—one in the National Museum—and literary descriptions make it possible to have an idea of what it looked like.

After Christianity became the official religion of the empire, Byzantine authorities took Athena's statue to Constantinople (A.D. 426). Later they transformed her temple into a church (sixth century). When the Crusaders came, they converted the Parthenon to a Latin church in honor of St. Mary of Athens (1209). Finally, the Muslims made it into a mosque (1460).

The Greek government is still restoring the Parthenon. It was extensively damaged in 1687. The Turks to whose empire Greece then belonged used the Parthenon as an ammunition dump. A shell from Venetian artillery struck the building and caused extensive damage. The Greeks are also trying to regain the Elgin marbles from the British Museum to complete the restoration. Views of the Parthenon are partially obscured by construction equipment.

If you want to see a full-size replica of the Parthenon, including the statue of Athena, there is one in Nashville's Centennial Park near the campus of Vanderbilt University. A wooden replica was built for a fair, but it became such a popular attraction that instead of being torn down after the fair, it was replaced by a replica made of stone.

North of the Parthenon is the **Erechtheum**. After the Persian destruction, it was decided to build a new temple of Athena Polias (Athena of the city) to replace the one that had been in the center of the plateau. This new temple (dedicated in 407 B.C.) housed the old statue of Athena from the temple destroyed by the Persians. The building is in the Ionic order, but has an unusual design: it is a double temple. The eastern half is dedicated to Athena and served as the principal temple of the city. The Parthenon never served this purpose though it was a much larger building. The western half of the Erechtheum is about nine feet lower than the eastern half. Here several gods and heroes were worshiped: Erechteus, the mythological king of Athens, his brother Boutes, the gods Poseidon and Hephaistos.

The most striking architectural element of this building is found in the southwest corner known as the porch of the *Korai* (maidens). Six columns support the roof of the Korai porch. Unlike the others of the building, they are not of the Ionic order. The columns are statues of the *Korai* standing on a high balustrade. They wear the dress of typical Athenian women of the fifth century B.C. Their hair is beautifully arranged and hangs down their backs. On their heads, they bear a Doric capital. These columns are known as the caryatids. Other examples are found in Delphi. The museum on the acropolis has a caryatid on display so you can get a closer look. Chicago's Museum of Science and Industry imitates this architectural form in its building. The Turks used this temple as a harem.

To the southwest of the acropolis is the Hill of the Muses with its **Philopappus Monument**. The people of Athens built this monument in A.D. 116 to honor Gaius Julius Philopappus, a Syrian who was a benefactor of Athens. They also honored him with Athenian citizenship. On the face of the monument is a relief showing Philopappus when he became a Roman consul.

Below the southeast corner of the acropolis one can see the ruins of the **Theater of Dionysus**. In the sixth century B.C., there was a temple to Dionysus in this area. Among the rituals that honored this god were dances, choral song, and recitations. From these rituals Greek drama was born. The first play was written and acted by Thespis in 534 B.C. Not long afterward, the ground north of the temple was terraced for seating. At the base of the seating area was a circular area known as the orchestra. Here the actors and dancers performed. The theater was enlarged and modified over the centuries. Its capacity was about fifteen thousand. The first seats were for the priests of Dionysus and important public officials. Inscriptions still visible on some seats reserve them for the priests of various cults. The remains visible today are of the Roman Period theater. The Romans remodeled it by adding a wall between the orchestra and the seats to protect the audience during gladiatorial contests. They also modified the orchestra so that it could show mock naval battles.

This building located west of the Temple of Dionysus was a healing center, an **Asclepion** (Asclepius was a legendary healer). Originally the building had two stories. The lower story led to a spring where people seeking a cure were to bathe to purify themselves before entering the shrine proper, which was on the second story. There the proper sacrifices were offered to Asclepius and those seeking a cure were to sleep. During their dreams, the god instructed them about what had to be done to effect their healing.

The southwest slope of the acropolis is the site of another venue for the performing arts: the **Odeion of Herodes Atticus**. Born in Marathon in A.D. 101, Herodes Atticus was a wealthy person with political influence because he was related to the imperial family by marriage. He wished to make his name immortal by underwriting important building projects in Athens. For example, he repaired the stadium that was in great disrepair. It was located just east of the Temple of Zeus. Built in honor of Regilla, Atticus' wife, this odeion was another one of his donations to the city. Completed in A.D. 161, it was a typical Roman theater though it had a roof. Its core was made of rubble and brick and it was faced with marble slabs. There were thirty-three rows of seats divided into two tiers. Its capacity was about five thousand. Only the seats in the first row had backs. These were reserved for civic leaders. The orchestra was a little larger than a semicircle. Behind the stage was a two-story building that was about sixty-two feet high. The side of the building facing the audience had niches for statues. The odeion has been restored and is used for musical productions—in particular, Athens' summer music festival.

Before leaving the acropolis, be sure to visit the small **museum** that is at the east end. It opened in 1878. After World War II, the original building was taken down and a larger structure was put up to display architectural fragments from the acropolis. Walking through the museum helps one to see the development of Attic art from the sixth to the fourth centuries B.C. Among the more important items are the friezes that adorned the old Parthenon in the archaic style and the caryatids from the Erechtheion.

Walking down from the acropolis will bring one to the **Roman Forum,** the market of the Roman Period, and **Hadrian's Library**. It is east of the agora and west of the Plaka. The library was a large rectangular structure located in the Roman Forum. The entrance, decorated with Corinthian columns, led to a large courtyard with a small pool and garden in its center. The actual library was at the end of the structure. It had a large central room where the books were kept, and smaller rooms off to the side.

Other Tourist Sites. If you have time, you should consider visiting other sites that Athens has to offer. You can get more specific information about any of these from the Greek Tourist Office (ETO) in Syntagma Square. Here are other places you should visit: (1) The National Archaeological Museum (1 Tosita St.); a collection of sculpture and ceramics from Archaic to Hellenistic Periods; the Mycenean gold masks and Minoan frescoes from Santorini; (2) the Byzantine Museum (22 Leoforos Vassilisis Sofias) which houses icons from the ninth to the seventeenth centuries and has exhibits on the development of church interiors; (3) the Temple of Poseidon at Sunion (48 miles SE of Athens); especially beautiful at dusk; intercity buses from Athens are frequent; (4) a ferry ride and a day at the beach on Aegina; (5) shopping in the Plaka; (6) the National Gardens near Syntagma Square; (7) the funicular to the top of Mount Lycabettos; (8) the Classical Period cemetery of Kerameikos; (9) the Cycladic Museum; 4 Neophytou Douka.

CENTRAL GREECE

Delphi

"As we were going to the place of prayer, we met a slave girl with an oracular spirit, who used to bring a large profit to her owners through her fortune-telling" (Acts 16:16).

Location. Delphi is located on a terrace (1,950 feet above sea level) of the Phaedriades ("shining rocks") range that outlines Mount Parnassus (8,100 feet), the dominant peak in the region. Mountains surround Delphi on three sides. To the south, there is a deep ravine that goes down to the Gulf of Corinth, about eight miles away. Dense olive groves that reputedly produce the best olives in Greece cover the ravine.

Delphi and Divination. Delphi is best known as a cult center of the god Apollo. But Apollo was not the first god that people worshiped there. Preceding him was the goddess Ge or Gaia, the Earth goddess. Already during this time, there was an oracle here. Her sanctuary was a cave that she shared with a python that protected her shrine. To take control of the shrine Apollo had to kill the python. Homer calls Delphi "Pytho" after this dragon. Acts 16:16 speaks about a slave girl with "an oracular spirit." A more literal translation of the Greek would read "a spirit of pythons." Evidently, the python associated with Delphi became the symbol of mantic activity in Greece. The woman who gave the oracles was known as the "Pythia."

The name Delphi comes from the place's human master, a king named Delphos whom Apollo also defeated to take complete control of the area. Apollo then came to Delphi as an "immigrant." Some suggest that his cult originated among the Hittites and then spread to the Greeks in Asia Minor, who brought this god to the mainland. There were other threats to the hegemony of Apollo. One came from Heracles, who eventually received his own altar in Apollo's temple. The historical basis of this legend is the attempts of the Dorians to take control of the oracle since Heracles was the Dorians' principal hero. The Dorians had great influence in Delphi and often the oracles favored Sparta, the main Dorian city. Dionysus also challenged Apollo. Their conflict ended with an agreement that Dionysus would take over the sanctuary every year during the three winter months.

People also worshiped Athena at Delphi. Her sanctuary is on a terrace to the southeast and below that of Apollo, an area known as *Marmaria*. She was worshiped under the title of *Athena Pronaia*, i.e., Athena who lived "in front" of Apollo's temple. While the cult on Marmaria may go back to the Mycenean Period (fifteen–thirteen centuries B.C.), the oldest temple found dates to the seventh century. Another temple replaced it a century later. An earthquake damaged the sixth-century temple in 373 B.C. and it was never restored. The area also had two small treasuries, several altars, and shrines to military heroes of Delphi. Between the temple and the treasuries is a circular building, the *tholos*. It is one of Delphi's most beautiful structures. It was built in the fourth century B.C. of Pentelic marble, but its function is unknown. Several friezes adorn it.

The Antiquities. Your visit to the site should include a tour of the area sacred to Apollo and a visit to the museum that houses the more important artifacts found during the excavations.

The **Sacred Way.** Follow the path from the entrance to the site up to the Temple of Apollo. In antiquity this path was known as the Sacred Way and was occupied by smaller cult places, treasuries, monuments, and groups of statues from various periods from the sixth century B.C. to fourth century A.D. At the beginning of the walk up the Sacred Way, one can see evidence that Christians also used the site for their worship.

Treasuries. Along the Sacred Way, there are several small temple-like buildings. These are the treasuries of the shrine. Excavations have uncovered the foundations of eleven such buildings. These were storehouses for votive offerings made to Apollo and his shrine by the cities of Greece. Also, delegations from these cities used the treasuries to store their equipment and baggage when they visited the shrine. The oldest of these is the treasury of Corinth built in the seventh century B.C. Very little remains of it. The Athenians built their treasury in the sixth century B.C. After their victory over the Persians at Marathon in 490 B.C., the Athenians built a new treasury on the same site. So much of it survived that it was possible to reconstruct it at the beginning of this century. Inscriptions cover the walls of the Athenian treasury. The most famous of these are two second-century B.C. hymns to Apollo, complete with musical notation. These are on display in the museum. The treasury of the Cnidians (sixth century B.C.) had two caryatids instead of ordinary columns on the ends of the long walls. These caryatids are on display in the museum.

The **Halos**. Between the treasury of the Athenians and that of the Corinthians was the Halos or festival place where a dramatic performance in honor of Apollo took place every eight years. The play depicted Apollo's slaying of the python and his stay in Thessaly where he had to be purified before he could return to Delphi.

The **Bouleuterion**. Next to the Athenian treasury was the site of the council chamber of Delphi. It dates to the early part of the sixth century B.C. when Delphi gained its autonomy. Thirty men made up the council, which handled the city's ordinary affairs. The oracle was considered so important to the whole of Greece that its administration and that of Apollo's temple were in the hands of the twenty-four members of the Amphictyonic League that represented twelve city-states of Greece.

The **Omphalos.** Along the sacred way, you will see an egg-shaped stone, the surface of which was carved to look like a network of knotted woolen cords. It was a copy of another such stone that was in the temple itself. Another example is in the museum. The word *omphalos* means "navel." Apparently some ancients thought of Delphi as the "navel" or center of the world. Some suggest that the origin of the *omphalos* lies in the Babylonian *kudurru* stones that were placed in fields to show ownership, but this is not certain. Others contend that the shape of the omphalos suggests a beehive that the ancients believed to be a source of self-generating life. Ezekiel spoke of Jerusalem as the "navel of the earth" (38:12). Some medieval maps depict Jerusalem as the center of the then-known world. There is a small *omphalos* in the nave of the Greek Orthodox church in the Holy Sepulchre.

Retaining wall. Surrounding the temple area is a wall built of polygonal stones. From the second century B.C. to the first century A.D. this wall served as a public archive for legal documents inscribed on the polygons. Most of the inscriptions deal with freedom granted to slaves that was effected through a fictitious sale to Apollo. Some commentators see this familiar procedure for freeing slaves as background for 1 Cor 7:22-23 in which Paul reminds the Corinthians that they have been called to be slaves to Christ and that they "have been bought at a price."

The **Altar of the Chians.** Just before turning into the temple area, one can see the base of an altar built by people from the island of Chios in gratitude for the liberation of their island from the Persians in 449. An inscription here says that the people of Delphi gave the people from Chios the right of *promanteia*. This meant that anyone from Chios seeking an oracle had the right to ask before others could make this request.

The **Temple of Apollo.** The first stone temple on the site went up in the middle of the 600s B.C. There may have been earlier temples made of wood or mud brick, but no trace of these has survived. Fire destroyed the seventh-century temple in 548 B.C. A new and larger temple went up in 505 B.C. It was Doric in style with fifteen columns along its long sides and six along the front and back. It was about 195 feet by 78 feet. In 373 B.C. fire and an earthquake destroyed this temple. Work on the replacement started in 366, was interrupted between 356–346, and completed to the extent that the building was dedicated in 339 B.C. It was built in the same style and had the same dimensions as its immediate predecessor. The rubble caused by this earthquake buried a statue that has become identified with Delphi. Presumably it stood in front of the retaining wall before the earthquake. It was a bronze statue consisting of the chariot drawn by four horses, in which stood a charioteer. A prince from Syracuse named Polyzalus gave it to the shrine to celebrate his victory in the chariot races of the Pythian Games of 478 or 474 B.C. Only small portions of the horses have survived along with the 5-foot, 10-inch figure of the charioteer. He is dressed in the long Ionic tunic worn by charioteers of the day. In his outstretched right hand he holds the reins. His eyes are white enamel with a black stone serving as the pupil. This statue is the most prized possession of the museum. The temple and its terrace were adorned with several other statues. Many of these can be seen in the museum along with friezes from some buildings on the site.

In A.D. 390 the Byzantine Christian Emperor, Theodosius, ordered the temple to be closed. His son Arcadius had the temple torn down and the contents of the treasuries disbursed. The site was abandoned and its buildings were covered with soil eroded from the surrounding mountains. Eventually a village called Kastri arose directly above the ancient site. In 1860 when archaeological soundings in the area showed promise of an important find, this whole village had to be destroyed and its houses rebuilt about a mile west of the site. Two years later this was completed and systematic excavation by the French Archaeological School in Athens began. Some work at the site continues because this important site still yields significant finds.

The **Theater.** In the northwestern corner of the temple area is a flight of stairs that lead to the theater. The first theater on the site was built in the fourth century B.C., but had no seats. Members of the audience simply arranged themselves on the slope above the orchestra. The first theater built of stone dates from 160 B.C. and was sponsored by King Eumenes II of Pergamum. Nero had the theater reconstructed in A.D. 67. He had the orchestra paved with marble and he set up marble slabs to separate it from the audience. Domitian built an imperial box. The theater has thirty-five rows and seats about five thousand. The seating has been preserved almost intact. The stage building has not survived.

The **Stadium.** On a terrace up the hill from the temple is the site of the races that were part of the Pythian Games. The first stadium dates from the

400s B.C. It consisted of a running track bordered by an artificial earthen embankment used by spectators. In the second century A.D. a stone structure seating seven thousand was built by Herodes Atticus, who also built the odeion on the southwest slope of the acropolis in Athens. The entrance to the stadium is from the east. Seating takes up twelve tiers along the north side and six along the south. The running track is six hundred Roman feet [= five hundred eighty-two English feet]. Stones with grooves for the runners' toes mark the starting point. Another set of stones marks the finish line. The track is wide enough to accommodate at least seventeen competitors running abreast. The stadium has been well preserved except for the south side seats, some of which have eroded down the hill.

The Pythian Games originally took place every eight years, but then later every four years. The official prize was a laurel wreath, but often victorious athletes had statues set up in Delphi or their hometowns. The latter sometimes rewarded their victorious representatives with various financial privileges. Other athletic competitions took place at the hippodrome on the Plain of Crisa below the site. The games also included musical competitions. These were held at the theater.

The **Castalian Spring**. East of the shrine to Apollo is the spring of the Nymph Castalia. Water comes down a rocky slope and leads into a basin cut out of rock. The spring was a resting place for pilgrims after their difficult trip up to Delphi. Its waters are cold even in the summer. Those seeking an oracle had to bathe in waters from the spring to purify themselves before entering the sanctuary of Apollo.

The Oracle of Delphi. The shrine to Apollo was renowned throughout Greece because of the oracle associated with it. Originally oracles were given one day a year—on the anniversary of the oracle's establishment. Later oracles were given each month—except during the winter when Apollo was not in residence at the shrine. People from all over the Mediterranean region came here to seek guidance about the future. Those seeking oracles ranged from emperors to peasants. They all had to follow a precise procedure. First, they had to bathe in the waters of the Castalian Spring as a purification. Next, they had to make an offering on the altar of the Chians. The poor offered a goat or a sheep; the wealthy an ox, boar, or other large animal. The victim's entrails were examined and if they appeared normal, the person making the offering was allowed to go on to Apollo's temple. If the entrails showed some abnormality, the pilgrim could not enter. Priests interrogated him to learn what he did to render himself unfit. Unlike some other oracles, the Delphic or Pythian oracle discriminated on the basis of gender. Women were not admitted to the oracle, but had to ask their questions through men.

Those admitted to the shrine of Apollo first had to wait in an anteroom. Pilgrims who had the rights of *promanteia* (priority) went first to a room *(oikos)* inside the temple and next to the room *(adyton)* where the Pythia was seated and oracles given. A priest received those seeking an oracle and wrote their questions on a tablet. These were to be presented to the *Pythia*, the woman who delivered the oracle. The Pythia was a woman of mature age chosen from

Delphi. There were no special qualifications except that she was to have been born free. She did not have to be a virgin, but after her selection she lived celibately in a special building at Apollo's sanctuary. To prepare herself for consultation, she fasted and then bathed in the Castalian spring. She then chewed laurel leaves and inhaled smoke from burning laurel wood. Cicero (*De divinatione*, I:38) wrote that she gave her oracles in a trance induced from inhaling gases from a cleft inside the *adyton*. Excavation has revealed no such cleft or chasm in the area. The Pythia sat on a tripod and gave her oracles which were no more than incoherent mumblings that the priests of Apollo "interpreted." These interpretations were given in hexameters and later in simple prose.

Of course, the priests who gave the interpretations were aware of the political machinations in Greece and therefore their interpretations were "informed," enabling them to give a right response. In complicated cases, the response was expressed ambiguously so that any failure could be blamed on the inquirer's misinterpretation of the oracle. Still, the oracle of Delphi was the most popular of all in Greece and it was frequented until the rise of Christianity.

The Bible on Divination. The Bible forbade the type of divinatory technique represented by oracles such as that at Delphi. These compromised the freedom of God in the process of communicating with human beings. Deuteronomy (18:9-14) is quite explicit in its rejection of divination, i.e., the use of various techniques to facilitate communication with the divine. According to Deuteronomy, when God wishes to speak with Israel, God will raise up a "prophet like (Moses)" (18:15). Actually the Bible allows three techniques for divine-human communication. The first is a lot oracle. The assumption is that God controls how the lots fall. In the Old Testament, the lot oracle is known as the *urim* and *thummim*. An example of their use is found in 1 Sam 14:36-44. The material and shape of these objects and the precise way they were used are unknown. In the New Testament, Luke describes the selection of Matthias to take Judas' place as involving the use of lots (Acts 1:26). Another legitimate technique is dreams and their interpretation. Joseph wins his freedom from Egyptian prison because of his God-given talent to interpret dreams (Genesis 40–41). God appears to Solomon in a dream (1 Kgs 3:5-15) and grants him wisdom to rule Israel. In the New Testament, Matthew has the annunciation of Jesus' birth take place during a dream that Joseph had (1:20-24). The astrologers received a message not to return to Herod during a dream (Matt 2:12) and Joseph is told first to take the child to Egypt to escape Herod and then to return the child to Palestine after Herod's death during dreams (Matt 2:13, 19). Finally, visions are another appropriate way that God communicates with human beings. Isaiah has a vision during which he accepts his call to be a prophet (Isaiah 6) and Peter has a vision about the end of the laws of *kashrut* (Acts 10:9-16).

That divination was popular in ancient Israel is clear from archaeology. For example, clay models of livers have been found at some sites, including Hazor. These were used as guides in the examination of livers as a divinatory technique. It is also clear from Deuteronomy's own legislation that would be unnecessary were not divination so popular. The problem with divination, in Deuteronomy's view, is not that it is superstitious. Note that Deuteronomy never says that divination does not work—only that the Israelites are not to use it. The problem with divination is that associated with it were rituals that would change the divinity's mind if the oracle was unfavorable. These *apotropaic* rituals—the wearing of an amulet, the saying of a prayer, the offering of a sacrifice—were touted as having the power to repel the effects of a negative oracle. Obviously, such ideas, though popular, were not acceptable by the "official" version of ancient Israelite religion as represented in the Bible.

In the biblical process of divine-human communication, human beings are usually passive. It is God who takes the initiative by calling a prophet and giving that prophet a word of judgment or salvation to speak to Israel. In divination, like that represented by the oracle at Delphi, human beings took the initiative. The god spoke when called upon to do so by human beings who engaged in a carefully orchestrated procedure to learn their fate through communicating with Apollo through the Pythia.

The Monastery of Osios Loukas (St. Luke)

Near Delphi is the village of Dhistomo. In 1944 the Nazis killed two hundred eighteen villagers in reprisal for partisan activity. Six miles east of this village is the monastery of Osios Loukas (St. Luke). The monastery is on a hill that offers a commanding view of the countryside. The monastery is named for a tenth-century A.D. hermit. His family was from Aegina, but they settled in this region during the Moslem invasion of Greece. Emperor Romanos II founded the monastery in 961 in honor of Osios Loukas who foretold his liberation of Crete. This is a religious shrine and a monastery. Appropriate dress is necessary. No shorts. Women are to wear skirts, not slacks.

Antiquities. There are three structures to be seen here: two churches and a crypt. It is a good opportunity to become familiar with the interior architecture and art of Greek churches and the Byzantine liturgical and aesthetic traditions that these reflect. Over the years the buildings have suffered from earthquakes. The last major restoration took place from 1958 to 1960. Some mosaics were not completely restored.

The **Church of Osios Loukas** dates to 1020. The foundations of its walls are stone with brick and stone above. The western door opens on a narthex whose ceiling has mosaics of the apostles. Mosaics on the wall depict the washing of the disciples' feet (John 13), the crucifixion, and resurrection. The church is cruciform. The ikonostasis that separates the nave from the sanctuary contains some icons from the 1500s. A seventeenth-century earthquake damaged the dome. A painting has replaced the dome's original mosaic. Attached to the north transept of the main church is the smaller **Church of the Theotokos**. It is the church built by Romanos in 961. The tomb of Osios Loukas is in the **crypt** that is below the main church though the saint's body is found in a small chapel along the north side of the main church.

THE PELOPONNESE PENINSULA

A two-hour bus ride west of Athens will take you to the Peloponnese Peninsula. There are several sites worth a visit: Corinth, Isthmia, Cenchreae, and Mycenae. The first three have important connections with the ministry of St. Paul. Mycenae may have been the place from which the Sea Peoples, also known as the Philistines, departed for Egypt and then the southern coast of Canaan. The Philistines were ancient Israel's main rivals for control of Canaan.

Corinth

"After this, (Paul) left Athens and went to Corinth . . . Paul remained at Corinth for quite some time" (Acts 18:1, 18).

Location. Situated fifty miles west of Athens, Corinth is just a few miles beyond the isthmus that connects Attica, the central part of Greece, with the Peloponnese Peninsula.

Significance. In antiquity, the most important city of the peninsula was Sparta, though Corinth's location guaranteed its prosperity. It was a transportation and commercial hub, a natural link between East and West. Already an important trade center in the 700s B.C., Corinth's importance continued into the Christian Era. Paul spent more time here than he usually did in cities he visited in the course of his missionary journeys. Part of the reason for this departure from his usual method of operation was the proximity of the games, held every two years since the 500s B.C. in nearby Isthmia. These games contributed much to Corinth's fame and wealth. Paul's use of imagery as related to athletic competition in 1 Cor 9:24-27 was no doubt inspired by the games he probably witnessed.

Ancient Corinth had two seaports and a reputation to match. One port was on each side of the isthmus. *Lechaion* on the Gulf of Corinth was to the north. From there, ships traveled to western Greece and to Italy. *Cenchreae* on the Saronic Gulf was to the east. This port connected Corinth to Athens and the eastern Mediterranean. Cenchreae was also the site of an early Christian community. In his Letter to the Romans, Paul urges them to welcome Phoebe, the bearer of his letter to them. Paul informs the Romans that Phoebe was the deacon at Cenchreae (16:1-2). Phoebe is the only person with a ministerial title of a particular Church found in the New Testament. The proximity of the ports made Corinth the type of city that catered to traders and sailors who spent long and sometimes difficult times at sea. It was a place where they could release their tensions after long journeys and before having to put out to sea again.

The Romans destroyed Corinth in 146 B.C. to prevent it from interfering with their plans for the region. Corinth was a member of the Achaian League and though the Romans defeated this league, a prosperous Corinth could still cause problems. In 45 B.C., after Rome's position in Greece was secure, Julius Caesar rebuilt the city and made it the capital of the province of Achaia (central and southern Greece). The site you visit will be the Roman Corinth.

Acrocorinth ("the top of the mountain") overlooks the road from Lechaion to Corinth (upper photo); and the Temple of Apollo, Corinth.

The Romans built their city over the old Greek city. The temple of Aphrodite was on the mountain above known as *Acrocorinth* ("upper Corinth").

Paul and Corinth. Paul's usual *modus operandi* as a missionary was to spend about one or two months at a principal city in a region he wanted to evangelize. He went to the local synagogue and usually managed to gather a few followers, who became the nucleus of a new church. Paul charged the members of that new church with the evangelization of the surrounding region. The apostle then went on to another city. Why did Paul spend so little time in a particular place? Perhaps it was because he believed that the end of the age was coming quickly and he had to spread the gospel before it was too late (1 Cor 7:29-31; 1 Thess 4:15-17). He was also convinced that Jesus was the Savior of Gentiles as well as the Jews. This made the field of his endeavor the entire known world. At the end of his life, he was planning more journeys to even more distant places (Rom 15:22-24). To fulfill his mission Paul had to be careful with his time. He broke this pattern of short stays twice. He spent two years and three months at Ephesus (Acts 19:8-10) and eighteen months at Corinth (Acts 18:11). His stays at these cities accounted for half the time Paul was "on the road" as a missionary between A.D. 48 and 55. Why did Paul stay so long at Corinth?

First, Corinth was a hub-city of the Roman Empire. It was a funnel through which traffic between the eastern and western parts of the empire passed. This made it possible for Paul to stay in one place and still spread the gospel by speaking with people who were passing through the city from widely different regions of the Empire. Second, besides its commercial enterprises, the city attracted visitors for other reasons. Pilgrims came for healing at the city's Aesclepion and sometimes stayed for months waiting for a cure. The Isthmian games brought in people from all over the empire. While Paul was in Corinth in A.D. 51, the games were celebrated just ten miles away at the shrine of Poseidon. Third, Corinth was the capital of the Roman province of Achaia (southern Greece). Of course, Corinth's bad reputation was a challenge for Paul. The Greek verb *corinthiazesthai* meant "to live immorally." A woman of easy virtue was called a "Corinthian girl." To fuel all this activity, there were thirty-three wine shops along the south side of the Roman Forum alone. Some historians, however, regard Corinth's reputation for loose morals derived more from Athenians' jealousy of Corinth's ascendancy in the face of their own city's decline. The often quoted saying of Strabo, "Not for everyone is the voyage to Corinth," probably has less to do with warnings about the city's sexual climate than its business atmosphere. Strabo's proverb implies that the amateur has to be careful in the highly competitive Corinthian economic climate.

Despite its supposed reputation for loose living, Corinth's religious activity flourished. It was home to temples dedicated to Aphrodite, Apollo, Isis, and Octavia (the deified wife of Augustus). The Hellenistic mystery religions were popular in Corinth as well. Where else did challenge and opportunity like that presented by Corinth face Paul? Paul's ministry must have been effective because it aroused the more conservative among the Jewish religious community at Corinth. Luke describes the efforts of some religious people to co-opt the Romans into silencing Paul (See Acts 18:12-17). The almost comic scene narrated by Luke is important because it supplies a datum that has been crucial in developing a chronology of Paul's ministry. Paul's opponents brought him before Gallio, the Roman proconsul of Achaia. According to an inscription found at Delphi that dates Gallio's term of office, it is likely that Paul's stay at Corinth took place sometime in A.D. 51–52.

The Isthmian Games. The Isthmian Games were one of the four great Panhellenic festivals. It ranked below the Olympic Games but above those celebrated at Delphi and Nemea. The games, which included events for women, took place every two years in the spring. Most athletes were professionals who participated for the financial rewards, though occasionally amateurs won events. Paul's first sustained use of athletic metaphors occurs in 1 Cor 9:24-27. Note especially the incorruptible crown that is the reward of Christian virtue as compared to the corruptible crown that the victors at the games receive. Champions at Isthmia received a crown made from withered celery. Spectators from out of town stayed in tents and Paul was a tent maker (Acts 18:3). This afforded the apostle an opportunity to speak with people from all over the Roman world and spread the Good News. Did Paul himself attend the games? Palestinian Jews objected to these spectacles, but the attitude of Diaspora Jews like Paul was more open.

The Antiquities. The Erastus Inscription. Begin your visit by walking through part of the excavations that have not been developed for visits by tourists— across from the entrance to the developed site. Be careful because the footing can be tricky. Above all, stay off the balks and exposed walls in excavated areas. The excavated area reveals several private buildings, some of which show they were homes of wealthy people. Notice the mosaics on some floors. There is a wide pavement running through this area. At the north end of the pavement that was laid before the middle of the first century A.D. is an inscription carved into acrocorinthian limestone. It reads ERASTUS PRO AED(ilitate) S(ua) P(ecunia) STRAVIT [L: "Erastus laid (this pavement) at his own expense in return (for the office) of aedile."] The letters inscribed in the pavement were probably filled in with brass, which was removed by looters. In Rom 16:23, Paul mentions an Erastus. Since students of Paul suggest that the Letter to the Romans was written from Corinth, it is possible that the Erastus of Romans and the Erastus of the inscription are the same person.

Theaters. Walking back up from the site of the inscription toward the entrance to the site of Roman Corinth, you will pass two theaters. The smaller one is an **odeion** from the first century A.D.; the larger structure is a **theater** proper and dates to the fifth century B.C. You will see better preserved theaters elsewhere.

Museum. Near the entrance to the site is a small museum that contains some artifacts found during the excavations of Corinth. There are examples of ceramic materials from the Greek and Roman Periods and a fourth-century B.C. stone dining couch. In the courtyard are examples of some statuary that graced

Inscription of Erastus, Corinth.

the public areas of the city. There is also an architectural fragment with a menorah and an inscription from the town's synagogue. Most come from the Roman Period. There is a small room off the courtyard that contains some votive offerings left by those who were healed at Corinth's **Aesclepion**. Perhaps Paul had these votive offerings in mind when he used the analogy of many members making up one body when he spoke to the Corinthian Christians about dissensions within their community (1 Cor 12:12-26).

Just outside the museum are some architectural fragments that help illustrate the differences among the architectural orders that can be seen in Greco-Roman monumental buildings. South of the museum is the **Temple of Octavia**. To the north of the site and at its highest point is the **Temple of Apollo**. It dates from the sixth century B.C. The Romans spared it when they destroyed the city in the middle of the second century B.C. Notice its monolithic columns. This is a difficult and expensive way to make columns. Usually columns are made by placing "drums" one on top of the other and then smoothing out the seams between drums to make them look like monoliths.

The **Roman Forum**. Below the Temple of Apollo is the Roman Forum. Like the agora of Athens, this was both a market and a civic center. There were stoa on the west, south, and northwest sides of the forum, though these have not been preserved very well nor have any been reconstructed as in the agora in Athens. On the west side of the forum there stood several temples. These, too, are in a poor state of preservation. In front of the south stoa there was a row of shops. In the center of these are the remains of the **bema**, the rostrum for the Roman proconsul when he held public audiences. It was in front of this bema that Paul's "trial" before Gallio took place (Acts 18:12-17).

The forum was also the site of several **basilicas**. These were rectangular monumental buildings whose interior space was divided into a central nave and two side aisles by two rows of columns. Sometimes there was another row of columns in the front and rear of these buildings as well. The government built them for the use of the citizenry for the conduct of public and private business. They were convenient places to meet. The basilicas were used to shelter people from the elements as they conducted public and private business. They could also serve a variety of public purposes. There was a basilica behind the south stoa, at the eastern end of the forum, and along the west side of the Lechaion Road. In Israel, both Jews and Christians adopted the architectural form of the Greco-Roman basilica and modified it so that the resulting structure could serve as a place of worship. At the eastern end of the forum, just before the Julian basilica, there are starting posts for foot races. Apparently there was a stadium in the area before the Roman Period.

Water Installations. After viewing the forum, leave the site through the propylaea at the end of the Lechaion Road. Like the propylaea at the acropolis in Athens, this structure served as the grand entrance to the forum. Along the east side of the Lechaion Road are several water installations. At the south end is the fountain of Peirene, which the springs of Acrocorinth fed. North of this fountain are the baths of Eurycles with a well-preserved public toilet. Waters from the baths served to flush the toilets. As the name implies, the Lechaion Road continued north to connect Corinth with its port on the Gulf of Corinth. At the south end of the forum, near the city council chamber *(boule)*, was an exit to the Cenchreae Road that led to the port on the Saronic Gulf.

The Corinthian Canal. Only a short distance from the site of ancient Corinth is the Corinthian Canal. This artificial waterway connects the Saronic Gulf to the east with the Gulf of Corinth to the west. Ships that pass through this three and one-half mile canal dug out in the 1800s save the time and fuel that would be needed to go around the peninsula. There were several unsuccessful attempts in antiquity to cut a canal here. Nero's attempt was the most famous failure. Because there was no canal in antiquity, small ships would be dragged across the four-mile wide isthmus on carts down a road known as the *diolkos*. Using this road, captains could shave two hundred miles off the journey around the Peloponnese peninsula. Land travel was no real alternative because of the mountains of central and southern Greece. The sea and the *diolkos* were the way to go. On your way to Corinth, be sure to stop at the canal. You should be able to spot the ruts made by the *diolkos*. You may even see an ocean-going vessel passing through the canal.

Cenchreae

"I commend to you Phoebe our sister, who is [also] a minister of the church at Cenchreae" (Rom 16:1).

Not far from Corinth are the remains of the harbor at Cenchreae. It is mostly under water, but it has been excavated. At the top of the hill at the eastern end of the harbor stood the temple of Aphrodite. The eastern end of the harbor had warehouses. One of these was converted to a temple of Isis. Between these two areas were stores and other commercial buildings. A church was built over one of the warehouses in the sixth century and it is possible to see the remains of some of its walls. Unfortunately, the site has not been developed for tourism. Acts 18:18 notes that Paul left for Syria from this port. Priscilla and Aquila accompanied him. Luke also adds the curious detail about Paul shaving his head here in fulfillment of a vow. When the first leg of his trip ended, Paul found himself in Ephesus (Acts 18:19). This is also the place where the deacon Phoebe lived and ministered (Rom 16:1-2).

Isthmia

"Every athlete exercises discipline in every way. They do it to win a perishable crown, but we an imperishable one . . ." (1 Cor 9:25).

If your schedule and the museum's open hours allow, be sure to stop at a small museum near the site of the Isthmian Games. Excavations are in progress so it is impossible to visit the site. Still, the museum has a plan of Isthmia and some important artifacts uncovered during the archaeological work. The museum is a ten-minute drive from ancient Corinth. The prize given to victorious athletes at the Isthmian Games was a garland of wilted celery. The image of this "perishable crown" led St. Paul to speak of the "imperishable crown" that awaited believers who persevere.

Mycenae

Location. Mycenae is an ancient site in the Peloponnese Peninsula about twelve miles from the Aegean Sea. It is located in a mountain glen between Mount Ayious Ilias to the north and Mount Zara to the south. Mycenae shows the early function of the city: to provide protection for surrounding agricultural towns, to engage in commerce, and to provide judicial services. It was a fortified city with dependent villages in the valley below. Its acropolis housed the king whose responsibility it was to defend these villages, settle disputes, and secure the favor of the gods. Later in the Classical Period, the city would also take on the function of promoting the ideology of the culture through institutions like the gymnasium and theater that are lacking at Mycenae.

Myceneans and the Bible. It is likely the Mycenaeans were among the groups that formed the population the Bible knows as the *Philistines* and Egyptian texts call the *Sea Peoples*. This conclusion is supported by the presence of Mycenaean pottery found at most Late Bronze Age sites in Palestine. While some of it came into the region by way of commerce, a significant amount is local ware made in the Mycenaean style. Other features of their material culture show that the Late Bronze Age migrants into Palestine had a material culture similar to that of thirteenth-century B.C. migrant settlements in Cyprus, which historians call "Achaean." This has led to the suggestion that the Mycenaeans first migrated from the mainland of Greece to Cyprus and then from there to the eastern Mediterranean coast. With the late twelfth-century B.C. collapse of Egyptian power in Palestine, these European migrants sought to take control of Egypt for themselves. Rameses III repulsed them. He then hired them as mercenaries to protect his eastern flank and settled them along the southern coast of Palestine. Forty years later, they defeated Rameses VI and sought to replace Egypt as the dominant force in Canaan. Five cities in the south (Gaza, Ashkelon, Ashdod, Gath, and Ekron) were the base of their power. When they began moving inland, they met the Israelite tribes. At first, the Philistines were dominant. This led to the establishment of the monarchy under Saul, whom the Philistines defeated at Mount Gilboa (see 1 Samuel 31). David was, at first, a member of Saul's court. Later, after a falling out with Saul, David became a Philistine mercenary (see 1 Sam 27:1-6). After Saul's death, David turned on his Philistine masters, defeated them, and established his dynasty in Jerusalem (See 2 Sam 5:17-25; 6-12; 2 Sam 7:8-17).

History. The site was occupied by 6000 B.C. The presence of a spring made it attractive for settlement. The citadel was fortified between 2000 and 1600 B.C. At that time two sets of shaft tombs were cut into the summit. These were royal tombs and may show that there were rival dynasties here. The city was at the height of its power from 1650 to 1150 B.C. The Mycenaeans were the heirs of the Minoan culture of Crete. The decipherment of Linear B, a text in the Mycenaean language, has led scholars to identify Mycenae as the locus of the earliest Greek culture on the mainland. The Mycenaeans established settlements throughout the mainland of Greece, which they controlled for five hundred years. They derived their wealth from commerce (a Mycenaean trading center was found at Ugarit). They also served as mercenaries in Egypt. They helped the Egyptians expel the Hyksos. Since the Egyptians paid their mercenaries in gold, this may be the source of the abundance of gold found at Mycenae. Thirty-three pounds were found in the royal tombs on the citadel alone. In 1200 B.C. an earthquake and fire partially destroyed the city. Another fire on the acropolis fifty years later led the Mycenaeans to abandon their city. The Mycenaeans migrated to Cyprus, Anatolia, and Palestine. Mycenaean colonies in the Mediterranean region show a destruction c. 1300 B.C. and a second wave of disasters in 1100 B.C. The exact reason for the fall of Mycenaean hegemony is unknown.

Homer's Mycenae. Homer wrote in the Classical Period (fifth century B.C.). The Trojan War that was the subject of his *The Iliad* could not have occurred earlier than the thirteenth century. Archaeology has shown that the city of Troy fell twice during Mycenae's heyday. Also, there may have been an historical basis for what Homer wrote about Mycenae's rival dynasties, but these events occurred much earlier—at the latest in the sixteenth century B.C. According to Homer, the leader of the Greek federation that defeated Troy was a Mycenaean king named Agamemnon. In describing the Mycenaean kingdom, Homer paints a picture of treachery, improper marriages, and revenge. (It is reminiscent of the Succession Narrative of 2 Samuel 9–20 and 1 Kings 1–2.) According to Homer, the rivalry for the throne of Mycenae centered on two brothers. The king was Atreus whose bitter rival was his brother Thyestes. The king invited his brother to a banquet whose main course was Thyestes' children. When the latter found out that he had unwittingly eaten his own children, he cursed his brother Atreus and his family. This curse brought ruin to the house of Atreus in the next generation.

Atreus' son Agamemnon succeeded him. While the latter was occupied with the Trojan siege, his wife Klytemnestra took a lover named Aigistos. Aigistos killed Agamemnon after a banquet given to honor him. Together Aigistos and Klytemnestra ruled Mycenae in Agamemnon's place. Later Orestes, Agamemnon's son, killed his mother and her lover. The two sets of royal tombs on the citadel may be evidence for rival dynasties in the city. Still, these tombs date from at least three hundred years before the siege of Troy that Homer describes. The *Iliad* then telescopes characters and events from an earlier period of Mycenae's history to the period, at least three hundred years later, of the Trojan War.

Early Excavations. The site of Mycenae was first excavated by Heinrich Schliemann in 1874–76. He was sure that his excavations revealed the tombs of Agamemnon and the other characters of Homer's story. After all, his earlier discovery of Troy proved that it was no mythological city. When he discovered the royal tombs inside the city and came upon a golden death mask, he wrote: "I have seen the face of Agamemnon." A picture of the mask is on the ticket you will receive for admittance to the site. The original is in Athens' National Museum. Schliemann worked before the development of pottery typology and other dating techniques. It is clear now that the tombs he discovered belong to an earlier period of Mycenae's history—much before the period that was the setting for Homer's story.

Antiquities. The visitor to the site observes the **cyclopean walls** (1350 B.C.) that surrounded the city. The city was built on a hill between two ravines that make the western side of the city its only vulnerable point. The top of the western gate has the **lion sculpture** (1200 B.C.), which is the oldest piece of sculpture in Europe. A tower to the west of the lion gate commanded the approach to the city. It also looked down onto the right side (the side unprotected by a shield that was held by the left hand) of anyone approaching with hostile intent. Inside the gate are **two circular burial areas** used to inter members of the royal house of Mycenae. Here were found nineteen skeletons: eight adult males, nine adult females, and two children. That these tombs housed the remains of Mycenae's rulers is evident from other finds: jewelry, vases, and masks of gold. Further up the hill is a **palace** and above that is a **temple**.

West and south of the citadel are the **beehive tombs**. They derive their name because the tops of the tombs (visible on the surface) are shaped like beehives. These tombs also reflect Egyptian influence. They resemble the pyramid tombs with their street that connected the funerary temple with the pyramid itself. The entrance to the tombs was flanked by two columns. Above the entrance was a pyramid carved into stone. Historians of the Classical Period did not realize that they were tombs and thought that they were treasuries. Sometimes they are still called this. One tomb popular with tourist groups is known as the "Treasury of Atreus."

The walkway *(dromos)* to the tomb is one hundred eighteen feet long. Its doorway is 17 feet 8 inches by 8 feet 10 inches. The lintel is thirty-one feet by four feet. It weighs almost one hundred and twenty tons. The diameter of the tomb is forty-two feet while the height of the beehive is forty-six feet. The interior of the tomb consists of layers of stone blocks between three and six feet in length that were offset against one another. When the structure was complete, the inside of the beehive was trimmed. The top stone is not a key stone. It can be removed without threatening the stability of the structure. The beehive was a symbol of life after death. When the ancients saw bees emerging from the hive after winter, they believed that new life was created miraculously in the hive. Perhaps they believed that by putting their kings in a beehive tomb, they would one day emerge alive again. Note that the *omphalos,* the navel of the earth that was found at Delphi, also has a beehive shape and even an entrance for the bees.

NORTHERN GREECE

In antiquity, this region was known as Macedonia. It was the region where the gospel was first proclaimed in Europe. Following the breakup of Yugoslavia, the southernmost region of that country proclaimed its independence and called itself Macedonia. The Greek government bitterly opposed this since it saw in the use of this name an implicit claim to the northern province of Greece, also known as Macedonia. After an intensive political and public relations campaign, the Greek government seems to have accepted that its northern neighbor calls itself Macedonia.

Philippi

"Paul and Timothy, slaves of Christ Jesus, to all the holy ones in Christ Jesus who are in Philippi . . ." (Phil 1:1).

Location. In antiquity, this city guarded a gap between low hills and a marsh through which an important Roman road, the Via Agnate, had to pass. Later, this road grew in importance as a commercial link between the ports of the Adriatic coast and Byzantium, the eastern capital of the empire. Near the city were valuable agricultural plains and the gold deposits of Mount Pangaeus. It is in the northeast part of Greece—not far from the borders of Turkey and Bulgaria.

History. The city's original name was *Krenides* ("Fountains"). Colonists from Thasos, the northernmost of the Greek islands, founded the city in the sixth century B.C. Two hundred years later, Philip of Macedon captured the city and renamed it for himself. It was not an important city until the Romans built the Via Agnate, an important line of communication for their legions in Greece. This road passed through Philippi. The town is most famous for the battle that took place here in 42 B.C. between forces led by Brutus and Cassius, two of those responsible for the assassination of Julius Caesar in 44 B.C., and the armies of Octavian and Mark Anthony. The latter two were victorious. Brutus and Cassius committed suicide, thus ending any hope for the republic. Veterans from the victorious army refounded the town with the name *Colonia Julia Augusta Philippensis*.

According to Acts 16, Paul had a vision in which a Macedonian appeared to him, begging Paul for his help. This vision impelled Paul to begin evangelizing Europe. He left Asia Minor for Macedonia and landed at Philippi's port Neapolis, which is the modern Kavalla. From there he began his ministry in Europe. When local diviners considered Paul a threat to their economic well-being, they had him and Silas thrown into prison (Acts 16:9-40). The date of Paul's first visit to the city was probably A.D. 49. Six years later he visited the city again (Acts 20:6), but Acts does not elaborate on his second visit. Paul addressed one of the letters he wrote while under house arrest in Rome to the Philippians (Phil 1:7).

Christianity prospered in the city, which became a metropolitan see. Though the city was abandoned in the 900s A.D., the local archbishop continued to claim Philippi as his seat until it was finally transferred to Kavalla in 1924.

Antiquities. French archaeologists began excavating the city in the 1920s and work continues at the site. They uncovered two basilicas, the Roman Forum, an octagonal church, a palaestra, and a theater. There is also a museum on the site that houses some of the small finds.

The **forum** was a paved rectangular structure (275 feet by 139 feet) with stoa on three sides. Only the foundations survive to the present. Near the forum were fountains, monuments to leading citizens, two temples and a library. South of the forum is **"Basilica B."** The building collapsed during its sixth-century A.D. construction when the architect attempted to cover its eastern end with a cupola. The western end of the building was salvaged and a portion of its narthex was used as a church in the 900s.

East of the forum is an **octagonal church**. Excavation continues so a final report on the structure has not been published. The church was entered from the Via Agnate by way of a massive gate. There was also a baptistry connected with the church. Earlier there were two phases of occupation. There was a previous octagonal structure on the site and below that was a fourth-century basilica dedicated to St. Paul. Usually octagonal churches marked holy places. It may be that the site memorialized the place where Paul stayed while in Philippi.

North of the road that runs through the site is **"Basilica A."** It was built in the sixth century A.D. and ruined that same century by a massive earthquake. Its stones were reused for other structures built in the area. Before reaching the terrace on which the basilica was built there is a Roman Period crypt which popular belief remembered as Paul's prison. Frescos of scenes from Paul's life decorate the reused crypt.

West of the entrance to the forum is the **museum**. The first floor exhibits finds from Christian Philippi while the upper floor houses finds from the earlier periods. Outside the museum there is a path that leads to the **acropolis**.

The 860-foot walk brings you to three massive towers built in the Medieval Period on the foundations of the fourth-century B.C. walls. The climb to the acropolis affords those who make it a fine view of the ancient Roman remains below.

The **theater** that is built on the slope of the hill below the acropolis dates to the foundation of the city. It was remodeled in the Roman Period. In the third century A.D., it was renovated again to turn it into an arena.

Thessalonica

". . . when I was at Thessalonica you sent me something for my needs, not only once but more than once" (Phil 4:16).

Location. This is a port city that rises from the Bay of Salonika. It is shaped like an amphitheater carved from the slopes of Mount Khortiatis. The city's population of one-half million makes it much smaller than Athens but still the second largest city of Greece. Its modern Greek name is Thessaloniki.

History. There was a small, unimportant town named *Therme* in the area which was refounded by Kassandros in 316 B.C. and named after his wife, Thessaloniki, a sister of Alexander the Great. It became the capital of the Roman Province of Macedonia. It was a logical choice because of its location on the Bay of Salonika. Among its most famous inhabitants was Cicero, who spent part of his exile here in 58 B.C. After Pompey parted ways with Julius Caesar, he sought refuge here in 49 B.C. The city supported Octavian and Anthony against Brutus and Cassius in the Roman civil war that followed the assassination of Caesar. The defeat of the republicans worked to benefit the city.

After leaving Philippi, Paul arrived here in A.D. 50 (Acts 17:1-9). The Apostle wrote several letters to the Church here which the NT preserves as First and Second Thessalonians. During a third-century persecution of Christians in the city, a Roman officer named Demetrius was executed. He then became the city's patron saint. Emperor Theodosius (379–395) converted to Christianity here and in 380 issued the Edict of Thessalonica, which ended the toleration of ancient Roman religion favored by Julian the Apostate. He also condemned the Arian heresy. In 390 Theodosius massacred seven thousand people from Thessalonica because the city's military commander was lynched after failing to control his soldiers. St. Ambrose required the emperor to do public penance for this crime. Justinian liked the city and made it the second city of the Byzantine Empire. The two apostles of the Slavs, Sts. Cyril and Methodius, hailed from this city.

Over the centuries, its strategic position marked Thessalonika for unwelcome attention by the Saracens, Crusaders, contending claimants to the Byzantine throne, and the Turks. The city managed to survive each invasion. In 1492, it accepted about twenty thousand Jews who were expelled from Spain by Ferdinand and Isabella. By World War II, the Jewish population of the city rose to sixty thousand. Most were deported to death camps in Eastern Europe by the Nazis during their occupation of Greece.

Detail of the Arch of Galleries, Thessaloniki.

Visit. There are several archaeological sites in the city that are worth a visit. The first is the early fourth-century A.D. **palace of Galleries**, that housed the emperor who started the persecution in which Demetrius was martyred. Located on the Navarino Square, the excavations of the palace can be seen from several vantage points on the square. Notice the octagonal building that probably served as a throne room. The **Arch of Galleries** on Agnate Road was built in A.D. 304 to commemorate the emperor's victory over the Persians in 297. It was part of a larger complex that included a palace, hippodrome, and mausoleum. The **Rotunda** is the most conspicuous ancient monument in the city. It was originally designed to serve as the emperor's mausoleum and was converted to serve as a church and a mosque. It was damaged by an earthquake and is undergoing repairs. The **Roman Forum** and **odeion** can be found at Dikastiria Square, the city's central square. **Agios Dimitrios** is the largest church in Greece and dedicated to the city's patron. The original building dates to the 400s. It was destroyed by a fire in 1917 but rebuilt according to the original plans between 1926 and 1948. Located on Ermou Street, **Agios Sophia** is an eighth-century church that reflects the transition in ecclesiastical architecture from the basilical form to the cruciform church. The city's archaeological building is on Hanath Square and displays sculpture from the Archaic, Classical and Roman Periods.

CHAPTER FOURTEEN

Turkey

GENERAL INFORMATION

Travel Documents. Those who hold a United States passport need a visa to visit Turkey. It can be obtained in advance from Turkish Consulate General offices or at the port of entry into Turkey. In 1996, the fee for the visa was $20. Nationals of other countries should contact the Turkish embassy or consulate about visa requirements.

Arrival. Most international airlines have direct or connecting flights to İstanbul's Atatürk International Airport. Some airlines also have flights that land at Ankara or İzmir. When one combines a trip to Turkey with one to Greece, it is possible to take a ferry from several Greek islands to Kuşadası, a port city about eighteen miles from the site of ancient Ephesus. It is also possible to take a train to İstanbul from Athens and other points in Europe.

Currency. Turkish currency is called the Turkish Lira (TL). Most banks will exchange traveler's checks and foreign currency for lira. Banks also maintain special offices in tourist centers to serve visitors. If you come from Greece and have drachma, note that Turkish banks are reluctant to accept Greek currency. This is probably part of the fallout from the animosity that exists between Greece and Turkey. This long-standing feud is currently being stoked by the strife between ethnic Turks and Greeks in Cyprus.

Postal and Telephone Services. You can find post offices in Turkey by looking for a sign with the letters PTT printed in black on a yellow background. These offices are open seven days a week. Besides the usual postal services, these offices will change currency or traveler's checks. One can also make international telephone calls from most post offices.

Health Matters. Special health precautions are usually not required, but there are sometimes problems in central or eastern Turkey that make some inoculations prudent. Check with your physician before you leave. Drinking water is chlorinated throughout the country but the distribution system sometimes causes problems. It is best to drink bottled water.

"The Center of World History." The Turkish Ministry of Tourism touts its country as the "Center of World History." The country's geographical position is one reason for this boast. It is located at a point where the continents of Europe, Asia, and Africa are closest to each other. Turkey straddles the point where Europe and Asia meet though only three percent of its vast area is in Europe. The Asian portion of Turkey is known as Anatolia. The country is roughly rectangular in shape and covers three hundred thousand square miles, 930 miles east to west and between 310 to 370 miles north to south. More than two-thirds of its borders are coastline. Turkey has land borders with Greece, Bulgaria, Georgia, Armenia, Iran, Iraq, and Syria.

Turkey is a parliamentary democracy with a free market economy. It has a population of sixty million (1995), 98 percent of whom are Muslims. The Republic of Turkey was founded in 1923 as a secular state, though the wave of Islamic fundamentalism that is surging across the region has touched Turkey as well. The country has been politically and culturally oriented to the West since the founding of the republic. Currently, however, there is a political and cultural struggle going on. Some Muslims reject Western influence and want the country to reflect an Islamic culture.

Who are the Turks? Because most Turks are Muslims, some people confuse them with the Arabs. Turks are members of a great linguistic and cultural family whose original home was in central Asia where they converted to Islam. They first came to the Eastern Mediterranean region as mercenaries in the tenth century A.D. They found the climate in that region preferable to that of Central Asia and so they remained in the Middle East. Under the leadership of the Seljuk family, Turkish nomads expanded westward, taking what is now Iran, Iraq, and Azerbaijan. They continued westward into the Byzantine Empire. By the 1200s, Anatolia became Turkish. Still, many other peoples remained in the region including Greeks, Kurds, and Armenians. Many of these adopted the Turkish language and became Muslims. Because the Turks did not have a concept of race that excluded anyone, they accepted those people as Turks.

Mustafa Kemal Atatürk forged the identity of modern Turks when he founded the Turkish Republic following the fall of the Ottoman Empire. This new political entity was based on economic, social, and political reform that brought the Turks into the modern world. Traditional Muslim dress was banned and Western clothing styles appeared. The Turkish language was written with the Western alphabet—not the Arabic characters that were used previously. The country's legal system followed Western rather than Islamic models. All this served to change an entire culture.

Who are the Turks? They are descendants of nomads from Central Asia and other peoples who adopted Turkish culture and language. They do not come from a single ethnic group any more than do the people of the United States.

Still, the vast majority speak Turkish and identify with Turkish culture. The largest group of non-Turkish speakers is the Kurds who live in the southeast of the country.

AN OUTLINE OF TURKISH HISTORY

Prehistory

Cave dwellings and stone tools and weapons at Karain	10500–7000 B.C.
The beginnings of agriculture in Anatolia	7000 B.C.

The Bronze Age

First settlement of Troy	3000 B.C.
The Hittite settlement and Empire	1900–1180 B.C.
Migration of the Phrygians	1250 B.C.
Migration of Greeks to the Aegean coast	1100 B.C.
Homer born at Smyrna	700 B.C.
Presocratic philosophers of Ionia	500 B.C.

The Persian Period

Defeat of the Lydians by Persians	546 B.C.
Revolt against Persians fails and Miletus destroyed	500–494 B.C.
Defeat of Persians by Alexander the Great	334 B.C.

The Hellenistic Period

The rule of the Diadochoi (Alexander's successors) in Anatolia	323–281 B.C.
Seleucid rule	281–263 B.C.

The Roman Period

Romans declare Anatolia their province of Asia	129 B.C.
Paul's missionary journeys begin	A.D. 47
Split of Roman Empire into Eastern and Western halves with the eastern capital at Izmir (Nicomedeia) by Diocletian (284–305)	250
Constantine makes Byzantium capital of the Empire and renames it Constantinople (now Istanbul)	330

The Byzantine Period

Theodosius divides the empire again and makes Anatolia the eastern center	394
Rule of Basil II: the height of Byzantine Empire	1025
Seljuk Turks defeat the Byzantine army and begin settlement in Anatolia	1071
Destruction of Constantinople of the Crusaders and the establishment of a Latin Kingdom	1203
Constantinople reverts to Byzantine control	1261

Ottoman Period

Ottoman Turks take Constantinople
and rename it İstanbul   May 29, 1453
The reign of Suleiman the Magnificent   1520–1566
Crimean War   1853–1856
Defeat of Central Powers in World War I
ends the Ottoman Empire   1918

Modern Period

Republic of Turkey proclaimed   October 29, 1923
Turkey joins NATO   1952
Turkish troops enter Cyprus and occupy half the island   1974
Pope John Paul II visits Turkey   1979
New constitution   1982

Turkey and Archaeology. Archaeology as a modern academic discipline traces its origins to the excavation projects of Heinrich Schliemann (1822–1890) in Turkey. Schliemann was a very successful German businessman. After he amassed his fortune, he devoted himself to his real love: the study of Greek antiquity. When most scholars considered the literature of antiquity to be useless in reconstructing history, Schliemann was convinced that Homer's stories about Troy in the *Iliad* were historically reliable accounts of actual events. Schliemann studied Homer and surveyed the topography of western Turkey to find the probable location of ancient Troy. He anticipated the techniques of modern archaeology by doing surveys and probes before beginning full-scale excavation projects. To the surprise of the scholarly world, Schliemann did uncover an ancient site that he was able to identify as Troy. He also excavated Mycenae in Greece.

Many of Schliemann's historical reconstructions were inaccurate and his archaeological method has serious flaws by contemporary standards. In particular, he failed to properly record the progress of his excavations. What made Schliemann different was that he was more than a mere treasure hunter. He sought to use excavation to reconstruct history. Schliemann sent the artifacts he found to museums in Greece and Germany, totally neglecting those in Turkey. The Turkish government wants what Schliemann found in his excavations returned to Turkey, but the museums that hold these antiquities are unwilling to part with them. Turkey itself is not blameless in this regard. Hezekiah's tunnel was excavated while Palestine was part of the Ottoman Empire. The inscription found in the tunnel was removed from the tunnel and sent to Turkey. It is now in the archaeological museum in İstanbul. The same museum holds the Samaria ostraca.

Turkey and Biblical Studies. The territory of the modern state of Turkey was the heartland of the Hittite Empire. The Hittites were Indo-Europeans who migrated into Anatolia around 2000 B.C. and became one of the great powers of the ancient Near East. While the Hittite empire collapsed in the twelfth-century B.C., neo-Hittite kingdoms took its place until these were absorbed into the Assyrian Empire in eighth century B.C. The chief rival of the Hittite Empire for hegemony in the ancient Near East was Egypt. The two countries exhausted themselves in fighting each other before Rameses II of Egypt and Hattusilis III of the Hittite Empire concluded a treaty ending the attempts by both powers to achieve absolute control of the Eastern Mediterranean region. The vacuum of imperial power caused by this treaty allowed several national states, including Israel, to emerge in Canaan.

One particular Hittite literary form important for OT studies is the treaty form. Most scholars maintain that the OT covenant form reflects that of Late Bronze Age treaties. The best preserved of these is the Hittite treaty form. The large number of these treaties that have been preserved testifies to their importance in social and political life in the ancient Near East. They were instruments for the creation and regulation of relationships between different political and social groups. In the OT, ancient Near Eastern covenant forms and language became important metaphors for the relationship of God and Israel.

The word "Hittite(s)" occurs fifty-eight times in the OT. But it is clear that these references speak of two groups. One is a group of people who settled in Canaan before the Israelite tribes. These are the "children of Heth," e.g., Gen 10:15; 23:10. One of these was a soldier in David's army and the first husband of Bathsheba, Solomon's mother: Uriah, "the Hittite" (2 Samuel 11). These Hittites are mentioned in the lists of peoples who lived in Canaan before the rise of the Israelites, e.g., Deut 7:1. There are several references to "Hittites" who cannot be residents of Canaan. These are the Hittites of north Syria and Anatolia. The Bible sometimes refers to them as "men of Hatti." Unfortunately, English translations render both "the children of Heth" and "the men of Hatti" as "Hittites." The "men of Heth" may be related to Anatolian Hittites, who may have migrated into Canaan and settled there. Still, the terms usually translated as "Hittites" in the OT refer to two different groups.

This region is also of interest to students of the NT. The Acts of Apostles has Paul preaching extensively in several regions and cities of Anatolia or Asia Minor, as the Romans called it: Galatia (1 Cor 16:1; Gal 1:2), Pamphylia (Acts 13:13), Ephesus (Acts 18:19), Iconium (Acts 14:1), Lystra (Acts 14:8). These are just examples of the many places that Paul evangelized the Asia Minor. The seven churches of Rev 1:4–4:22, especially 1:11 were all in Anatolia. The coming of Christianity transformed Anatolia both religiously and politically. Constantine the Great established the capital of his Christian Empire in Byzantium, which he renamed Constantinople.

Note on Place Names. In the section that follows, some sites are mentioned in the Bible while others are not. The latter are included because they give visitors a good idea of the Greek and Roman cultural milieu in which Christianity arose. Also, they are often included in tourist itineraries—especially when visitors spend more than just a couple of days in Turkey. Sites that are mentioned in the Bible will be listed according to the Greek names rather than their modern Turkish names. The latter are given in parentheses. The names of sites not mentioned in the Bible will be given according to current usage.

İSTANBUL

Location. This city whose name means "city of Islam" is unique because it extends into two continents: Europe and Asia. Through the center of the city runs the Bosporus Strait. It is at the intersection of the land route from the Balkans to the Middle East and the sea route from the Mediterranean to the Black Sea. This has made İstanbul a most important commercial center.

History. In 667 B.C. a group of Athenian colonists settled in the region. They named their settlement "Byzantion" (L: Byzantium) in honor of Byzas, one of the first settlers. The Persians captured the settlement and ruled here from 512 to 478 B.C. after which the Greeks regained control. For the next two hundred years, Athens and Sparta took turns at controlling the city. In A.D. 330 Constantine the Great chose Byzantium as his capital and the city became known as Constantinople, i.e., "the city of Constantine." In 1054 Pope Leo IX excommunicated Michael Cerularius, the patriarch of Constantinople. He, in turn, excommunicated the pope. There was a short-lived reconciliation after the Council of Florence in 1452. But popular sentiment was against any accommodation with Rome. In 1965 Paul VI and Anthanagoros, the Ecumenical Patriarch, rescinded these excommunications, but the rift between East and West continues over the papal primacy. The Fourth Crusade never reached the Holy Land. Instead, the Crusaders sacked Constantinople in 1204 and set up a Latin kingdom that lasted for fifty-seven years. On May 29, 1453, the city fell to the Ottoman Turks, who renamed the city İstanbul. They converted Hagia Sophia, one of the greatest churches in the world, to a mosque, symbolizing their victory over the Christian Byzantine Empire. Today Hagia Sophia is a museum. Ankara superseded the city as Turkey's capital in 1923. Though like Turkey as a whole, the city is overwhelmingly Muslim, but it is the seat of the Ecumenical Patriarch (Greek Orthodox), an Armenian Orthodox patriarch, and a Roman Catholic archbishop.

Antiquities. The **Camlica Hill** on the city's Asia sides provides a panoramic view of the entire city. The city is home to several palaces the most famous of which is the **Topkapi**. The fifteenth-century complex of buildings and gardens was the first palace built by the Ottomans after they gained control of the city. (Open 9:30–5:00 daily except Tuesday.) Among the city's museums, the most important are the **Archaeological Museum** which displays artifacts from Anatolian civilizations dating back to the 500s B.C. (Open 9:30–5:00 daily except Monday) and the **Hagia Sophia (Aya Sofya) Museum**. Built in 535, this was the city's largest church. After the fall of Constantinople, it was converted to a mosque with the addition of the minarets. It no longer serves as a place of worship. (Open 9:30–4:30 daily except Monday). Those who admire Byzantine mosaics and frescoes will enjoy a visit to the **Kariye Museum**. Originally this was the Church of St. Savior and later a mosque. (Open 9:30–4:30 daily except Tuesdays). The **Blue Mosque** (Sultan Ahmet Camii Mosque) was built on the site of the Byzantine Period hippodrome and partly on the site of the imperial palace. The building is among the finest examples of Turkish architecture.

Mary, as depicted in a 12th c. mosaic, Hagia Sophia Museum, Istanbul.

AEGEAN COAST

Antioch in Pisidia (Yalvaç)

Name. There were several cities in the Eastern Mediterranean named "Antioch." These were cities built or hellenized by Seleucid kings. For example, when Antiochus IV made Jerusalem into a Hellenistic city, he called it "Antioch in Jerusalem." The two Antiochs that figure prominently in the NT are "Antiochus of Syria," located in Turkey on the Orontes River near the border with Syria, and "Antioch of Pisidia," located in south central Turkey.

Location. The archaeological remains of the ancient city are northeast of the town of Yalvaç in south central Turkey.

History. The ancient city dates to the third century B.C. but was an unimportant settlement until the Roman Period. Augustus settled veterans from his legions here in 25 B.C. The Romans beautified the city with buildings related to worship of the emperor. Acts 13 mentions that Paul visited the city. Some Pauline scholars hold that the place Paul visited in Acts 16:1-6 and 18:23 was also Antioch though the text does not name the city. Paul's first visit took place in A.D. 47. Pisidian Antioch was a logical stop for Paul whose goal was to visit the major cities of the empire before taking the gospel to Rome itself. Paul found this city attractive because it was settled by some of the leading Roman colonial families. The emperor Tiberius was once an honorary magistrate of the city. The city's fortunes waned in the seventh to eighth century A.D. under pressure from invading Arabs and Turks.

St. Paul in Antioch. Acts 13 depicts Paul preaching for the first time as a Christian missionary. Since he preached in the city's synagogue, he reminded his audience that Jesus was the son of David whose coming was the subject of prophecy. He describes the crucifixion and resurrection as the fulfillment of prophecy. The sermon was so effective that a large crowd of Jews and Gentiles assembled on the following Sabbath to hear Paul. His popularity turned the leaders of the Jewish community against him. What success Paul had is hard to measure since there is no archaeological trace of Christianity in Antioch until the fourth century A.D. There is, however, the apocryphal *Acts of Paul and Thecla,* which details the martyrdom of Thecla, one of Paul's converts from Antioch.

Visit. There is little visible on the site except for the foundations of a second-century A.D. **triple-arched gate**. Also visible are two **Byzantine basilicas,** one of which was a church. There is a small **museum** in Yalvaç that displays the small artifacts from the site.

Aphrodisias (Geyre)

Location. The ruins of Aphrodisias are fifty miles southwest of Denizli and just south of the village of Geyre. It is in a valley created by a tributary of the Meander River.

History. There has been human habitation here since the Chalcolithic Period (fourth millennium B.C.). In the Bronze Age (1200 B.C.), the city was known as Ninoe. The name derives from the Assyrian name for Ishtar, the goddess of love and war. The Greeks identified this Semitic goddess with their own Aphrodite so the town was renamed Aphrodisias during the Hellenistic Period, though it did have several other names earlier in the Greek Period. The city became the center of Aphrodite's cult. But it was in the Roman Period that the city reached the apex of its prosperity. The early Roman emperors were the city's patrons. Most of the archaeological remains come from the Roman Period. In the Byzantine Era, the city became the residence of a bishop and its name changed again. It was known as Caria from which the modern Turkish name is derived. The city declined along with the fortunes of the Byzantine emperors. By the fifteenth century, it was no more than a village. Excavations began in the 1930s, but since 1961, when American archaeologists took over, important progress has been made and the results have been near spectacular.

Visit. The **Sebastion** dates from the first half of the first century A.D. It was dedicated to Aphrodite and honored the imperial family, the principal members of which were deified. The structure consists of two parallel porticoes (220 feet long and 33 feet high) that flank a thirty-nine-foot pavement. The east end of the pavement leads to a Corinthian-style temple. The city's eight-thousand-seat **theater** dates from the first century B.C. and is well preserved. It was remodeled in the second century A.D. to accommodate the gladiatorial contests that Roman audiences loved. Also on the site are **baths,** the **Temple of Aphrodite** (first century B.C. to first century A.D.), the city's **stadium,** constructed in the first century A.D. with a capacity of thirty thousand, and a **tetrapylon,** which marked the city's main north-south street with a processional street that led to the Temple of Aphrodite. A **museum** holds some of the small finds from this very rich site.

Didyma

Location. From Miletus, the site of the sanctuary of Apollo Delphinios, there was a road called the *Sacred Way* that was twelve miles to Didyma, the site of another shrine to Apollo. The final section of this road was lined with statues that honored the priests and priestesses of Apollo. These statues are in the British Museum.

History. A shrine existed on this site before the arrival of the Greeks. When they arrived, they claimed the site for Apollo and an oracle, rivaling that in Delphi, was established here in the eighth century B.C. The shrine has an international reputation. The one biblical connection with the site occurred in the seventh century B.C. After the Pharaoh Neco defeated Josiah at Megiddo in 608 B.C. (see 2 Kgs 23:29-30), he sent a thanksgiving offering to this shrine. King Croesus of Lydia (560–546 B.C.) sent gold offering to both this shrine and the one at Delphi. When the Persians conquered Ionia in 494 B.C., they destroyed Didyma's shrine. Alexander the Great ordered another to be built and

Seleucus Nicator began the project. Visitors to the site see the remains of this Hellenistic temple. The Romans honored the shrine to Apollo but the Christians opposed it. In 385 Emperor Theodosius prohibited all divinitory practices. The temple was never completed though the cella was used as a church until the 1400s.

The Antiquities. Though the **temple to Apollo** was never finished, what remains is in good shape. Here visitors cannot only look at the temple from the outside, but they can also walk inside its precincts—something that most people in antiquity could not do. This was the third largest building erected in the Hellenistic Age. Only the temple of Artemis in Ephesus and that of Hera on Samos were larger.

There are forty columns in the platform in front of the temple's entrance. Several are not complete and one can surmise the process of erecting and finishing columns by examining the columns closely. Outside the temple on each side there were two rows of columns with nineteen columns in each row. There are also two rows of columns in the rear of the temple with ten columns in each row. A few have fallen because of earthquakes. One can enter the inside of the temple by one of two enclosed ramps. The oracle room was between these passageways. Opposite this was the *naiskos* or *adyton*, which was a small building that housed the statue of the Apollo. (It was the equivalent of the Holy of Holies in the Jerusalem Temple.) One can see the base of the walls plus a few courses of stone that stood on this base. The building does not have a roof.

Ephesus (Selçuk)

"While Apollos was in Corinth, Paul traveled through the interior of the country and came to Ephesus where he found some disciples" (Acts 19:1).

Location. Like most Greek colonies in Anatolia, Ephesus was found along the coast. It was situated at the point where the Cayster River entered the Aegean Sea. Because of the silting up of the river, the site of ancient Ephesus is now about twenty miles from the sea.

History. Evidence for the earliest occupation at the site is limited to some Mycenaean graves from the 1300s B.C. The first permanent settlement in this area was along the north slope of Mount Pion (northeast of the theater) by the Ionian Greeks in 1000 B.C. The Lydians under King Croesus destroyed the city in 550 B.C. The rebuilt city was on the plain near the Temple of Artemis. In 301 B.C. the site of the town was moved to the plain west of Mount Pion. This area was formed by the silting of the harbor. This is the same area of the Roman Period city. The city's era of greatest prosperity coincided with the rule of Augustus in Rome. It received the title "the First and Greatest Metropolis of Asia" and was revitalized with new construction. The city's fortunes began to suffer in the third century A.D. as the Parthians and Goths undermined

Roman hegemony. Also two severe earthquakes (fourth and seventh centuries) led to partial depopulation of the city. Though it survived, Ephesus' days of glory were in the past.

Paul and Ephesus. Paul left Corinth to visit Antioch (Acts 18:22). To reach Antioch he embarked at Cenchreae, Corinth's eastern port, for a direct route across the Aegean Sea to Ephesus. From there he continued to Antioch by land. During his short stay at Ephesus, Paul was impressed with the city and promised to return (Acts 18:21). He did return and stayed for thirty months (Acts 19:8-10). Why did Paul stay so long in this city when his usual practice was to remain in one place for only a month or two?

Ephesus held that same attraction for Paul as Corinth but to a greater degree. Its population of 250,000 placed it among the largest cities in the Roman world. It was the capital of the Roman Province of Asia, and was a commercial and banking center. Through it passed goods from the north and the east. Part of Ephesus' importance derived from its export of agricultural products that grew in the fertile Meander River Valley. The city was also an important pilgrimage center for the worship of the goddess Artemis (L: Diana). The temple built in her honor at Ephesus was one of the seven wonders of the ancient world.

Ephesus was a center of learning in the Greco-Roman world. The library of Celsus is testimony to that, but Ephesus' scholarly reputation is older than that second-century A.D. building. It was also home to some of the presocratic philosophers whose questioning about the "one and the many" began the metaphysical quest, and it was home to the historian Herodotus. Its location made it a meeting place for ideas from the East and the West. In contrast, it was also renowned for the superstitious. In antiquity, the expression "Ephesian books" referred to magical, occult, and superstitious texts. Luke notes that one reaction to Paul's preaching is that several Ephesians abandoned their magical practices and burnt their books whose value came to "fifty thousand silver pieces" (See Acts 19:13-19). Like Corinth, Ephesus presented Paul with a challenge and opportunity that he had to exploit.

Paul was not the first to bring Christianity to this city. He says that he opposed the Christians at Ephesus who did not believe in the resurrection (1 Cor 15:32). Luke says that when Paul came to Ephesus for a longer stay, "he found some disciples there though they had been baptized with the baptism of John" (Acts 19:1-17). It was Apollos who instructed the Ephesians in "the new way of the Lord," but Luke notes that he knew only of John's baptism (Acts 18:24-28). Priscilla and Aquila were the resident ministers of the city (Acts 18:19). In 1 Tim 1:3 the first task Paul gave to Timothy was to discourage idle religious speculation at Ephesus. Another early Christian minister at Ephesus was Onesiphorus (2 Tim 1:18). Paul implies that he wrote First Corinthians while in Ephesus (See 1 Cor 16:8-9). Some students of Paul suggest that the apostle wrote Philippians, Philemon, and possibly Galatians here as well.

John and Ephesus. The tomb of John on the Citadel attests to the popular association of the apostle John with this city. This also is the source of the association of Mary with Ephesus. John is identified with the "disciple whom Jesus loved" and to whom he entrusted the care of his mother (John 19:26-27). Mary's tomb is located in Ephesus as well. (Note: There are two places in Jerusalem that also claim to be the site of Mary's tomb.) This association is based not on evidence from the New Testament, but from second-century Christian writers who favor placing John in Ephesus at the close of his life. These same writers identify the apostle John as the author of the Book of Revelation as well as the Fourth Gospel and the Johannine letters.

Ephesus is one of the seven Churches of Asia that are specifically mentioned in the Book of Revelation. After commending the members of the Church of Ephesus for their patient endurance, the seer of Patmos calls them to repentance since he asserts that they have "turned aside from (their) early love" (Rev 2:1-7).

Judaism and Ephesus. Evidence for a thriving Judaism in Ephesus is evident from Jewish, Christian, and Roman literary sources. Josephus mentions Ephesus several times and the Book of Acts and some of Paul's letters attest to controversies between the Jews and Christians of the city. It is difficult to reconstruct the character of Judaism in Ephesus. No synagogue has been found and other material remains uncovered by archaeologists are minimal.

The Antiquities. There are three sites in the area of ancient Ephesus that merit a visit. The first is **the Greco-Roman city** and the **Church of Mary**. It is among the more spectacular and complex archaeological sites that you will visit. Responsibility for excavation of the site has been given to an archaeological team from Austria. (That is why many of the explanatory signs at the site are in German.) It will take two to three hours to complete the visit. Before setting out, it is imperative that you have a hat, water, and sunglasses. The reflected heat and glare from the ancient limestone structures can be a problem without these precautions. A second site is known as the **Citadel.** On its summit is the Church of St. John. The third site is Selçuk's **museum,** which houses the artifacts found during the excavations at Ephesus. The most important of these are the two statues of Artemis.

The **Roman City.** Visitors walk down an ancient street that seems cluttered with public buildings of all types. There are some private homes just above on the lower slopes of Mount Koressos. They have been excavated and show elaborate construction. They have courtyards with pools and fountains. Also evident are the sleeping quarters of the houses and their dining rooms. Their interiors, faced with marble and ornamented with mosaics, show that they were the homes of the wealthy. In the same area are a few shops. These homes were in use from the first to the sixth century A.D. These were open to the public once, but because of souvenir hunters who damaged the area, they have been closed. There is also some controversy about how the Austrian archaeologists reconstructed these buildings.

Near the entrance to the site, there is a **gymnasium**. While this served as a social and athletic center, it also was a locus for philosophical discussion. The gymnasium was an important element in any Hellenistic city. It was one avenue for socialization and the propagation of Hellenistic ideology. That is why First Maccabees considers the building of a gymnasium in Jerusalem as the work of "breakers of the law" (1:10-15). This book recognizes that the gymnasium was not simply a place for "working out"; it represented a genuine threat to Judaism for it led the Jews who frequented it to assimilate the Hellenistic culture it represented (e.g., see especially 1 Macc 1:15). In the Roman Period the gymnasium and baths were places for relaxation, entertainment, and education. Six baths and gymnasia have been uncovered at Ephesus: (1) the Harbor Baths and Gymnasium, (2) the Vaduz Gymnasium, (3) the Theater Gymnasium, (4) the Varius Baths, (5) the Scholastikia Baths, and (6) the East Gymnasium. A Roman bath contained several rooms: (1) the *caldarium* (hot water pool), (2) the *tepidarium* (warm water pool), (3) the *frigidarium* (cold water pool), (4) the *apodyterion* (the changing room), (5) the toilet, (6) *natatio* (swimming pool), and (7) *unctorium* (place for massage). The gymnasium was usually attached to the bath.

West of the gymnasium are the ruins of the **prytaneion**, which was the town hall of Ephesus. It was demolished in antiquity to provide stones for rebuilding the town's bathhouse. It was in the ruins of this building that the two statues of Artemis that can be seen in the museum near the site were found.

Another important feature of Hellenistic cities were places where theatrical and musical performances took place. Next to the prytaneion was the **odeion** of Ephesus. Odeia were structures with a relatively small seating capacity (1,400). Usually musical performances were given there. But the performances were not without their religious associations since the gods were usually honored—sometimes with a sacrifice—at the beginning of the performance.

Along Ephesus' main thoroughfare, you will see some of the city's public fountains and wells. Among the most impressive are the **nymphaeum** (second century A.D.) and the **Fountain of Trajan** (A.D. 110). Three aqueducts constructed by the Romans during the reign of Augustus fed these fountains. Before the aqueducts were built, the water requirements of the city were met by a nearby spring and cisterns.

On the south side of the street are the remains of several **Roman Period temples**. Several temples such as one in honor of Hadrian and another in honor of Domitian served the imperial cult at Ephesus. Other temples on the site served traditional Greek cults: a temple to Artemis (Diana), to Hestia (goddess of fire), Serapis (an Egyptian import; this temple was later adapted for use by Christians), and a temple to Zeus and the Cybele (the mother goddess).

The **Scholastikia baths** were built in the first or second century A.D. and remodeled in A.D. 400. Before their remodeling these baths had a brothel attached to them. One can still see directions cut into the pavement, steering customers to it. Their name derives from the name of the woman who sponsored their reconstruction.

Not far from the baths is the **Library of Celsus**, which is one of the visual highlights of a visit to Ephesus. Built between A.D. 110 and 135, the monumental character of the structure is still evident. Its facade (sixty-eight feet long and fifty-two feet high) is eighty percent original stone. It faces the east for

Façade of the Library of Celsus, Ephesus.

better lighting. The ground floor served as a reading room. The scrolls were kept in cabinets. Its collection was small by the standards of the day (fifteen thousand scrolls; the library at Alexandria had hundreds of thousands of scrolls). Tiberius Julius Aquila built the library in honor of his father, Tiberius Julius Celsus, who served as proconsul of Asia. Celsus' family paid not only for the construction of the library but supplied its operating budget. This budget included financing for annual choral performances to honor Celsus whose sarcophagus was under the apse of the building. By A.D. 400, it had been abandoned and was filled with debris. Its exterior served as a backdrop for a fountain built by the proconsul Stephanus.

Remains of the great Roman theater of Ephesus.

North of the library are the remains of the Hellenistic **agora** that served as a market through the Roman Period. It was close to the harbor and many shops. At the southern base of Mount Panion was the "State Agora" that served as the civic center of Ephesus. The Greeks built it, but the Romans remodeled it extensively. It is located across from the Odeion.

North of the library is the **theater** of Ephesus. It was begun in the Hellenistic Period, but completed only in the second century. It had a seating capacity of twenty-four thousand. Its acoustics are a marvel. A person on the stage can speak in normal tones and be heard by people sitting in the seats of the last row. It was extensively renovated in the Roman Period to have it serve Roman audiences. For example, the orchestra was enlarged to accommodate animal and gladiatorial fights. The theater served not only for artistic performances, but as a meeting place for the city assembly and for gatherings in times of crisis. Because Paul's preaching threatened one of the chief industries of Ephesus (making miniature shrines of Artemis), one of the craftsmen aroused the ire of the Ephesians. In their anger, they dragged two of Paul's co-workers into the theater. Paul wanted to go to them, but friends dissuaded him. Eventually the town clerk managed to quiet the crowd (Acts 19:23-40). There is no evidence that Paul preached in the theater. The only text that mentions Paul and the theater states that Paul did _not_ go there to preach or defend his associates (Acts 19:30). The theater is used for productions today. As of 1994, it has been closed for extensive repairs. Early in that year, a rock concert took place in the theater.

The combination of an oversold house and the loud music did some structural damage.

At the front of the theater begins the **Arkadiane**, a colonnaded street that went from the center of the city to the harbor. It was named after the Byzantine Emperor Arcadius (A.D. 395–408) who renovated it.

On the way to the parking lot of the site, there will be some washrooms on the left. A road next to these washrooms leads to the remains of the **Church of Mary**. The building was a second-century A.D. basilica that was transformed in the early Byzantine Period to a church. A baptistery was added to the structure at that time. In the apse of the church is a plaque commemorating the visit of Paul VI here in 1964. The Council of Ephesus took place here in 431. This Council condemned Nestorius, who claimed that the humanity and divinity of the Logos remained so distinct that Mary was the mother of Christ, but not of God. The Council proclaimed that Mary was the Mother of God by giving her the title *Theotokos* (God-bearer).

Also excavated are the Byzantine baths (sixth century), the stadium (first century A.D. and extensively renovated in A.D. 200–300), and the Vedius gymnasium (A.D. 150). These structures have not been prepared for visits by tourists. The archaeologists are currently reconstructing the buildings here and they may be integrated into the touristic site soon.

The Citadel. St. John's Church. A second-century tradition located the death of John in Ephesus. This church houses the tomb of the apostle. The first church on this site was built in the 300s. In A.D. 500, Justinian enlarged it. The church also has a baptistery with a small pool.

The **Temple of Artemis** (Artemision). From the area in front of St. John's church, one has a good view of the remains of the Artemision. The shrine to Artemis was in use for twelve hundred years and underwent many developments. The first shrine on this site was built in the 700s B.C. This building was destroyed and rebuilt. The rebuilding was completed in 550 B.C. The new temple was the largest structure in the Greek world. It was destroyed by fire in 356 B.C. on the very night Alexander the Great was born. Alexander ordered the temple rebuilt after he visited Ephesus in the early fourth century B.C. This building was four times larger than the Parthenon in Athens. The Goths destroyed it in A.D. 263 and rebuilt it only to be dismantled by Christians in the sixth century to provide stone for their churches. Some of its architectural fragments traveled as far as the church of Hagia Sophia in Constantinople and the church of St. Catherine of Alexandria in the Sinai. The fourth-century temple was 228 feet by 422 feet and contained 127 columns, each of which was six and one-half feet in diameter and sixty-five feet high. One column has been reconstructed to give visitors an idea of the size of the temple. The goddess who was worshiped here was the Greek Artemis who assimilated some characteristics of the pre-Ionian goddess, Cybele, the mother of the gods. The importance of this goddess to the Ephesians is clear from Acts 19:27-28, 34-35. The cult of Artemis satisfied both the social needs of the city and the piety of individuals. It did not focus on fertility and sexuality and there is no evidence that it involved sexual rituals.

Also visible from the area in front of St. John's Church is the **Isa Bey Mosque.** This Muslim place of prayer dates from the 1300s.

The Museum. The visit to Ephesus concludes with a stop at the local **museum** in Selçuk. Here two well-preserved statues of Artemis, found during the excavations, are on display. There are also other artifacts from the excavations at Ephesus.

Hieropolis (Pamukkale)

"Epaphras sends you greetings; he is one of you . . . always striving for you in his prayers . . . I [Paul] can testify that he works very hard for you and for those in Laodicea and those in Hierapolis" (Col 4:12-13).

Location. This site in western Anatolia is twelve miles north of the town of Denizli. Its Turkish name means "cotton castle." The name is a metaphor for the chalk terraces formed by the limestone-rich hot springs here. The water cascades down the hillside and forms what looks like a petrified waterfall. The warm (93° F) waters that fill the pools formed by the hardened limestone are said to alleviate rheumatism and various skin problems.

History. The town of Hieropolis dates to the second century B.C. and is named for Hiera, the mythological ancestor of the royal family of Pergamum. It was destroyed by an earthquake in A.D. 60 and rebuilt almost immediately. The town depended on the various components of the wool industry for its wealth. There was a large Jewish community in the town and Col 4:13 mentions the Christian community that probably developed out of it. Legend locates the martyrdom of the apostle Philip here in A.D. 80. The Emperor Justinian had the bishop of Hieropolis stamp out the remnants of Greco-Roman religion in 500. Many temples were destroyed and altars demolished. With the arrival of the Turks, the city was abandoned.

Visit. The remains of the ancient city spread out over a large area and some climbing is necessary to see the antiquities. A complete visit would take about four hours. At the southern end of the site is a **museum** near the **Roman baths.** Behind the museum is a sixth-century A.D. **basilica,** which served as the city's cathedral in the Byzantine Period. East of the basilica is the town's **cardo.** A small portion of this colonnaded street is visible. In the same area are the **Temple of Apollo** and the **Roman Theater.** A 700-foot climb up the hill to the southeast is the fifth-century **martyrion of St. Philip.** There are some large circular tombs in the northwest corner of the site.

Environs. About fifteen miles from Pamukkale and two and one-half miles from Honaz is the site of ancient **Colossae.** In antiquity both Hieropolis and Laodicea eclipsed it. There are few remains but the ancient city is remembered because of Paul's letter to the Christian community there. The double "s" in the city's name is a relic of a pre-Greek language so the town was probably settled before the Greeks arrived. It was known for its fine wool. By first century A.D., however, it was no longer an important city. Christianity came to Colossae through the efforts of Epaphras (Col 1:7), who was one of Paul's associates (Philemon 23). It is not certain that Paul ever visited the city. Its wool trade was taken away by Laodicea and it was damaged by earthquakes and ruined during the Arab and Turkish incursions in the region. By the ninth century A.D., the site was abandoned.

Also nearby is the site of ancient **Laodicea** (Rev 3:17). Most of the sites's architectural fragments were reused in later buildings and the site is not worth a visit. The city was a renovation project of Antiochus II (261–246 B.C.). He rebuilt an earlier Hellenistic settlement called Diospolis and renamed it after his wife Laodicea, though he divorced her shortly after completing the project. The city was in an ideal location. It was at the junction of roads that led to the Euphrates and Lydia on the north and the Aegean and Pamphylia on the south. Its main commercial enterprise was the wool industry. Laodicean wool was soft and black. Laodicea was also a source of an important medicine, "nard" (see Cant 1:12; 4:14; Mark 14:3; John 12:3). Epaphras was probably responsible for bringing Christianity here (see Col 4:12-13). Though the Book of Revelation condemns the city, it became an episcopal see and the site of a fourth-century council. The city never recovered from the effects of a fifth-century earthquake. A few Turks replaced the small Greek population in the 1100s and renamed the city Ladik. Eventually they abandoned the site and moved to nearby towns.

Miletus

"From Miletus [Paul] had the presbyters of the church at Ephesus summoned" (Acts 20:17).

Location. Miletus lies in the southwest corner of Turkey, five miles from the sea and thirty miles due south of Ephesus. In antiquity, like most other Greek settlements in Anatolia, Miletus was located along the coast. It was a peninsula with four harbors. By the fourth century A.D. the silting of the harbors by the River Meander ended their usefulness. The silting continues to the present.

History. According to ancient historians, Minoan Period immigrants from Crete founded Miletus. It became a Mycenean outpost when settled by these mainland Greeks in the fourteenth century B.C. Homer implies that Miletus fought against the Greeks during the Trojan War (c. 1250 B.C., see *Iliad*, 2.868ff). The Ionian Greeks went to Miletus in the tenth century B.C. and exploited its location along the sea. It became their most important city with colonies as far away as Egypt and the Black Sea. Miletus also controlled several offshore islands including Patmos. The level of Miletus' material culture at this time was high as shown by the pottery and sculpture found from the Ionian Period.

It was among the first cities in the ancient world to mint coins, and its alphabet was adopted universally by the Greeks. It was the home of the presocratic philosophers, Thales, Anaximander, and Anaximenes (sixth century B.C.). Another famous son of Miletus was Hippodamos (fifth century B.C.), the great city planner, who devised the grid-system that was used to plan cities like Priene. Miletus' main exports were wool and furniture. The Persians conquered Ionia in 546 B.C. Miletus led the Ionian cities in revolt against the Persians in 499 B.C. This led to the city's destruction. The city was rebuilt according to the Hippodamian grid, but it had lost its place of prominence to Ephesus. Miletus still was an important city with a population estimated at sixty thousand. Alexander captured the city in 334 B.C. and later it passed into the hands of the Romans. This city has three impressive agoras, four harbors, two important temples: one dedicated to Athena and the other to Apollo. A great gateway leading from the harbor was built near Apollo's temple just before Paul's arrival.

According to the NT, Paul stopped at this city twice. The first time receives a mention in Acts 20:15-17. It was at the conclusion of his third missionary journey. He bypassed Ephesus and stopped at Miletus to where he summoned the elders of the Church of Ephesus. He wanted to use Miletus' better harbor to find a ship that would take him quickly to Jerusalem for the feast of Pentecost. Second Timothy 4:20 also mentions Paul in Miletus, though this may not imply another trip.

The Antiquities. The site is currently under excavation and most of it is not available for viewing by tourists—except for the **theater** and **baths**. It is one of the best-preserved and most impressive Greek structures in Turkey. While a theater existed in Miletus from the Hellenistic Period, the structure that now stands is an extensive Roman Period reconstruction of the earlier edifice. The benefactor responsible for underwriting the reconstruction was Faustina, the wife of Marcus Aurelius (A.D. 161–180). She went to the city around A.D. 164 and was so impressed with it that she became a valuable benefactor. The seating capacity of the theater, which was built into the side of a hill, was fifteen thousand. In the fifth row of seats there is an inscription that has been read as "Place of the Jews, the so-called God-fearers." The New Testament used the expression *God-fearer* (e.g., Acts 10:1) to speak of a Gentile who was sympathetic to Judaism. The transcription of the inscription and its interpretation, however, are matters of some dispute.

From behind the theater it is possible to see some other structures that recent excavations have uncovered: the sanctuary of Apollo Delphinios (the dolphin was an animal sacred to Apollo), the city's **agoras** (the south **agora** was the largest in the Greek world, covering eight acres), and **bouleterion**. Another structure that can be visited is the **Faustina Baths**, which were also a donation from the wife of Marcus Aurelius. Southwest of the bath was the **stadium** that dates from the second century B.C. It is 627 feet long with a seating capacity of fifteen thousand. About 545 yards south of these structures is the beginning of the *Sacred Way*. This road connected Miletus' temple of Apollo and his temple in Didyma, ten miles away. It was the setting in the spring for processions between these two sanctuaries. It was paved during the reign of Trajan (98–117). This street is currently under excavation.

Pergamum (Bergama)

"To the angel of the church in Pergamum . . . I know that you live where Satan's throne is, and yet you hold fast to my name and have not denied your faith in me . . ." (Rev 2:12-13).

Location. Ninety miles north of İzmir, along Turkey's west coast, the modern city of Bergama lies directly above one of the most important cities of the Greco-Roman Period: Pergamum.

History. Greeks founded Pergamum in the eighth century B.C. The city became prominent following the death of Alexander the Great in 323 B.C. Pergamum was an important city in the territory ruled by Lysimachus, one of Alexander's generals (the Diadochoi) who carved up his empire among themselves. The city aligned itself with Rome against the Seleucid Empire in the second century B.C. and with Rome's victory, Pergamum was given control of some Seleucid territory. Attalus III (138–133 B.C.) bequeathed his kingdom to the Romans, whose control in the region had been growing. The city prospered under Roman rule. Among its most notable citizens was Galen, the physician (A.D. 129–220). Roman emperors were among his patients. The city began to decline in the first century A.D. It was damaged by an earthquake and this prevented it from competing successfully with commercial rivals in the region. "Satan's throne" spoken of in the Book of Revelation was probably the great altar of Zeus in the city's principal temple. It survived the judgment spoken of in Revelation and was the seat of a bishop during the Byzantine Period. Like the rest of the region, it suffered from the incursions of the Arabs and Turks. The latter took the city in the 1300s.

Antiquities. The German Archaeological Institute has been excavating the site since 1878. Unfortunately, the archaeological remains of ancient Pergamum are widely separated. Visiting them all requires about two days. Most visits are more limited. The **acropolis** is northeast of Bergama. Of particular interest on the acropolis are the **altar of Zeus and Athena** (third century B.C.) built to celebrate the city's victory over the Celts, the **upper agora,** the **Temple to Athena** and the **Hellenistic theater.** In the city of Bergama, one can find the **Kizil Avlu** (the Red Hall). The actual function of this huge structure is still a matter of debate. Some consider it to be a Roman Period library while most believe it to be a Roman Period temple, dedicated to the Egyptian gods Serapis, Harpocrates, and Isis. Worship of these gods was popular in the first centuries of the Christian Era. The temple complex includes places for ritual bathing and spaces for processions and assemblies. The city's **archaeological museum** exhibits finds from excavation in the area. Among the most impressive is the colossal statue of the Emperor Hadrian. To the west of Bergama, there is an **Aesceplion** that functioned during the Hellenistic and Roman Periods. Such healing centers were popular in the ancient world. The most famous was at Epidarus in Greece. There were similar centers in Corinth, Athens, and even Jerusalem. People who came to Pergamum's Asclepion came not only for healings but also had the opportunity to visit the city's theater and to engage in philosophical discussion here and other places in the city. During the Byzantine Era, a church was built on the temple to Asclepius.

Priene

Caution. Priene was built on a steep hill. The way up to the city is lined with the old pavers from the city that are in various sizes, shapes, and states of repair. It is not a long or difficult climb, but you will be more comfortable if you wear sturdy walking shoes rather than sandals or other footwear without much ankle support.

Location. This site is eighty miles south of İzmir, near Turkey's west coast. When this city was built in 350 B.C., it was much closer to the sea than it is now. Its harbor was called Naulochos. The silting caused by the River Meander led to the city's decline at the end of the Roman Period. The city was built on terraces carved into the side of Mount Mycale (Samsun Dağı).

History. It was first an Athenian colony and then passed to the control of Pergamum. It came into the Roman orbit in the middle of the second century B.C. The Romans made few alterations to the city except for the theater and some public buildings. Because the Meander silted up near Priene, the base of its wealth was gone and the city began to sink into decline during the Roman Period. It had its own bishop during the Byzantine Period so the city must still have had limited importance. It was abandoned sometime during the Ottoman Period.

Antiquities. Though this city is not mentioned in the Bible, it is worth visiting because it has all the typical features of a Hellenistic city on a smaller scale than one sees at Athens or Ephesus. Because the area has fewer visitors than those two cities, one can better appreciate the architecture of the monumental buildings. Also, the city was built according to the Hippodamian grid. Streets all meet each other at right angles. Although other cities in the ancient world were laid out in this pattern, Priene is the best surviving example.

Among the structures that you will visit is a small **theater** that was in use from the 300s B.C. It was remodeled three times. The archaeologists are restoring the structure behind the orchestra. South of the theater was the city's **gymnasium**. To the west of the gymnasium is the **Temple of Athena** that was considered an architectural model in its day. The city also has temples of Zeus, Olympias, Demeter, Cybele, Isis, Serapis, and Anubis. The latter three cults were imports from Egypt. The city's **bouleuterion** is among the best preserved from antiquity. One can see the seating (450 capacity) and the small altar in the center. A large portion of the site reveals private houses. One can also see the foundations of several **stoa** and two **agoras**, two **gymnasia**, and a **stadium**.

Sardis (Sartmustafa)

"To the angel of the church in Sardis . . . I know your works, that you have the reputation of being alive, but you are dead" (Rev 3:1-2).

Location. Some eighty-three miles inland from Ephesus and sixty miles from İzmir, the ruins of the ancient city are extensive and spread over a large area. The Greek and Lydian city lies west of the acropolis while the Roman city is on a terrace to the north.

History. In antiquity, this city was famous as the capital of the Lydia. The Lydians claimed to be descendants from the Assyrian sun god, which has led some to consider them to be a Semitic people. Their language is Indo-Germanic in origin, related to Phyrigan and Etruscan. In any case, they probably were invaders who took over an earlier Greek settlement of the Maeonians. Their empire lasted from 680 to 547 B.C. and all sorts of legends grew up around Lydia and its last king Croesus (560–547 B.C.). Croesus supposedly consulted the Delphic oracle when the Persians threatened his empire. The oracle responded in its usual ambiguous manner when it told Croesus that if he attacked Cyrus, the Persian, he would destroy a great empire. Croesus attacked but Cyrus defeated him. The oracle was correct. Croesus did destroy a great empire—his own. One of Croesus' achievements was the issuance of coins whose value was guaranteed by the state. The coins were made of electrum, an alloy of gold and silver. The Lydians then invested money, the basis of commerce from their time on. They also invented dice—a good way to separate people from their money.

The only explicit references to this city in the Bible are in the Book of Revelation (1:11; 3:1, 4). Still some biblical historians suggest that the Sepharad mentioned in Obadiah 20 was Sardis. (Medieval rabbinic tradition holds that Sepharad was Spain. Today the Sephardic Jews are those who are descendants of Jews who settled in Spain and were expelled in the fifteenth century A.D.). In any case, there was a significant Jewish community in Sardis. Both Josephus and archaeological remains testify to that.

The Persians incorporated Lydia into their state. Alexander the Great returned the region to the Greek orbit. In 133 B.C. the city came under the control of Rome. Sardis became a regional capital with many beautiful buildings. Despite its negative assessment in Revelation, the Christian community prospered and the city was the seat of a metropolitan bishop. The last bishop attested lived in the fourteenth century when the city slipped into obscurity.

Antiquities. The most impressive antiquity on the site is the **Temple of Artemis**. The temple that visitors see dates from the fourth century B.C. and replaced the earlier Lydian one that the Greeks destroyed. The temple is unusually large: 330 feet by 155 feet. Its interior space was divided into a nave with two aisles by two rows of twenty Ionic columns. There is another important third-century A.D. basilica that was transformed by the city's Jewish community into a place of worship. The existence of a synagogue in the center of the city attests to the standing of the Jews in the city. One can also visit the city's **gymnasium,**

theater, and **stadium,** which date from the Roman Period. The **agora** functioned from the eleventh to sixth century B.C.

Smyrna (İzmir)

*"To the angel of the church in Smyrna . . . I know your tribulation
and poverty, but you are rich . . ."* (Rev 2:8).

Location. Turkey's third largest city and second busiest port is found along the country's Aegean coast.

History. The city goes back to the third millennium B.C. In the Bronze Age, it was part of the Hittite Empire. During the Greek Period, it was among the most important cities of the Ionian Federation. When the Lydians conquered the city in the sixth century B.C., Smyrna experienced a serious decline and was an insignificant village until the fourth century B.C. when Alexander the Great had the city rebuilt. Smyrna flourished during the Roman Period, but the Ottoman Turks took the city in the fourteenth century. Though it has been devastated several times from earthquakes and fires, the city survived and was rebuilt. Its location insured its survival. The Greeks claimed the city after the fall of the Ottoman Empire in 1922, but the Turks were able to recapture it.

Antiquities. The **Archaeological Museum** houses artifacts found throughout the region, including Ephesus. Across the street is the **Ethnological Museum** which helps visitors appreciate Turkish culture as revealed through its handicrafts. In the city Basmahane district, one can see the remains of the Greco-Roman **agora.** On the summit of the Kadifedale hill stands a medieval castle that offers a spectacular **panoramic view** of the city, the harbor, and the surrounding hills. The Roman Catholic **Cathedral of St. John the Evangelist** dates from the nineteenth century and was financed in part by the people of Lyons, France.

THE MEDITERRANEAN COAST

Aspendos

Location. The site is about four miles from the modern village of Belkis.

History. It is likely that the city was founded by Greek migrants following the disruptions caused by the Trojan War. The name of the city is not Greek so it is probable that the Greeks simply took over an already existing city. In the sixth century B.C., the city fell to Cyrus the Persian. In 467 B.C., the Athenians took the city but they surrendered it to Sparta at the end of the Peloponnesian War in 404 B.C. The city welcomed Alexander the Great in 333 B.C. When the Romans took the city two hundred years later, it fell on hard times because the Romans neglected it until the time of the empire when the city enjoyed a revival. Most of the structures visible on the ancient site come from the Roman

Period. The city's wealth came from the grain produced in the region. While Aspendos continued to be important during the Byzantine Period, it never had its own bishop. The Turks conquered the city in the seventh century and abandoned it in the eighteenth century.

Antiquities. The antiquities are widely scattered on the site. The centerpiece is the fifteen-thousand-seat **theater,** the best-preserved from the Roman Period. It is still in use today. Its architect was Zeno who was commissioned by Marcus Aurelius (A.D. 161–180). Near the entrance to the site are substantial remains of a third-century A.D. Roman **bath** complex. Less well preserved is the **gymnasium** from the same period. One can also see the **agora** and a **basilica,** which was the city's administrative center. Just as impressive as the theater is the city's **aqueduct,** a portion of which is near the city's north gate. This great engineering accomplishment brought water from the Isaurian Mountains to the north.

Attalia (Antalya)

"After proclaiming the word at Perga they went down to Attalia" (Acts 14:25).

Location. A favorite with vacationers, Antalya is known as the "Turquoise Riviera." In antiquity the region was known as Pamphylia (see 1 Macc 15:23; Acts 2:10; 13:13; 14:24; 15:38; 27:5). The city is in the central area of Turkey's Mediterranean region. Its population (270,000) doubles during the tourist season.

History. Attalus II (160–139), king of Pergamum, founded this city and named it after himself. He needed an outlet to the Mediterranean, and Side, the only other port in the region, was protected by Rome. The Romans annexed this city late in the second century B.C. Paul visited the nearby Perga (Acts 13:13, 14; 14:25) and sailed to Antioch from Attalia. Apparently, though, Christianity did not take hold here since the city did not have its own bishop until the eleventh century. The emperor Hadrian came to the city in A.D. 130 and the arch commemorating that visit still stands. The Crusaders used the port to store supplies for their activities in Palestine. During World War I, the Ottomans ceded the city to Italy, but the Turks took the city back in 1921.

Antiquities. At the highest point of the old section of town is the **fluted minaret,** which dates to the 1200s A.D. and was built by the Seljuk Turks when they settled the region. **Hadrian's Gate** is a monument from an earlier period. The Romans built this triple-arched structure to commemorate the visit of the emperor Hadrian to the city in A.D. 130. The city's **archaeological museum** houses artifacts from the region with particular emphasis on statuary from the Roman Period. One can also see finds from the Karain Caves which illuminate the period of the earliest human occupation in Turkey. Also on display are the remains of St. Nicholas who was buried in nearby Demre. His tomb was robbed several times by the Crusaders so it is doubtful that what is on display are actually the saint's relics.

Iconium (Konya)

"In Iconium [Paul and Barnabas] entered the Jewish synagogue to-
gether and spoke in such a way that a great number of both Jews and
Greeks came to believe" (Acts 14:1).

Location. This city of over a half a million is in south central Anatolia, about
one hundred and seventy miles south of Ankara. It lies between the mountains
of Phrygia to the west and the plain of Lyonia to the south and east. The city
lies on a fertile plateau 3,770 feet above sea level. Its location on a road linking
Rome with Macedonia, Achaia, and the Middle East guaranteed that it would
be an important commercial center.

History. The city goes back to the third millennium B.C., which makes it one
of the oldest continuously inhabited cities of the world. The Seleucids who
ruled the city from the fourth century B.C. introduced Greek culture and language. Rome incorporated the city into its empire in 65 B.C. Paul's visit had a
great impact on the city as attested by Acts and by material remains that can
be seen in the museum. The second-century NT apocryphal text *The Acts of
Paul* is set in Iconium, though it offers more information about the ascetical
practices and enthusiasm of the century after Paul than about Paul's time. The
story centers on Thecla, a convert who asked Paul for baptism. In 235 a local
council was held here. From 1000 to 1300, Konya was the capital of the Seljuk
empire and was an important religious and cultural center. Marco Polo visited
the city and attested to the quality of its carpets. During the 1200s an order of
Islamic mystics popularly known as "the whirling Dervishes" were founded
here. The city suffered because of raids by Arabs from the seventh to the ninth
centuries. It prospered under Seljuk rule though the Crusaders controlled the
city briefly. The city became part of the Ottoman empire in the fourteenth century.

Antiquities. The city's **archaeological** museum houses finds from the region
and its collection of Roman sarcophagi is impressive (Daily except Monday;
9–5:30). The **Mevlana Museum** is part of a complex that contains the tomb of
Mevlana (Celaleddin Rumi, 1200–1273), a Sufi philosopher and theologian.
The word "Mevlana" is an honorific title meaning "Master." Mevlana taught
his disciples tolerance, love, and the quest for perfection. His son Veled founded
"the whirling Dervishes" who try to achieve ecstasy through dance. After
Atatürk secularized the country, the order was disbanded and their residence
was turned into this museum.

Perga (Perge)

". . . Paul and his companions set sail and arrived at Perga in
Pamphylia" (Acts 13:13).

Location. Perge is fifteen miles east of Antalya and was a river port on the
southern coast of Anatolia.

History. Like several other cities in the region, Greek migrants fleeing the disruption caused by the Trojan War founded the city. It is mentioned in a thirteenth-century B.C. Hittite treaty as Parha. The city came into its own after it welcomed Alexander the Great in 333 B.C. The Seleucid dynasty ruled the city after Alexander's death, but the Romans displaced them in 188 B.C. and gave the city to the king of Pergamum. In A.D. 43, the city was formally included in the Roman Empire. Paul and Barnabas visited the city. It was here that John Mark left their company and returned to Jerusalem (Acts 13:13). Later Barnabas suggested that Mark rejoin them. When Paul refused, they parted company (Acts 15:36-41). Bishops from this city attended the Councils of Nicea (325) and Ephesus (431). The city was devastated by Arab raids and was virtually abandoned by the seventh century, though there was a small Christian community here in the 1400s.

Antiquities. The city was famous for its temple to Artemis Pergaea, but excavators have not been able to locate it. They have uncovered the city's **Greco-Roman theater**, which was built against the hillside and has seating for fourteen thousand. Northeast of the theater is the **Roman stadium** built in the second century A.D. with seating for twelve thousand. Northeast of the stadium are the **baths** built during the reign of Hadrian, and a **nymphaeum** built by Septimus Severus (193–211). East of the baths is the fourth-century A.D. **agora**. In the agora, there are a small circular temple, colonnaded streets, and water-channels. There are paths that begin at the nymphaeum that lead to the city's **acropolis**. The remains here date from the Roman and Byzantine Periods, though it was occupied from the beginning of the city's history.

Side

Location. This city lies along Turkey's southern coast on a rocky peninsula that juts into the Gulf of Antalya. It forms part of the Turkish "Riviera."

History. In antiquity, people built their towns so that they could be defended easily. Often this meant building them on an "acropolis." Climbing up the slopes of a hillside made attack risky. Side offered settlers an alternative. This town was built on a narrow peninsula. Walls protected it from attack by land and sea. Its harbor offered an escape route if invaders breached the walls. Although Greek colonists settled here in the seventh century B.C., they could not impose the Greek language on the indigenous population. The language spoken at Side, which has yet to be deciphered, was Anatolian in origin. Greek did not replace it until the time of Alexander the Great. After Alexander's death, Side was first ruled by the Ptolemies. In 218 B.C. the Seleucids took it. It prospered because of its standing as a commercial center. It was also a center of culture and learning. The Romans took control of Side during their campaign to rid the area of pirates in the first century B.C. The Romans made the city the seat of their governor and beautified Side. Most of the antiquities that are visible today are remains from the Roman Period. Beginning in the 600s A.D., Arab raiders cost the city its prosperity. Occupation appears to have ended here after a series of earthquakes in the twelfth century.

Antiquities. Just outside the **north gate** of the city is a second-century A.D. **nymphaeum** that was fed by an **aqueduct** that brought water from the north. After entering the city by the north gate, one can see two **colonnaded streets**. The one that goes in a southwesterly direction leads to the city's **agora** at the center of which stood a **temple to Tyche**. Along the southwest side of the agora is the Roman **theater**. It had forty-nine rows that accommodated fifteen thousand people, making it the largest theater in Pamphylia. North of the agora were the **baths** that now house the local archaeological **museum**. South of the theater is the **state agora (Roman forum)**. Here the public business of the city was conducted. Near the city's harbor are two second-century A.D. **temples**. One was dedicated to Athena and the other to Apollo.

CENTRAL ANATOLIA

Ankara

Location. This city is situated in central Anatolia at the feet of the Pontus Mountains. The NT knows this region as Galatia. Its population is 2.6 million and it is the country's second largest city.

History. This is Turkey's capital. Though it has been continually inhabited from the Bronze Age, it was a small town until it became the capital of the newly created Turkish Republic in 1923. There was a town in the region during the Phrygian Period (thirteenth century B.C.). During the Persian Period, it was known as Ancyra. In the third century B.C., a Celtic tribe migrating from across the Dardanelles made this city their capital and called it Galatia. The Romans conquered this city in 189 B.C. Augustus renamed the city after himself, calling it Sebaste, which is Greek for Augustus. During the Byzantine Period it was the seat of an archbishop and the location of several local councils. It passed back and forth between Christians and Muslims until the Ottoman Turks secured the area. They called the city Engüriye which Europeans pronounced "Angora." After the demise of the Ottoman Empire, its original name reemerged.

Antiquities. Of most interest to visitors is the city's **Museum of Anatolian Civilizations** (also known as the Hittite Museum). It displays artifacts that detail the presence of the various cultures of Anatolia from the Hittite to the Ottoman. (Daily 9–5, except Monday). A most imposing structure is **Atatürk's mausoleum**. Completed in 1953, it reflects the attempt to fuse ancient and modern architectural styles. The building's art depicts the transition from the traditionalism of the Ottoman Period to the modern Turkey that Atatürk established. A small museum displays some of Atatürk's personal effects (Daily 9–12; 2–6). The **Ethnographic Museum** has an impressive collection of Turkish crafts that goes back to the time of the Seljuks (Daily 9–12:30; 1:30–5:30, except

Monday). The **Citadel** was probably built by the Galatians in the third century B.C. It served the Byzantine emperors when they were trying to hold off the Turkish incursions. One can browse through the old shops in the **Cikricila Yokusu** for examples of Turkish folk art.

Thyatira (Akhisar)

"To the angel of the church in Thyatira . . . I know your works, your love, faith, service and endurance, and that your last works are greater than the first" (Rev 2:18-19).

Location. The ancient city in Western Asia Minor was located in the plain of the Lycus River at the junction of roads that led to Lydia and Mysia. The remains of the ancient city are seven and one-half miles southeast of the central Anatolian town of Aksaray.

History. The material and literary remains of Thyatira are too few to allow a reconstruction of this town's history. The city seemed to have thrived from the second century B.C. until the third century A.D. It was an important center of the wool trade. Inscriptions list the names of several dyers and fullers in the city. Acts mentions Lydia of Thyatira as a trader in purple dye (16:14-15, 39). The references to the city in Revelation about the blazing eyes and brass feet of "the Son of God" (2:18) may be allusions to a statue of Apollo or Helius found on coins from the city.

Antiquities. There is little to attract visitors today. The antiquities date from the Byzantine Period. There is a **fortress** on top of the hill and several **monasteries** cut into the side of the hill. The eleventh-century A.D. **Church of the Bell** is also cut into rock. It has a triple apse and a two-story narthex.

Glossary

Anatolia. The Asian portion of the modern Republic of Turkey. It was one of the crossroads of the ancient Mediterranean world and had many historical and cultural connections with Syria-Palestine. It was the home of the Hittite Empire (second millennium B.C.). In the first millennium, the Greeks colonized it. The Romans knew it as *Asia Minor*. It was evangelized by the first Christians including Paul. The seven churches mentioned in Revelation were located here.

ark. The central cult object of a synagogue. Within it are kept Torah scrolls read during the service.

Asclepion. A shrine in honor of the deified Greek physician Asclepius. The original shrine was at Epidarus. Athens, Corinth, and Jerusalem had shrines as well. People, hoping for a healing, stayed for months at such a shrine which had rooms for ritual bathing, dining, and a dormitory for pilgrims. The healing usually took place while the pilgrims were asleep and dreamt of their cure. After receiving their healing, pilgrims left a votive offering at the shrine. Sometimes it was a ceramic model of the body part that was cured.

Ashkenazi. A Jew of Eastern European extraction.

ashlar. A building stone that has been worked with either a smooth or a bossed surface.

agora [G; L: forum]. The marketplace of a city. It was a place where people met to conduct all types of business. Besides being a commercial area, it served as a social and political center as well.

basilica. A Greco-Roman monumental building, rectangular in shape, whose interior space is divided into a central nave and two side aisles by two rows of columns. Sometimes there will be a row of columns along the back side or around all four sides. Both Jews and Christians used the basilica form in building their places of worship in Palestine.

bouleuterion. The city council chamber of a Hellenistic city. The name is derived from *boule*, the Greek word for city council.

cardo. The main north–south street of a Roman-Byzantine city. The word means "hinge."

caravansarei [A: khan]. An inn used by caravaners in antiquity. It was usually a two-story rectangular building with an open courtyard in the center. Pack animals (camels and donkeys) would be kept in the courtyard. Rooms on the first floor served to warehouse the goods carried by the animals, and the second-floor rooms sheltered the people. The best preserved examples of caravansarei are in Acco's old city.

caliph. The Muslim title given to the individual who claimed religious and political authority over the Islamic world. This title was abolished by the Turks after the demise of the Ottoman dynasty when Turkey became a secular state.

cartouche. An oval frame enclosing the hieroglyphs of Egyptian royal names.

casemate. A double wall. During peacetime, the space between the walls is used for housing or storage. During war, the space is filled with stone or other debris. A casemate wall stands up better to battering than a solid wall.

cella. The central room of a Greco-Roman temple in which the statue of the divinity was placed. It is equivalent to the Holy of Holies in the Temple of Jerusalem.

Decapolis (G: "Ten Towns"). A group of ten Hellenistic cities, most of which were on the east side of the Jordan River and the Sea of Galilee. Beth She³an (Scythopolis) was the one city west of the Jordan. Jesus visited the region of the Decapolis during his ministry (Matt 4:25; Mark 7:31).

decumanus. The principal east–west street in a Roman-Byzantine city.

ein or **en** [A: ain]. spring.

ethrog. A citrus fruit that looks like a large lime. During the Roman-Byzantine Period it was a Jewish religious symbol since it was taken to the synagogue during the Feast of Booths *(Sukkot)* in obedience to Lev 23:40.

Fatimid. An Arab dynasty whose capital was Cairo. Hakim the Mad, a Fatimid caliph, destroyed churches and forbade pilgrimages and thereby provoked the Crusades.

First Revolt. A Jewish revolution against Roman rule in Palestine that broke out in Caesarea in A.D. 67. It spread throughout Palestine. Josephus was a leader of Jewish forces in Galilee until he realized that the revolt was doomed. In A.D. 70 Jerusalem fell to the Romans, who destroyed the Temple.

First Temple Period. Roughly equivalent to the period of the monarchy. More strictly from the time of Solomon's building of the Temple (c. 960 B.C.) to its destruction by the Babylonians in 587 B.C.

frieze. An ornamental feature of monumental buildings from the Greco-Roman Period. These were reliefs found usually above the columns of these buildings. In Greek and Roman temples, friezes depicted the assembly of the gods, mythology connected with the god worshiped in the temple, or some historical event. The frieze of the synagogue of Capernaum depicted only floral and geometric patterns because of the prohibition of images.

glacis. A sloping extension to the outer wall of a city. It prevents undermining of the wall, and forces attackers to expose the entire body when storming the city.

Haram es-Sharif (A: The Noble Sanctuary). The Arabic name for the Temple Mount in Jerusalem. Here are located the Dome of the Rock (sometimes called the Mosque of Omar) and the Aksa Mosque.

haredi (pl: **haredim**) (H: "those who tremble"; see Isa 66:2, 5). Ultraorthodox Jews. The men wear black coats and hats. They have a strong presence in Jerusalem. The secular Jews resent the *haredi* attempts to force religious observance.

Hasmonean. The name of the dynasty of Jewish high priests and kings who were the descendants of the Maccabees. The name of the dynasty derives from Hasmoneus whom Josephus identifies as the grandfather of Mattathias, the first leader of the revolt against Seleucid rule in 167 B.C. Herod married into this family and then killed the last male Hasmonean so that he could claim the throne. Augustus recognized Herod as king in 33 B.C. and so the Herodian dynasty replaced the Hasmonean.

hippodrome (L: circus). A race course for chariots. Such an edifice was usually part of important Greco-Roman cities. Josephus asserts that there was one in Jerusalem though it has not been discovered by archaeologists. There was a hippodrome in Caesarea Maritima. The crusaders reused its seating to provide stones for their fortress. The foundations for the seats have been partially excavated. One can still see the obelisk that stood in the center of the structure.

in situ (L: "in place"). An archaeological formula which means that an artifact was found "in the place" where it was stood in antiquity.

Ionia. The Greek name of the central sector of Turkey's west coast. It was colonized by Greeks about 1000 B.C. It gave its name to an order of Greek architecture, the Ionic order which is simpler than the Corinthian but more elaborate than the Doric.

Josephus. A Jewish historian and apologist. He was a leader in the First Revolt against Rome, charged with the defense of Galilee. When he realized that Jewish resistance was futile, he went over to the Romans. He wrote several works [*A History of the Jews* and *The Jewish Wars*]. His intended audience was the Roman world and he tried to show that the

Jews were a noble people with a proud and honorable history. They were not revolutionary barbarians that Roman stereotype made them out to be.

kibbutz. A collective, agricultural settlement. Members own no personal property and contribute their work to the kibbutz, which provides for their needs.

khan. See **caravansarei.**

King's Highway. A commercial road that connected Egypt with the rest of the ancient Near East by passing through Damascus. It ran along the eastern edge of the Transjordanian highlands.

Kotel (H: wall). The name by which Israelis refer to the Western Wall. They eschew the term "Wailing Wall" as a remnant of a no-longer-relevant past.

lulab (H: palm branch). A Jewish religious symbol sometimes found on mosaics or on stone decorations of synagogues. The lulab in those contexts will depict the palm branch bound with myrtle and willow branches. These were brought to the synagogue during the Feast of Booths *(Sukkot)* in accordance with Lev 24:40.

Mamlukes. Turkish slaves *(mamluk* means "owned") who turned themselves into an army. They ended Ayubid rule in 1250. Their sultan was Baibars (1260–1277). His successor, al-Ashraf Khalil, took Acre in 1291 and ended Crusader rule in Palestine.

menorah. The seven-branched candlestick that was an element of the Temple. It became an important Jewish religious symbol and now serves as the symbol of the State of Israel. The eight-branched candlestick is more properly called a *hannukiah* since it is used for the eight nights of the Hannukah Festival.

mikveh (H: pl: mikveot). A Jewish bath used for ritual cleansing. Many were found just outside the southern entrance to the Temple.

minaret. The tower of a mosque from which the call to prayer given by the muezzin goes out five times a day.

mirhab. A niche found in mosques that point the way to Mecca and so orient the worshipers for prayer. Early examples were not niches, but slabs of marble set up against the wall facing Mecca.

Mishnah (H: repetition). A codification of oral legal traditions, some of which went back to those of the Pharisees of Jesus' day. The work was probably done at Sepphoris by Judah the Prince about A.D. 200.

mithraeum. A shrine of the god Mithras whose worship was popular among Roman soldiers. It consisted of a picture or frieze of Mithras killing a bull. Sometimes there would also be an opening in the roof for a mithraeum that allowed a ray of sunlight to illumine the picture of

Mithras on the summer solstice. A mithraeum was found in Caesarea, built along the sea, in one of Herod's warehouses which the soldiers reused for the worship of Mithras.

moshav (H: settlement). A cooperative agricultural settlement. Individual families own their homes and other private property, but the fields, equipment, and other property connected with the moshav's work are owned collectively.

muezzin. This man stands in the minaret of a mosque to call Muslims to prayer five times a day. Mohammed detested bells so he thought of this means to remind people of their duty to prayer. Today it is rare for a muezzin to make these calls in person. Many mosques use tape recordings. Almost all use loud speakers to magnify the call to prayer, whether live or on tape.

odeion. A small theater from the Greek and Roman Periods. It was used for musical productions.

Ptolemies. The rulers who descended from Ptolemy, one of Alexander's generals, who ruled in Egypt. They contended with the Seleucids for control of Palestine.

Second Revolt. A revolt against Roman rule in Palestine (A.D. 132–135). It was provoked by Hadrian's plan to level Jerusalem and build a new city on the site. Though the revolt enjoyed initial success and support from Rabbi Akiba, it failed. Hadrian followed his original plans. The Old City of today follows the street plan of Hadrian's *Alia Capitolina,* the name he gave to his new city. The leader of the revolt was known as Bar Kochba (Aramaic: the son of the star) whom Akiba proclaimed the Messiah.

Second Temple Period. From the rebuilding of the Temple following the return from Exile (515 B.C.) to the destruction of the Temple by the Romans in A.D. 70.

Sephardi. A Jew of Spanish extraction. After their expulsion from Spain in 1492, Sephardi Jews moved to North Africa, Italy, Holland, and other places in Europe.

Seleucids. Rulers descended from Seleucus, one of Alexander's generals, who ruled Mesopotamia. The wrested control of Palestine from the Ptolemies. Antiochus IV Epiphanes, who precipitated the Maccabean Revolt, was a Seleucid.

shofar. The ram's horn trumpet used particularly during the High Holy Days. It is a Jewish religious symbol in the Roman and Byzantine Periods.

stoa. A long open building with a roof supported by one or more rows of columns parallel to the back wall. Stoa were public buildings used for commercial, religious, social, and political purposes.

Sukkot (H: tabernacles, booths). The pilgrimage festival that comes after the fruit harvest (see Deut 16:13-17). It ends with the feast of Simhat Torah ("the joy of the Torah"), which brings to a close the fall Jewish holidays that begin with Rosh HaShanah (the New Year).

sultan. A Muslim title given to the secular ruler of the Ottoman Empire. It was abolished when Turkey became a republic after the First World War.

synagogue (H: bet knesset "building of assembly"). A single-purpose monumental building used for Jewish worship. The liturgy of the synagogue was not sacrificial, but consisted of prayers and readings from the Scriptures. Priests were not needed for the liturgy so the synagogue was a lay institution. The origins of the synagogue are still a matter of some debate. Archaeological evidence in Israel leads to the conclusion that synagogues as single-purpose buildings date to the middle of the second century at the earliest. The synagogues mentioned in the New Testament and Josephus were probably multi-purpose community buildings that could be used for worship. No building whose identification as a synagogue is undisputed has been found in Israel, though structures at Gamla, the Herodium, and Masada are identified by their excavators as synagogues.

Talmud (H: learning). A compilation of rabbinic legal traditions developed from the fifth to the seventh centuries in Babylon and Palestine. The Babylonian Talmud was completed and serves as the basis of rabbinic study and the source of Orthodox observance.

tel (H; A: tell). An artificial mound created by successive layers of occupation at a site. A tel can be differentiated from a natural hill because the top of the former is usually flat. Cities in the Bronze and Iron Ages were located on hills, near a reliable water supply, usually along trade routes. Because sites meeting these requirements were few, the same site would be reused after it was abandoned because of military or natural disasters.

triclinium. The formal dining room in a home from the Roman and Byzantine Periods. Guests reclined around tables that were set up along the walls of the room. The museum at Sepphoris encloses a triclinium that is adorned with a most beautiful mosaic.

Via Maris ("The Way of the Sea") or Coastal Road. One of the two principal commercial roads that connected Egypt with the rest of the ancient Near East. It ran along the Mediterranean coast. It turned inland near Megiddo and then passed along the northern tip of the Sea of Galilee, passing through Capernaum. One branch continued due north and another branch went east. See also the King's Highway.

wadi (A; H: nahal). A river bed. It is dry except during the rainy season.

List of Illustrations

All illustrations are from The Liturgical Press archives collection, unless otherwise noted.

Front cover. The Old City of Jerusalem as seen from the Mount of Olives. The Russian Orthodox Church of Saint Mary Magdalene (foreground) and the Dome of the Rock. Photo by Robin Pierzina O.S.B.

Back cover. Worshipers at the Western Wall, Jerusalem. Photo by Robin Pierzina O.S.B.

ii–iii. Detail of Jerusalem from the Madaba Map mosaic, Jordan. Photo by Columba Stewart O.S.B.

xiv. Modes of transportation in the lands of the Bible.

28. The many faces of the Holy Land (clockwise, beginning at upper left): Bedouin woman adorned with her jewelry. A Samaritan high priest with Torah scroll on Mount Gerizim. Jewish boy wearing a phylactery. Photo by Robin Pierzina O.S.B. Greek Orthodox monk.

60. Moslem girls at the Damascus Gate market, Jerusalem.

67. The Old City of Jerusalem as seen from the east.

72. Via Dolorosa, near the Ecce Homo Arch.

74. Map: Jerusalem at Holy Week.

76. Dome of the Rock. Photo by Hugh Witzmann O.S.B.

81. Interior of the Dome of the Rock.

85. Jewish worshipers at the Western Wall. Photo by Robin Pierzina O.S.B.

90. The stone of unction at the entry to the Holy Sepulchre.

95. Kidron Vally tombs.

100. Bethany churches.

Index of Biblical References

Index of Persons

Abraham, 137, 138, 203, 213, 221, 226
Aesclypius, 278
Ahab, 183, 202, 224, 272
Ahaz, 96
Akiva, 146, 198
Albright, W.F., 99, 102
Alexander the Great, 143, 154, 155,
  172, 253, 255, 280, 289, 291, 292,
  320, 324, 330, 337, 340, 341, 343,
  344, 347, 354
Alexander Yannai, 145, 149, 206, 272,
  293
Ammonites, 234, 235
Antiochus IV, 117, 143, 155, 292, 294,
  329
Arabs, 104, 114, 121, 122, 139, 143,
  150, 151, 172, 184, 197, 198, 199,
  202, 207, 209, 211, 213, 214, 257,
  279, 323, 329, 341, 346, 347
Arafat, Yassir, 215
Archelaus, 145, 146
Arculf, 163, 195
Arius, 256–257
Assyrians, 96, 143, 145, 183, 202, 228,
  233, 326
Athanasius, 256–257
Augustus, 145, 146, 147, 199, 228,
  329, 331, 348, 352

Babylonians, 101, 143, 145, 222, 228,
  233, 271, 351
Bagatti, Bellarmino, 37, 163, 164
Bar Kochba, 123, 220
Bedouin, 122, 128, 137, 207, 209, 213,
  232, 245, 248
Ben Gurion, David, 133, 141
Benedictines, 93, 113, 192, 196

Benjamin of Tudela, 94
Byzantines, 13, 99, 120, 136, 139, 146,
  163, 172, 185, 192, 207, 208, 213,
  218, 230, 257, 266, 324, 327

Caiaphas, 149
Carmelites, 152
Chagall, Marc, 106, 109
Christians, 89, 92, 120, 146, 149, 150,
  161, 163, 167, 177, 179, 197, 213,
  232, 249, 257, 296, 331, 333, 337,
  347, 348
Constantine, 88, 89, 91, 197, 218, 256,
  324, 326, 327
Copts, 256, 257, 281
Corbo, Virgilio, 177, 179, 234
Crusaders, 88, 116, 117, 118, 119, 120,
  121, 139, 143, 146, 147, 149, 151,
  153, 163, 167, 168, 184, 192, 197,
  198, 199, 210, 211, 236, 240, 245,
  272, 273, 300, 324, 327, 345, 346,
  352

David, 91, 97, 113, 125, 133, 134, 149,
  153, 158, 172, 186, 206, 216, 218,
  220, 221, 226, 233, 234, 235, 250,
  267, 271, 277, 316, 326
Druze, 51, 52, 184, 208, 211, 232

Edomites, 133, 135, 233, 234
Egeria, 43, 163, 164, 177, 188, 194,
  197, 242, 243
Egyptians, 117, 145, 150, 254, 256,
  257, 260, 271, 273, 280
Elijah, 150, 151, 152, 192, 199, 226
Elisha, 150, 222, 226, 228
Erastus, 312

366

Index of Geographical Names

Index of Subjects

DIVISION OF CANAAN

Miles 0 — 40
Kms 0 — 40

Sidon

SIDONIANS
LEBANON MTS.
HITTITES
ARAMEANS

Damascus

▲ MT. HERMON

Tyre

DAN
Dan (Laish)

MEDITERRANEAN

ASHER

NAPHTALI

Hazor

SEA

Lake
Galilee

MANASSEH
(EAST)

Ashtaroth

MT. CARMEL ▲

ZEBULUN

MT.
TABOR ▲

Dor
Megiddo
Shunem
Endor
ISSACHAR

Jezreel
MT. GILBOA ▲

Ramoth

MANASSEH
(WEST)

Jordan River

Jabesh

Shechem

GAD

AMMONITES

Joppa

EPHRAIM
Shiloh

Bethel
Ai
Gilgal
BENJAMIN
Gibeah
Jerusalem

DAN

Jericho
Rabbah

Ashdod
Libnah

Bethpeor

Bethlehem

REUBEN

Ashkelon

PHILISTINES

Gath?
Lachish

Hebron

Dead

Gaza

JUDAH

Engedi

Sea

Gath?

MOABITES

Beersheba
Hormah

SIMEON

The Negev

EDOMITES

© United Bible Societies, 1976

377

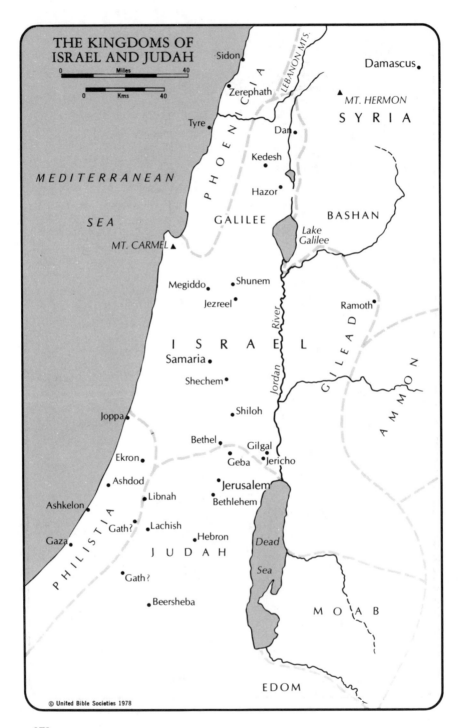

THE KINGDOMS OF
ISRAEL AND JUDAH

Miles
0   40

0   Kms   40

Sidon

Damascus

Zerephath

LEBANON MTS.

MT. HERMON

SYRIA

Tyre

Dan

PHOENICIA

Kedesh

MEDITERRANEAN

Hazor

GALILEE

BASHAN

SEA

Lake
Galilee

MT. CARMEL

Megiddo   Shunem

Jezreel

Ramoth

I S R A E L

Samaria

GILEAD

Shechem

Jordan River

AMMON

Shiloh

Joppa

Bethel

Gilgal

Ekron

Geba   Jericho

Ashdod

Jerusalem

Ashkelon   Libnah   Bethlehem

PHILISTIA

Gath?   Lachish

Gaza

Hebron   Dead

JUDAH

Sea

Gath?

MOAB

Beersheba

EDOM

PALESTINE IN THE
TIME OF JESUS

0 ____ Miles ____ 40

0 ____ Kms ____ 40

MEDITERRANEAN

SEA

Sidon

Zarephath

LEBANON MTS.

PHOENICIA

Tyre

SYRIA

Abila

ABILENE

Damascus

▲ MT. HERMON

Caesarea Philippi

Ptolemais

GALILEE

Chorazin

Capernaum

Magadan

Cana   Tiberias

MT. CARMEL ▲

Nazareth

Nain

▲ MT.
TABOR

Bethsaida

Lake

Galilee

Gadara

Caesarea

SAMARIA

Samaria

MT. GERIZIM ▲

Joppa

Salim

Aenon

▲ MT. EBAL

Sychar

TEN TOWNS

Gerasa

Jordan River

Arimathea?

Ephraim

Emmaus

Jerusalem

Azotus

Ascalon

Gaza

JUDEA

Hebron

Jericho

Bethany

Qumran

Bethlehem

Bethany

PEREA

Dead

Sea

IDUMEA

NABATEA

© United Bible Societies, 1978

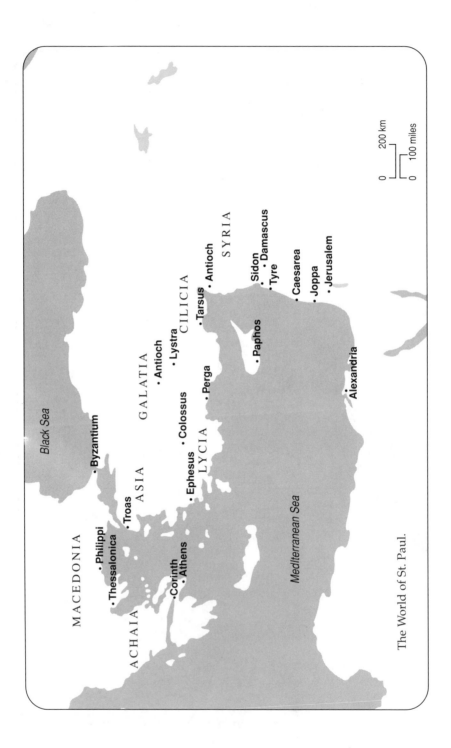

The World of St. Paul.